WOMEN CHALLENGING UNIONS:
FEMINISM, DEMOCRACY, AND MILITANCY

Women Challenging Unions is a collection of original papers that presents a vision of an invigorated and vibrant labour movement, one that would actively seek the full participation of women and other traditionally excluded groups, and that would willingly incorporate a feminist agenda. This vision challenges union complicity in the gendered segmentation of the labour market; union support for traditionalist ideologies about women's work, breadwinners, and male-headed families; union resistance to broader-based bargaining; and the marginalization of woman inside unions.

All of the authors share a commitment to workplace militancy and a more democratic union movement, to women's resistance to the devaluation of their work, to their agency in the change-making process. The interconnected web of militancy, democracy, and feminism provides the ground on which unions can address the challenges of equity and economic restructuring, and on which the re-visioning of the labour movement can take place.

The first of the four sections includes case studies of union militancy that highlight the experiences of individual women in three areas of female-dominated work: nursing, banking, and retailing. The second and third sections focus on the two key arenas of struggle where unions and feminism meet: inside unions, where women activists and staff confront the sexism of unions, and in the labour market, where women challenge their employers and their own unions. The fourth section deconstructs the conceptual tools of the discipline of industrial relations and examines its contribution to the continued invisibility of gender.

LINDA BRISKIN teaches in the Division of Social Science, York University. She is co-author of *Feminist Organizing for Change: The Contemporary Women's Movement in Canada*.

PATRICIA McDERMOTT teaches in the Division of Social Science, York University. She is co-editor of *Just Wages: A Feminist Assessment of Pay Equity*.

EDITED BY LINDA BRISKIN
AND PATRICIA McDERMOTT

Women Challenging Unions: Feminism, Democracy, and Militancy

UNIVERSITY OF TORONTO PRESS
Toronto Buffalo London

© Linda Briskin and Patricia McDermott 1993
Published by University of Toronto Press Incorporated
Toronto Buffalo London
Printed in Canada

ISBN 0-8020-2872-1 (cloth)
ISBN 0-8020-7376-X (paper)

Printed on acid-free paper

Canadian Cataloguing in Publication Data

Main entry under title:

Women challenging unions : feminism, democracy
and militancy

Includes index.
ISBN 0-8020-2872-1 (bound)   ISBN 0-8020-7376-X (pbk.)

1. Women in trade-unions – Canada. I. Briskin,
Linda, 1949–   . II. McDermott, Patricia.

HD6079.2.C3W65 1993   331.4′78′0971   C93-094604-9

Contents

Part Three
Unions and Women Workers

Part Four
Studying Women and Unions

Foreword

JUDY DARCY

In a speech ten years ago I recall saying how complex the issue of women and unions was because it is a topic that is so political, yet so personal. At the time women were making great strides in getting unions to tackle gender-equality issues in work and society; but it was still considered a sign of weakness to talk about the impact of the union on our private lives – on our emotions, our families, and our relationships.

What is ground-breaking about this book is that it deals with such a wide variety of women's struggles and women's lives in the labour movement. The range of experiences, from nurses and auto-workers to bank and garment workers, helps legitimize the challenges that all of us have made to our unions. In areas of racism, occupational health and safety, and even collective bargaining, the theories often give way to personal experiences. And that makes it easier for me to talk about my own experiences in the labour movement.

Whether we challenged the status quo from within or from outside the labour movement, there is now a richness and diversity to the story of women in unions that makes for an exhilirating subject. It didn't feel quite that way ten years ago. The economic hardship of women and the ghettoization of women's work were on the feminist agenda. And my union was an obvious venue to deal with them. But it wasn't easy. I remember my first CLC convention in 1974 when any female felt she was taking her life in her hands if she walked through certain sections of the convention. Those were the days when women only merited a few short paragraphs in a policy paper on human rights. Any women who spoke felt she had to bend over backwards by saying, 'I'm not one of those women's libbers, but ... I remember being told by a higher-up male trade-union official that when I cried a little in a very emotional strike meeting, I wasn't displaying 'tough leadership qualities.' When I took my four-month-old son to a union convention I was told, 'Get your priorities straight.'

Today, as president of the Canadian Union of Public Employees (CUPE), Canada's largest union (and I hope without sounding like a Pollyanna), I can tell you with confidence that those stories are well and truly part of history – because in the past twenty years I have seen and experienced women forging a new history for the labour movement. It's true that I grew up in a union whose membership is half-female and that our members, whose jobs involve services to the public, are progressive both as unionists and advocates of a strong public sector. But when I say that two years ago I was elected president, and Geraldine McGuire was elected secretary-treasurer, of CUPE, without the fact of two women holding the top jobs even being an issue, it can be said that our union has come a long way.

The long way was paved by the work and efforts of hundreds of CUPE women who had to establish themselves as a force in their own union. We started by fighting to make equality issues a priority for our union and organizing to elect women to executives and committees. Our CUPE National Executive Board is now 50 per cent women and we also have two visible-minority members. We have had affirmative-action practices in place for several years that provide for at least 50 per cent women in our training program for new staff representatives and at least 50 per cent women for instructor training programs. And we are making serious efforts to train and hire visible-minority workers, too (this year our trainee representative program includes ten women and five visible-minority workers out of fourteen participants), though I would be first to say we have a long way to go on both fronts.

I certainly don't want to give the impression that sexism and racism don't exist in CUPE and many of our locals. But we do have a very strong mandate to fight even more forcefully than before to tackle all these interrelated equality issues, be they sexism, racism, or discrimination against lesbians and gays or people with disabilities.

As a feminist in the labour movement, I have certainly felt political and personal barriers. But I was walking the picket lines with women who faced even more barriers. I had supported women on the picket line as a student activist and feminist before I knew much about unions. But after I got involved in my library local, I found the labour movement was a comfortable movement for me. It helped to ground me, forcing me to live my politics on a day-to-day basis. The movement was a crucible where I watched women, shy and reserved, radicalized by their involvement, transformed by union opportunities.

That's been one of the most exciting aspects of union life for me, seeing the changes in workers who were given a chance to develop skills, build confidence, and actually become different people. It's the same kind of developmental change that happens to people on a picket line, for as we know a strike is an educational experience like no other. How the labour movement develops its activists and leaders and enriches their lives is still an aspect of unionism that people understand the least.

As more and more women have moved into leadership positions in unions, we've seen a difference in the tone of the debates in the labour movement and in the way decision-making is approached. We have begun to get men with so-called power to listen to women with so-called power – and to listen to each other. And this has meant that the door has been opened wider to the notion of sharing power with others.

Substantive policy issues and decisions are not all worked out by the heads of the big unions in the back hall. Now the issues are on the table, they're confronted squarely, and people listen to each other more instead of always stereotyping each other's positions.

There have been huge barriers, yes. And there still are. But I'd like to suggest we've come further than even some of this book's contributors would allow. I see (some!) lessening of turf wars in the labour movement, more concentration on collective goals, more genuine debate and thinking things through, arguing with persuasion rather than force. And although an article in this volume suggests that bargaining gains for women have been largely confined to areas where legislative standards mandated them, I don't think this is the case. Many of the changes that have resulted in legislation (pay equity, for example) came only after hard bargaining – including strikes – by unions.

That's the good news. The bad news is that as neo-conservatism takes hold in Canada, the equality that's been won is being threatened. Our biggest challenge right now is to be vigilant enough so that equality issues aren't pushed to the background because of the obsession with competition and deficits and the juggernaut of international capital.

I happen to think the women's agenda will continue to be front and centre because the women's movement is too strong in Canada. We're too well organized, we've come too far, every step has been heartfelt and hard won. We made pay equity a key issue and now it's central. We've put violence against women on the agenda as a major social issue. The roots are all firm, in spite of the great pressure to turn back. There is nothing to indicate that Canadian women will allow back-pedaling.

Tough times like these make it all the more clear that economic issues are women's issues. That's why our union stands forcefully for a national child-care program as a major component of gender equality and a major prerequisite for economic renewal. It is also crucial for us to organize women in the child-care and health-care sectors. In child care, because wages and conditions are still so abysmally poor that they affect the quality of care. In the hospital sector, because the unionized, well-paid jobs that now exist are being down-graded, contracted-out to low bidders, or wiped out altogether in a so-called deinstitutionalization that simply transfers responsibility for health and social services back to the family (that means women).

I'm tremendously optimistic about the future for women within the labour movement. But I'm also constantly aware that the day-to-day struggle is difficult and painful and that women still make incredible sacrifices in their own workplaces and homes. It may be that we are winning the struggle for equality on paper, while the 'personal' side of the equation remains a huge challenge. I have to confess that I talk about it today much the same way I did ten years ago, with a sense of frustration and not many solutions.

Can you be a union activist and still have a personal life? None of us has found a satisfactory answer yet. I do know that the support system is crucial. It's very important for my colleague Geraldine and I to go into one of our offices regularly and close the door and say: 'Gee, I was proud of what you did out there today.' Or for us to have a good cry and then a good laugh together and know how much we need each other's support and encouragement and the support and encouragement of others. That means continually finding new ways to involve more women in leadership and decision-making so that our gains become permanent and entrenched.

The acknowledgment of that need for support has translated into another impact by women on the labour movement: the drive to build coalitions and a new-found sense of solidarity, both here and internationally. I think of the 1993 CLC statement on International Women's Day, which revitalized me (and also gave me goose bumps). It speaks of our unbreakable links with women everywhere because sexism and racism recognize no borders; when mass rape is a weapon of war, when 80 per cent of the world's refugees are women, and women live so disproportionately in poverty, we have so much more to do.

'And for those of us who are white,' reads the statement, 'the first challenge is to confront our own racism, our own lack of understanding which makes us blind and hence makes our sisters invisible. As all of us commemorate March 8, we have to keep in mind that genuine liberation cannot be achieved for some and not for all. We are realizing, more and more, that "as we go marching," no one should be left to watch from the sidelines as the parade passes by.'

What an exciting parade it has been, as Canadian women have opened up their unions and made the needs of women and feminist values integral to the labour movement. We've made our unions into powerful tools for change – and defined our own power in the process. From this base, we must build unions that empower all women.

Acknowledgments

We would like to thank the Gerstein Foundation, the Social Science and Humanities Research Council of Canada, and the Faculty of Arts at York University for their generous financial support for this project.

We would also like to thank all those who participated in the seminar series on 'Women and Unions: Industrial Relations, Collective Bargaining and Union Militancy' from which this book was generated.

LINDA BRISKIN
PATRICIA McDERMOTT

INTRODUCTION

The Feminist Challenge to the Unions

LINDA BRISKIN and
PATRICIA McDERMOTT

The labour movement in Canada is facing one of the most serious challenges it has ever confronted. Fierce global competition and economic restructuring have meant not only a loss of jobs in the industrial and manufacturing sector – the traditional base of union support – but also the creation of more non-standard part-time, part-year service work, often in difficult-to-organize small workplaces; the shift to homework, off-shore production, and contracting out; and the demand by employers for more flexible labour. These trends suggest an increase in the feminization of labour (more jobs like traditional women's work) and the feminization of the workforce (more women workers), and produce a further polarization of available work – good jobs for the few and bad jobs for most.[1] Furthermore, the ideology and practices of 'international competition' have exacerbated the intransigence of employers, and increased their direct attacks on the rights of unions.

Gender issues, then, are centrally implicated in the process of economic restructuring. As a result, the relations between women and unions are undergoing a striking transformation at the core of which is the critical recognition of interdependency: women need unions and unions need women. The key demand of women workers for economic independence, that is, for a decent living wage to support themselves, and in many cases their dependents, threatens to be reduced, under the grim reality of economic restructuring, to an urgent call for the right to work. Like men, women workers have always needed unions to help equalize the relationship between labour and management, but in this period this need has taken on a desperate edge.

For women, unions also provide an arena in which they can actively engage with fundamental issues affecting their home and work lives. In the process, union activity fosters not only personal empowerment but political awareness and collective solidarity, a point emphasized in rich detail in the chapters which discuss women's involvement in the 1988 nurse's strike in Alberta (Coulter), in the bank workers' mobilizations in the west and the east (Baker), and in the Eaton's strike (McDermott). For example, Margaret, a bank worker interviewed by Patricia Baker, talks of how union activism changed her: 'Oh my God I've changed a lot. I wouldn't even sit and talk to you years ago. I was so shy ... I've learned so much since being in the union ... It opens your eyes about what's going on everywhere ... I can't believe where I was and where I came from.' Baker suggests that 'with the strike experience and with community support, the women came to realize their worth as people and as workers ... By mobilizing themselves and winning broad community, labour, and national support, these women experienced the power of collective action.'

Unions need women for many reasons. Perhaps the most obvious is that the labour movement needs women as new members. Economic restructuring, in eroding the largely male, industrial union base, has raised serious questions about the labour movement's ability to survive. As the rate of unionization declines – although this decline has not been anywhere near as serious in Canada as in the United States – unions are now looking to women workers for revitalization and growth, and to new sectors of the economy to replace their traditional support.

Although women's participation in the paid labour force has risen rapidly since the Second World War – they now constitute over 45 per cent of the workforce, only 30.3 per cent of women workers in 1990 were in unions, compared with 38.6 per cent of male workers. In her paper on 'Patterns of Unionization,' Julie White calls for a 'fourth wave' of unionization in the previously ignored private service sector where so many women are employed. Craft workers, she points out, organized in Canada in the late 1800s, industrial workers largely in the 1930s and 1940s, and public-sector workers in the 1960s and early 1970s. White suggests that the time is now ripe for the labour movement to organize the unorganized. Historically, however, unions have not been effective at organizing service work or women workers. In the attempt to encourage more women to join unions, the labour movement must now confront problems that women workers have struggled with for decades, and develop innovative organizing strategies which take account of women's work and women's experience.

In fact, we are arguing that unions will need to incorporate a feminist perspective into their ideology, practices, policies, and strategies in order to survive, indeed, flourish, in the current conditions. Carl Cuneo, in chapter 5, sees 'feminism today as the most creative energy within the labour movement' and in their contribution to this book, Jane Stinson and Penni Richmond (chapter 6) argue that the feminist project in unions is directly related to the future health of the labour movement, and that an alternative approach to unionism, based on feminist values that foster more participatory and inclusive decision-making, is needed for unions to grapple successfully with the challenges ahead.

Engaging with a feminist perspective will mean that unions must pay close attention to the issues that women have raised – sexual harassment, child care, maternity leave, affirmative action, pay equity – and continue to expand the definition of legitimate union issues; struggle for increased representation of women and racial minorities in elected positions and in all the structures of the union movement; address the barriers women face in becoming active in unions – in particular, those related to the double day and sexual harassment; re-examine and re-invent union process to move towards greater democracy, inclusivity, and participation; and finally ensure that union policy is translated into practice within the collective bargaining process and that demands to improve the conditions of women and other marginal workers are made a priority. Gains in collective bargaining depend upon a multi-pronged strategy which emphasizes the links between legislation and bargaining, and simultaneously builds alliances with those fighting for similar issues in the community-based women's movement and in other progressive movements. At the same time, the ability of women unionists to access the collective bargaining process will depend upon the transformations in representation and process noted above, a point underscored by Pradeep Kumar in chapter 10.

We use the term 'feminism' in a generic way to refer to the challenge to gender-based inequity. However, we recognize that a multiplicity of feminisms situated on a complex political spectrum struggle for a place within the union movement, each bringing a different approach to prioritizing union issues, expanding women's participation in leadership positions, developing new process mechanisms, and organizing with the community outside the labour movement. Read together, the articles in this collection illustrate just such a range of feminist politics and practices.

As a result of the organized pressure of women union activists in the last two decades, unions have made enormous strides; indeed, from an optimistic vantage point we might say that the face of the Canadian labour movement has been transformed. Many of the following articles document these changes and provide us with grounds for hope about the future.

A feminist agenda, then, not only suggests ways to attract and keep women members, and members from other groups traditionally excluded from organized labour, but, more important, it offers a point of reference for a re-visioning of the labour movement which goes far beyond 'letting women in.' Taken as a whole, the organization of power in the unions is under serious scrutiny; indeed, so is the very meaning of unions.

It may seem naïve to argue that equity must be made a priority during recessionary times, yet the papers in this volume suggest there is little choice. The challenge of equity is at one and the same time the challenge of economic restructuring. Restructuring produces more divisions among workers, many of them gender-based; these must be actively resisted in order to protect wages and working conditions and to prevent erosion of the labour movement. But it is only through solidarity that such resistance is possible. What the movement of union women has demonstrated in the last decades is that solidarity can only be built on equity.

Despite an important record of changes, serious problems remain. A common pattern emerges: unions begin by developing new policies and educational programs; they move towards questions of representation, first at the leadership level and then in relation to union staff; and then stall at innovations in collective-bargaining demands and process – the most critical arena for unionized workers. After thoroughly analysing the degree of success of collective bargaining in addressing key concerns of interest to women workers, Kumar concludes that not only has progress been 'agonizingly slow' and mostly confined to areas where legislation has mandated change but that the very commitment of unions to bargaining gender issues is in serious question.

We believe unions can play a much greater role in promoting gender equality than they have in the past. What are some of the areas of resistance that prevent deeper changes? The following discussion will consider four points: union complicity in the gendered segmentation of the labour market; union support for traditionalist ideologies about women's work, breadwinners, and male-headed families; union resistance to broader-based bargaining; and patriarchal, bureaucratic, hierarchical, and often fundamentally anti-democratic union structures and practices which marginalize women inside unions.

Evidence suggests the widespread acceptance of, and complicity in, the perpetuation of the gendered segmentation of the labour market by unions. Thus male-dominated unions have not made women workers and the sectors in which they work an organizing priority. Unions have also been less than enthusiastic about measures which would specifically challenge labour segmentation, for example, pro-rated benefits and job security for part-time and part-year workers, and affirmative-action programs that would integrate women into more highly paid male jobs, as well as into the staff positions of union bureaucracies. This lack of enthusiasm has often been expressed as a refusal to re-examine practices around seniority to protect newly hired women or members of racial minorities. A sad example is revealed at the Stelco plant in Hamilton, Ontario, where after the successful struggle to get women 'Back into Stelco' in 1979–80, few remain following a wave of layoffs.[2]

Despite its seriously outdated perception of both the composition of the contemporary family unit, as well as the role of women's earnings in keeping her partner and/or dependents out of poverty, the patriarchal belief in the reality and ideology of a male-headed family persists. This belief underlies the right-wing challenge to women's right to waged work, which in turn has provided ideological justification for differential job access and lower pay. In fact, Rosemary Warskett, in chapter 12, illuminates the gender bias inherent in the trade-union movement's understanding of wage fairness itself; she unpacks three approaches to the distribution of wages – for skill, for living, and for family head – all of which have a deleterious impact on women.

Another thread in this ideology is the tenacious conviction that women identify mainly with family, and that housework and child care ought to be women's responsibilities, which has meant that unions have played little role in attempting to challenge the sexual division of labour in the household. Nor have they used the collective-bargaining process to respond innovatively to the often conflicting demands of household and workplace; in fact, they have often supported work structuring that exacerbates the tension between them.

Furthermore, the stereotype has endured that women are disinterested in unions, despite the fact that women have demonstrated their militancy through participation in first-contract struggles and in strikes in their communities and workplaces; and their union activism through their willingness to challenge conventional leadership and bureaucratic practices of unions. Industrial-relations practitioners have certainly contributed to this stereotype. Ann Forrest, in chapter 16, documents how the discipline has refused to 'catch up with the evidence,' which actually suggests that today women 'are *more* inclined to join unions than men.'

Blaming women, however erroneously, for the pattern of their participation in unions has made invisible the unique difficulties of organizing the sectors in which women work and has meant that unions have not developed organizing strategies grounded in the differences between women's work and consciousness, and men's work and consciousness. Pat Armstrong, in chapter 15, uses the example of nursing work to demonstrate that traditional union approaches, shaped by industrial settings, have not been able to meet the needs of people-centred, caring work. She argues that rather than making women's work more like men's, the unions must re-think union organizing to create structures that reflect the caring skills and vocational commitment typical of much women's work. For nurses, such new structures must also take account of the ways in which disciplinary procedures, assessments of skill, hiring and evaluation practices, and decision-making structures differ not only from industrial work but also from the traditional male professions of law and medicine. Without these kinds of shifts, women in caring work will not be persuaded that unions can meet their needs.

A third area of resistance to fundamental union change concerns broader-based bargaining. In her critique of labour law in chapter 11, Judy Fudge suggests that the unions have faced employer-biased state policies that contribute to making the sectors of the economy in which women predominate difficult to organize. Labour boards encourage the fragmentation of bargaining structures. Through the 'community of interests' policy which shapes appropriate bargaining units, they often place female office workers in separate, and consequently smaller and less powerful, units than those of male plant workers of the same employer; or designate part-time and full-time workers as separate units, thereby reducing their bargaining strength. This tendency to fragment, rather than consolidate, bargaining structures clearly weakens the labour movement's ability to respond to the challenge presented by contracting-out, homework, and the dramatic increase in casualized and flexible employment relationships which globalization engenders.

The union movement must also take some blame for the fragmented structures that currently exist, for it has never put broader-based bargaining on its own agenda in any meaningful way. Caught up in jurisdictional disputes and with a clear tendency to protect a specific union turf rather than consider the long-term health of the labour movement as a whole, unions have done little to counteract the desire of capital, along with an accommodating state, for more fragmented structures. In her paper on the Canadian garment industry, in chapter 14, Armine Yalnizyan points out that, although the rate of unionization in this sector has declined from 80 per cent to 20 per cent in just thirty years, three unions struggle to represent garment workers and have remained resistant to the idea of merging into one structure. The topic of union mergers also raises the often heated and sensitive debate about whether national or international unions can best serve members in Canada.

Finally, union structures and practices continue to be male-dominated. In chapter 4, Linda Briskin points out that 'male power generates and is reinforced by bureaucratic, hierarchical, and competitive ways of organizing which combine to produce certain kinds of organizations, patterns of decision making, and an emphasis on particular issues. Thus, male power and privilege, male leadership, and traditional organizational forms intersect and function to exclude and disadvantage women.'

Stinson and Richmond document the sexism and discrimination experienced by women who work for unions; Cuneo's chapter on 'Trade Union Leadership' provides evidence of the continued mechanisms of sexism and their impact on women in union leadership. For example, many women activists feel excluded and uncomfortable in the culturally male settings of smoke-filled bars. The near ritualistic practice of making critical decisions about union strategies 'over a beer' sends a clear message to women that it is the 'old boys' network' that really matters in union politics. And male spouses often object to their partners' after-hours socializing. Others have been sexually harassed, and in some cases even sexually assaulted, by male unionists who also apply a heavy-handed double standard to the sexual activities of women unionists.

These four areas underscore the paradigm shift that is necessary for union transformation and offer a point of reference for reading the chapters that follow. We have also identified five themes that weave a connecting thread through these chapters. Although there are many others, we flag these five because they highlight both the feminist critique of the labour movement and the potential for the successful integration of women into this movement. The first theme of 'making gender visible' and the closely related second theme of 'challenging the male standard' provide tools of analysis that explicitly focus on gender. The third and fourth themes – 'separate organizing' and 'building alliances and coalitions' – are complementary strategies for moving forward to a transformed labour movement. The final theme – 'militancy and democratic process' – highlights the feminist vision of a democratic and participatory labour movement that nurtures the militancy and activism of women, indeed, of all workers.

MAKING GENDER VISIBLE

A foundational premise of this book is that gender is always significant and must be taken account of in any analysis of trade unions and workplaces. The goal is to make visible the operation of gender. In so doing, we liberate a deeper understanding of the reality of gender-specific oppression and simultaneously challenge the inherent naturalism which often organizes the societal understanding of gender dynamics.

This naturalism is present in union attitudes towards certain 'women's' issues. For example, leave to take care of sick children is often considered a 'women's issue' because of the widespread belief that child care is women's responsibility. When this item comes to the bargaining table, gender politics accord it a low priority because it is assumed to be of concern only to women, and not to the whole membership. The labour movement could challenge this naturalism by maintaining a commitment at the bargaining table to child-care-related issues and by negotiating not only maternity leave but also paternity and parental leave.

Making the significance of gender visible will help overcome the persistent tendency simply to ignore women and their demands. As

Anne Forrest points out, the texts and journals in the field of industrial relations remain 'stubbornly silent' on the subject of women and unions, and treat the gendered division of labour as 'entirely natural.' Why, asks Forrest, has women's comparatively lower rate of unionization not been problematized 'particularly when wages and working conditions are so abysmally poor – the very conditions that industrial-relations scholars would regard as causative factors in the organizing drives of men'?

The commitment to making gender visible rests on the assumption that women have gender-specific needs, different ways of organizing, different expectations, and different priorities. For example, in their discussion of their experience as staff members within the labour movement, Jane Stinson and Penni Richmond suggest that the gender of union staff influences work style. In the dominant male model, the staff act as authority figures, experts, and 'white knights' who charge in to rescue weak locals. In contrast, women staff tend to promote a participatory approach whose aim is to develop the confidence and skills of members.

Making gender visible requires a reconceptualization of the analytic tools used to study union and workplace practices. For example, in her chapter on the Eaton's strike, Patricia McDermott suggests that female-dominated workplace disputes, especially those in the service sector, cannot be understood without reference to gender (and sectoral) specificity. Such a gender-specific analysis not only alters how we study industrial disputes involving women and assess strike tactics, but also has the potential to change how unions organize women.

Indeed, evidence in this book suggests the increasing significance of gender as a variable: in the feminization of labour (more jobs like traditional women's work), the feminization of the workforce (more women workers), the feminization of unions (with increasing numbers of women members), and indeed the feminization of militancy.

CHALLENGING THE 'MALE STANDARD'

Closely related to the theme of making gender visible is the need to challenge the tendency to use the male as 'the standard.' This tendency takes two pernicious forms: first, the assumption that the experience of men is generic to both women and men, an assumption which makes the significance of gender completely invisible; and second, the assumption that men's reality should establish 'the norm' against which women are measured, thereby implying that women are atypical and should change to conform to the male model. Both tendencies, well documented in the feminist literature on sociology, philosophy, law, and politics, privilege men's experience.

A striking illustration of treating the male standard as the norm is described in chapter 13 by Karen Messing and Donna Mergler. They argue that the traditional approach to workplace health and safety has assumed men to be the 'proud possessors of a monopoly on occupational risks'; women's occupational problems have often been ignored, or named as 'women's problems' and thereby minimized as health problems. The classic solution has been to exclude women from dangerous jobs, rather than to change or improve jobs, which would not only provide equal access but also increase the safety level for all workers. For example, pregnant women are re-assigned to 'risk-free' work, despite the fact that working conditions unsafe for pregnant women are rarely safe for other workers. Rejecting the male standard could help move health-and-safety discourse to the demand for 'zero tolerance' of workplace hazards for both men and women.

The acceptance of the male standard is also evident in pay-equity initiatives that usually involve the revaluing of work. In chapter 12, Rosemary Warskett notes that in the process of evaluating jobs, the danger lies in the acceptance of the employers' often male-biased assessment of what is valuable. As feminist critiques of pay-equity exercises have pointed out, male skills are often inflated, while the skills characteristic of women's work go unacknowledged and unrewarded. Furthermore, male-dominated union bargaining committees often collude with employers in maintaining the male standard; and, even in circumstances where women's jobs may be assessed as more valuable than their male co-workers, the way pay equity has typically been implemented in North America has meant that male wages are accepted as the norm and women's are brought up to it.

Using male experience as the norm is also implicit in the organization of union activism, which often assumes that the activist is male and has a wife at home to care for him and his children. Thus, union positions which involve travel and weekend meetings – what Stinson and Richmond refer to as 'greedy work' – function to discourage the participation of women who shoulder the bulk of domestic and care giving responsibilities. Bargaining sessions that regularly go all night and sometimes for weeks on end – a long-standing tradition in the labour movement – structurally maintain collective bargaining as almost exclusively male.

In general, then, subsuming women under the heading 'worker,' which in reality means male worker, has made it legitimate for unions to build their organizing strategies around full-time, male workers in the primary and secondary sectors and to ignore female-dominated service work. Since part-time, precarious employment is fast becoming the norm, unions must now shift their focus to a new 'standard' worker – one long neglected at the bargaining table and never before an organizing priority. Furthermore, union women are no longer prepared to adapt to a labour movement that requires them to 'fit in,' but are calling on that labour movement to change to accommodate them.

The challenge to make gender visible and remove the male standard has undermined the very notion of a generic worker with a homogeneous and self-evident set of interests. This orthodox approach is gradually being replaced by a recognition of the multiplicity and variety of workers with often contradictory interests arising out of the intersecting realities of race, class, gender, sexual orientation, age, ability, language, and region.

SEPARATE ORGANIZING

Almost every paper in this volume touches on the critical theme of separate organizing, critical because of the media-inspired discussion of 'post-feminism' which questions the value of women's organizing, and specifically of separate women's committees within organizations.[3] Surely, so the argument goes, basic feminist principles have become so firmly entrenched in everyday discourse and practices that it is no longer essential for women to organize, analyse, and strategize without men. Yet, as Linda Briskin points out in chapter 4, 'women's relation to power is fundamentally different than men's.' In fact, separate organizing is the strategic reflection of gender significance and specificity. Separate organizing within unions remains an essential strategy if women are to further their goal of increased access to decision-making power and to implement their vision of a transformed labour movement. Cuneo sees 'separate organizing as a special form of activist leadership.' The Black women activists interviewed by Ronnie Leah (chapter 7) underscore the need for separate organizing to ensure that race issues are not overshadowed by gender issues.

Briskin stresses that the success of separate organizing depends on maintaining a delicate balance between autonomy from the structures and practices of the labour movement – a necessity to maintain the 'radical edge' – and integration into those structures in order to gain resources and legitimacy. Separate organizing can take place within one union, a union federation, or the labour movement as a whole. For example, the tendency for some largely female teachers' and nurses' unions not to join provincial labour federations suggests a degree of separate organizing. Although the reasons for not formally joining a labour federation are complex and deserve more study, such a choice can be seen as an attempt to balance autonomy and integration. Similarly, the bank workers involved with SORWUC, a self-consciously separate and feminist union, as well as the two locals in Nova Scotia which rejected the CLC's jurisdictional plans to turn them over to the United Steel Workers (Baker, chapter 3), were also seeking a degree of autonomy from the mainstream labour movement.

BUILDING ALLIANCES AND COALITIONS

At the same time as feminist activists within the trade-union movement must engage in some form of separate organizing to maintain a cutting edge to their demands for change, evidence suggests the importance of building links both within the labour movement and with progressive forces outside union structures. Although calling for both separate organizing and coalitions might appear contradictory, the distinction between separate organizing as a strategy and separatism as a goal (Briskin, chapter 4) helps us to see how they are complementary. Building alliances from the base of separate organizing ensures that the demands of the dominant group – in this case, white male workers – will not overshadow those of more marginal workers – white women and women of colour, gays and lesbians, and so on.

The call to build links is at the heart of many of the strategic reflections in this volume. Karen Messing and Donna Mergler note that linking health-and-safety committees and women's committees could produce a powerful and reciprocal combination. The redesign of work to make men's jobs safer could mean that more women would be able to integrate into non-traditional work – a long-standing goal of the women's committees. Ronnie Leah documents the increasing convergence of human-rights and women's committees, linking the emphasis on race, ethnicity, and sexual orientation of the former with the focus on gender in the latter, thus strengthening the capacity of both groups to address the complexities of diversity.

Penni Richmond and Jane Stinson stress that creating links among union staff, leadership, and membership will help ensure that feminism in theory within union structures becomes feminism in practice. In particular, establishing a new relationship between the traditionally female clerical staff and the women who have recently entered the upper levels of the union hierarchy – often into better-paid specialist jobs – will be instrumental to this process.

Armine Yalnizyan's paper on the garment industry underscores the need both for international cooperation and for stronger ties to progressive community-based organizations. Global restructuring, in particular the shift to off-shore production, makes it crucial for women to connect across national boundaries. At the same time, the current growth of homeworking in Canada highlights the necessity for new organizing strategies, the success of which will depend upon strong and enduring links to community-based organizations and groups.

Undoubtedly the most fruitful and enduring alliance has been between the movement of union women and the community-based women's movement, each having an important impact on the other – the former responding to the demands of feminism and the latter to the demands for a class-specific understanding of women's realities. Despite their importance, however, these connections are complex and have not been free of tensions.

Pamela Sugiman, in chapter 8, explores the interplay of unionism and feminism in the Canadian Auto Workers (CAW) union over a thirty-year period and demonstrates the ambivalent relationship many trade-union activists have to feminism. In the 1960s and 1970s, especially in their struggle to win protection against sex discrimination in the Ontario Human Rights Code, CAW women activists drew on a feminist ideology and methods of mobilizing then current in the women's movement; they also built alliances with middle-class feminists, the NDP, and groups such as the Voice of Women, and organized around a broad range of issues. Yet these activists simultaneously articulated a discomfort with naming themselves feminists.

Although the United Nurses of Alberta (UNA) has never become formally affiliated with women's organizations, Rebecca Coulter notes, in chapter 2, that the UNA cooperates on many projects with these groups. Indeed, the National Action Committee on the Status of Women (NAC) was very supportive during the 1988 strike. Although the UNA has never identified itself as a feminist organization, and indeed Coulter suggests the relationship between feminism and nursing remains 'uneasy,' she argues that the striking nurses have clearly benefited from the gains of the women's movement – specifically feminist analysis. For example, the now-established understanding that nursing work is undervalued and underpaid are rooted in feminist analysis of the labour process.

MILITANCY AND DEMOCRATIC PROCESS

Strike action is often seen as the quintessential symbol of union militancy; throughout the history of the labour movement, women workers have engaged in this form of action. Yet a commitment to strike action is insufficient to address women's concerns as workers or as unionists. Women workers face three parallel struggles – to organize into unions, to fight for workplace rights, and to win a fuller place inside the union movement – the common themes of which are the linked demands for empowerment and democratization.

This militant focus on more democracy is not surprising given women's historic pattern of exclusion from decision making. Women call for a form of democracy that would not only allow them fuller access and more power in the workplace and union, but would also take account of their gender-specific realities. In this interconnected web of militancy, democracy, and gender the ground on which the revisioning of the labour movement can take place is illuminated; for example, the high expectations for full participation in their unions voiced by women activists challenge the apathy inherent in the service mentality of business unionism and shift the ground of union power structures. Similarly, women on strike are often militant in gender-specific ways which, when recognized, inspire innovative organizing strategies.

Furthermore, there is a strong connection between the demand for democratic, participatory processes within the labour movement and the militancy needed to challenge employers. A number of papers in this collection make the connection between the desire for democratic participation within union structures and solidarity in the face of employer intransigence. For example, in her analysis of the roots of militancy in the United Nurses of Alberta (UNA) Rebecca Coulter isolates the highly democratic and participatory demand-setting process (an early stage of collective bargaining) within the UNA as 'the flashpoint for nurses' militancy' and a key element in explaining both the solidarity of the membership and their willingness to strike.

The feminist struggle for democratic process within the labour movement is critical: it will be the key to gaining and maintaining access to, and a voice within, the labour movement; it will empower women to stand firm when confronting their employers; and it will help provide the vision for a new kind of unionism.

CONCLUSION

We have structured this book to move from the personal and particular to the more analytic and general. Thus, the first section focuses on case studies of union militancy and activism that highlight the experiences of individual women in three areas of female-dominated work: nursing, banking, and retailing. We begin with these chapters because the compelling voices of women unionists are rarely heard in the discourse on unions, particularly in academic analysis. This commitment to hearing silenced voices is deeply embedded in the scholarly traditions of women's studies. Indeed, the emphasis on letting women 'speak for themselves' has been part of an epistemological challenge to social-science methodology, which has been concerned about the absence of women's voices and experience, about the assumption that men's experience is generic, and about the tendency for 'experts' to interpret women's experience for them.

Starting with these papers also highlights women's resistance to the devaluation of their work and their agency in the change-making process – as union activists committed to both workplace militancy and a more democratic union movement. These images provide a reference point against which the rest of the chapters can be read; many of them emphasize more structuralist arguments and identify barriers and constraints which disempower women.

The second and third sections focus on the two key arenas of struggle where unions and feminism meet: inside the unions, where women, as activists and staff, confront the sexism of union bureaucracies and hierarchies; and in the labour market, where women, as wage workers and union members challenge both their employer and their own unions. The fourth section shifts attention to the study of women and unions, deconstructing the conceptual tools of the discipline of industrial relations and highlighting its contribution to the continued invisiblity of gender.

We have tried to balance contributions that highlight particular realities – for example, the Canadian Auto Workers union and the garment industry – with pieces which speak at a more general level – about wage fairness or separate organizing. Nevertheless, it is inevitable for a topic so wide in scope in a country so regionally diverse that an anthology will be incomplete in its coverage. We note with regret the absence of an overview of feminist organizing in Quebec unions, and of studies which examine everyday practices at the local level.

We are also concerned about the unfortunate homogenization implied in the use of the term 'women.' Despite the presence of an article which deals directly with race issues for union women (Leah, chapter 7), and despite a sensitivity to the multiple realities of women in many of the other articles, we are aware of the dangers of using generic categories; in fact, we make this criticism of traditional approaches to the study of workers and unions in this introduction. In order to reflect the experiences of all women, and to understand them more fully, we need more particular studies which examine the differential impact of union and workplace policies and practices on women of colour, immigrant women, lesbians, old women, women with disabilities, and so on, and which highlight their culturally and class-specific organizing strategies. We hope this volume will encourage scholars and activists to turn their attention to such studies.

Feminist claims for equity have often been founded on the simple but overwhelming assertion that women constitute 50 per cent of the population yet are in subordinate roles in almost all spheres of social, political, and economic activity. The fact that by the end of this decade half the labour market will consist of women is surely a reality upon which women will stake their claim for equality in the workplace and within unions. The combined challenge of equity and economic restructuring requires that the labour movement seize the opportunity offered by a growing female labour force with an emerging feminist consciousness.

This book documents union resistance to change but also advances a vision of an invigorated and vibrant labour movement which would actively seek not only the full participation of women and others traditionally excluded but the incorporation of a transformative feminist agenda.

NOTES

1 See Economic Council of Canada, 'Good Jobs Bad Jobs: Employment in the Service Economy,' Ottawa 1990.
2 See Meg Luxton and June Corman, 'Getting to Work: The Challenge of the Women Back into Stelco Campaign,' *Labour / Le Travail* 28 (Fall 1991).
3 It is instructive that at the September 1992 conference on 'A Gender Perspective in the European Trade Union Confederation (ETUC),' organized by the Women's Committee of the ETUC and held in Milan, a major focus was on whether to maintain separate structures for women or to mainstream.

PART I
WOMEN ON STRIKE

1

The Eaton's Strike: We Wouldn't Have Missed It for the World!

PATRICIA McDERMOTT

I'm a different person now, really, this strike changed me completely ... If you'd asked me before the strike if I could have done this I would have said 'no way.' Now I feel very accomplished in some way.

On 30 November 1984 the employees of six Eaton's department stores in southern Ontario went out on a strike that lasted nearly six months. It was a strike that captured the public's imagination and mobilized Canada's labour movement more than anything had done in years. The Canadian Labour Congress (CLC) organized a boycott of Eaton's and sponsored a national tour of four strikers who helped spread interest in their dispute across the country. The strike also caught the attention of the Canadian Catholic Bishop's Committee, as well as the Anglican Church of Canada, and both of these organizations issued unprecedented statements supporting the strikers. The strike inspired the creation of the Women's Strike Support Coalition, which brought together women from both the labour and the women's movement in a committee that organized numerous highly successful support rallies including a spectacular concert at Toronto's Massey Hall attended by over three thousand people.[1] This strike was also significant because it involved the same union, the Retail, Wholesale and Department Store Union (RWDSU), that had come so close to organizing Eaton's flagship store in downtown Toronto in 1952.[2]

The organizing drive began with a chance encounter in late 1983 between Mike Dunlop from the RWDSU and an Eaton's employee at the Bramalea store near Toronto. Mike and his wife were buying a videotape recorder and asked if the employee would throw in a few free cassettes with the purchase. In response, Paul Wanamaker said it would have to come out of his own wages, and on his salary even a few tapes would make quite a dent. In the conversation that followed Wanamaker revealed that Eaton's workers had not received a raise in more than two years, but were expecting one shortly.[3] Mike Dunlop's wife commented 'something to the effect that, "well you're the union man, help this guy out. He needs a union."'[4] After some discussion Mike agreed to give Paul a call once the raises were announced. When they came through in early 1984 they were very disappointing, with some people receiving only a few cents an hour increase. It was clear that the time was ripe for an organizing campaign and within a month the store was unionized.

The certification of the Bramelea store acted as a catalyst for organizing in the other five Eaton's outlets, as well as for several dozen Simpson's and Zellars department stores. The drive at the six Eaton's locations has been described as 'an organizer's dream,'[5] during which 'the workers all but organized themselves.'[6] The success of this drive is clearly illustrated by the fact that the organizers were able to sign up well over 70 per cent of the employees in most of the fourteen full- and part-time units, thus allowing each to be certified without the need for a representation vote by the Ontario Labour Relations Board.[7]

Although the organizing drive was clearly successful, the same cannot be said of the strike itself. If the gains made as a result of striking are used as an indicator, the strike was arguably a failure since the strikers were offered the identical contract after the dispute ended as they were when it began. Furthermore, since all Eaton's bargaining units were eventually decertified, the strike must also be considered a failure.

Another way to judge the success of a strike, however, is the extent to which it inflicts an economic penalty on the employer. From this point of view it may be that the Eaton's strike was at least a partial success. There is some evidence that the national CLC-sponsored boycott of Eaton's was starting to work. Although Eaton's is a privately held firm and therefore does not have to issue a public annual statement of profits and losses, when the strikers returned to work many mentioned that the internal figures about sales were seriously down from normal levels. Although it is difficult to say how effective the boycott was, it would appear that a national boycott takes a considerable time to work and has to be repeatedly reinforced in media coverage. In the strikers' assessment the boycott was an extremely good strategy for a retail strike. It gave them something to ask individual consumers to do to support their cause and it became a key focus for the strikers on the line every day.

There were also suggestions that some decline in sales was likely caused by the loss of so many trained personnel, such as 'section heads' who were responsible for managing departments and who were heavily represented among the strikers. In interviews with strikers, there were numerous references to their departments 'being in a mess' or 'in total chaos' when they returned to work. As one striker commented, 'To make money in retail you have to keep careful accounts about returns, keep on top of new orders, make sure the stockroom is in order. From what I can tell, many of the basic routines needed to run a money-making department hadn't been done for months.'

Of the approximately nine hundred potential strikers, estimates suggest that only about five or six hundred came out to the picket lines on the first few days of the strike. Some, who supported the strike, stayed home rather than picket, while others got new jobs. It was clear, however, that the workforce inside the stores was seriously diminished at the start of the strike. Eaton's quickly hired new employees and increased the hours of their large pool of part-time student employees, who appeared not to support the strike to the extent that the long-term, 'regular part-timers' did. By the end of the strike it is estimated that there were about two hundred strikers picketing regularly.

It is this group of strikers, the 'die-hard' core, who were responsible for making the Eaton's strike a partial success. The ability to maintain vigorous picket lines throughout the strike was critical for continuing the media coverage necessary to keep public attention focused on their dispute and, in turn, support the boycott. The series of support rallies and concerts all depended on there being strikers covering the lines every day. Perhaps the best evidence that there was a significant degree of public awareness being generated by the strike were, as noted earlier, statements supporting the strikers from both the Canadian Catholic Bishops' Committee and the Anglican Church of Canada. Not only do they illustrate that the national boycott was likely gaining support, but also harming the company's social reputation as well as its economic health. Eaton's has always presented itself as a fine, upstanding employer closely tied to the somewhat aristocratic Eaton family. It must have been a shock to management and Eaton family members alike to have the social-policy bodies of two large churches refer to the strike and essentially take the strikers' side in the dispute.

It is, of course, obvious that a strike plays a key role in the world of industrial relations. The threat of the collective removal of labour power has proved to be at the heart of achieving better wages and working conditions for over a century. Even in settings where workers do not have the right to strike,[8] 'illegal' strikes have regularly shown their power to make gains at the bargaining table. Thus, the ability to demonstrate to the employer that the membership of the union is behind the threat to strike and is capable of conducting a strong, well-run picket line, remains a critical element of successful collective bargaining.

Throughout the interviews on which this paper is based,[9] strikers frequently commented that, as one noted, 'I don't think people thought we could do it.' Indeed there was a popular assumption that a group of recently organized, largely female, service-sector workers would not be able to sustain a first-contract strike for a lengthy period.[10] As one prominent RWDSU organizer commented: 'I thought maybe if we were lucky we could keep things going for two or three weeks ... but I've got to be honest, I think I underestimated these people. I think we all did. And I even think they weren't sure they could do it themselves.'

The Eaton's strike offers an opportunity to examine a rare event through the eyes of, as one striker referred to her co-strikers, 'an extraordinary group of ordinary people ... your basic moms, wives, sisters, and girlfriends.' There have been many significant female-dominated strikes throughout Canadian history, yet few have been in the private, service sector. A service-sector strike, involving largely part-time, low-paid female workers with little background in the labour movement, is particularly important because it offers insights into a key group of workers that the labour movement is depending on for growth as industrial economies become rapidly dominated by service work.

Because this strike was in the service sector and conducted in settings through which many members of the public had to pass daily, new techniques had to be learned to deal with people who crossed the picket line. It did not take long for the strikers to question industrial style picketing tactics they were expected to use. They learned to run successful picket lines in their own right and to develop creative ways to sell their cause to the public. As the months wore on and the strike spilled over into their personal lives, they had to adjust their roles as mothers, wives, and friends to the world of a strike. Through the interviews, we see how they confronted friends and relatives who continued to shop at Eaton's and the series of personal changes such a strike can bring.

This paper will explore the strikers' experiences and perceptions of themselves as striking members of a union. Our focus will be on how they changed between that first chilly day of what turned out to be one of Ontario's coldest winters in years and the disappointing settlement in May 1985. What was it like that first morning for a group that had never been on strike before? What tactics worked to build support for their dispute? What did they do on all those picket shifts, six days a week, month after month? How did they keep their spirits up? How did the strike affect their roles and responsibilities within the home? Were their friends and relatives supportive? The answers to these questions are critical for a deeper understanding of the nature of militancy that is likely to characterize female-dominated, service-sector strikes and will hopefully lead to more successful collective-bargaining power for organized women workers.

THE METHODOLOGY AND PEOPLE INTERVIEWED

The interview data presented in this paper are based on tape-recorded sessions with strikers who remained on the picket line until the last day of the strike in May 1985 and returned to work at Eaton's. Interviewing began immediately after the strike ended and continued for six months through to January 1986. The bulk of the interviews are from the Toronto-area stores: fifteen each from Shoppers World and Scarborough Town, the two largest stores; eleven from Eglinton-Yonge, a comparatively smaller store; six from Bramalea, a relatively large store and the first unionized; three from St Catharines; but none from the small warehouse store in London, Ontario.

The interviews ran from one to two hours in length and were generally held in the respondent's home. Since the majority of Eaton's workers are women, and indeed most of the 'die-hard' strikers were women (approximately 95 per cent), it was decided to interview a majority of women. Thus, forty-four of the fifty interviews were with women and the focus in this analysis will be on these data.

Most of the strikers who stayed out on the line to the last day of the strike were mothers with children. Two-thirds of those interviewed had children living at home and many said they were attracted to retail work because it was 'close to home' and offered flexible hours more conducive to family life than a nine-to-five office job. Very few had ever been in a union, and only a handful had ever been on strike before. In keeping with the traditional profile of Canadian retail workers, all those interviewed were white and about three-quarters Canadian-born. They ranged in age from twenty-five to sixty-seven, although most of those interviewed were between thirty and fifty.

Most of the strikers were in families in which their relatively low pay represented a significant part of the family income. About two-thirds of those with spouses had partners who held what social scientists would classify as 'working class' jobs, while the other third had partners with clearly 'middle class' occupations. Of those interviewed, twenty-seven had worked at Eaton's for ten or more years and the average length of service for the fifty people interviewed was eleven years. There were relatively few part-time students on the picket line, despite the large number of students employed by Eaton's in recent years, since the company, like so many other large retailers, had moved to a high proportion of young part-time workers. Although students obviously could not put in the same time on the picket line as those who were not in school, they were clearly underrepresented among active picketers. When asked about this matter, many interviewers said that the students did not 'see themselves working at Eaton's forever.' These are people, said one interviewee, 'who will quit because their work schedule conflicts with their basketball practice.' Among those interviewed in this research, there were only two students.

THE FIRST DAY

Many of the strikers said their reaction to the first day on the line was a mixture of embarrassment, humiliation, and a sense of bewilderment at being there:

My first thought was 'Oh this is degrading. Absolutely degrading – to put on a sign and walk around.' You see, I've never pictured me being on a picket line. It was just ridiculous and yet there I was. So for the first few days my major reaction was, 'What have I done?'

I was embarrassed ... What was going through my mind was 'What are people thinking of us?' Here we are walking on the sidewalk, in full view of the public ... parading up and down in front of a store ... It just seemed very strange.

Linked to the reactions of embarrassment and humiliation was also a strong sense that they wanted to 'look respectable' – a desire, they quickly learned, that came to be incompatible with keeping warm. Almost every respondent made some comment similar to these two:

There I was ... heels on, silk scarf, my good coat. Trying to project an image of respectability when all the time I thought, 'I'm going to freeze to death.'

Everyone was dressed the same way. I think we thought, 'Well, we're going to be out there, and people are going to look at us.' And we sort of thought, 'We should dress up.' We sort of wanted to present our case by the way we looked. But what a comparison, the way we looked that first week and then how we looked at the end of the strike.

The desire to project a 'respectable' image appeared related both to how they saw their work and to their perceptions of strikers. Most saw their work as 'white collar' and 'professional' while they saw people on strike, as one commented, as 'a rough bunch ... steel workers with hard hats.' Most of those interviewed were quite shocked by the things that people yelled at them from passing cars, a fact which tended to reinforce for some their own views of people on strike. As the weeks wore on, however, many mentioned that they eventually 'learned to swear' at those who harassed them on the line and described the process as 'toughening us up,' learning to 'hold our own,' and 'not being such wimps.' As one noted: 'We were mothers who taught our kids not to use those words, and they were being used to describe us ... hookers, assholes, commies. People giving us the finger ... Oh that was hard to take. But you got used to it. Eventually you learned to give them the finger.'

Perhaps one of the most important and distressing aspects of the first day of the strike was how poorly prepared the strikers were for the basic mechanics of being in, let alone running, a strike. A few mentioned that they had been drafted to make signs; however, they had been given virtually no instructions about where to picket, what to do, and what action has legal. Most described the first day as chaotic and confusing and many were annoyed that they had been given so little information by their union. Several felt that, if 'even a small flyer' had been handed out explaining the basics, everything would have gone more smoothly. In fact, some of those interviewed actually felt more people would have come out to picket the first day and ended up staying out on the line if they had known what they were getting into. One striker described how on the first morning she was told she was a picket captain: 'I said, "Fine ... so what does a picket captain do?" ' Another recalls how a police officer showed a group of strikers at the Shoppers World store how to picket: 'I remember him saying "Well, put a sign on and just walk up and down." Then he told us we could slow traffic to explain our strike ... but we weren't supposed to stop it for long. I thought, "Why is a policeman explaining to me how to strike; my union should have done this." '

As the winter set in, the cold weather played a role in the almost physical transformation of the strikers, as one interviewee noted, 'from "a group of ladies" to "real strikers" serious about what they were doing.' They learned to dress for the weather, borrowing clothes, and especially boots, from husbands and older sons. There were many, many stories about boots: how people cried as their favourite seven-year-old Italian leather boots were destroyed by the road salt; how one day at Shoppers World a whole picket shift appeared bootless – their boots had all shrunk at the same time after a particularly slushy period; and, at the Scarborough Town store, the most famous pair of boots of all, 'Ruth Lutes's moon boots' – an old pair of her son's one-inch-high 'platform boots' that were a man's size eleven. Ruth, who takes a size seven, said she felt 'taller, and more powerful somehow, in those crazy boots.'

The boot stories illustrate the in-jokes that became an important part of picket-line culture for the strikers. Most of them talked about their daily routines: where they ate, how the restaurant staff was so supportive, how this donut shop became their 'home away from home,' and so on. One picket line at the Scarborough Town store had a trailer that was brought to the site each day to provide shelter and a place to cook and make coffee. This trailer became an important social setting where the strikers, as one noted, 'cooked, cried, and thawed out.'

When asked what they talked about every day, a typical response was, 'Everything! recipes, kids, husbands, clothes, how we hated Eaton's, our lives, our dreams, just everything.' It became clear that, despite the inevitable 'what are we doing out here?' depression that set in from time to time, the strikers became very close to their immediate picket shift, to the extent that they began to feel they were showing up for picket duty so they would not let 'the girls' down. Many described occasions when they dragged themselves out of bed and thought, 'What's the point?' and then, as one typical interviewee commented:

I'd say to myself, 'Look everyone else is going to be there, Dorothy, Bernice, ... Everyone else is just as tired of this whole thing as you. We're in this together so get going.' And it seemed to work. The morning shift on my line were a very reliable group ... very reliable.

You became very close to the people you saw every day. Closer, I'd say, with a group than I've ever been in my life. You knew you were experiencing something special that would stay with you forever. These are people I came to trust.

For many of those interviewed this was the first time in their lives they had become so close to a group of women. They all described how, after talking so much day after day, they came to know their immediate picket shift, as one expressed it, 'almost better than anyone I had ever known.' Another noted: 'After the first month or so of talking you really got to know about everyone's life ... Then for the next month you could build on this knowledge and the conversations became very intense and we would actually psychoanalyse each other. You know, "Well maybe you resented him because of the way your first husband treated you" ... things like that?'

One of the strikers at Scarborough Town commented that she 'felt sorry' for those who voted for the union (as most had), but never came out or never stayed out. She said each would have 'been a better person' if they had 'stood up to their commitment.' This was a frequently recurring theme. This group of strikers tended to see themselves as 'people of their word' who, as one striker put it, 'did what they said they were going to do.' They saw the strike as a commitment they had made, 'sort of a promise to each other,' or as 'a deal I made with myself.' It is not surprising that these strikers should perceive themselves in this way. They were indeed people who had 'stuck it out over the long haul' and who were on the line every day, rain or shine, and in many case sleet and snow.

LINKS TO THE WOMEN'S MOVEMENT

Most of these women were also exposed, for the first time in their lives, to the organized women's movement. The strikers were asked to lead the International Women's Day March in Toronto in 1985. There were numerous comments from those interviewed about not realizing that this march was held every year and many were staggered by the size of the march – well over six thousand people. A prominent striker, Maria Cavalli, addressed the crowd on behalf of the strikers and described how she was overwhelmed by seeing so many women together cheering for the strikers: 'When they [women] have the support of other women that truly care ... All of a sudden your adrenalin flows, and your morale goes up ... A woman needs a woman. Only another woman can understand what you're really going through ... Like that big rally at Women's Day, that was unbelievable, that was something you really felt. Just to see that sea of women ... that was fantastic.'

There were many links to the women's movement through support work right from the start of the strike. In the first weeks of the strike members of the employment committee of the National Action Committee on the Status of Women (NAC), in conjunction with the Toronto-based feminist musical group the Red Berets, organized the singing of especially adapted 'striking' Christmas carols in front of the Eaton Centre in downtown Toronto. The Women's Strike Support Coalition, formed at an Organized Working Women's conference in early January 1986 and including feminists from both the women's and the labour movements, was responsible for many of the most successful support rallies held throughout the strike.

Although a basically cooperative relationship eventually developed between those doing support work for the strike within the RWDSU and those doing support work in the women's movement, several of the unionists and activists interviewed acknowledged a noticeable degree of tension between the two. One of the best examples of this tension was the announcement at one of the early Coalition meetings by the two RWDSU employees assigned to the Eaton's strike, Donna Johanssen and Geri Sheedy, that as far as the RWDSU was concerned, they could only attend weekly Women's Strike Support Coalition meetings 'on their own time.' Although both Johanssen and Sheedy continued to work actively with the Coalition until the end of the strike, there were many incidents of them explicitly being told that

RWDSU work 'came first.' As the strike wore on, however, there appeared to be a much higher degree of trust between the largely male staff of the RWDSU and the Women's Strike Support Coalition. This was especially demonstrated in the cooperation needed to mount the ambitious Massey Hall concert.

SERVICE- OR INDUSTRIAL-SECTOR PICKET-LINE TACTICS

Early on in the strike, workers from male-dominated unions came out to the Eaton's picket lines to show solidarity in the evenings and on weekends. In the first weeks, most of the lines experienced some conflict between the women strikers and the men from other unions over how picketing should be done. The male unionists basically felt that the traffic going in and out of the busy shopping malls should be slowed down considerably to put pressure on Eaton's as well as hurt other retail outlets, who would then complain to Eaton's to settle the strike. Here is one striker's dilemma about how she felt:

I remember the construction workers used to come and help us out on Saturday ... They would stop the traffic to let people know we were there, but in essence, that action of stopping the traffic ended up turning against us ... People told us they were supporting us until they had to wait so long ... It also increased the abuse we took. 'Hi, I'd like to tell you about our labour dispute ... Hi, asshole, I'd like to tell you how I'm now late for work' ... In theory the men may be correct, but that's a pretty big mall. What about all the other businesses that were being hurt too?

In the end this line, as did most others, decided it was best not to slow cars, even though it meant some supporters from male-dominated unions would not come out any more – 'They just thought it was useless,' recalled one women. The striker whose comments we have just heard returned to this discussion of tactics in the latter part of her interview. Although she was 'quite sure' that they had made the right decision – not to slow down cars – she admitted to 'some nagging doubts,' which she expressed in this manner:

When the construction workers were there, I've got to be honest, there was a little bit of a sense of power. One time a car that had nearly hit one of us swung by and the construction worker with me kicked the car and a piece fell off. Twenty minutes later the fellow who had been in the car came walking over and picked up the piece and left, but he didn't say anything. I don't think he dared say anything ... And I remember thinking that this was kind of a good feeling, you know, like power.

In commenting on this tension between what tactics were appropriate, key RWDSU organizer Carole Currie supported the strikers 'one hundred per cent' in their decision not to slow traffic: 'I think a lot of those people (male support picketers) were thinking about industrial sites where the only place the cars were going was the worksite ... The dilemma was that we had a lot of members in those malls who were supporting us and they had to go to work ... So the strikers were right. It was their strike and they knew their clientele. They knew where their sympathy was and they knew how to get it.'

In terms of getting support, the strikers did develop some extremely creative ideas to capture public attention and win support. One of the most successful was the 'Strikers Uncrate the Sun Day' at the Scarborough Town store. This event, a parody of an annual marketing campaign, 'Eaton's Uncrates the Sun,' was staged on one of the coldest days of the year. The strikers sat in deck chairs, with sun glasses on, played with beach balls and hung bathing suits and beach towels on a long clothes line. The event attracted media attention and got rave reviews from passers-by all day. 'Nearly everyone who drove by laughed and waved. It was a huge success. We had a ball and I think we got more support for the strike that day than any other.'

The strikers all enjoyed the support rallies organized by the Women's Strike Support Coalition, especially the ones at their own stores. In terms of tactics, however, there was one incident about which most strikers felt strongly, again highlighting for them a 'different approach' to the kind of strike they wanted to run and to the tactics of some of the otherwise 'much appreciated' support from those primarily in male-dominated unions. This incident occurred at a large rally for the Scarborough Town store and involved 'some guys from the CAW' (Canadian Automobile Workers) letting some mice loose inside the store. Most of the strikers interviewed objected to the prank and many thought it was 'childish.' One typical comment was that 'it was disgusting and it got very bad press.' 'It may be a cliché,' noted one striker, 'but women tend to dislike mice running around – I don't think a woman would have thought up this idea.'

As this example illustrates, many strikers developed a keen sense of how they wanted to portray their strike to the ever-present media.

Some became quite sophisticated in analysing how something would look in the newspaper and how to talk to reporters. At the first Women's Strike Support Coalition rally, held in February on the same morning in six different sites in southern Ontario, metre-half high Eaton's credit cards were cut up in a symbolic gesture to support the Eaton's boycott the CLC had launched. One striker commented on how these huge cards created 'a wonderful visual effect for the press' and another noted that these cards 'made it very likely that the [news]papers would use a photo when they covered the piece.'

MORE 'CREATIVE' TACTICS

Despite the fact that one could argue that the strikers chose a less confrontational style on the line, they also engaged in numerous, as one striker referred to them, 'ah, shall we say, more 'creative' tactics.' One of these was simply taking things back – things that had been purchased in the month or two leading up to the strike, or gifts 'unthinking relatives and friends' had given them for Christmas. One striker commented that she felt like a fool because of the way she used to buy slightly damaged merchandise 'just to help Eaton's out a little – a loyal worker.' She said it felt great returning a stepladder to Eaton's and then going out and buying one from Sears. As part of the returning process the salesclerk asks why the product is being returned. Several of those interviewed said they always enjoyed saying, 'Because I'm on strike against this company,' when asked their reason for returning an item.

Another more disruptive tactic was to go into an Eaton's store and put together a large purchase, have the order put through and then say that they had forgotten something and walk away. One striker who did this regularly had a 'delinquent' Visa card she used especially for this exercise. When they told her they were 'dreadfully sorry' but her card was not accepted, she would just say, 'Oh well, too bad,' and leave. Another tactic was to 'rearrange' counters and clothing racks so that things were mixed up, causing more work for the store's scab labour.

The strikers' more militant side was also shown to people who were very rude or 'nearly knocked us down' as they whizzed past their picket line. One line kept a huge stack of hard-to-remove, round, blue 'Boycott Eaton's' stickers ready for people who were particularly obnoxious. They would wait until the people had gone into the store and then go and put stickers on their car. There were a few rumoured incidents of holes being punched in tires and some cars being scratched; however, none of those interviewed knew anyone who was involved. On the whole they felt that they were, as several noted, 'a pretty tame bunch.'

As the strike dragged on, personal anger and frustration led some individual strikers to do things they would 'never dream of doing' before the strike. On her way home late one night a striker put boycott stickers all over a neighbour's truck because he told her he was totally against the strike and she was lucky to have a job. Another, while driving to Guelph one day repeatedly cut off an Eaton's delivery truck and slowed down so the driver would have to see her Boycott Eaton's bumper sticker. She says she 'knows it was crazy, completely nuts. I could have killed myself. I just got so angry when I saw that Eaton's symbol.' Another spoke of 'very militant' dreams in which she 'kidnapped one of her managers and threatened to bomb the store.'

As noted, however, the strikers strategically opted for less-confrontational methods to win support for their dispute. They decided that a strike held outside a large shopping mall could not afford to slow traffic and still win over people to the idea of not shopping at Eaton's. They decided that humour and 'being polite' were, on the whole, the best techniques to win over the undecided shopper. They also realized that it did not really matter how they looked but, as one noted, 'how we handled ourselves out there ... how we presented ourselves to the customers and the press.' They also learned that one of the most important things about running a good strike was to picket regularly, an activity that many found could become a fulfilling and even enjoyable experience.

ON THE HOME FRONT

Despite the close bonds that eventually formed between the strikers on the line, as one noted, 'You still had to go home at night and if there was no support there – that was tough.' Support from family and friends was a critical element in keeping strikers coming out to the line and their spirits up. Indeed, a strong case could be made that without this type of support, particularly from one's spouse and children, it would have been very difficult to stay out throughout the strike. When asked how their spouse felt about them being on strike, most married women said that their partner 'was great.' Sue Arduino, a picket captain at the Eglinton-Yonge store was pregnant throughout the strike. She recalls her husband being very understanding: 'My husband was fantastic. I mean, I didn't pay a lot of attention to him. You know, I would come in, say 'hi,' grab a bite and then be on the phone all night with the strike ... It's supposed to be a romantic time, this young couple expecting their first baby.' Another striker commented: 'I think your husband had to be supportive or you really couldn't be there. This thing was very disruptive to your home life. Piles of dishes, laundry and ironing everywhere. No time to make dinner, no time to shop. Looking like a lumber jack everyday and talking non-stop about one thing – the strike ... It would get to anybody – you had to have supportive people on the home front or you were very miserable.' One very active striker at Scarborough Town, Maria, felt that she would not have made it through the whole strike without the help of her husband and friends. When she got depressed, her husband would say, 'Come on, that's not the Maria I know.' Her children thought she made a 'great radical' and brought grandchildren to the picket line on weekends. One of her best friends put a Boycott Eaton's sign in her variety-store window, and then when she saw her on television one day, she called and said 'Maria, you were so great I've put two signs in my window – one on each side.'

It was not always such a supportive environment, especially for those who did not come out or stay out on strike. A lot of those interviewed told stories about how some husbands essentially pressured their wives back to work. As one commented, 'Well they're Greek and he just said, "Enough is enough – you're going back tomorrow." ' Another interviewee's best friend confided to her that she just could not take the fighting and tension at home and had decided to go back in, but came out at lunch breaks to walk the line. 'I know she felt terrible, but what could she do?'

Some of the family tension was undoubtedly related to the financial stress caused by the strike. It is also likely that some husbands saw the strike as a threat to their control in the home. As one striker noted, 'No dinner on the table, piles of laundry in a corner, the house a mess – meanwhile a wife galavanting around to support rallies.' It seemed clear that the strike had to become a family affair to enable a striker to remain on the line. Given the male-dominated power dynamics in many families, coupled with women's domestic role as 'chief cook and bottle washer' and primary caregiver in the home, women strikers more than men strikers require an accommodating domestic setting to be able to devote energy to a strike. One story of a non-supportive husband came from a striker who did not want to be interviewed in her home, but came over to a friend's house for a joint interview. Her husband was an accountant who was described as being very 'anti-union.' To make matters worse, her stepson worked at Eaton's throughout the strike. She recalls a typical, tension-filled discussion about the strike: 'It was one of the first Saturday mornings and he, my stepson, asked me if I was going to the picket line that day. "Of course" I said. Then he asked if I'd give him a ride. So, in sort of a joking way I said, "I'm not driving a scab to work." So my husband got angry and said, "Don't you let her call you that. If you want to work, you work." So I thought, "Oh God, is this what it's going to be like?" And it was, all the time.'

FRIENDS: 'YOU WIN SOME AND YOU LOSE SOME'

Perhaps the most emotional parts of each interview were when strikers described how a close friend or relative had shopped at Eaton's during the strike. They all felt very strongly about the boycott and were hurt when they saw or found out someone close to them had shopped in an Eaton's store. One striker recalled going to a birthday party for her husband and when he opened the box it was from Eaton's. She said her face 'just dropped' when people saw what had happened; they said, 'Don't worry, don't worry it's not from Eaton's we just used an old box.' She was relieved, but surprised to experience such intense emotion that was brought on by thinking someone had shopped for her husband at Eaton's. One of the most poignant stories comes from a striker from Shoppers World who saw her sister-in-law buying a coat in the store. She described feeling 'crushed and betrayed.' On her way home from the line she gathered together some literature on the strike and stopped by her sister-in-law's house:

As soon as I stepped in she looked up and said, 'Hi, how are you?' 'Well,' I said, 'I'm kind of upset. I saw you shopping in the store today.' ... She got quite uppity and said, 'I don't like being spied on ... or being told where to shop.' So I looked her in the eye and said, 'At a time like this you count on the support of your family and friends. I'm here because I don't think you really understand why we are out there. I can't tell you or anyone else where to shop. I'm just asking for your support' ... I was starting to cry so I just turned and left. I didn't see her for months after that.

A similar story comes from Betty at Scarborough Town Centre. She saw one of her closest friends shopping in Eaton's – in her own department. So she confronted her: 'Ruth, you're not shopping at Eaton's, are you?' and she said, 'Yes I am'; so I just said, 'Thanks a lot for keeping me out in the cold,' and walked away. In a few days her friend phoned:

She said 'Well, you know how difficult it is to buy Martin clothes.' I said, 'It's a lot more difficult for people on the line to pay their bills. You don't have a mortgage. Your kids take singing lessons – $50 a lesson. You have everything! This strike is about people who don't.' I just couldn't help myself that's just the way I felt. I didn't see her until the strike was over and she came up to me in a florist's. 'I guess it's hello and goodbye.' I just smiled and she said she wanted me to know that she hadn't shopped there since that day. I said, 'Well that's nice.' I couldn't bring myself to say, 'Oh forget it.' Maybe one day I'll be able to be friends with her again; we were for fifteen years.

Suzanne at Eglinton-Yonge describes an encounter with a long-time friend who bought her make-up at Eaton's during the strike. She ended a lengthy interchange, and a long-term friendship, with a theme heard throughout the interviews: 'I don't care if you believe in unionism or not, you don't have to, but you should believe in me ... If you were out on a picket line, I never would have crossed it ... I have things that I have to do in my life and all I'm asking from you is a little support. I'm just asking you to stay out of that Goddamn store!'

Many of those interviewed felt that the boycott was particularly important for them because it was 'about shopping.' Since women do most of the shopping they felt that the challenge they faced was to reach out to women, as consumers, and convince them that Eaton's was not a good employer of women. Therefore, it hurt more when 'housewives' would push by the picket line into Eaton's. They felt a special sense of betrayal when it was 'someone just like yourself.' Students you could forgive; 'What did they know?' Even 'expensively dressed career women or business men' were also more easily forgiven; but someone who looked like she could be working beside you one day – 'that hurt more for some reason.' It also seemed especially important for strikers when women showed support. One striker recalls an older woman who came over and put two twenty-dollar bills in the strike-support bucket: 'She said she thought we were wonderful and was with us all the way. She had been in the telephone operators' strike at Bell years ago and said her retirement was much better now because of that strike. It made us feel wonderful all day. Things like that sort of took the cold away.'

I'VE CHANGED, I'M A DIFFERENT PERSON

Without being prompted in any way the strikers repeatedly mentioned being 'a different person.' 'The strike changed my personality, I went from being mouse to mouth,' noted one. 'I used to be mousy, now I'm more aggressive,' commented another. The observation that many of the strikers felt they had changed was often related to their new-found awareness of politics, the media, and the women's movement. Many also said it involved their increased ability to confront friends, family, and in many cases members of the public in pursuing support for their dispute. Commonly heard phrases were 'I had my eyes opened' or 'I became aware of how the world works.' Some of those interviewed noticed not only a transformation in themselves, but in those around them. Here are two lengthy quotes that capture the repeatedly made point about how the strikers described the change they experienced as a result of the strike:

It was very eye-opening, it was very mind-opening ... I don't find things tolerable like I used to – like sexual harassment. I've talked to a lot of strikers on different lines and they say that as women they will never be uninvolved again ... So they've learned that. And I think that in itself is a big plus because we've been put down so long in that company. We became subservient. We didn't open our mouths. We were afraid of everything ... of management coming at us with a complaint.

The people I've known in the store and been friends with have changed a lot ... Women I would have considered before the strike indecisive are now much more assertive. I think they always had this quality, the character to stand up for something, but I think the strike brought that out in them. That makes me happy because they're not standing back and taking this crap which I think they've done for many years ... The strike has brought that assertiveness to the front.

Besides the personal change, there were also extensive comments about 'people seeing them differently.' Many noted that their children, for instance, 'thought they made a great radical' or 'couldn't believe it was me marching in all the rallies.'

CONCLUSION

What can be learned from a detailed look at this strike? The first thing, of course, is that female department-store workers are more than capable of a strong and lengthy showing on the picket line; however, they do need basic information about how to run a strike and what to expect on the line to get the strike off to a good start and to ensure that as many people as possible are attracted to join the picket line from the outset. It is also clear that a female-dominated strike is quite different than one primarily involving men. Women will develop their own strategies about how best to run their strike and to win support for their cause. These interviews also suggest that women need and enjoy warm companionship from their co-strikers to develop the necessary commitment to stay out on strike. Indeed, it is these social commitments that can become a motivating force in maintaining a long strike. Given their domestic roles, women strikers, likely more than male strikers, need support from their family and friends, as well as from the intense relationships they develop on the line, to be able to sustain a lengthy labour dispute.

In their interviews the strikers have painted a detailed picture of a long, female-dominated strike that can be shared with women workers who are nervous about joining a union because, as is so often heard, and indeed was echoed by many of the strikers themselves before they joined the union, 'unions mean strikes; I don't want to go on strike.' In response, a typical Eaton's striker would likely note: 'My God. I'm not saying it wasn't hard. Six months in the freezing cold. It was hard alright ... all those creeps giving you the finger ... but it was also wonderful. We became so close ... we changed so much. I know I speak for the rest of us at my store when I say we wouldn't have missed it for the world!'

Since the credible threat of strike action is one key element of successful collective bargaining, it is critical that women workers develop a perception of themselves as able to sustain strike action in support of their negotiating demands. Not only is it important for them to see themselves in roles in which they confront their employers, it is also critical that they know that a strike can be an exhilarating and transformative experience for those involved. Understanding how gender shapes labour militancy, in a very practical way, can prepare both unionists and members alike for concerted workplace action in female-dominated settings. This understanding could be useful for both union organizing as well as preparing current members in largely female workplaces to look to the strike as a realistic option when faced with an intransigent employer.

NOTES

1 The Women's Strike Support Coalition (WSSC) was formally launched at an Organized Working Women's (OWW) conference in early January 1985. The WSSC met weekly throughout the strike to coordinate support work. It must be noted that although the committee got the idea for many support activities, there were numerous people, including many men, involved in mounting an actual event. For example, one of the key organizers for the Massey Hall Concert was writer Rick Salutin, who used his extensive contacts in the Canadian arts community to pull together an impressive list of performers which included, among many others, actor Eric Peterson, singer Nancy White, and the rock group Parachute Club.

2 Eileen Tallman Sufrin, *The Eaton's Drive: The Campaign to Organize Canada's Largest Department Store 1948 to 1952* (Toronto: Fitzhenry & Whiteside 1982)

3 David Olive, 'Trouble at Canada's General Store,' *Toronto Life*, March 1985, 33–5, 51–60

4 This version of the story differs slightly from the one presented in the media, which does not mention the role that Mike Dunlop's wife played in initiating the discussion about a union. This account of the legendary chance encounter was from a joint interview with Carol Currie and Gerri Sheedy, 14 Nov. 1985.

5 *Globe and Mail*, 23 Feb. 1987

6 Anne Forrest, 'Organizing Eaton's: Do the Old Laws Still Work?' *Windsor Yearbook of Access to Justice* 8 (1988): 190–213.

7 The Ontario Labour Relations Board will approve an 'automatic certification' if the union wanting representation rights has signed up more than 55 per cent of the bargaining unit.

8 Strikes are illegal, for example, in cases where the government has removed the right to strike statutorily from a group of public-sector

workers, or in situations in which employees strike 'mid-term,' that is, when the contract has not expired – thus making a strike illegal under Canadian labour law.

9 This paper is part of a larger project, a book on the strike.

10 Bradley J. Pragnell, *Organizing Department Store Workers: The Case of RWDSU at Eaton's, 1983–1987* (Kingston: Queen's University Industrial Relations Centre, Research Report no. 22, 1989)

2

Alberta Nurses and the 'Illegal' Strike of 1988

REBECCA PRIEGERT COULTER

On 25 January 1988, more than eleven thousand staff nurses who were members of the United Nurses of Alberta (UNA) directly challenged the province's *Labour Relations Act*, which prohibits strikes by hospital workers, and began an illegal strike that was to last for nineteen days. Because the willingness of union members to strike is an important measure of worker militancy, the ability of the UNA to call an illegal strike and sustain it in the face of extremely punitive retaliatory measures by employers and the state is compelling evidence that Alberta nurses are the most militant members of an occupational group of women that has become increasingly militant over the past few years.[1] Indeed, for UNA, the 1988 strike was the seventh one, and the fourth involving hospital nurses, since the union's founding in 1977.[2]

The 1988 strike provides a key entry point for understanding the organization and politics of the United Nurses of Alberta and opens up questions about how a professional women's union[3] positions itself with respect to both the male-dominated union movement and the women's movement in Canada. What is it that explains the solidarity and militancy of Alberta's unionized nurses? To explore this question this chapter begins by looking at UNA's formative experiences with collective bargaining and government intervention and then discusses the conditions which contributed to the nurses' ability to call and maintain the illegal strike of 1988. It moves next to outline the events leading up to the strike and provides a brief history of the strike itself. Finally, the strike and its aftermath are examined in the context of a discussion of UNA's relations with the labour movement and women's organizing.

UNIONIZING ALBERTA NURSES

Prior to 1977, the Alberta Association of Registered Nurses (AARN) was the only organization which gave nurses a province-wide collective voice. Established in 1916, the AARN, like contemporary nurses' organizations elsewhere, used occupational closure strategies in an effort to attain professional status for nursing. That is, by attempting to control standards of nursing practice and the education of nurses, the AARN hoped to establish nursing as an independent profession which could lay claim to acceptable levels of remuneration for its members as well as allow nurses control over their own work.[4] However, by the mid 1960s the salaries and conditions of work in the province compared unfavourably with many other provincial jurisdictions, and Alberta nurses began to organize bargaining units at the hospital level to seek redress. Between 1964 and 1966 twelve Staff Nurse Associations were certified by the Board of Industrial Relations and thirty-eight were recognized voluntarily by hospital boards. This grass-roots and locally initiated approach to organizing undoubtedly contributed to nurses' sense of ownership of 'their' union. Within the AARN, a Provincial Staff Nurse Committee (PSNC), which excluded management nurses, was created to handle collective-bargaining activities.

In the late 1960s and early 1970s disputes between nurses and their employers intensified as the nature of the nursing work changed and hospitals became larger and more bureaucratized. In 1972, the growing militancy of rank-and-file nurses was demonstrated by the decision of the AARN to remove its ban on strike action by nurses. Finally, as a result of a growing division within AARN between the management nurses who controlled the Provincial Council and the PSNC, the PSNC broke away on 6 May 1977 to establish an independent union, the United Nurses of Alberta.[5]

The timing of and the context for the creation of a separate union for staff nurses was significant. In 1975, the federal Liberal government began the process of reducing funding for health care. Increases in funding were tied to the GNP rather than to the real costs of health care. Block funding replaced cost sharing and transfer payments from the federal government to provincial governments were reduced. During this period (1975–8) the federal government also instituted its program of wage and price controls. Both cutbacks in funding for health care and wage controls were used by employers to argue against wage increases and improved working conditions for Alberta nurses. The inability or unwillingness of the AARN to respond forcefully to the employers, and the nature of the conflict between management and staff nurses within the professional association, further distanced staff nurses from the cautious approach to collective bargaining favoured by the AARN and enhanced the solidarity of staff nurses.

When the UNA moved into its new office in June 1977, province-wide negotiations were in progress and had reached the conciliation stage. Few in the new union felt that conciliation would result in significant gains for hospital nurses. On 4 July 1977, the union began a legal strike at seven Alberta hospitals. Within four days the provincial government intervened by declaring a public emergency and ordering the nurses back to work. With no strike fund and only two months' worth of dues in the bank, the nurses could not afford to defy the government order and returned to work. The government set up an emergency tribunal to award a settlement binding on both parties and appointed Mr Justice Bowen as the arbitrator. This first strike established a pattern of UNA militancy and government intervention that led directly to the 1988 strike.

Nurses benefited financially from the Bowen award. Given a 9 per cent wage increase at a time when the province, following the federal government's lead on wage controls, had legislated a 6 per cent ceiling, UNA became one of the few unions to gain exemption. The provincial cabinet had to issue a special Order-in-Council allowing employers to pay the full 9 per cent increase. At the same time, Mr Justice Bowen rejected UNA's demand for an automatic dues-collection clause. He said that because nurses were professionals 'they would not require any coercion of any kind to own up to their obligations and pay their required dues, and therefore the clause was unnecessary.'[6] Ironically, this decision increased the union's visibility in its formative year. Union leaders had to campaign actively for members and nurses had to make a conscious decision to join the union by signing a release allowing employers to deduct union dues from their pay cheques.

UNA, then, was born under circumstances which quickly focused attention on a number of key elements including the presumed split between professional and union activities, the question of striking, and the role of the government in settling disputes. The union's first foray into strike action did not lead to a negotiated settlement but did produce a substantial wage increase. This outcome can only have solidified support for the union. Within the context of cutbacks to health-care funding, the high visibility of the union movement's opposition to wage controls, and the increased militancy of other professionals such as teachers in the 1970s, nurses received validation for their decision to unionize.

The ten years following the founding of UNA were marked by a number of negotiated settlements and a several strikes during which the provincial government exercised increasingly repressive measures against the union. A collective agreement which included provisions for the application of the Rand formula was reached through negotiations in 1978–9. The next round of negotiations did not go as well, and in April of 1980 UNA began a legal strike at seventy-nine hospitals. After three days members were ordered back to work. This time they refused the order and challenged its validity in the courts. While the case was being argued, negotiations resumed and a settlement was reached.

A central issue in the 1980 negotiations was the professional-responsibility clause. Alberta's *Nursing Profession Act* makes it clear that nurses have a professional responsibility for the quality of patient care. Nurses can lose their licences to practise if it can be shown that they did not provide appropriate care. Originally part of a strategy that sought dignity and decent wages through professionalization, the concept of professional responsibility is now a means through which nurses attempt to exercise some real control in their workplace. Arguing that a professional-responsibility clause is necessary because it relates directly to their legal liability for patient care and their ability to protect their licences to nurse and hence their livelihood, nurses can use such a clause to demand better standards of care and increased staffing on hospital wards. In fact, professional-responsibility clauses represent a melding of the organizational strategies of professionalization and unionization for control in the workplace. It is no surprise that hospital employers have opposed such clauses as a direct attack on management rights. As a result of the 1980 strike, however, Alberta nurses won a professional-responsibility clause along with a 39.8 per cent wage increase over two years, improved work scheduling, and fifty other contract improvements.[7] Union activity and the willingness to strike had paid off for nurses, but the provincial government again had shown its proclivity to interfere with the bargaining process.

In 1981 a new round of bargaining began. Indicative of a new confidence in their worth and power, the nurses demanded a 40–52 per cent wage increase over two years, voluntary overtime and improved scheduling provisions, new health and safety measures, and 229 other changes or new items. In the absence of a settlement by December 1981, the union held a strike vote among its 8300 hospital nurses and, although some locals voted not to strike, the overall results gave UNA a strike mandate. At this point, Alberta's minister of labour intervened and using provisions of the *Labour Relations Act* ordered a Disputes Inquiry Board. This board was to hold hearings into the outstanding items and make recommendations for a settlement. Both parties, UNA and the Alberta Hospitals' Association (AHA), were ordered to attend the hearings of the Disputes Inquiry Board.

When the board brought down its recommendations, the minister of labour ordered a government-supervised vote among UNA members. However, UNA, in keeping with its constitution, had already decided on its own vote and directed its members to boycott the government vote even though the government threatened to impose the results of its own vote regardless of how few nurses actually participated. Ultimately, the government backed down and the results of the UNA vote were accepted.[8] This vote rejected the recommendations of the Disputes Inquiry Board. A few days later the Labour Relations Board refused UNA's request to conduct a second strike vote in those locals which had previously voted against the strike but wanted a chance to reconsider. On 16 February 1982, 6000 nurses at 69 Alberta hospitals went on strike.

On 10 March the government acted to stop the strike. Bill 11, which was an order to force nurses back to work immediately, was introduced and passed on the same day. The bill included severe antiunion sanctions including large fines, the threat of decertification, and restrictions on individuals with respect to working for or holding office in a trade union. The legislation also ordered both parties to appear at a tribunal which would issue a binding settlement. The nurses decided to return to work and in July the tribunal awarded a 29 per cent wage increase over two years, improved scheduling, a safety clause which stipulated that nurses should not have to work alone, and access for nurses to hospital boards. No gains were made on the question of voluntary overtime.

The following spring Bill 44 was passed by the Alberta legislature. The bill amended the *Labour Relations Act* to remove the legal right to strike from all hospital workers including nurses. The legislation provided for compulsory arbitration as a settlement mechanism and specified that awards had to reflect government fiscal policy. The legislation included stiff monetary penalties for unions and union members who decided to defy its conditions and a provision which allowed an employer to apply to the Labour Relations Board for a six-month cessation of dues collection. Nurses believed that the legislation was aimed directly at them and while the next two rounds of bargaining resulted in negotiated settlements between UNA and the AHA, it was only a matter of time before the union would confront the punitive conditions of the new legislation directly.

Baptized in a strike and growing through the experiences of two other hospital strikes, members of UNA developed a strong sense of solidarity. Heavy-handed government intervention only succeeded in building a strong oppositional culture within UNA, for nurses grew increasingly angry about any interference with their right to free and unfettered collective bargaining. Since nurses always seemed to be the first occupational group subjected to a range of fines and sanctions, UNA's membership developed a strong sense of its own power. Government sanctions also contributed to a process in which nurses began to reflect on the gender specificity of their work and their union practices. Margaret Ethier, president of UNA from 1980–8, put this understanding bluntly. Commenting on Bill 11 she said, 'I believe it was pure and simple revenge, and I can understand that. After all, [Premier] Lougheed's boys don't take kindly to being out-smarted by a bunch of women.'[9] Becoming 'bad girls' was increasingly less threatening to nurses and, indeed, was fast becoming part of the union culture.[10]

The union leadership has worked very hard at fostering grass-roots development and involvement. UNA's demand-setting process is open and democratized, with the result that nurses understand and become committed to the union's bargaining position. A bargaining year starts with meetings in each of the hospital locals in which members go over the current agreement and come up with a list of changes and additions that they want. By June each local has sent a list of its demands in to the elected negotiating committee. This committee compiles the demands from all the locals, considers them, and makes recommendations about the demands. The demands from all locals along with the committee's recommendations are then sent back to each of the locals for discussion and consideration. The locals then send delegates to a provincial demand-setting meeting where the negotiating committee presents its set of proposed demands for that round of bargaining. Approximately four hundred delegates meet over three days to consider the negotiating committee's recommendations. Delegates may make changes to the committee's recommendations, but all changes must be based on demands which originated with the locals in the first place. No new demands can be introduced. Each proposal is thoroughly debated and requires a two-thirds approved in order to be included in the final list of demands. The final set of demands coming out of this delegate meeting is then sent back to the locals for ratification, and once it has been approved by at least 50 per cent of the locals and 50 per cent of the members, the package becomes UNA's opening position at the bargaining table.

After negotiations with the AHA begin, UNA members are informed about developments quickly through phone fan-outs, meetings, mailings, electronic mail, and articles in the union's *Newsbulletin*. During the course of negotiations, at least one reporting meeting is held. Elected delegates from the locals meet with the negotiating committee to receive information and to give advice and direction.

During negotiations, if the employers make an acceptable offer of settlement, the negotiating committee may sign a Memorandum of Settlement. The committee then calls a reporting meeting to present the memorandum and recommend its ratification. If the delegates at the meeting agree with the recommendation, the memorandum is sent out to the locals for a ratification vote. If the employers refuse to table an acceptable offer, the negotiating committee calls a reporting meeting, presents the details of the stalemate or impasse, provides an assessment of the bargaining that has occurred to date, and recommends that a strike vote be held in all affected locals. Because UNA categorically refuses to recognize any third-party intervention in negotiations, the only choice before members is to accept the employers' last offer or to go on strike for an improved offer. If the vote supports strike action, the negotiating committee sets the strike and all affected locals are called out. If strike action is rejected by the members, the negotiating committee goes back to the table and accepts the employers' last offer. The memorandum is then sent out to the locals for ratification.[11]

Two principles govern UNA's approach to collective bargaining. The first is that no roll-backs or concessions will ever be considered by the union. The second is that the union rejects all government interference in the form of arbitration, conciliation, or mediation and claims its right to strike as though no legislation to the contrary existed. Clearly UNA has a powerful commitment to free collective bargaining and to a process which 'allows members of UNA to make decisions at every point ... about what they will work for and what they will not.' The union leadership recognizes that it is the open and democratic process of demand setting and reporting back which 'inspires and motivates the members.'[12] Hibberd, noting that the union has utilized the work skills of its members, especially their communication links, to build solidarity and collective commitment to negotiating packages, agrees that the demand-setting process allows 'maximum involvement in the generation of demands, and in the ratification of the final negotiating package,' and it is the process which generates widespread support among members.[13] Put another way, the members experience a strong sense of ownership with respect to bargaining demands because they have been actively involved at each stage.

During the 1980s other events served to increase nurses' solidarity. The much-publicized case of child deaths in Toronto's Hospital for Sick Children, the scapegoating of one nurse, Susan Nelles, and the lack of respect and consideration accorded nurses during the hearings of the Grange Royal Commission confirmed for nurses that their expertise and work were unrecognized and undervalued.[14] As Growe puts it, the Grange Commission marked 'the point in history when the largest organized group of women in Canada lost their innocence'[15] and began to see the realities of their gender and work locations with more clarity.

While nurses are increasingly educated to value holistic, individualized care, hospital work systems are bureaucratically organized with an emphasis on rapid task completion and compliance with established policies and procedures.[16] Like many women workers, nurses have been left with many responsibilities but little authority, and they work within a hierarchical structure that vests most power in the hands of the doctors and administrators who are removed from the day-to-day realities of patient care. As Wilma Scott Heide points out, 'health policy decisions and funding are made in the context of a value system that is white, patriarchal, and capitalist.'[17] As a result, few resources have been directed towards those areas that nurses feel need attention. This helps account for the fact that nurses in the 1970s and 1980s turned to the potential of collective bargaining to effect change in their workplace and work lives. They were fed up with under-staffing and over-work, with inadequate supplies and equipment, with threats to their health and safety, and with the emphasis on business efficiency rather than patient care.

In many ways, the 1988 strike ended up being about all those things. After the strike was over, the president of UNA, Margaret Ethier, stated that nurses had gone on strike for better wages and working conditions 'including the important working condition of being treated with respect.' However, she also observed,

We did not go on strike to protest the health care cutbacks; to show the public that the taxes they pay for proper health care are often spent on anything but patient care; to show that it is becoming more difficult, if not impossible, for nurses to provide quality care, or even safe care for our patients.

We did not go on strike to change the law; to expose to the public the unfairness of current labour laws ...

We didn't go on strike to inspire other nurses and other trade unionists and individual members of the public; to set an example of what can and should be done when people believe enough is enough; to make people realize that sometimes it is necessary to face and deal with conflict and confrontation ... to show the strength that can be derived from a group that is fully committed to common goals – in spite of their personal, political and social differences.

These were not the reasons we went on strike, but the effect of our strike was that we achieved all of the above.[18]

THE 'ILLEGAL' STRIKE OF 1988

While the union's history, the collective memory of the nurses, the material circumstances of nursing, and the specific social and economic climate all made the 1988 strike possible, it was the union's democratic processes which provided the flashpoint for the nurses' militancy. Negotiations began in the fall of 1987 for a new collective agreement. Among the items taken to the table by UNA were ones concerning nurse safety, patient care, and the professional-responsibility article. The employers came to the table proposing many take-aways. In January 1988 the UNA negotiating team received a final offer from the employers, an offer which demonstrated that the proposed roll-backs would not be withdrawn. A reporting meeting was called for 5 January 1988 in Calgary. During discussions of the employers' offer, delegates at the meeting came to the conclusion that their negotiating team had agreed to a provision dealing with short- and long-term disability and Workers' Compensation that amounted to a take-away. Reiterating the cardinal rule that the union would never accept roll-backs, take-aways, regressions, or concessions, delegates at the reporting meeting sent the negotiating team back to the table to tell the employers that the disability provision was not acceptable and that no memorandum of settlement would ever be ratified if it contained that clause. At the same time, a vote on the employers' last offer was set for 22 January with a ballot reading 'Are you willing to go on strike for an improved offer?'

The negotiating team returned to the table and informed the employers of UNA's decision. As a result the employers went to the Labour Relations Board and charged UNA with negotiating in bad faith. At the same time, the AHA asked the LRB to find the union in breach of the legislation which outlawed strikes in the hospitals. The employers took the position that the wording on the ballot consti- tuted a threat to strike, an act which was prohibited by law. On 22 January at 3 AM, the LRB handed down a ruling which said that the wording on the ballot did, indeed, constitute a threat to strike and hence the vote would be illegal. The LRB issued a cease-and-desist order prohibiting the strike vote scheduled to begin that morning.

Between 3 AM and 7 AM UNA utilized its phone fan-out system to inform members of the LRB ruling, and at 7 AM voting started in defiance of that ruling. Nurses were outraged that they could so easily lose the democratic right to vote. As one veteran nurse put it, nurses 'are women with a lot of resolve. We're not putting up with this.'[19] In fact, all 104 eligible hospital locals held the vote with a large voter turn-out. Of the 11,436 nurses eligible to vote, 8,688 defied the ban. Heather Smith, a UNA negotiator in 1988 and now UNA president, observed, 'It's not that we don't take the threats seriously, it's just this time we feel we have to be firm and stand our ground.'[20] In essence, the nurses began engaging in an illegal act the moment they cast ballots. Of those voting, 76 per cent voted to go on strike. On this basis, the negotiating committee called for a strike to commence at all hospitals at 7:30 AM on 25 January 1988.

From the first day of the strike, nurses faced punitive retaliatory actions and these actions quickly escalated. For example, some employers immediately applied to the LRB for permission to cease collecting union dues for six months. At the same time, unions from across Canada began sending telegrams and letters of support, and

Dave Werlin, president of the Alberta Federation of Labour, promised that Alberta workers would support UNA financially. On the second day of the strike the courts granted an injunction against picketing at three Calgary hospitals and one thousand nurses responded by turning up at those hospitals to walk the line. On the third day some individual nurses were served with civil contempt-of-court charges and by the end of the strike over seventy-five individual charges were laid and heard. On the same day, the Alberta government, through the acting attorney-general, charged UNA with criminal contempt. The minister of labour also named a mediator, but because of UNA's opposition on principle to third-party intervention, the union rejected the mediator. Instead, the union asked for an 'independent facilitator' who would have some real power to influence the government with respect to monetary issues and increased funding. A facilitator, Chip Collins, was appointed on 31 January.

On 1 February UNA appeared in court on criminal contempt charges. The government requested a $1 million fine and sequestration of the union's bank accounts and assets. According to UNA, sequestration had never been used in North America. On 4 February UNA was fined $250,000, which sum was to be paid within five days on threat of sequestration. The magnitude of this sum was symbolized by the inability of the cash register to produce one receipt for UNA's secretary-treasurer when she went to pay the fine on 9 February. Instead, she got two receipts for $90,000 and one for $70,000. By the end of the strike the union had paid a total of $400,000 in fines for criminal contempt and $26,750 for civil contempt.[21]

While UNA was making court appearances, so, too, were locals and individual nurses. On 10 February, for example, ten locals and individual members of varying numbers from most of the locals were found in civil contempt and fined. On the same day, employers, who had been keeping up a steady barrage of disciplinary letters to members of small locals, stepped up their action and began to terminate nurses' employment. Three nurses in Fort Vermilion–High Level were told that termination notices were in the mail; Barrhead terminated thirteen nurses; four nurses in Rocky Mountain House and seventy-five in Lethbridge were told they would be fired if they did not report for work within forty-eight hours. In Lac La Biche a black van actually drove all over the town to deliver termination notices.[22] Punishment and fear were being employed as strategies to break the union and the nurses' solidarity.

These strategies were unsuccessful and despite a bitterly cold winter, nurses remained on the picket lines across the province. David Harrigan, vice-president of UNA, estimated that only about 10 per cent of the nurses were scabbing.[23] As one nurse with eighteen years' experience said, 'We really hate being out here. But we have no choice. What do we do?' Another nurse with fourteen years of service spoke of her stomach being in knots when she had to do picket duty, and said she was pessimistic about how successful the strike might be. None the less, she backed the strike because 'I'm supporting my fellow workers right now. The other girls I work with, this is their work, their life, their only means of money.'[24] A much younger nurse said, 'I'm angry. It is not right. We were pushed into a corner ... We didn't have a choice.'[25]

An editorial in the *Calgary Herald* concurred. Nurses 'have not received a square deal from their employers, who have given the impression that one class of essential worker can be treated as indentured servants with impunity.'[26] Another commentator noted that 'the nurses won the battle for public opinion hands down.'[27] The most tangible evidence of wide support was the more than $500,000 raised from donations both big and small. Pensioners donated the dollar or two they could afford, a group of employees at a McDonald's in California passed the hat at work and sent the money to the strike fund. Other individuals, groups, and unions sent money to the Friends of Alberta Nurses Society (FANS), set up by the AFL to ensure that donations would not be sequestered.

By 10 February UNA and the AHA had all but reached a settlement. The only sticking point was the employers' insistence on retaining the right to stop collecting union dues. UNA members report hearing the president of the AHA say to reporters as he left the hotel, 'They have to be punished somehow.' On 11 February an improved offer was tabled by the AHA and employers withdrew their applications to suspend dues collection. On 12 February UNA members voted to accept that offer and a negotiated settlement was reached. The nurses returned to work the following day.

CONCLUSION

The union now terms the 1988 settlement a 'tread water' one. Over a 27-month contract, wage raises of 8 to 10.9 per cent, depending on seniority, were won, but vacation entitlements remained unchanged.

For UNA 'the most important victory was forcing the employer to remove the takeaways from the table.' At the same time, the union leadership believes that the benefits of the 1988 strike were reflected in the gains made during the 1990 round of negotiations.[28]

The 1988 'illegal' strike was significant, too, because it captured the imagination and support of a wide range of people and highlighted UNA's relationships with other unions and with the women's movement. Women's groups and unions rallied to the cause, literally and figuratively, and put pressure on the provincial government to provide funds for a settlement. The National Action Committee on the Status of Women (NAC) and its member groups sent telegrams and letters to the premier urging a rapid settlement. As Edmonton Working Women put it, 'the country's attention was captured by the courage, strength and unity of the members of the United Nurses of Alberta who went on an illegal strike. They defied the law to defend their own democratic rights, and to oppose the erosion of workers' rights on all fronts ... [and to] fight for the patients' rights to quality, publicly funded health care.'[29]

While the union and women's movements rallied to the cause during the 1988 strike, UNA consistently has eschewed formal affiliation with either. UNA cooperates with the Alberta Federation of Labour on many projects but co-exists with, rather than joins, the federation. Affiliations with the CLC, the CCU, and the CFL have all been discussed and rejected, ostensibly because of the monetary costs of membership. The decision not to affiliate with the CLC was reinforced when observers sent to the CLC convention in Montreal were troubled by the actions of several large unions on the floor and in the backrooms, especially with respect to the treatment accorded the Edmonton Firefighters who were attempting to break away from their international union. The UNA observers came away convinced that the trade-union movement in Canada was male-dominated and not democratic enough. UNA's position that 'nurses will speak for nurses' and its reluctance to affiliate officially with the CLC suggest a consciousness and practice developed out of a workplace where for too long nurses have had to take orders from (male) doctors and have occupied a place in a patriarchal institution which is low in power, prestige, and status.[30] In the end, Alberta nurses are not prepared to trade the benefits of separate organizing and independent decision making for membership in a trade-union organization where nurses would likely face gender struggles comparable to those that confront them in the workplace.[31]

While nurses have begun to develop some consciousness of themselves as women workers and have used some of the conceptual tools of feminism to understand and explain their lives, UNA has not been identified, nor has it identified itself, as a feminist union. The first executive director of the UNA, Bob Donahue, was Metis and senior nurses recall him talking about the similarities between the oppression of aboriginal peoples and the oppression of nurses because they were women.[32] Although nurses may have agreed with this analysis, UNA has not become an active participant in the women's movement in the way that the Federation of Women Teachers' Associations of Ontario has. For example, UNA has not joined NAC, at least partly because the union does not wish to risk an internal split on the abortion issue.[33] But the failure of nurses to identify with the women's movement might also be explained partly by the fact that socialist feminists have tended to overlook the work of women employed in traditional professions or have regarded such women as privileged, while liberal feminists have inadvertently down-graded the importance of nursing through programmatic demands which focus on women's entry to non-traditional (that is, male) professions such as medicine and law.

During the 1988 strike women's groups 'discovered' nurses and provided considerable support for them. None the less, striking nurses primarily identified as workers and unionists and were not inclined to see their experiences in the context of any larger women's struggle. For example, Barb Strange, president of the local at the Calgary General Hospital said, 'This dispute has become a power struggle ... They're not just worried about keeping costs down. They have the mentality that they are the masters and we're the servants and how dare we step out of line.'[34] While we could read gender into her observations, it is not explicitly there, whereas the use of the master/ servant analogy recognizes class and traditional boss/worker dimensions.

It is clear, however, that striking nurses benefited from the gains of the women's movement. Although the relationship between feminism and nursing remains 'uneasy,'[35] public discussion which focused on how women's caring and nurturing work was devalued and on critiques of the organizational and power structure of hospitals were based in feminist analysis and on the gender-specificity of nursing work. Further use of feminist analysis would allow nurses to develop expanded understandings about attitudes towards them and about their work as *women's* work. If nurses, as women workers and women unionists, want to move forward with a broad social agenda for health care, they will have to 'harness their visions of a preferred future to a larger understanding of power relations in health care, including *the interaction of the sexual division of labour* with bureaucratic methods of organizing work'[36] (my emphasis).

Indeed, shortly after the strike, some nurses began to question whether collective bargaining provided all the tools necessary to take care of their workplace concerns. Irene Gouin, vice-president of UNA Local 79 in 1988, reflected on the gains and losses associated with the strike. 'We're going to have to take much more initiative in between strike action. This is the fourth time we've gone to bargaining and very few health care, patient care, and employee safety concerns have ever been achieved at the table. We're going to have to try and find some other avenues to do that.'[37] Indeed, since the 1988 strike, UNA's leadership has begun to assess what strategies in addition to collective bargaining will aid nurses in achieving their goals.[38]

Lessons from women's-movement organizing might suggest ways in which nurses could reconsider their relationship with other women workers in the hospital setting in order to make significant changes in patient care. As White has pointed out, women hospital workers (as opposed to men) have an 'attachment to healing.'[39] However, the hierarchical structure of hospitals separates nurses from nursing assistants and other health-care workers, and nurses have not been active in breaking the divisions down. In fact, nurses use, rather than challenge, demarcationary practices of occupational closure or exclusion to separate themselves from other health-care workers below them in the hierarchy.[40] As Allen has argued, this approach is 'masculinist' and 'professionalist' in orientation and can actually be 'viewed as in *opposition* to collective bargaining or unionism.'[41] Organizing with other women in the workplace might prove a beneficial strategy for nurses seeking fundamental changes in health care, for this strategy would enhance the collective power of all hospital workers. Put another way, perhaps nurses should organize not only within their profession but across their sector, much as the Ontario Secondary School Teachers' Federation has begun to organize not just teachers but all workers in secondary schools.

In Alberta, the wages and working conditions of nurses have been improved through the astute use of traditional collective-bargaining strategies and the willingness of UNA members to directly challenge government intervention in negotiations between employees and employers. The solidarity of nurses and their union consciousness were strengthened further through the shared experience of an 'illegal' strike. And bridges, some shakier than others, were built among UNA, other unions, and the women's movement in 1988. To what extent the lessons of the strike will shape nurses' efforts to control their work, improve patient care, and transform the health-care system remains to be seen.

NOTES

1 See, for example, Larry Haiven, 'The State and Nursing Industrial Relations: The Case of Four Western Canadian Nurses' Strikes,' unpublished paper presented jointly to the Canadian Sociology and Anthropology Association and the Society for Socialist Studies annual meetings, Kingston, June 1991; Sarah Jane Growe, *Who Cares? The Crisis in Canadian Nursing* (Toronto: McClelland and Stewart 1991); Judith M. Hibberd, 'Organized Political Action: The Labor Struggle in Alberta,' in Alice J. Baumgart and Jenniece Larsen, eds, *Canadian Nursing Faces the Future: Development and Change* (St Louis: C.V. Mosby Company 1988), 489–99. On Australian nurses see Liz Ross, 'Sisters Are Doing It for Themselves ... And Us,' *Hecate* 13, no. 1 (1987): 83–99.
2 The other three strikes involved nurses at the Hardisty Nursing Home (1981), the Parklands Nursing Home (1982), and in eight health units across the province (1985). Nurses in eight health units were locked out in 1982. See Trudy Richardson, 'United Nurses of Alberta History' (Edmonton: United Nurses of Alberta 1992).
3 The membership of the UNA is 97 per cent female. Although the 3 per cent male membership may exercise 'more influence than their numbers would indicate,' there is no doubt that the UNA is a union of women. Interview with Trudy Richardson, UNA education officer, 9 March 1992
4 For a discussion of nurses' strategies of professionalization or occupational closure, see Anne Witz, *Professions and Patriarchy* (London and New York: Routledge 1992) and David G. Allen, 'Professionalism, Occupational Segregation by Gender and Control of Nursing,' *Women and Politics* 6, no. 3 (Fall 1986): 1–24.
5 See Richardson, 'UNA History,' for events leading up to the formation of UNA; see Growe for events leading up to the formation of nurses' unions as distinct from professional associations.

6 Quoted in United Nurses of Alberta, 'Brief on Collective Bargaining,' February 1992

7 Richardson, 'UNA History,' 8

8 As a result of this conflict, the law was later changed. The new law made it illegal for unions to refuse to take part in a government-supervised vote. The government also was given the power to impose its vote results as a way to settle disputes.

9 Quoted in Don Braid, 'Strike Has Tories in Tight Corner,' *Calgary Herald*, 26 Jan. 1988, A8

10 Growe 134

11 This description of the bargaining process is based on UNA 'Brief on Collective Bargaining,' and an interview with Richardson, 9 March 1992

12 UNA, 'Brief on Collective Bargaining,' 12

13 Hibberd 494

14 Elaine Buckley Day, 'A 20th Century Witch Hunt: A Feminist Critique of the Grange Royal Commission into Deaths at the Hospital for Sick Children,' *Studies in Political Economy* 24 (Autumn 1987): 13–39; Dorothy E. Smith, *The Conceptual Practices of Power: A Feminist Sociology of Knowledge* (Toronto: University of Toronto Press 1990), 101–3; Growe 26–43

15 Growe 39

16 Alice J. Baumgart and Jenniece Larsen, 'Introduction to Nursing in Canada,' in Baumgart and Larsen 8; M. Louise Fitzgerald, 'Nursing,' *Signs: Journal of Women in Culture and Society* 2, no. 4 (Summer 1977): 818–34; Pat Armstrong, 'Where Have All the Nurses Gone?' *Healthsharing*, Summer 1988, 17–19; Marie Campbell, 'Management as "Ruling": A Class Phenomenon in Nursing,' *Studies in Political Economy* 27 (Autumn 1988): 29–51

17 Wilma Scott Heide, 'Feminist Activism in Nursing and Health Care,' in Janet Muff, ed., *Socialization, Sexism, and Stereotyping: Women's Issues in Nursing* (St Louis: C.V. Mosby Company 1982), 256. See also Ann Game and Rosemary Pringle, *Gender at Work* (Sydney: George Allen and Unwin 1983), 94–118; Eva Gamarnikow, 'Sexual Division of Labour: The Case of Nursing,' in Annette Kuhn and AnnMarie Wolpe, eds, *Feminism and Materialism: Women and Modes of Production* (London: Routledge 1978), 96–123.

18 Quoted in Rebecca Coulter and Trudy Richardson, 'Militancy and Alberta Nurses,' *The Year Left*, forthcoming

19 'Nurses to Walk Out,' *Sunday Herald*, 24 Jan. 1988, A1–A2

20 'Nurses Defy Law,' *Calgary Herald*, 23 Jan. 1988, A1–A2

21 The UNA appealed the fines for criminal contempt, but in 1992 the Supreme Court of Canada, in a 4–3 ruling, let the fines stand.

22 Details of the strike are drawn from Coulter and Richardson.

23 'Emergency Problem,' *Calgary Herald*, 1 Feb. 1988, A1

24 'Nurses Plan Mass Rally,' *Calgary Herald*, 31 Jan. 1988, A1–A2

25 'Nurses Insist They'll Walk the Line Despite the Fine,' *Calgary Herald*, 6 Feb. 1988, B1

26 'Strike Is Unnecessary,' *Calgary Herald*, 26 Jan. 1988, A4

27 Jack Spearman, 'Arrogance Trips Conservatives,' *Calgary Herald*, 16 Feb. 1988, A4

28 Richardson, 'UNA History,' 15

29 Interview with Irene Gouin in 'Alberta Nurses Victorious in "Illegal Strike,"' *Challenging the Barriers: Edmonton Working Women Newsletter*, Spring/Summer 1988, 4

30 Interview with Trudy Richardson, 9 March 1992

31 For discussions of the problems confronting women who work in mixed-sex unions, see several other chapters in this book. Also, see Cynthia Cockburn, *In the Way of Women: Men's Resistance to Sex Equality in Organizations* (Ithaca, NY: ILR Press 1991).

32 Interview with Trudy Richardson, 9 March 1992

33 Ibid., 15 May 1992

34 'Moore Suggests Pact Way To Go,' *Calgary Herald*, 6 Feb. 1988, A1–A2

35 Janet Kerr and Jannetta MacPhail, *Canadian Nursing: Issues and Perspectives* (Toronto: McGraw-Hill Ryerson 1988), 60; William K. Carroll and Rennie Warburton, 'Feminism, Class Consciousness and Household-Work Linkages among Registered Nurses in Victoria,' *Labour / Le Travail* 24 (Fall 1989): 131–45

36 Baumgart and Larsen 10

37 'Alberta Nurses Victorious,' 5–6

38 Interview with Trudy Richardson, 15 May 1992

39 Jerry P. White, *Hospital Strike: Women, Unions, and Public Sector Conflict* (Toronto: Thompson Educational Publishing 1990)

40 Witz 44–8

41 Allen 12

3

Reflections on Life Stories: Women's Bank Union Activism

PATRICIA BAKER

Unionization among Canadian bank and financial workers[1] is well documented by academics and activists. Of particular interest to them has been the unions' limited success among financial workers, generally attributed to the following factors: bank managements' anti-union activity; the structure of branch banking in Canada and banks' increasing reliance on technological innovation; the structure of Canadian federal labour legislation; rivalries among interested unions; and the challenges of organizing women white-collar workers in small, scattered private-sector workplaces, with few traditions of trade unionism.[2]

My approach in this paper is different. Here I focus on union activism as an experience for individual women financial workers who have actively participated in unionizing their workplaces. By examining their experiences and reflections on those experiences, we see facets of their activism that are invisible on a larger scale, but which are crucial to our understanding of the problems of bank-worker unionization. Feminist researchers have acknowledged within recent years that women's stories provide valuable direct documentation of women's lives, and in particular their workplace lives.[3] This paper explores one aspect of working life among women financial workers – the development and impact of union activism – by presenting selected episodes of bank unionization in four women's lives: their involvement in bank unionism, their experiences with, and understandings of, its successes and failures, and their analyses of the potential for bank-worker unionization. My hope is to see how these women have challenged not only Canadian banks and other financial institutions, but also traditional, male-dominated union philosophies and strategies.

I have chosen to discuss interviews conducted in 1991 with four women – Sara, Anne, Elizabeth, and Margaret.[4] The circumstances of these four women's lives and their experiences of bank unionism present interesting contrasts as well as some striking similarities, giving us insight into the development and significance of bank unionism for them. All four women have been actively involved, at different times, in unions which have been major players in bank unionism. Sara and Anne were active in the Service, Office, Retail Workers Union of Canada (SORWUC) in the late 1970s and early 1980s; Elizabeth and Margaret are currently involved in the Union of Bank Employees (UBE) and have been so since the mid-1980s.

The remainder of this paper is organized into four sections: the historical context for these women's experiences; their political involvements before bank activism; their experiences of bank unionization, including reflections on and analyses of its successes and failures; and prospects for bank unionization in the future.

HISTORICAL CONTEXT

Unionizing Canadian bank and financial workers began[5] promisingly enough in the late 1970s, when a number of unions vied for the right to represent bank workers. Among the earliest and best-known unionizing successes were initiated by SORWUC, a small, feminist, independent national union based in British Columbia. By mid-1978, the United Bank Workers section of SORWUC had a membership of more than 600 located in 26 branches (24 in British Columbia, 2 in Saskatchewan).[6]

The Canadian Labour Congress (CLC) began its bank-organizing campaign in 1977, establishing the UBE as a direct charter of the CLC. With both the CLC and SORWUC organizing bank workers, the process was complex, stormy, and controversial.[7] Ironically, the main casualties of the struggle were unionized bank workers. In 1978, SORWUC was unable to meet its ever-growing financial commitments and, faced with problems from the banking industry, withdrew from branch organizing and negotiations. Since that time, the CLC (under whose auspices much of what limited bank organizing there has been since has taken place) has been no more successful. In 1988, for example, union membership in the financial industry as a whole (including banks, credit unions, caisses populaires, and so on) comprised only 3.4 per cent of paid workers.[8] This particular historical relationship between the two union organizations provides the setting within which we can examine the experiences of Sara, Anne, Elizabeth, and Margaret.

POLITICAL INVOLVEMENTS: BACKGROUND

Sara and Anne in British Columbia

At the time of my interviews, Sara and Anne lived in Vancouver;[9] each had a long history of political activism, and had met and become friends in the late 1970s because of their political involvement. Sara spent most of her youth in Saskatchewan, then moved to Toronto at seventeen, where she took a job in an insurance company. Two years later she moved to British Columbia. Sara has spent her adult working life as a clerical worker. She described her political awakening to me: 'I was a feminist and a socialist from when I was a teenager ... so as soon as I ended up figuring out that I probably was going to spend the rest of my life as a clerical worker, I got quite into organizing them ... When I was still in high school I used to do things like go to picket lines ... I was really active, actually, in the young CCF of Saskatchewan.' As a feminist, Sara's union activism began as, and continued to be, specifically oriented to the particular problems confronting women in the paid workplace.

Sara's first direct union involvement was with an independent newly formed feminist union, the Association of University and College Employees (AUCE), during her employment at the University of British Columbia (UBC) in the early 1970s. At about the same time she participated in SORWUC's creation. SORWUC was formed in 1972 out of the Working Women's Association (WWA), which in the early 1970s was actively supporting the struggles of non-unionized women who were trying to unionize. SORWUC was created with a specific mandate to unionize working women in traditionally non-unionized sectors. Sara became active in SORWUC, and in particular its bank-worker unionization.

Anne was raised in a small town in southern Ontario, where she lived until she was eighteen. After one year of university, she hitch-hiked to Vancouver in the late 1960s, where she wanted to 'get involved in anti-war activities.' Anne recalled the Ontario roots of her political and union activism:

I worked part time in a hospital washing dishes in a small town in southern

Ontario, when I was fourteen or fifteen, and there was an increase in the minimum wage law and they didn't increase our wages. And I remember calling the Department of Labour being really angry ... And I remember getting all the dietary girls together, department girls, and saying they have to pay us more. And we went to the head of the kitchen, the dietician, and she said that they didn't have to because we were just students and I said no, that was not an exemption any more. And I remember that we ended up seeing the hospital administrator ... I remember the administrator was really mad about seeing us ... So why did I do that? My mom's real strong and ... [my sister and I] ... were to be whatever we wanted to be and nobody could stop us ... My dad's a union person from way back so we weathered quite a few strikes in our household ... So unionism was always in our family.

And the Women's Movement knocked me over ... As soon as I heard that we should be doing it together I said, 'right' ...

Like Sara's, Anne's union consciousness was formed by her development as a feminist and her involvement in the women's movement. Anne's first adult opportunity to act on this consciousness came about when she tried to unionize a restaurant in which she worked. It was at this time too that Anne met Sara. 'I was organizing a union at Smitty's Pancake House where I was waitressing ... I got very drunk with a woman who knew [Sara] and we just sort of met accidentally, and she was saying that she shouldn't be drinking so much because she had to go to the founding convention of this Working Women's Association the next day. And I said, "Oh, what do they do?" and she described how they were women who thought that women needed their own union. And I said, well that's interesting because I'm trying to sign up the women where I work ... And she said, "Oh you should meet my friend [Sara]. She knows a lot about unions too." So I did.'

Shortly after this meeting, Anne was fired from the restaurant for her union activity. Anne turned to Sara for help in launching an unfair-labour-practice complaint. Although the complaint was unsuccessful, Sara supported Anne throughout the case, and as a result they became firm friends.

Sara and Anne were both active in the successful unionization of AUCE at UBC and at five other universities and colleges in the area. Both women (and other activists in AUCE and WWA) recognized that crucial to AUCE's survival was its involvement in a broader movement to unionize women workers. SORWUC's formation was part of this larger strategy. As Anne explained it to me: 'The only way that we felt AUCE was going to survive ... was if we could get downtown office workers unionized as well so that we could all support each other ... So a bunch of us ended up leaving UBC and ... getting jobs downtown ... the reason I decided to get a job in the banks was the Working Women's Association had been leafletting downtown ... and there had been several responses from women at [one bank] who had ripped the coupon off the bottom and sent them in for more information. So the first place I went to was the [bank] and was hired right away.' The drive to organize bank workers was under way.

Elizabeth and Margaret in Nova Scotia

Elizabeth and Margaret's personal and political backgrounds are quite different from Sara's and Anne's. Elizabeth and Margaret have always lived in and around a small (population about 5500) rural community in Nova Scotia. Neither (by their own admission) had been politically active or politically aware until their UBE activity in the mid-1980s.

Elizabeth was born and raised in the Nova Scotia community where she now works. She left the community to attend university, and returned home to find employment where the number of jobs available to women were limited. She took the job as a teller at a bank branch in town about eleven years ago, because it was considered a reasonably good and well-paying job for a woman. However, by 1986, bank workers at the branch were still enduring chronically low wages and capricious managerial favouritism, especially in merit evaluations and promotions. One specific event convinced Elizabeth that the branch needed a union: management's decision to hire someone from another bank to fill a position for which employees in the branch were qualified. Elizabeth made contact with the local CLC organizer, who helped Elizabeth and her co-workers unionize the branch as a unit of UBE Local 2107.

Elizabeth had no previous experience with unions, feminism, or political activity. Her initial involvement with UBE was the catalyst for her development as a committed union activist. Further, Elizabeth's union experience helped her conquer some of her earlier fears and strengthened her beliefs and commitments: 'I'm not as afraid [now] ... I wouldn't get up in front of a group or do anything like that. So now I know that you can do it if you really believe in what you're doing ... I'm much more political than I was ... I was interested in [politics] and such but now I'm more [actively involved].'

Margaret was also born and raised in a rural Nova Scotia county close to the town where she and Elizabeth now work. Margaret worked at a variety of part-time clerical and service jobs. She then attended university for less than a year, but dropped out to take up her job at the local credit union. She has worked at the credit union from the age of eighteen (since 1978) in a variety of capacities: teller, customer-service, term-deposits, and loans clerk, and most recently as an accounting clerk.

Margaret's first union experience came in 1987 with her active participation in the certification of her credit union as a unit of UBE. The circumstances which prompted Margaret and her co-workers to unionize were deteriorating working conditions – including the increased hiring of part-timers, the erosion of benefits, and finally the hiring of someone from outside the credit union for a management position for which there were qualified credit-union employees – and the example of Elizabeth's unionized bank branch. Owing to their unfamiliarity with unions, Margaret and her co-workers turned for advice and support to Elizabeth, who had been instrumental in her own branch unionization.

Like Elizabeth, Margaret had no union experience prior to her participation in unionizing the credit union. When I asked Margaret if she thought the experience of union activism has changed her, Margaret responded by contrasting her attitudes and behaviour before her union involvement with her life today:

Oh my God I've changed a lot. I wouldn't even sit and talk to you years ago, I was so shy. You'd never believe how I've changed ...

I've learned so much since being in the union. I never even used to read a newspaper! That's the God's honest truth. Before we unionized I was just in my own little world ... I've always been concerned about the way people treat people, though. But now, with unions you're so involved ... it opens your eyes about what's going on everywhere because it actually does affect you ... I can really say I've learned so much from being in the union ... Oh my God! I can't believe where I was and where I came from and the point I'm at now.

Because Elizabeth's and Margaret's Nova Scotia community is small and tightly knit, Margaret knew Elizabeth before their respective unionization experience. But as Margaret and Elizabeth became prominent unionists (in their respective workplaces) and active in their common union local, they have also formed a close friendship and a good working relationship. Margaret spoke to me with great warmth about the relationship she has established with Elizabeth: 'We get along really good ... Her and I are like two comrades in crime. We're always up to something and going somewhere. [Another credit union employee] says we complement each other.'

To summarize, the paths to bank-union involvement for Sara and Anne were substantially different than those for Margaret and Elizabeth, and were travelled fifteen years earlier. To a large extent, Sara's and Anne's participation in the unionization process grew out of their involvement in the burgeoning women's movement of the 1970s. They recognized the significance of bank-worker unionization as part of a larger political agenda to unionize women workers. By contrast, bank unionization has been a novel and transformative experience for Margaret and Elizabeth, one they were willing to undertake in order to improve their long-term working conditions in a rural area where they expect to live out their lives. These different paths do converge, however. As we will now see, the convergence of these women's diverse experiences is clearly illustrated in their reflections on, and analyses of, their experiences of unionization itself.

EXPERIENCES OF BANK UNIONIZATION

Sara and Anne

Sara's and Anne's relationship to bank unionization is a historic one. They were among the most active members of SORWUC in the late 1970s and early 1980s, and played key roles in organizing bank workers, negotiating union contracts, and taking local and national leadership positions. In 1977, Sara was elected national president of SORWUC, and became a prominent spokesperson and negotiator during SORWUC's drive to organize bank workers. Anne held several leadership positions at different times, including SORWUC national president, president of the bank workers' local of SORWUC, vice-president, secretary, and treasurer. I asked Anne what life was like for her while she was active in SORWUC:

I think I ranted and raved a lot. I think I just talked and argued bank-worker organizing every waking minute. I would leaflet [at bank branches] before I went to work, if I didn't have a breakfast meeting. This was during the bank-worker organizing, so say a three-year period [1976–9]. And then go to work [at a branch in downtown Vancouver] with just unrelenting pressure at work. We actually had a supervisor that was sent down from our regional office that directly supervised myself and another one of the union women, so it was just constant harassment ... On my lunch hour I usually met with other bank workers downtown. That was one of the things that was really great about that branch I was at. I was right downtown so I was within walking distance of a lot of other bank workers and right across the street from our union office, so I always had a meeting or went over to the union office to eat my lunch. And then in the evenings I usually had a lot of phoning to do to organize meetings or to talk to other organizers, or just organizing. And on the weekends I hung out with other bank workers who were organizing, usually drinking a lot in the pub. I mean we did tons of work in the pub, you know, just trying to figure things out and strategize. That was usually with our partners, so it was a social event, but our partners were very much part of the bank workers' organizing drive. I mean they had equal say in terms of the strategizing. So it was very much of a community sort of organizing effort. So the people I hung out with during that period, their lives were organizing the bank as well. So that's what I did. And then when my partner at the time got fed up with bank-work organizing we split up. And that's just the way it was. And it was so powerful what was happening because for a good part of that time the fight was really on. We ... were winning all kinds of small victories. So it was terribly exciting.

For Anne and Sara, union activism in SORWUC was an all-con-suming process, a process to which they were entirely dedicated. The networks of resistance and organization which they created and in which they participated were lively and rich. More generally, the unorthodox approach to organizing undertaken within SORWUC reflected and reinforced the intensity and cooperation recalled by Anne. That is, SORWUC was conceived of and operated as a grass-roots union: 'We didn't want a union run by highly paid professional union leaders ... Locals of the union were given complete control of their own affairs and the right to secede from SORWUC upon majority vote of the local membership. The new union encouraged members in each workplace to write their own contract proposals and conduct their own negotiations for a union contract.'[10]

The union was organized so as to enhance members' self-reliance and minimize their reliance on legal experts and paid union staff.

Furthermore, SORWUC bank organizers were also bank workers, and so were well-acquainted with the problems facing women who worked in banks. In make-up and philosophy, then, SORWUC provided for women a unique alternative to the CLC.

Sara's SORWUC recollections, and in particular her self-identification as a union leader, communicated to me the impact of the collective unionization process undertaken by SORWUC: '[Being a leader] means taking initiative and being prepared to be ... exposed ... But ... one thing that I really learned in SORWUC and AUCE was that ... working collectively works way better. That it's just way easier ... First of all, you're more likely to come up with the right decision when a bunch of people are involved in making the decision. And even if it turns out to be wrong you're better off if you can share the blame ... I guess I think the most important thing about the union leadership is ... trying to facilitate the membership [to make] the decision that really represents what they want.'

Anne, too, accepted her responsibilities as a union leader. She explained to me the balance between a sometimes difficult learning process and working more effectively with Sara and her other bank and union colleagues:

I think I was seen as a work leader as well in my branch ... On the teller line, if there was sort of a complaint that we all had then it was ... brought to me and I was told what I should do about [it]. Go tell the supervisor this and that. If we had meetings I was designated to speak up. Actually in my workplace it was ... quite hard on the other union organizer, that I was seen as the leader. Because she was the more senior. I hadn't been there very long so she used to get a lot of harassment like, well if you're not sure about this why don't you go and ask Anne ...

I don't think I'm a really good leader when it comes to stuff like being a president of a local ... I think I'm better at [a] negotiation committee or something like that. [Sara was] just wonderful as president ... She's more inclusive. She's better at compromises or negotiating compromises. I was always leading the most hard-line section of the union which can sometimes be divisive. I think that's something I learned actually to get better at, over the bank-worker organizing drive, was to get sort of representative and less sort of individual as a leader.

It was really stressful [being a leader]. I remember one thing which I used to do all the time which was when I had a meeting with the manager that day, or with the labour board, I always wore a shirt that had a high collar or a turtleneck because I got all splotchy when I had to speak or when I had to deal with a nasty situation ... And I used to really concentrate on my hands because they always shook ... So yeah, it was difficult. It was hard.

As is evident in these quotations, Sara and Anne learned from, and complemented, each other's bank-worker unionization experiences in a variety of ways. As feminist unionists they worked to create an alternative union to meet the needs of women bank workers, and developed a particular sense of their own involvement in that process. Further, their view of their leadership capabilities is compatible with other observations concerning feminist leadership. For example, Miriam Edelson[11] suggests ways in which feminist leadership can promote grass-roots democracy and support within a union: 'The notion of a distinctive feminist leadership lies in providing members opportunities to develop their own power and the self-reliance required to effect democratic changes in the union.'

The extent to which SORWUC's bank-worker unionizing activities were successful was primarily due to the initial effectiveness of the collective and individual strategies to which I have alluded: grass-roots, feminist organizing by workers intimately acquainted with the problems and concerns of women bank workers, and with a commitment to democratic leadership.

These strategies were not enough to sustain SORWUC, however. As a small, inexperienced union, it faced a series of insurmountable difficulties: prohibitive costs of branch organizing and negotiating; entanglements, by the banks, in a series of costly legal battles over certifications and unfair labour practices;[12] and the withdrawal by the CLC of financial and other assistance, once it became clear that SORWUC wanted to maintain its national union status, and would not merge with an existing union or become a directly chartered local of the CLC, as desired by the CLC leadership.[13] These circumstances were effective in draining SORWUC's energies and morale from bank-unionizing efforts.

The CLC's withdrawal of financial assistance proved fatal to SORWUC's bank-organizing drive. In 1978, unable to meet its financial commitments and faced with relentless opposition from the banks, SORWUC withdrew from branch organizing and negotiations. By the beginning of 1979, all of its twenty-six certifications were withdrawn, though some of the units were absorbed into the UBE.[14]

SORWUC did not abandon bank organizing entirely. In keeping with its commitment to provide viable alternative unions for women workers, SORWUC changed its strategy. In the early 1980s it regrouped, chartered a new local for all financial workers, and concentrated on organizing and educating bank workers in the Vancouver area through leafletting and meetings.[15] Nevertheless, SORWUC had little long-term success in organizing bank workers. In 1988, it ceased to exist. Throughout the 1980s and 1990s, what limited bank unionizing there has been has taken place largely within the CLC.

My interest in this paper is to see how SORWUC's history and fate have been interpreted by Sara and Anne, and in particular how their SORWUC experiences shaped their analyses of the potential for future bank-worker unionization. In my recent interviews with Sara and Anne, they had much to say about how they experienced and understood both the short- and long-term impact of SORWUC's involvement in bank-worker organizing. Here I will provide brief comments on the immediate personal impact on them of SORWUC's withdrawal from bank organizing. I leave Sara's and Anne's longer-term analyses for the final section of this paper.

Anne recalled the period after SORWUC withdrew from bank organizing as personally very difficult, yet hopeful as well:

[In 1979] we pulled out of negotiations and then for a year we wrote that book [An Account to Settle, by The Bank Book Collective] and that was just incredibly time consuming. There [were] really just five or six of us [including Sara] ... And it was sort of a catharsis for us; to do the analysis as quickly as possible but it was also really depressing. Really hard time personally for those women that were involved. Yeah, that was tough that year. And then it was like we all sort of took a break; didn't see each other for quite a while. But I'd say they're my closest friends now. I don't see them as much as I see some other women but ... they're my closest friends. [We share] lots of dreams. Of what it would be like if we won!

I guess the one thing that I have from that period that I'll have forever is the women friends. I mean no one is as close to me as those women ... It was a very intense ... time.

Sara's recollections of her SORWUC activism and its outcome were also both circumspect and optimistic:

I think it was generally a positive experience. There [were] some ... contradictions ... in SORWUC that were hard to figure out ... I'm not sure whether we could have done things differently ... SORWUC was sort of a cross between or a combination of a union and a feminist working women's organization. And some times that was hard from the point of view of ... we should make what decisions ... It was hard to have a lot of volunteers involved without giving them some decision making power. On the other hand I think it's a real principle of unionism that the people who have to live under the collective agreement should be the ones who are involved in decisions ...

I think it was, on the whole, a pretty positive experience ... I keep running into things that you could ... credit to the old SORWUC organizing, whether it's people who are now active in other unions but got their first experience at SORWUC or ... clauses in collective agreements.

For both Sara and Anne, participation in SORWUC and the unionization of bank workers was an intensely memorable experience. In many ways their experience has been replicated in more recent efforts to unionize bank workers, and perhaps most dramatically in Elizabeth's and Margaret's experiences of bank-worker unionization.

Elizabeth and Margaret

Margaret's and Elizabeth's involvement in bank-worker unionization is recent and ongoing, and is one episode in the CLC's efforts to organize bank workers in various regions of Canada during the 1980s. As mentioned earlier, Elizabeth was instrumental in the unionization of her bank branch in 1986. She has remained extremely active in her local, having been involved in every round of negotiations, and as branch steward. At present, Elizabeth is the vice-president of Local 2107.

At the time this paper was written, Elizabeth was the only one of the four women to have been directly involved in a bank workers' strike. This strike occurred from November 1987 to February 1988, when Elizabeth (and ten of her twelve co-workers) walked a picket line to obtain a 15 per cent wage increase, to attain wage parity with tellers at other Nova Scotia banks.

The strike gained a great deal of support both locally and nationally.[16] Elizabeth's role in the strike was crucial as a negotiator and as national spokesperson for her branch. The strike ended near the end of February when the strikers voted by a narrow margin to accept a wage increase of 7.3 per cent over nineteen months, with a cash signing bonus – a substantially smaller package than their original demand. The acceptance of this contract was controversial. According to various sources, and contrary to the CLC's official claims, representatives from the CLC coerced the women into accepting the limited settlement.[17]

Despite the disappointments of the settlement, the strike had a positive impact on the women. With the strike experience and with community support, the women came to realize their worth as people and as workers – a realization many women never experience, given the systematic undervaluing of women's work and lives in our society. By mobilizing themselves and winning broad community, labour, and national support, these women experienced the power of collective action. Their empowerment continues to be manifest in their ongoing support for a union in the branch.

What was true for all the women strikers was especially true for Elizabeth. Her union activism in UBE has been a profound and transformative experience for her, a dramatic contrast to her earlier unawareness about and hesitancy towards political activism. She has developed a sophisticated understanding of unionizing, negotiations and labour politics, and the community in which she lives, and a clearer sense of how she is involved as an activist, and why: 'I think that forming a union and especially going on strike you realize that if you think it's important enough then go for it and fight for it. It doesn't matter. I think that that's something that I've learned. I don't think it's something that would have come, you know, say six or seven years ago. I would have been angry but I wouldn't have done anything about it.'

Elizabeth also reflected on the importance of community support for the bank workers' union and their strike, and how that support has influenced her relationships with the townspeople: 'I think people ... see you differently. Well I think now they see you! ... Before you were kind of invisible ... people you meet on the street will be kind of smiling when they talk to you ... I think people give you a little bit more credit now than they did before. I think they actually consider that you might [be] intelligent ... Some people have actually said, "Oh, you should run for the NDP here" ... I mean years ago you'd never have gotten that, you know ... It's been really good. It was a real good experience.'

Despite her actual and acknowledged prominence and experience in union activism in her branch, and the respect she has acquired, Elizabeth viewed her leadership as largely circumstantial, due to the fact that she is single and has limited family responsibilities:

I've never considered myself a leader ... I don't really care to be, I could work very well in the background. But I think it's just ... circumstances were right in my case ... I was older, I've been there a long time ... to be older and still to be single [she lives with her sister] and not have any children ... I was ... [almost] the same age as the ones older than me, I just don't have the family responsibilities ... They didn't look at me ... as a smart aleck young kid trying to tell them ... what to do ... I had the time to do it ... There are women there probably who are just as capable as I am, but they just don't have the time ... If it ... meant that I had to go to a meeting to meet somebody or call somebody or leave town ... and it meant that I didn't put supper on that night, nobody cared ... I didn't get static from a husband or kids if I was away a lot, or this was taking up a lot of my time ... I take it upon myself to go to all kinds of things that normally if I had a family I wouldn't really be able to do.

The fact that Elizabeth is more or less free of expected domestic responsibilities, and can therefore devote time to union activity, is by no means coincidental. Research has shown that it is difficult for women to become actively involved in unions; because of their double burdens of paid work and domestic duties, many women simply do not have the time to participate in union negotiations, meetings, or conferences, particularly when these are held, as is often the case, on evenings or weekends. Many unions have yet to accommodate these responsibilities in the scheduling of union activities, the provision of child care, and so forth.[18] As a single woman with no children, Elizabeth has been freer to become involved in her union, and has certainly made the most of the opportunity.

It was clear to me when I interviewed Elizabeth in the winter and summer of 1991, that she has had, and plans to continue having, a major role to play in the union at her branch. She feels a strong sense of responsibility to the branch, her co-workers, and the union: 'I'd like to see ... a good strong union ... I think I started something and I should see it through ... I wouldn't ever want to leave and see it fail.'

Paradoxically, and as we shall see below, Elizabeth's support of branch unionism and more generally of the unionization of bank workers has evolved into a sophisticated criticism of the CLC's bank-unionization strategy, and a vision of bank unionizing not unlike that shared by Sara and Anne.

Margaret's involvement in unionization is both similar to, and different from, Elizabeth's experiences. In 1987, Margaret instigated the unionization of her credit union with Local 2107, with advice and support from Elizabeth. Margaret remains active in the union, and is currently local president.

Despite Margaret's obvious activism and her leadership position in the local, she, like Elizabeth, does not see herself as a leader. Interestingly, though, Margaret's comments on her leadership style resemble Sara's and Anne's evaluations of leadership: 'I run things kind of different. I like to have input from everybody ... That's why I don't think I'd make a good leader. I'd like to have everybody's opinion ... I don't like seeing people, one person or two people, have all the power. I don't think it's fair ... But sometimes you have to have somebody make a decision ... I don't like to make decisions without consulting members that are involved in the union.'

As was the case with Elizabeth, Margaret's involvement with the union encouraged her to participate more extensively in related political activities: 'I've been always on the negotiating committee [for the credit union] ... I was vice-president [of Local 2107] and now I'm president of the local ... Right now I'm also ... a board member, executive board member for the Labour Council. And I ran in an election in the summer for area vice-president for our area from the Labour Council ... I lost by one vote ... There's still another election for the same position in October. [The Nova Scotia Federation of Labour] know[s] how active [Elizabeth] and I are. They can't believe we're so active for a small local.'

Margaret's activism, both within and outside her union, is reinforced by the union support she has found among her co-workers. When I asked her if there has ever been an attempt to decertify the credit union (a practice not uncommon in bank unions), Margaret immediately replied: 'Never! We're unbelievable ... we're so strong ... They [the credit union workers] ... really believe that they would be so much worse off without a union ... I mean it's not the union of unions. It's not great ... But if we didn't have it we'd be so much worse. At least we get some powers, you know. If we all stand together ... If you really stay together you can work wonders.'

Elizabeth's and Margaret's experiences with union activism, while not situated in the long-standing personal traditions of feminism and political activism which form part of Sara's and Anne's background, embody some of the qualities found in Sara's and Anne's comments: learning the value of collective organization, and making a commitment to local cooperation and to principles of democratic leadership.

Furthermore, as we shall see in the final section of this paper, Elizabeth's and Margaret's personal development as union activists has led them to develop more radical principles and union strategies for bank workers, principles and strategies similar to those elaborated by Sara and Anne.

Margaret's quotation immediately above suggests an ambivalence about the CLC's ability to represent satisfactorily the interests of bank workers, which will be the subject of the last section of this paper. On the one hand, a common sentiment expressed by the four women activists I interviewed is that unionization is absolutely necessary for financial workers in particular, and women in general, to gain a measure of control over their working lives. On the other hand, it is by no means clear that the conditions exist within which this goal has been, or perhaps can be, realized. SORWUC is gone; and as Margaret notes, the UBE has by no means been the 'union of unions' for bank workers. This dilemma will become clearer in the following section in examining these four women's reflections on and critical analyses of the successes and failures of bank unionism and its prospects for the future.

DOES BANK UNIONISM HAVE A FUTURE?

Superficially, at least, the union frameworks within which these four women have operated appear to be quite dissimilar. Sara's and Anne's involvement with SORWUC kept them outside the mainstream labour movement and made them the targets of severe criticism from trade unionists, some progressive groups and individuals, and the Canada Labour Relations Board for giving up their bank certifications. Conversely, Margaret's and Elizabeth's much more recent union activism has always been situated squarely within the UBE. However, as a consequence of the CLC's approach to bank organizing, Margaret and Elizabeth too have been isolated from mainstream bank-unionizing activity. We now examine how this isolation arose, in order to see how a common understanding of the possibilities for future bank unionism has developed among these four women.

Despite – or perhaps because of – their intense commitment to their unionized workplaces, Margaret and Elizabeth have at times been critical of the CLC's bank-organizing strategies. As Margaret remarked to me, while she and her credit-union colleagues have steadfastly supported the union in their workplace, she has become disillusioned with the lack of support and services received from the CLC: 'That is I think ... the worst and the hardest thing to fight rather than management is that union members get disillusioned. And it's only people like [Elizabeth] ... and myself and a few others at work that worked really hard to try to bring people around and say look, ... it's up to us ... We were naive ... I can't count the number of reps we've had with the CLC and the turnover there ... Basically what we had to do was do it on our own. Stand on our own two feet really quick. And we learnt all the ins and outs and the politics and the bureaucracy and everything.'

Frustrated by the irregular availability (because of staff turnover and limited numbers of staff servicing the Atlantic region) of a regional CLC staff representative to assist with the running of their union, Elizabeth and Margaret (and their co-workers) learned to manage on their own. This self-reliance has fostered a collective strength, sustaining their unionized workplaces since 1986 and 1987 (a relatively long time for bank unions), and has produced their critical analysis of the CLC's efficacy in bank unionizing. In short, Elizabeth and Margaret have become dissatisfied with what the CLC has had to offer them. As Elizabeth commented: 'I really don't find that they listen to ... the grass roots ... I think they are so far removed from the actual workers that they have no sense of what those workers are actually going through. I think they have an idea that "we know what's best for you, so you listen to us."'

In one respect, at least, concerns about the CLC's interest in the union's well-being seem well founded. In December 1989, the CLC decided to give bank worker jurisdiction to the United Steelworkers of America (in the Atlantic region and Ontario), and to the British Columbia Government Employees' Union. According to Elizabeth, Nova Scotia bank workers were not consulted. A ballot was sent to all unionized bank workers in the province, who were urged to vote for the Steelworkers (the only union on the ballot). The vote was held on a unit-by-unit basis. This is how Elizabeth described hearing about the vote: 'When I got this notice, I had come back from vacation and the notice was in my desk. The first thing I thought of was, oh my goodness if [another unionized branch in Nova Scotia] gets this they're not going to know what to do. Because there really wasn't much education going on when we first joined the union ... I called the shop steward [at the other branch] ... and she was just lost. She said, "We thought we were the only ones in the province who didn't know what was going on," 'cause this was such a sudden thing. We knew that ... they were ... looking for another union of course, but thought we were going to get some say in it.' According to Elizabeth, many unionized bank workers in Nova Scotia mistakenly believed that if they did not vote for the Steelworkers, they would have no union at all. Consequently, they voted 'yes' to the Steelworkers. Elizabeth also felt that the suddenness of the vote and the lack of communication and information among the unionized branches about the vote made this outcome inevitable. However, Elizabeth's branch and Margaret's credit union both refused to vote for the Steelworkers, precisely because they were given no choice. As a result, at the time this paper was written, these two units were all that remained of UBE Local 2107 in Nova Scotia (a situation which, according to Margaret, disturbs the CLC leadership sufficiently that the unionists of Local 2107 are referred to as 'the problem people because [they] didn't do what [they] were told').

As a result of this jurisdictional shift, Elizabeth and Margaret were now effectively isolated from bank unionization in the province. As Elizabeth put it: 'We [the bank branch and credit union] were the only ones who in the end voted to stay as a direct [charter of the CLC] ... We said no, we're not going with [the Steelworkers]. So now we don't have any place to go. We either stay with the CLC forever or we ... go with Steel. We don't have a choice. Jurisdiction was given to [the Steelworkers] ... If I were to approach another union ... and they would say, "Yes, we'll take you over," Steel has to give our release, and we're not even part of Steel.'

To a large extent, the structural isolation experienced by all four women is, in large part, due to the challenges they have posed to the mainstream labour movement. Their experiences of bank activism served to reinforce for Sara and Anne, and to develop in Elizabeth and Margaret, the conviction that women, and in particular women bank workers, should have union structures that recognize and deal with the working conditions with which they contend. In their opinion, these structures do not yet exist within the mainstream labour movement.

The various activist experiences of these four women have generated some very specific and similar analyses of possible unionization strategies for bank workers as women. In my opinion, the similarities among them are especially interesting given the fact that, at the time this paper was written, Sara and Anne had never met or spoken to Elizabeth and Margaret. The four women know of one another's activities through the media or through third parties such as myself.

One point on which all four women agree is that, in answer to the question posed by the title of this section, yes, bank unionism does have a future. Their vision of that future is also shared, but has yet to be realized: bank workers need their own union. As Sara put it: 'I think ... basically the last few years have proved that SORWUC was right about the way to organize banks ... I think that bank workers should have their own union ... The CLC still hasn't realized that banks have to be organized by bank workers. I mean they don't even hire bank workers as organizers. It's not as if there aren't bank workers with organizing experience. I mean this has been going on now for fifteen years.'

Anne is certain she would like once again to be involved in organizing bank workers, and feels that the model SORWUC tried to use would be most appropriate: 'I'm firm that we made the right decisions in organizing on our own. I think that we made the right decisions in pulling out. I think that ... tactically we might have done it ... different. Just in terms of trying to meet with more bank workers ... I want to talk to every single bank worker that's joined a union and talk to them about why we thought we should do it this way. But we did the best we could.'

Margaret's and Elizabeth's experiences of unionism have been exceptionally positive and empowering. However, the traditional mainstream structure within which that unionism has taken place has not been so salutary. Elizabeth was critical of the CLC's role in the settlement of the strike at her branch. She felt the local CLC staff representatives asserted authority as established trade unionists and as men to persuade the majority of women to vote for a limited settlement. Elizabeth was convinced that the strikers could have stayed out longer, given their continuing local and national support. Whether a longer strike would have resulted in a better settlement is now a moot point. What is important here is the impact the decision to settle has had on Elizabeth's analysis of the CLC's commitment to unionize bank workers. Furthermore, both she and Margaret have been frustrated by the decision to transfer bank-union jurisdiction to the Steelworkers. As Elizabeth said: 'I don't have anything against the Steelworkers ... I think they must be a successful union with all the members that they've got, but even if they were good for us, even if they were the best union for us ... the whole labour movement seems to be missing the idea that what we're talking about is that we didn't make the decision. That we didn't make that decision and we want to decide who's good for us ... Nobody is listening to us ... We're [not] looking for somebody to take care of us ... we're just looking for somebody to help us take care of ourselves or to teach us how.'

These circumstances, in combination with a lack of ongoing servicing and support from the male CLC staff workers and a high turnover of CLC staff representatives, brought Elizabeth and Margaret to conclusions similar to those of Sara and Anne. As Elizabeth pointed out: 'I really believe that there's something wrong with the system ... The only way that workers, especially that women workers, can make any gains at all is through [a] union ... I believe that there are certain times ... for bank workers to unionize. And I think now ... it would be really easy for someone to do if they had a full-time organizer ... My ideal would be, I think, [that] bank workers should form their own [union] ... I've always felt that the best place for us was on our own and outside the CLC. What you could do if you were all together [unionized] and by yourself [in one union].'

Margaret, too, believes strongly in a union to accommodate the specific needs and circumstances of bank workers, indeed of all financial workers: 'I would like to see that all the banks and credit unions that are now organized leave the affiliates that they're with and join one big union of our own ... Oh, I think it would be so exciting to have our own union. Just fantastic. And then you'd have specialized people that worked in banks and credit unions going out organizing other banks and credit unions. [It's] absolutely necessary [that bank workers organize other bank workers]. We know how the banks tick. We know what makes them work ... I couldn't go into a steel plant and figure out what they're doing and what they need in their negotiations and contracts ... How can they come into ours? ... I think it creates so [many] problems, because they don't know what they're talking about.'

An important strategic component for all four women was the recognition that bank workers' needs, as women and as workers, be met in the process of unionization. As Elizabeth said:

I'd like to see the success of the bank workers. Because, you know, I think that it would give women a real boost, if a group of women could take on a financial institution and be successful ... And I think it would give women that work within the banks a boost themselves because ... I see ... what happens [to them] is what happened to me. Most of them have worked only at the banks all of their lives. And they have a great way at the bank of making you ... think that you should be grovelling to them ... We proved when we were out on strike, that ... we make the money for the bank. But they [bank management] ... think ... anybody could do what you're doing ... and over the years ... I think that it had an effect on [the women] ... I think it [unionization] would give women in the bank a sense of ... just how much they know ... It's amazing the knowledge that they have ...

I'd love to see it [unionization] succeed because I think it's ... the one thing that terrifies the bank, is to think that they could all be unionized and that these women would actually start to think for themselves.

In a similar vein, I asked Anne what her dreams for bank workers were. Without hesitation she replied: 'Oh, for me, number one is equal pay ... economic independence. I want the women who I work with to be able to ... make decisions in their lives without having to worry about being able to make it from one pay cheque to the next ... It drives me wild how money, poverty run our lives. I mean more and more women are choosing to make the decisions that are best for them even though they know they are going to live in poverty. But it's just not fair.'

SOME FINAL THOUGHTS

In reflecting on Anne's, Sara's, Margaret's, and Elizabeth's stories, I have been struck not only by the great differences in their lives – in political experience, geographic location, their historical and present-day relationships to unions and unionization – but also by the remarkable similarities of their knowledge and vision which have come as a consequence of their involvement in unions. Certainly, these four women's impact on bank unionization, and its impact on them, is only one part of a larger and much more complex process. The four stories do, however, leave us with some interesting strategic issues to ponder. These four women, separated in space and through circumstance, came to similar conclusions about the power and the possibilities of women's collective action. Given the lamentably limited degree of success achieved thus far in bank unionization, and the difficulty in pinpointing one particular cause for this situation, I feel that we would do well to listen to the analyses provided by women who have directed their energies towards solving what is for them an immediate problem: how collective action can best be furthered to promote women bank worker's interests. The womens' suggestion that bank workers need their own, autonomous union has the potential to resolve this dilemma, though it is not without both practical and political difficulties. On the one hand, if bank workers take the initiative to organize themselves, the possibility exists for them to make effective and positive connections between local activism and a larger-scale union movement, as well as to achieve real improvements in, and control over, their working lives. On the other hand, such a massive unionization task would require considerable financial and material resources, scarce in a time of recession, high unemployment, and shrinking union membership. Furthermore, the political challenge, of course, is whether such a union could be accommodated within a mainstream union structure like the CLC. Many feminist unionists have argued that women's needs and interests cannot always be met within mainstream unions;[19] these four women's experiences lend support to that view. Clearly, women union activists in Canadian financial institutions face many obstacles on the road to unionization. It is my hope that those obstacles are not insurmountable.

NOTES

The research for this paper was made possible by a Women and Work Strategic Research Grant (1991–4) from the Social Sciences and Humanities Research Council of Canada. My thanks go to Linda Briskin, Pat McDermott, Malcolm Stebbins, and three anonymous reviewers for their thoughtful and painstaking editorial comments and helpful suggestions. Responsibility for the final product is, of course, my own.

1 This group includes workers in federally chartered banks, trust companies, caisses populaires, and credit unions.
2 Patricia Baker, 'Banking Transformed: Women's Work and Technological Change in a Canadian Bank,' Ph.D. thesis, Department of Anthropology, University of Toronto, 1987; 'Unionizing Canadian Bank Workers: Time for a Change?' paper presented at the international colloquium Gender and Class, University of Antwerp, Belgium, 18–20 Sept. 1989; 'Some Unions Are More Equal than Others: A Response to Rosemary Warskett's "Bank Worker Unionization and the Law,"' *Studies in Political Economy* 34 (Spring 1991): 219–33; The Bank Book Collective, *An Account to Settle: The Story of the United Bank Workers (SORWUC)* (Vancouver: Press Gang Publishers 1979); Elizabeth

J. Shilton Lennon, 'Organizing the Unorganized: Unionization in the Chartered Banks of Canada,' *Osgoode Hall Law Journal* 18, no. 2 (1980), 177–237; Graham S. Lowe, *The Canadian Union of Bank Employees: A Case Study* (Toronto: Centre for Industrial Relations, University of Toronto 1978); *Bank Unionization in Canada: A Preliminary Analysis* (Toronto: Centre for Industrial Relations, University of Toronto 1980); Allen Ponak and Larry F. Moore, 'Canadian Bank Unionism: Perspectives and Issues,' *Relations Industrielles* 36, no. 1 (1981): 3–34; Rosemary Warskett, 'Bank Worker Unionization and the Law,' *Studies in Political Economy* 25 (Spring 1988): 41–73

3 Susan N.G. Geiger, 'Women's Life Histories: Method and Content,' *Signs* 11, no. 2 (1986): 334–51; Sherna Berger Gluck and Daphne Patai, eds, *Women's Words: The Feminist Practice of Oral History* (New York: Routledge, Chapman and Hall 1991); Karen Sacks, 'What's a Life Story Got to Do With It?' in The Personal Narratives Group, ed., *Interpreting Women's Lives: Feminist Theory and Personal Narratives* (Bloomington: Indiana University Press 1989)

4 I interviewed Sara, Anne, and Margaret in the summer of 1991, and Elizabeth in the winter of 1991. I also had several informal conversations with Elizabeth that summer. All names used here are pseudonyms.

5 There were attempts to organize bank clerks as early as the first two decades of this century. From then until the 1970s, there was little interest in or attempts to organize bank employees nationally in Canada. (For more detailed accounts of the history of bank unionization in Canada, see Graham S. Lowe, *Bank Unionization in Canada; Women in the Administrative Revolution* [Toronto: University of Toronto Press 1987].) The first major organizing breakthrough among bank employees came in 1967, when the Office and Professional Employees Union (OPEU) was certified to represent about 1000 employees at the Montreal City and District Savings Bank. This was the only union in the banking industry until 1976. By the late 1970s, six unions were organizing bank workers: SORWUC; the Canadian Union of Bank Employees (CUBE); the Office and Technical Employees Union (OTEU); the Association of Commercial and Technical Employees (ACTE); the United Steelworkers of America (USWA); and the Retail Clerks International Union (RCIU). By December of 1979, the Confederation of National Trade Unions (CNTU), with roots exclusively in Quebec, had signed up twelve branches as well. See Baker, 'Banking Transformed.'

6 The Bank Book Collective

7 For more details, see Baker, 'Some Unions Are More Equal than Others'; The Bank Book Collective; Lennon; and Rosemary Warskett, 'Legitimate and Illegitimate Unionism: The Case of SORWUC and Bankworker Unionization,' a paper presented to the political-economy sessions of the Canadian Political Science Association, Hamilton, June 1987; 'Bank Worker Unionization and the Law.'

8 Statistics Canada, *Industrial Organization and Finance Division Labour Unions Section. Annual Report of the Minister of Industry, Science and Technology under the Corporations and Labour Unions Returns Act (CALURA). Part II. Labour Unions. 1988* (Ottawa: Minister of Supply and Services Canada 1990), 40

9 Sara still lives in Vancouver, but Anne moved to Seattle at the end of the summer of 1991.

10 The Bank Book Collective 10

11 Miriam Edelson, *Challenging Unions: Feminist Process and Democracy in the Labour Movement* (Ottawa: CRIAW/ICREF 1987), 6

12 The Bank Book Collective; Warskett, 'Bank Worker Unionization and the Law'

13 The Bank Book Collective

14 Ibid.

15 Personal communication, SORWUC members, 11 Dec. 1988; SORWUC, 'UBW Account Reopened,' *S.O.R.W.U.C. News*, April 1981, 6–8

16 For details on the extent and nature of the strike support, see Patricia Baker, 'Union and Community: The Case of the Bank Workers in [a community in Nova Scotia]'; paper presented at the CESCE annual meetings, Ottawa, 20–23 May 1989

17 For details on this strike, see Baker, 'Union and Community' and 'Unionizing Canadian Bank Workers.' According to a number of my informants, it was at the meeting at which the vote on the bank's offer was held that the CLC staff representative strongly urged the women to accept the bank's offer. Whatever their misgivings may have been, a small majority of the women voted to accept the offer. My informants suggested that these women were intimidated by their staff representative's considerable union experience – that is, as an experienced union person, he was viewed as having authority to make such a decision, whereas the women, with their own extremely limited union experience, did not. This explanation is rather conjectural, but does reflect several of the women's overall uncertainty about and inexperience in the conduct of a strike.

18 See, for example, Gerard Griffin and John Benson, 'Barriers to Female Membership Participation in Trade Union Activities,' *Labour & Industry* 2, no. 1 (1989): 85–96.

19 Margaret Beattie, 'The Representation of Women in Unions,' *Signs* 12, no. 1 (1986): 118–29; Dorothy Sue Cobble, 'Rethinking Troubled Relations between Women and Unions: Craft Unionism and Female Activism,' *Feminist Studies* 16, no. 3 (1990): 519–48; Edelson

PART II
THE POLITICS OF GENDER WITHIN THE
UNION MOVEMENT

4

Union Women and Separate Organizing

LINDA BRISKIN

A significant turning-point for women's organizing in the Canadian unions was the women's conference of the Canadian Labour Congress (CLC) held in 1990 and attended by six hundred delegates, the theme of which was 'Empowering Women.' The conference focused on developing strategies to increase empowerment through collective action in unions, the workplace, and the community. The organizers of this conference made a decision to have separate workshops for those men in attendance. This issue became controversial on the floor of the convention: men belligerent about what they saw as segregation and reverse discrimination; some women, often from male-dominated unions, supporting them; and many women angry about being distracted from the business at hand. The blow-up at this conference provoked a debate across the country; what is so instructive is the response of the union leadership. Rather than supporting the men and condemning the organizers, they saw in men's reaction a justification to support *increased* separate organizing for women.

In vigorously defending the decision to place the brothers in their own workshops, CLC Executive Vice-president Nancy Riche explained that the men only workshop was based on the assumption that men could learn from each other and would use the opportunity to strategize together to develop ways to support women in their struggle for equality. She stated unequivocally that the Women's Conference was not the place for these men to expect their sisters to set aside the agenda to try to accommodate them. The enthusiastic reception to Riche's strong language was evident in the response of one tired and frustrated delegate who said that 'the most supportive thing the men could have done was to have sent women to the conference.'[1]

As a result of these events, the British Columbia Federation of Labour (BCFL) passed a motion allowing for women-only conferences. Marion Pollack, an activist from the Canadian Union of Postal Workers (CUPW) in British Columbia said:

The events at the 1990 conference have already opened an important door for women unionists ... The B.C. Federation of Labour sponsored a recent conference entitled 'Breaking the Cycle: Women and Violence'. This conference was advertised as 'women only,' and was attended only by females. It was extremely popular ... Surprisingly, very few men complained about the women-only nature of the conference. In my opinion, the designation of the conference as 'women-only' was a direct result of the debates and hullabaloo at the 1990 CLC women's conference.[2]

The CLC executive board granted the CLC women's committee the right to organize such conferences; the BCFL and CLC now join the Public Service Alliance of Canada (PSAC), which has had such a policy for some years.

This example demonstrates an interesting shift in the practices and dominant discourse of the union movement around the issue of women's organizing – towards a greater legitimation of 'separate organizing.' Simultaneously, it highlights the ongoing resistance to such practices. This paper documents the support for and resistance to strategies of separate organizing, and presents an analytic framework for interrogating the practices, ideology, contribution, and tensions of such organizing. The emphasis, then, will not be on the *issues* of women's organizing inside the union movement, for example, sexual harassment, pay equity, or child care, but on the *strategy* of separate organizing.

Separate organizing takes a variety of forms within the union movement: an informal women's network or caucus in a union; a formal, sometimes elected, provincial or national women's committee; a women-only educational conference; a women's local of a mixed union or a women's auxiliary; or a women-only union like the Federation of Women Teachers' Associations of Ontario (FWTAO).[3] Separate organizing is often supported by union resources and facilitated by equal-opportunity coordinators, women's bureaus, and so on.

Despite the significant differences among them, we can imagine such instances of separate organizing along a continuum in their 'degrees of separateness.' Grouping them under the rubric of separate organizing for the purposes of this paper makes visible a rich history that is intrinsically related to gender-specific experience. Despite its usefulness, such a formulation is also problematic because it assumes a unifed category of 'woman' and a homogeneity to women's experience. Historically specific studies are necessary to tease out the multiplicity of women's experiences of separate organizing based on race, class, sexual orientation, ethnicity, and age; such studies would help to underline, for example, the race-specific experience of gender.

In a discussion of separate organizing, it is critical to distinguish between separatism as a *goal* – an end in itself, and separate organizing as a *strategy* – a means to an end. Separatism often includes an explicit refusal to work with men and usually focuses on the building of alternative communities as a solution rather than on the transformation of dominant social structures. By contrast, separate organizing is a strategy of empowerment for women in their struggle to alter the political and economic configurations. Union women have mostly argued for separate organizing rather than separatism; however, separate organizing by union women has often been discredited on the assumption that it is separatist. The conflation of the two means that separate organizing by women is often seen as a divisive strategy in the union movement, rather than as a means to strengthen, not only the voices of women, but of the union movement as a whole.

Separate organizing by women has a long and complex history in the women's movement, in the community, and in the union movement. This history has often been both invisible and inaccessible – not surprising given that women's organizing has been under-researched and under-theorized in all sites where it has occurred. Situating a study of the separate organizing among union women in this larger context allows us to see both the continuity of the principle of separate organizing and the multiplicity of different forms, locations, and institutions in which it has occurred. So, for example, consciousness-raising groups developed by the women's liberation movement of the 1960s and 1970s provided the model for informal women's committees in unions.

It is significant that more than fifteen years of women's committees and caucuses in the unions, and some success in pressuring unions to take up women's issues, has not led to a decline in such organizing. In fact, the trajectory has been to seek more arenas in which women can organize separately. We can document growing acceptance and legitimation of separate organizing – at least in the public discourse of unions – and increasing institutionalization and formalization of structures to facilitate it: constitutional clauses to incorporate women's committees, policy statements to address women's concerns, allocation of staff and financial resources, and so on.[4] Support among union women and men, and also among union leadership, is manifested in the widespread existence of educational programs and conferences for women, as well as women's informal caucuses and formal committees. Even CUPW which resisted the organization of a national women's committee for years, passed a motion in 1990 to set one up – with guaranteed funding.[5]

Optimistically we might suggest that unions have come to recognize the need for separate organizing as a basis from which women can become full participants in the union. They may also have come to see that gender-specific organizing, far from dividing the union, has made the union movement stronger. How deeply embedded these changes in consciousness are is difficult to gauge, but it can be argued that women's separate organizing has changed the way unions organize and educate the rank and file; it has expanded the understanding of 'union' issues, thereby supporting that current of social unionism which is critical to the long-term health of the union movement. It has also helped to legitimize coalition building with groups outside the union movement as union women have organized successfully with the community-based women's movement in coalitions such as the Equal Pay Coalition, Canadian Daycare Advocacy Association, March 8th Coalition, and Ontario Coalition for Abortion Clinics.

Women's separate organizing in the unions has also provided a strategic foundation for responding to issues around race and racism, as well as sexual orientation and homophobia. Increasingly women and men of colour, lesbians and gay men, and native peoples are organizing 'separately' inside the union movement. Evidence in this regard is striking. In 1990 the Canadian Union of Public Employees (CUPE) broke new ground with its work on employment benefits for gay and lesbian workers and their families. An August 1991 article in *Xtra* reports on the formation of 'Lavender Labour,' a lesbian and gay labour network in the United States and indicates that the 'OFL offers same sex spousal benefits to its employees and is a member of the Coalition for Lesbian and Gay Rights in Ontario ... The Ontario and BC Federations of Labour are actively pursuing issues around gaybashing, sexual harassment and contract language.'

To detail the organizing of union women of colour is beyond the scope of this paper. But it is interesting to note the impact of such organizing on the OFL. The OFL Document no. 2 from the 1987 Convention, 'A Statement on Equal Action in Employment,' takes up employment equity for all equity-seeking groups. In 1988 the Women's Committee of the OFL sponsored a conference on 'Building Bridges for Affirmative Action' which focused on women with disabilities, native women, and visible-minority women. The OFL Document no. 2 from the 1991 Convention on 'Challenging Harassment' takes up racism, sexism, homophobia, and violence against women.

At this historical conjuncture, it is not entirely clear what linking gender-specificity to race, class, ethnicity, and sexual orientation will mean for organizing inside the unions and for organizing the unorganized. Most certainly, it will mean complexifying our understanding of separate organizing. This separate organizing must be championed by feminist union activists, who need to recall their struggle to legitimize separate organizing and to resist arguments that separate organizing by women of colour is divisive.

Indeed, it is in the interests of unions to fully support such efforts. The democratic, participatory thrust inherent in structures of separate organizing encourages the involvement of what is often an apathetic membership. Separate organizing provides the basis for different constituencies to come together from positions of strength; for example, consider the discussion of the links between health-and-safety committees and women's committees in the Karen Messing and Donna Mergler piece in this volume; and the convergence of human rights and women's issues in the piece by Ronnie Leah, also in this volume.

Further, in a time of attacks on the right to unionize, and of serious decline in unionized manufacturing jobs, unions are realizing the importance of expanding their constituencies of *active* members and increasing their appeal to the unorganized, many of whom are immigrant women and people of colour. Union support for separate organizing will make unions more attractive to these constituencies.

Studying the *phenomenon* of separate organizing precipitates out important strategic questions: under what conditions do women call for separate organizing? under what conditions is this kind of organizing successful? These questions underline the point that separate organizing neither succeeds nor fails by virtue of being 'separate'; rather a complex of contextual circumstances impact on its relevance and viability. Two themes emerge, then, which inform the next two sections: the importance of gender-specific experience in shaping organizing strategies; and the significance of institutional location to the success of separate organizing. The paper argues that the success of separate organizing in the unions depends upon maintaining a balance between 'autonomy' from the structures and practices of the labour movement and 'integration' into those structures.

SAMENESS AND DIFFERENCE: GENDER SPECIFICITY AND SEPARATE ORGANIZING

Women's relationship to separate organizing has been marked by a deep ambivalence which reflects the struggle to be integrated as equals into the structures of institutions and the recognition that women are discriminated against as women and may need special measures to make such integration possible. This section will consider three claims: that separate organizing is a form of ghettoization; that separate organizing is a necessary corrective to the 'deficits' in women; and finally that separate organizing is a pro-active positive appropriation of women's experiences. This discussion underlines that support for, or rejection of, separate organizing can be informed by a variety of political approaches.

1. Ghettoization

A persistent thread in the resistance to separate organizing has been grounded in the contention that it reinforces rather than addresses discrimination, that is, to organize separately *produces* gender discrimination rather than responds to it. Embedded in the claims about ghettoization are two assumptions: that *integration* into male-dominated structures on the same terms as men is *the* strategic orientation for winning 'equality'; and that gender differences are fundamentally insignificant. Despite continuing ideological support for this kind of position, it is possible to trace the shift *in practice* away from the ghettoization perspective as it fails to produce results.

For example, Roberta Till-Retz suggests that the view that separate structures are 'ghettos to keep women quiet, ineffective, and "talking only to themselves"' resulted in the Swedish unions abolishing their women's divisions in the 1970s and in a 'wholesale rejection of every form of special structure or special consideration for women. There were no "women's issues," but only "family issues" or "equality issues." It was hoped that Swedish social policy would enable women to emerge freely and naturally to union leadership. *But this has not happened ... and many Swedish union women privately favor quotas and other special efforts to get women into union offices'* (emphasis added).[7] In her work on the organizing of women activists in the Canadian region of the UAW in the 1960s, Pamela Sugiman talks about 'the campaign for the elimination of all gender distinctions in UAW contracts.'[8]

Inspired by the general ideological foundations of industrial unionism – universality, impartiality, democracy, and thus, gender-neutrality – many women claimed that they deserved the *same* terms of employment as working men. In the early stages of their struggle, they promoted a narrow conception of equality that emphasized uniformity, denied preferential treatment, and thereby overlooked the historical structural context of gender differences and inequalities.[9]

Sugiman recounts the activists' increasing disillusionment with this approach and their turn to feminism which allowed them to address 'women's *particular* position in work and society' (emphasis added).[10] As the integration strategy fails to produce results, it is modified through a shift towards the deficit model and the belief that being more *like* men can produce 'equality.'

2. The Deficit Model

Separate organizing has at times been justified by a 'deficit model' analysis which suggests that women workers, as a result of socialization patterns, are poorly equipped to take on leadership roles in the union movement, that is, the problems women face in unions are a result of some inadequacy in women themselves.[11] Unlike the ghettoizaton model, this approach does recognize the significance of gender difference and the need for some separate organizing; however, it focuses on 'women changing' – in fact, on *individual* women changing – rather than on 'unions changing.' Ruth Milkman makes this point in her assessment of the Coalition of Labour Union Women (CLUW) in the United States:

CLUW's approach presumes that the key difference between women and men is that women lack leadership skills, self-confidence and therefore power. While taking account of the fact that women have 'family responsibilities' that obstruct their union activity, CLUW does not view this as a basis for a critique of established organizational forms within the labor movement, but rather as an additional handicap which women must somehow overcome. As the CLUW slogan 'A Woman's Place Is in her Union' implies, all the needs of women can be taken care of within the existing framework of trade unionism. The problem with unions is only that women do not have a large enough role in them; the solution is for women to equip themselves to compete more effectively, on the established terms, for leadership.[12]

Although the deficit model has informed many union educational programs for women, and much of the debate about women and union leadership, the ground is shifting as women activists politicize and organize collectively – a shift manifested in the changing focus of some union educational programs for women. The programs which focus on 'changing women' by improving their self-esteem, developing their assertiveness, and training them in union procedures are increasingly being replaced by others with a deeply political edge which concentrate on developing an activist politicized feminist constituency in the unions. This is evident in a new six-day course called 'Women of Steel' developed by District Six of the the United Steelworkers of America (USWA) in cooperation with the Ontario Women's Directorate (1991). Discussions of assertiveness training and dealing with stress are secondary to, or perhaps interwoven with, the focus on institutional and family obstacles facing women, the history of women in unions, the relationship between the labour movement and the women's movement, envisioning a transformed union movement, and making political change outside the union. Noting this shift is not meant to underestimate the contribution of education programs which focus on 'changing women,' but rather to highlight the problematic strategic message embedded in such an approach – a message which not only blames the victim but also assumes that being like men is the solution for women.

3. A Pro-Active Politic of Separate Organizing

Increasingly, separate organizing is a pro-active choice on the part of women in order to strengthen their voices, respond to their particular concerns as activists or workers, and create a context to draw on organizing strategies that come out of their experience. This politic of separate organizing is informed by a recognition of the gender-specific character of experience which, in this context, means that women enter unions differently than men because of the nature of their workplace and household/family experience; that their work bridges the public and the private, and each impacts on the other; and that the pervasive violence women experience in both public and private spaces shapes not only workplace and family experience but also women's political strategies. In short, women's relation to power is fundamentally different than men's. It is not surprising, then, that women identify different issues as significant to them, and organize and resist in distinct ways.[13] This politic of separate organizing recognizes that the problems women face in unions are a result of structural and ideological discrimination, and that women must organize *collectively* – bringing to this process their own gender-specific knowledge – in order to effect institutional change. This is not meant to be a biologistic argument but one which sees women's experiences as socially constituted. It acknowledges women as a constituency and the discrimination that women qua women face.

This politic rejects gender blindness and the assumption that 'gender-neutral' integration – on the same terms as men – is either possible or offers a solution. It moves beyond the belief that gender can be made irrelevant through good intentions; indeed, it recognizes that gender-neutral approaches can actually reinforce the status quo because they make invisible the deeply embedded character of sexism. Strategies that take gender into account are necessary to reflect women's experience and overcome women's disadvantage, and to highlight the functioning of structural inequality. Separate organizing is one such strategy.

Recognition in the union movement of the gender-specific character of experience is increasingly evident.[14] We see this trend in recent union campaigns around violence against women which have expanded their focus from employer harassment and internal procedures to deal with co-worker sexual harassment to the general issue of violence against women. For example, a 1991 campaign about violence against women organized by the BCFL used this caption: 'Let's break the pattern of violence against women. As trade unionists, we're working to achieve justice and equality in our society. Violence against women undermines that work. It's not a private matter – breaking this pattern is *everybody's* business.'

The Canadian Auto Workers (CAW) sponsored a women's conference on the issue of violence against women in August 1991, passed a resolution committing the CAW to the goal of creating 'zero tolerance level of sexist treatment of women', and did a mass distribution of posters and buttons with the slogan 'Violence: Break the Silence.' To mark December 6, a national day of remembrance and action on the issue of violence in commemoration of those women who died in the Montreal massacre in 1989, the CAW urged its locals to conduct educationals, participate in local events around December 6, and support their local shelters and rape crisis centres through fundraising and volunteer work.[15]

This focus on the *general* issue of violence against women signals several important shifts in union thinking about women's concerns. Most significant for our discussion here is a firm recognition of the gender-specific character of experience. This focus appreciates that women's experiences inside and outside the workplace are inextricably linked (the strategic reflection of which are coalitions between the movement of union women and the community-based women's movement). It also demonstrates that the conventional boundaries of business unionism which emphasize wages and fringe benefits are not adequate to women's concerns. Indeed, the campaigns about violence against women have not been couched in the language of business unionism. In contrast, in the campaign in the unions for support of reproductive choice and access to abortion in the mid-1980s, the narrowly defined workplace focus of business unionism was accommodated in the recurring arguments that union endorsement was justified because 'abortion is a workplace issue.'

Furthermore, the campaign for abortion access was largely initiated by community-based women's groups working in concert with union women who often spoke from the margins of their unions. In contrast, union staff and leadership are taking more initiative on this recent campaign on violence. For example, the CAW literature is all signed by then union president Bob White, and in an October 1991 letter addressed to local union presidents, secretaries, women's committees, and so on about the CAW's co-worker harassment policy, White forcefully states: 'The most vulnerable members in the workplace should not have to carry this issue on their own. *It is the local leadership that should take up this issue on their behalf and insist that the harassment stop.'*

There is not only growing recognition of the gender-specific character of experience, but also an increasing legitimacy for organizing strategies which take account of gender. The Service, Office and Retail Workers Union of Canada (SORWUC) stands as only one of many concrete examples of women developing unique organizational strategies. SORWUC was an explicitly feminist union which, in the 1970s, took on the enormous task of organizing bank workers in Canada. It focused on the banks as a sector of women's low-wage work that had been virtually ignored by the trade-union movement. SORWUC felt that women had to organize women: because women had respect for the work of women; because women organized differently with more participatory decision-making strategies and with a recognition of the limits placed on women workers by the double day; and because women focused on different issues such as pay equity, child care, and sexual harassment. SORWUC was able to organize many bank branches where others had failed. Its success was related to the recognition of the importance of gender-specific methods of organizing and of the specificity of women's concerns.[16] In the United States, District 925, now affiliated to Service Employees International Union (SEIU) but growing out of 9 to 5, the National Association of Working Women, has become 'the preeminent example of the new style of female organizing.'[17]

Not only are the district's organizing materials and themes decidedly female, so are its staff. The results of the District's efforts indicate an unmistakable identification by working women with this new organization. In little over four years, the District has organized 6,000 workers, predominantly in university, public sector, government, and school white and pink collar jobs. The District has set a national example for organizing by focusing on issues of direct concern to working women – VDT hazards, pay equity, job undervaluation, child care – and by developing female-run campaigns and rank and file leadership.[18]

Equally interesting in this regard is the new politic of leadership emerging among feminist unionists. Informed by the organizing strategies of the grass-roots women's movement, this politic 'supports decentralization of the power traditionally associated with leadership positions ... It is an inclusive rather than exclusive politic; it relies on participation more than on representation. It moves toward greater democracy and openness of union structures and decision-making; it underscores accountability and operates on the basis of a strong and active link between leadership and constituency. And it operates with a consciousness of gender, and of the specific barriers which women face in the household, the workplace and the union.'[19] These examples suggest an increasing degree of comfort with pro-active separate organizing.

However, important issues remain unaddressed. For example, is pro-active separate organizing informed specifically by a feminist politic? This question signals other points: about the multiplicity of feminist politics, the distinction between feminist and gender consciousness, and the use of a label like 'feminist' which is not necessarily adopted by women union activists. This paper has also not engaged particularly with the responses of men to separate organizing which have disputed the evidence of sexist discrimination, called separate organizing divisive and reverse discrimination, and attempted to discredit, by marshalling homophobia and anti-feminism, those women in favour of it.

Nor has this paper considered that separate organizing by women workers which is structured by occupational segregation. For example, nurses – an almost entirely female profession – did not *choose* to organize separately; thus, it would be inaccurate to include them within a discussion of *pro-active* separate organizing. Nevertheless, it is probably the case that because the nursing profession is sex segregated, the work stereotypically identified with women and their 'nurturing' qualities, de-valued on this basis, and underpaid relative to doctors who have traditionally been men, certain kinds of gender-specific concerns will precipitate out.

We can conclude this section by taking a lesson from women's organizing in the past. In a provocative argument on female institution building and the failure of American feminism in the 1920s, Estelle Freedman concludes:

The strength of female institutions in the late nineteenth century and the weaknesses of women's politics after the passage of the Suffrage Amendment suggest to me that the decline of feminism in the 1920s can be attributed in part to the devaluation of women's culture in general and of separate female institutions in particular. When women tried to assimilate into male-dominated institutions, without securing feminist social, economic, or political bases, they lost the momentum and the networks which had made the suffrage movement possible. Women gave up many of the strengths of the female sphere without gaining equally from the man's world they entered.[20]

The fact that women's separate organizing provides a power base from which women can effect change is central to the discussion in the next section about the conditions under which the strategy of separate organizing is successful.

AUTONOMY AND INTEGRATION: THE DILEMMA OF SEPARATE ORGANIZING

Women's separate organizing is not only about gender specificity and gender power but also represents a challenge to organizational practices. Male power generates and is reinforced by bureaucratic, hierarchical, and competitive ways of organizing which combine to produce certain kinds of organizations, patterns of decision making, and an emphasis on particular issues. Thus male power and privilege, male leadership, and traditional organizational forms intersect and function to exclude and disadvantage women. This is not just because those in power are men, but because male power, which is socially constituted, functions organizationally in specific ways. Since women's separate organizing simultaneously contests gender power and organizational structures, it is experienced by men as a serious challenge.

It is not surprising, then, that there is a convergence, on the one hand, of demands by rank-and-file unionists for more democracy and by union women struggling for more voice, and, on the other hand, of resistance to women's organizing by both patriarchal and bureaucratic interests. Dierdre Gallagher, a long-time feminist activist in the union movement, makes this link: 'There is still an unwillingness to let women share power, and a fear – a real fear – of sharing power with women. In some ways, it is a fear of democracy itself, because women's push within the labour movement has represented a demand for a more democratic union. These people who fear democracy, fear women.'[21] Put another way, some of the resistance to women's organizing inside unions has been to the implicit rank-and-file challenge to entrenched leaderships.

Separate organizing is about gender *and* about organization. This is why organizing 'separately' is not itself enough to guarantee success; the location of the separate organizing in the structural web of the institution is critical. I would argue that the success of women's separate organizing in unions depends upon maintaining a balance between the degree of autonomy from the structures and practices of the labour movement, on the one hand, and the degree of integration into those structures, on the other. Too little integration and the separate organizing is marginalized; too much integration and the radical edge is necessarily softened. Relatively successful integration produces the level of legitimacy necessary to ensure access to adequate resources. The autonomy axis provides the foundation for a strong voice about women's concerns and the context for building alliances between the movement of union women and the community-based women's movement. To the extent that separate organizing and such alliances are successful, the autonomy axis can become an additional source of legitimacy.

In her study of the separate waitress locals of the Hotel Employees and Restaurant Employees International Union (HERE) in the United States from around 1900 to the 1930s, Dorothy Cobble draws some similar conclusions about the context in which 'separate organizing' is successful. Specifically, she contrasts the impact of separate women's locals with women's committees in mixed locals and concludes unequivocally: 'In the end, without the autonomy, power, and institutional legitimacy enjoyed by the separate female locals, the impact of women's committees was episodic and ephemeral. Without a majority vote within the local or a separate institutional base of power, women could neither change the priorities of the male leadership, nor could they act independently. Moreover, the basic legitimacy of women's committees was always in question.'[22] In contrast, the separate locals 'played a critical role in stimulating leadership among waitresses ... The decrease in waitress activity from the 1930s onward closely paralleled the decline in female locals.'[23] In this example, we can see that the overly integrated women's committees were de-legitimized.

Cobble is also concerned about how separate organizing was legitimized. She points out: 'Unlike women's locals in other industries which included women from many different trades, waitress locals had an 'occupational homogenity' and a legitimacy as a craft-based organization. Because the sexual divisions were also perceived as 'craft' divisions, waitress locals received the same treatment and were accorded the same benefits as any other craft based local.'[24] The craft-like organization of their work 'ensured that the 'ghettoizing' impact that can accompany separatism was minimized and the positive aspects of female institution building were maximized.'[25] This paper focuses on the location of separate organizing in the institutional web of the union; but Cobble reminds us that the structure of work also shapes the meaning and success of such organizing.

It is interesting to consider several current and Canadian examples: the Service, Office and Retail Workers Union of Canada (SORWUC) and the Federation of Women Teachers' Associations of Ontario (FWTAO). Both are examples of separate organizing and both have been seen to represent a significant challenge in this regard. Although SORWUC did have some male members, it was a feminist-initiated and women-led union; the FWTAO is a women-only organization. The balance of autonomy/integration, resources, and legitimacy, played out quite differently in each case, helps us to reflect both on the successes of, and the resistances to separate organizing.

A comparison between FWTAO and SORWUC can be used to highlight the tensions among autonomy/integration, legitimacy, and resources; however, I recognize serious limits to making such a comparison. For the differences between the two groups are striking: the status of the FWTAO as a women-only union is protected by a by-law of the Ontario Teachers' Federation (OTF) (it is one of five affiliates of the OTF, each with equal status); SORWUC struggled to survive. By virtue of its status, FWTAO has a stable resource and membership base; SORWUC did not. FWTAO organizes professional women with relatively high salaries rather than low-wage clerical workers. SORWUC took on the whole labour movement in its challenge to the CLC for its right to organize separately; FWTAO faces only the Ontario Public School Teachers' Federation (OPSTF), the affiliate of the OTF which organizes the male elementary-school teachers. However, despite the strengths of FWTAO, and perhaps because of them, it has faced fifty years of serious challenges and continues to fight for its right to exist.

The experience of SORWUC illustrates the necessity of both a stable resource base and a legitimized structural location to the success of women's separate organizing. Despite its victories in organizing the banks, the lack of a stable resource base, jurisdictional disputes with the CLC which prevented it from establishing a legitimized structural location in the union movement, and the constraints of labour legislation interfered with the ability of SORWUC to pursue its organizing campaigns. What this suggests is that SORWUC had too much autonomy from the labour movement: it was not adequately integrated. It did not, then, have the legitimacy to claim resources from the union movement. Unfortunately, the available avenues for integration overly threatened the autonomy of SORWUC.[26]

In sharp contrast, the FWTAO functions with an effective balance between autonomy and integration, a balance which has produced legitimacy of voice and which has been made possible by its access to a stable resource base. The structural location of the FWTAO is key to its strength. It is both autonomous from other teachers' unions – a fully separate union – *and* integrated as an equal member into the larger umbrella structures such as OTF. It has equal status at the bargaining table with the OPSTF that is, they bargain together, but as two separate autonomous units.[27] This degree of autonomy produces not only a degree of legitimacy – FWTAO is seen as a force with which to contend – but also a strong voice to represent the *specific* concerns of women teachers in the primary sector. The stable resource base makes this structure of autonomy and integration viable; without it, the FWTAO might have to compromise its politics to maintain legitimacy.[28] In the FWTAO the ingredients are present for effective 'separate organizing.' Indeed, its success has provided it with the space to be a strong feminist voice both for women teachers and in the women's movement, and helps to account for the longevity and intensity of the challenge by the OPSTF to their separate status.[29]

If the goal of women's separate organizing is empowerment, the evidence presented here suggests that the legitimacy which emerges from maintaining the delicate balance between autonomy and integration is an important ingredient.

CONCLUSION

The discourse on women and unions has shifted dramatically over the last fifteen years. Originally women's increased participation was promoted because discrimination against women was seen to weaken the labour movement.[30] The arguments used at this stage emphasized that all union members were the *same* and should be treated as such. This position assumed it was possible to produce equality through the same treatment despite differential access to power, privilege, and resources. 'Equal' and the 'same' have often been conflated in women's struggles to make change, thus obscuring not only the gendered character of experience but also the specificity of women's oppression.

Increasingly the debate has moved from what is good for the unions to what is good for women unionists, that is, to a discourse of women's *rights* which accepts that women qua women face discrimination. This position has meant a growing acknowledgment that unity will be built through a recognition of difference and of differential access to power, and that the union movement will be strengthened by some degree of separate organizing by women.[31] In this context, the strategic possibilities for harnessing the power of separate organizing by women are dramatically increased.

NOTES

I wish to thank Patricia McDermott and all those who attended the workshop on The Politics of Gender within the Trade Union Movement (March 1992) for their insightful comments on an earlier version of this paper.

1 Jane Jetson, 'Coming to Terms with Power: Male Backlash Mars Event,' *The Capital Siftings*, 30 Nov. 1990. Other information about this event came from an interview with Penni Richmond, director of the Women's Bureau of the CLC (3 April 1991) and 'Women, Protest and Power,' a series of articles on it in *Our Times*, March 1991.
2 Letter to the Editor, *Our Times*, May 1991
3 See Debbie Field, 'The Dilemma Facing Women's Committees'; Arja Lane, 'Wives Supporting the Strike'; and Meg Luxton, 'From Ladies Auxiliaries to Wives' Committees'; all in Linda Briskin and Lynda Yanz, eds, *Union Sisters* (Toronto: Women's Press 1983). See also Alex Brown and Laurie Sheridan, 'Pioneering Women's Committee Struggles with Hard Times,' *Labor Research Review* no. 11 (Spring 1988) for a discussion of the Women's Committee of IUE Local 201, established informally in 1976 and one of the longest-lived union women's committees in the United States.
4 Marina Boehm, *Who Makes the Decisions? Women's Participation in Canadian Unions* (Kingston: Queen's University, Industrial Relations Centre 1991) details the history of some of these changes. Naomi Baden analyses 'the extent to which a commitment to women has become *institutionalized* within the labour movement.' She focuses on the number of women members, the number of elected women officials, the number of national-union female staff and the types of jobs they do, and the types of programs, departments, budgets, and other resources committed to women's concerns. See 'Developing an Agenda: Expanding the Role of Women in Unions,' *Labour Studies Journal* 10, no. 3 (Winter 1986): 229–49.

5 For a discussion of women in CUPW, see Julie White, *Mail and Female* (Toronto: Thompson Publishers 1990).

6 See Kit from the Research and Equal Opportunity Departments, February 1990. Also in 'Sexuality: A Trade Union Issue?' *Labour Research* (June 1991), a new survey shows unions increasingly taking up lesbian and gay concerns in the United Kingdom.

7 Roberta Till-Retz, 'Unions in Europe: Increasing Women's Participation,' *Labor Studies Journal* 10, no. 3 (1986): 253–4

8 Pamela Sugiman, ' "That Wall's Comin' Down": Gendered Strategies of Worker Resistance in the UAW Canadian Region (1963–1970),' *Canadian Journal of Sociology* 17, no. 1 (1992): 10

9 Ibid. 10–1

10 Ibid. 13

11 The 'deficit model' is criticized as a strategic approach to dealing with discrimination against girls in school in Jane Gaskell, Arlene McLaren, and Myra Novogrodsky, *Claiming an Education: Feminism and Canadian Schools* (Toronto: Garamond 1989). See chapter 1.

12 Ruth Milkman, 'Feminism and Labor since the 1960s,' in Ruth Milkman, ed., *Women, Work and Protest* (Boston: Routledge and Kegan Paul 1985), 313

13 There is an extensive feminist literature on the issue of women's different ways of knowing, much of it based on Carol Gilligan's seminal work *In a Different Voice* (Cambridge, Mass.: Harvard University Press 1982). For a discussion of organizational strategies in the women's movement, see Nancy Adamson, Linda Briskin, and Margaret McPhail, *Feminist Organizing for Change* (Toronto: Oxford 1988); for a discussion of 'female styles of work' in the union movement, see Ruth Needleman, 'Women Workers: A Force for Rebuilding Unionism,' *Labor Research Review* no. 11 (Spring 1988).

14 In discussion, Karen Messing made the important point that as we make visible the gender-specific character of women's work, we allow for more attention to the gender-specific character of men's work, for example, around the issue of reproductive hazards. Gradually, we move to eliminate the notion that there is a generic worker.

15 From a letter by Peggy Nash, assistant to the president, CAW (30 Oct. 1991), providing an update on CAW activities following up from their national conference, addressed to all Local presidents, secretaries, women's committees, and so on

16 From an interview with Jean Rands, a founding member of SORWUC conducted on 7 May 1991. See also Patricia Baker, 'Some Unions Are

More Equal than Others: A Response to Rosemary Warskett's "Bank Worker Unionization and the Law,"' *Studies in Political Economy* no. 34 (Spring 1991).

17 Baden 245

18 Ibid. It is interesting to note the links between women's organizing inside and outside the unions. 'One of the appeals of the District 925 model for organizing has been its commitment to women workers *prior to* and *outside* of unionization efforts. 9 to 5, the National Association of Working Women, the sister organization of District 925, is a separate entity and is not union affiliated. It advocates the formation of pre-union organizations which focus on self-help and assertiveness training; it also undertakes public and community organizing around issues of concern to women workers in a particular locale. Such a multi-faceted approach to women's concerns lends credence to the organization when it does advocate unionization' (245).

19 Linda Briskin, 'Women, Unions and Leadership,' *Canadian Dimension,* Jan./Feb. 1990, 39

20 Estelle Freedman, 'Separatism as Strategy: Female Institution Building and American Feminism, 1870–1930,' *Feminist Studies* 5, no. 3 (Fall 1979), 521, 524

21 Dierdre Gallagher, 'Affirmative Action,' in Robert Argue, Charlene Gannage, and D.W. Livingstone, eds, *Working People and Hard Times* (Toronto: Garamond Press 1987), 354

22 Dorothy Cobble, 'Rethinking Troubled Relations Between Women and Unions: Craft Unionism and Female Activism,' *Feminist Studies* 16, no. 3 (Fall 1990), 534

23 Ibid. 521

24 Ibid. 521–2

25 Ibid. 522

26 For a discussion of the impact of the labour-relations system on organizing bank workers, see Rosemary Warskett, 'Bank Worker Unionization and the Law,' *Studies in Political Economy* 25 (Spring 1988). For an analysis of some other factors in the failure of SORWUC, see Baker, 'Some Unions Are More Equal than Others ...' Baker focuses in some detail on what it meant that SORWUC did not have an established structural location in the Canadian labour movement and, indeed, the impact of this fact on the CLRB rulings. She also notes that when 'it became clear that SORWUC would not join the CLC and lose its independence by merging with an existing union, CLC financial assistance was withdrawn' (p. 224).

27 Barbara Richter, an executive staff member in the Collective Bargaining Department of FWTAO makes this point in her testimony before the Ontario Human Rights Commission. See vol. 43 (1990), 5961.

Juriansz [OPSTF lawyer]: In this joint session there is no opportunity for domination?
Richter: No
J: Even though men and women are present together in one meeting?
R: Yes, they are present together because they have a separate structure and come to that meeting as equals in equally established and recognized in law organizations and that is a fundamental difference between a meeting of two executives of two organizations and men and women meeting together.

28 The fear of compromise is part of the defence put forward by the FWTAO to the challenge of sex discrimination by Linda Logan-Smith and Margaret Toman. This challenge, supported by the OPSTF, is currently in front of the Ontario Human Rights Commission.

29 The longevity and intensity of these challenges are documented in the official transcript of the testimony of Florence Henderson (former executive director of the FWTAO and on staff with that organization from 1965 to her retirement in 1985) in front of the Ontario Human Rights Commission. See vols. 18–30 of the transcript, 1990.

30 Boehm notes this tendency in the early union promotion on women and unions (p. 43).

31 The increased acceptance of separate organizing in Canadian unions is in sharp contrast to developments in the United States. Ruth Milkman argues that the U.S. labour movement 'has a deep rooted mistrust of any efforts to assert the special interests of a group within the membership.' Milkman 309

5

Trade Union Leadership: Sexism and Affirmative Action

CARL J. CUNEO

'The old boys ... are very very bureaucratically entrenched labour leaders ... They have been full-time union presidents or union business reps or [in] some position of full-time union work for years. They're very high up, very powerful, very well paid ... These people are very far removed; they haven't been in the workplace for years and years. ... They're very, very strong [and] in control. They all band together, and they want to keep the control of their positions. They don't want to lose their positions, ... to lose the control of being on, say, the CLC executive. So they have found ... an old union maxim that [there's] strength in numbers amongst the old boys banding together. They want to keep things exactly as they are.' [CUPW official's description of male officials on the CLC executive council]

INTRODUCTION

Women have historically been denied equal access with men to official positions in the labour movement.[1] Women's representation among elected and appointed union officials has barely, if at all, kept pace with their increasing participation in the official labour force and in unionized jobs. The reasons for the continuation of this gender inequality are rooted in complex historical, social, and social-psychological factors – such as the patriarchal practices of the labour movement, the sexism of both male and female unionists inherited from society, an unequal domestic burden at home, women's greater child-care responsibilities, and a gender division of paid work that underrepresents women in many industrial-sector jobs, thereby reducing their role in the leadership of industrial unions. Despite these barriers, women have been making considerable progress, and are increasingly represented in many official union positions, especially at the local and regional levels. Many trade unions, labour federations, and congresses have developed programs (such as child care at union meetings, lunch-hour union meetings, assertiveness training, women's committees, and affirmative action) to facilitate the participation of women.

In this chapter I make four points. First, we need to broaden the way we look at union leadership. It should be viewed not just as the positions unionists occupy, but also what they do in these positions, and what unionists do who do not have official positions. In other words, what actions and initiatives do they engage in to lead the union, regardless of whether or not they are elected officials or paid staffers. This issue has always been important for male unionists. It is especially important to consider for women because many barriers specific to women's participation are especially important when we ask what leaders really do rather than just what positions they hold. Second, sexism is one such barrier. It disempowers women by hindering their deeper involvement in union activities. It is often experienced as private and personal, and is then not acknowledged, named, or studied, and thus solutions are not sought; yet it is systemic, requiring structural changes in the way unions operate. Women have been successful in pushing some unions to take measures against sexual harassment and violence against women. But much remains to be done. Third, the struggle against sexism takes many forms. One is structural – setting up affirmative action, or designated positions, for women (and for visible-minority women), empowering them at all levels of leadership, from the local union to the CLC. Affirmative action is a response to many different barriers women face. Its use against sexism is justified because sexist structures, practices, and attitudes are difficult to change simply by amending constitutions, passing by-laws, or introducing convention resolutions. While these are important, more forceful and focused measures, like affirmative action, are required to deal with a problem that does not seem to have a quick solution. Fourth, a special kind of activist leadership – separate organizing through women's committees and caucuses – has been employed to implement the campaigns against sexism and to support affirmative action. This activism has empowered women, as they otherwise might not have been.

Data for this paper are drawn from a project based on in-depth qualitative interviews with 252 women union activists at the Canadian Labour Congress; the national, regional, and local levels of 18 unions; city and district labour councils; and the federations of labour in British Columbia, Alberta, Saskatchewan, Ontario, New Brunswick, and Nova Scotia. Documentary materials were also collected from these organizations. This analysis of leadership, sexism, and affirmative action is a small part of a much larger study of gender in the Canadian labour movement outside Quebec.

WHAT IS UNION LEADERSHIP?

The purpose of this section is to situate *empowerment* and *separate organizing* – both crucial for understanding the struggles around sexism and affirmative action to be discussed later – in a typology of union leadership.

Union leadership has traditionally been viewed as *holding* office, *occupying* or *filling* a position, in the CLC, in the provincial federations of labour, and at the national, regional, and local levels of specific unions – such as the United Steelworkers of America, the Public Service Alliance of Canada, or the Canadian Union of Public Employees. These offices include formal positions on many committees – such as political-action, educational, constitutional, and women's – at all levels of the labour movement. Union office holders may be organizers, negotiators, health and safety reps, pay-equity specialists, and so on.[2] One is recruited into such positions by nomination, acclamation, election, or appointment.

The weakness of this traditional view is that it often does not deal with the *content* of leadership – what one *does or does not do* in these formal positions. We often make the mistake of assuming that those holding official positions actually *do* lead. However, some unionists occupy official positions, but fail to lead by mobilizing union members around specific actions and campaigns.

We thus need to supplement the traditional view by looking at leadership in a second way – as a *process*, a *dynamic* of engaging in activities, *whether or not one occupies a formal position*. Thus, the *rank and file can lead* (for example, by opposing inactive officials and urging the union to initiate a number of policies). Many voluntary activities – from doing mindless paperwork around union offices to helping to organize strikes and demonstrations – are essential parts of *'union leadership'* or *'activism,'* which is the capacity and willingness to act, and the practice of taking the initiative, of beginning new actions, of going on the offensive, of making things happen rather than waiting for them to happen.

There are three overlapping issues to consider – union participation, holding formal union office, and leadership/activism. The squares within squares in figure 1 represent four stages of participation: I, Non-Participation; II, Non-Activist Participation; III, Activist Participation; IV, Separate Organizing, a special kind of activist participation. Each inner square builds on the basis of the outer squares, but also adds a new, sometimes contradictory, dimension: the three levels of participation (II, III, IV) build on the base of a previously inert section of the rank and file, but also convert it into something completely different – a more militant membership; Activist Participation (III) grows out of a base of Non-Activist Participation, and converts it through mobilization; Separate Organizing (IV) is a special form of Activist Participation that denies sameness in tactics across gender lines and affirms solidarity among women. The Rank and File box (A) overlaps all four stages of participation; the Union Official box (B) overlaps only the three participation squares (II, III, IV), since officials are, by definition, participants, though not necessarily activist. The location of the Union Official box within the Rank and File box symbolizes their close connections, both positive and negative. Elected officials (stewards, local presidents, secretary-treasurers, and so forth) are usually unpaid and keep their jobs within the workplace while doing volunteer work for the union; they are still rank and filers. Paid union staffers are often recruited from the workplace that they represent and work closely with elected officials and the rank and file in processing grievances and negotiating contracts, among other duties.

We'll start by looking at the largest square (I. Non-Participation): some rank-and-file members are indifferent or hostile to unions for a variety of reasons – latent individualism, pro-business attitudes, the failure of their own union to resolve successfully a grievance at work, dissatisfaction over poor wages, fringe benefits, or working conditions which are blamed on their union, and time pressures associated with combining household work with paid work. Such members don't attend union meetings, or vote on contract ratification or in union elections; they don't sit on committees, perform voluntary union work, or run for union office. The anti-union non-participants don't even direct their anger into activist opposition to incumbent leaders or their policies; they simply 'stay away.' One woman union steward

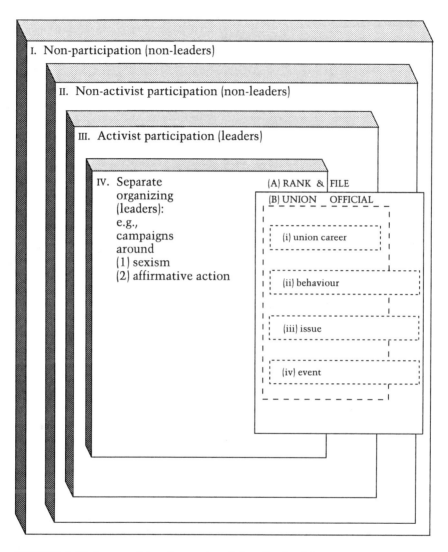

FIGURE 1 Union participation and activism/leadership

from the Alberta Union of Provincial Employees (AUPE) seemed to describe the non-participants of square 1 thus: 'The concern I have with the labour movement is there's too many sheep. There's not enough people who are prepared to be leaders.'

Three concepts are central to this discussion. *Power* is the capacity to pursue successfully one's own interests and attain one's goals, even against opposition from others; those who exercise power have considerable control over their own lives. *Authority* is one kind of power; it is the exercise of power by virtue of holding a formal office. Authority is vested in an office or position (such as president) by union constitutions, by-laws, and amendments voted on at membership meetings and conventions. Thus, authority is the legitimate or rightful exercise of power. Members not in office – the rank and file – can exercise the informal power of mobilizing and organizing, even though they do not always possess formal authority recognized under the union constitution to do so. *Empowerment* is the process of democratizing power and authority. It involves enhancing the power of formerly powerless union members, such as women, visible minorities, and the disabled. New sources, forms, and centres of power, such as women's committees and visible-minority caucuses, are created within the membership. Empowerment may involve the decentralization of power away from office holders. It is gained through mobilizing and organizing the rank and file, which has to *'take* power' or to invest power in itself rather than *be* mobilized or organized by union officials.

Union 'leaders' and 'activists' (III and IV in figure 1) empower themselves and others through self-organization and attempts to organize others. Since they do not have to hold a union office to do this, leaders/activists can be union officials *or* members of the rank and file. They potentially challenge union hierarchies and entrenched privileges of power. *Union leadership/activism* may thus be defined as the process of taking the initiative, suggesting progressive policies, stimulating constructive discussion and debate, mobilizing and empowering the rank and file, democratizing union structures, expanding the horizons of the trade union, setting examples for others to follow, creating solidarity among union members, healing divisions, establishing coalitions with other unions and community groups, and acting as effective spokespersons representing the union or labour organization to outside agencies and organizations, such as government and employer groups. In contrast to business unionist managers, leaders/activists are more dynamic and militant, searching for alternative ways of doing things. 'Business unionist managers' have authority and exercise power by virtue of holding official union positions, such as president, vice-president, secretary-treasurer, and so on, but are not interested in mobilizing the rank and file or demo-cratizing union structures. Yet they go through the formal motions of democracy.

In figure 1, one kind of union participation (no. II) is non-activist and is engaged in by part of the rank and file and by union managers; the other two (nos. III and IV) are characterized in terms of activism and leadership, and are the focus of this chapter in the campaigns against sexism and for affirmative action. There seems little doubt that many union members and officials can be categorized as either activists or non-activists; they often gain a reputation among their union brothers and sisters for being one or the other. However, the same person can be activist in one way, at one time, or on some issues – urging recalcitrant members to vote for measures against sexual harassment at conventions – and non-activist in another way, at another time, or on other issues – wanting to keep the old guard in office from election to election. Their activism may come to the fore during particular events, like strikes, after which they may lapse into non-activism. They may have been activist during one part of their union career, and non-activist in another part. So, union mem-bers and officials are usually neither exclusively activist nor non-activist all the time, on all issues, and in all events. For this reason, in figure 1, the Rank and File (A) and Union Official (B) boxes are subdivided into behaviour (ii), issue (iii), and event (iv) segments which overlap the four stages of participation (I to IV). The degree of union participation and activism/leadership of rank and filers and officials varies enormously on each of these characteristics. A union-career segment (i) overlapping the three levels of participation (II to IV) is shown for the Union Official box only, suggesting that an office holders's activism can vary greatly throughout her career. The dis-tinction between activism/leadership and non-activism/non-leader-ship thus seems to describe the behaviour, careers, and policies of union members and officials, as well as the issues they act on and events they engage in, rather than just their persons or biological entities.

Non-activist participants (II) are of two types – Rank and Filers (box A) and Union Officials (box B). Rank-and-file non-activists are differ-ent from non-participants (I) in that they minimally participate in union affairs by attending meetings, especially to vote on contracts. But their involvement ends there. They do not push for democratiz-ing union committees, nor do they attempt to mobilize the rest of the rank and file. Non-activist officials are the union managers mentioned previously: they discourage activism among the rank and file, which they see as a potential threat to their incumbency. A woman steward from the Alberta Union of Provincial Employees stated that 'union leaders don't want more leaders out there because it's going to challenge their power. I wasn't a threat 'cause I wasn't after power.' This attitude typifies the patriarchal business unionist leadership in male-dominated sectors of the economy, such as construction, in the breakaway Canadian Congress of Labour (CCL), not to be confused with the Canadian Labour Congress (CLC). Such male leaders are content to administer their collective agreements, although they will go on strike to force better economic concessions from employers. However, they hardly ever venture into coalitions with community groups on issues such as racism, sexual orientation, or even free trade, and invite the incumbent government's minister of labour to address their conventions. Yet other male-dominated sectors, such as auto and steel, have produced activist union leaderships.

Three main kinds of activist union participation are evident in figure 1. There is the self-organization among *rank and file* activists who participate in union affairs without holding formal union office. They are not mobilized by someone else, but mobilize themselves; they empower themselves and others through their activism, such as in campaigns against sexism and for affirmative action (to be discussed later in this chapter). They critique the policies or non-policies of inactive union managers (II), and push the union to organize the unorganized rather than just raiding other unions' jurisdictions. They join committees voluntarily or start new committees by networking with other union members. They are often members of non-union community groups (such as the Canadian Abortion Rights Action League), and encourage other union members and officials to do joint projects with such groups. Their leadership is social unionist from a rank-and-file, grass-roots location. In the past it has taken the form of an activist opposition to incumbent union officials, often through alliances and blocs supporting rival candidates for office. Today its strongest expression is a militant feminism that challenges patriarchal and bureaucratic business union managers, as in the demand for affirmative-action posts for women and visible minorities.

The second kind of activist union participants are *officials* who democratize union structures and mobilize and *empower* the rank and file. They are 'on the lookout' for rank and filers with signs of activism, who are then often targeted as future potential leaders, and sent to labour schools, seminars, and workshops to learn the technical skills of formal leaders. This is a social-unionist leadership which may or may not be male-dominated, but which, in contrast to 'union managers,' engages in a much more creative use of union by-laws, constitutions, and traditions to develop innovative contracts with employers (for instance, on pensions, plant shut-downs, and child care). Activist officials also seek alliances with other unions and non-union community groups on a variety of issues – fighting the North American Free Trade Agreement, the GST, racism, and sexism, and promoting solidarity with Third World struggles (for example, the ANC in South Africa). Activist officials encourage the self-organization of women through women's caucuses and committees, and support new union policies on gender-related issues (such as day care, abortion, sexual assault, workplace sexual harassment, maternity/ paternity leaves, and flex times for union meetings to get more women to participate). Official and rank-and-file activists in nos. III and IV try to mobilize union members in nos. I and II; non-activist union managers in no. II prefer to keep them demobilized.

The third type of activist participation or leadership represents a coming together of women among rank and filers in box A and officials in box B to create *separate organizing* (IV) in women-only caucuses, committees, workshops, seminars, and conferences. Although some men (and women) have criticized separate organizing as weakening union solidarity, it is justified on several counts: continuing sex discrimination; blockage of women's access to union offices; the necessity of women providing themselves with a safe haven away from their union brothers to discuss and take actions on the basis of their personal experiences with sexual harassment and assault; for developing their leadership skills; and, most important, for mobilizing themselves politically, as well as others – especially the non-activist rank and filers in no. II, and the non-participating women of no. I. Some of the most creative energies and innovative policies in the labour movement today have emerged through women's separate organizing. Most of the campaigns against sexism and for affirmative action – to be discussed in the next two sections – were initiated and carried out through the separate organizing of women's committees and caucuses.

Feminism and gender seem to lie at the heart of any discussion of union leadership. The non-activist business union managers of no. II are more often men than women; the activist officials of no. III are both women and men. Today many activist rank-and-file leaders in no. III are women; they are more likely than men to be unpaid for what they do, and engage in the temporary, voluntary activities that come and go with the many union events, crises, and emergencies. A senior Saskatchewan official in the Canada Employment and Immigration Union (CEIU), a component of the Public Service Alliance of Canada (PSAC), described the major unions in her province: 'Most of the male members that are there are full time presidents or whatever and they're paid, right. Most of the women that are there – it's just part of their volunteer [work].'

The informal, activist, processual conception of leadership is vital to feminism in the labour movement.[3] It forms part of the critique of non-activist union officialdom, which is seen as stagnant and protective of its patriarchal privileges of power. 'Power' and 'empowerment' are central issues in this critique. Business unionism is often viewed as a mechanism for maintaining male, bureaucratic power in the labour movement; but social unionism can be equally patriarchal and bureaucratic, though more democratic and progressive. Although bureaucracy is often seen as patriarchal, and democracy as feminist, feminism can make good use of bureaucracy in pushing for constitutional changes to fight sex discrimination or developing rules giving women greater access to union offices (such as affirmative-action positions). Patriarchy can also flourish under both bureaucracy and democracy. Needless to say, some democratic structures, especially in large unions, can be quite bureaucratic. This is particularly true for representational rather than direct democracy.[4]

Activist leadership in the sense defined in this paper is seen as a way of empowering, not only women, but all union members. As one senior official in Ontario from the Communications and Electrical Workers of Canada put it: 'An active member is somebody who is trying to empower others.' In the words of an employment-relations officer from the Saskatchewan Union of Nurses: 'You empower people where people learn how to do more things for themselves ..., [where] people go through a whole process of taking more control over their working lives and consequently over their personal lives.'

While much of women's empowerment comes from self-organizing through the informal political activism of the rank and file, 'ultimate power' in the labour movement rests in the formal positions at the top. The irony is that women cannot completely empower themselves by remaining excluded from formal positions, which hold the key to policy-making decisions in the labour movement. As a local president of the Union of Canadian Transport Employees, another component of PSAC, stated, 'If you're not in a [formal] position of power, it's very hard to get anything changed. So, in my local, I'm the president, my first vice-president is a woman, my secretary is a woman and quite a few of my stewards are women, and I've done that deliberately.' A staff person with the CLC stressed that without women in key leadership positions, it would be impossible to have women's interests reflected in union policies: 'There needs to be more attention to the women's perspective in the policy and stuff that's written by the fed. But ... it's basically really hard to do that stuff if you haven't got women involved in all the key positions and able to then reflect some women's perspective into it.' The danger is that, by becoming formal union officials, women (as well as men) may – but not necessarily – buy into the formal, bureaucratic, and patriarchal conceptions of authority held by union managers, and hence demobilize themselves.

The remainder of this paper will illustrate the preceding points by focusing on two issues – sexism and affirmative action – important in any consideration of women's trade-union leadership. In the structures, culture, and day-to-day practices of the labour movement, sexism impairs women's ability to learn activist/leadership skills among the rank and file. It thereby helps to destroy the fertile ground necessary for the cultivation of a potential activist pool of women for recruitment to official leadership positions. It also operates in a more formal area, preventing incumbent women union officials from carrying out their duties and advancing their careers. Because sexism is so systemic, ingrained, and resistant to change, it requires an energetic and forceful response in a variety of ways. One of these, to be discussed later in the chapter, is the designation of affirmative-action slots for women at the formal leadership level. Though affirmative action is a response to many different kinds of barriers women face, it is an especially potent weapon against sexism because other measures may take much longer to bear fruit. It declares a space within the union hierarchy partly immune to the effects of sexism. Men running for office cannot employ sexist practices to exclude women from such positions, though the effects of years of sexism may still have prevented women from eventually seeking office.

In the next two sections, it is important to keep in mind four salient points from the present section. First, women's struggles against sexism and for affirmative action have emerged out of an *activist leadership* that crosses the rather artificial boundaries between rank-and-file and union office holders. They thus bring together the traditional, formal view of leadership with the informal, dynamic view discussed earlier and illustrated in figure 1. Second, *empowerment* is central to understanding the battles around sexism and affirmative action. While sexism *disempowers* by hindering women's involvement in informal activism and formal positions, affirmative action is one specific response to sexism that potentially *empowers* or *re-empowers* by creating a reserved social space for women within formal leadership realms. Third, in the struggles against sexism and for affirmative action, women have employed *separate organizing*, both as a political tactic to develop a greater focus and concentration on a specific goal and as a safe environment away from men. It has helped to democratize unions by increasing the representation and power of a previously marginal section of the labour movement. Fourth, while sexism exists in the *informal* practices of unions and throughout their *formal* hierarchical structures, affirmative action is largely a *formal* response to problems existing in informal and formal areas of union activity.

SEXISM

Sexism in the labour movement can take a variety of forms, from the macho atmosphere in pubs, bars, and 'watering holes' at labour conventions to sexual harassment and assault, all of which *disempower* women by impeding their union careers or forcing them to quit the labour movement. It is a systemic problem that exists not only in the intentions and attitudes of union members, but also in the structures and organizations by which they govern themselves. As such, it requires more than education to eradicate; it requires wholesale changes in the structures through which unions operate. This is one reason why I argue in this chapter that setting up affirmative-action positions – a structural change – may be seen as one among many responses to sexism.

Despite professing the legitimacy of women's presence in the labour movement, some male unionists still cannot accept women occupying *union offices*, and let these women know this, making it difficult for them to perform their duties. This covers all union positions – from office staff to elected executive members. A woman staff rep in the Public Service Alliance of Canada reported: 'In the [union] office, ... if I pick up the phone and there's a male, he'll automatically assume that I'm not a rep, that I'm office support ..., and he'll want to speak to a rep. Men are somewhat surprised when I say, '... I am a rep and how can I help you?' Sometimes they'll say they want to speak to the boss, and when you explain to them that there is no boss, well then they'll [say] ... 'Isn't there a man in your office?' [I reply]: 'Well, yes, there is, but he's not the boss, what do you want?' There'll be some men who will simply refuse to deal with me, not on the basis of anything other than they want to talk to a man.' Another woman from the same union had to cope with the pressures brought on by the responses of some men to her election as vice-president: 'It wasn't just ordinary pressures and responsibilities; ... I was a woman who defeated an 'old boy' at the convention ... It was having to contend with a lot of sexism that manifested itself in real terms with people trying to undermine my effectiveness by consistently questioning things that I was doing and decisions that I was making. And so I was always in a very defensive position and that's really exhausting; it kind of wears you down.'

There is a double standard for sexual behaviour in the labour movement. Men, whether married or single, can have affairs with impunity without having their union careers destroyed. Women, however, are expected to have a higher standard by not having affairs, or there's 'hell to pay.' Men have used sexual affairs, real or imagined, to destroy women's careers. This problem was summed up by an executive member of the Canadian Union of Postal Workers (CUPW): 'If a woman ... should fall in love, or fall in lust, with a man ..., and this gets around, she's seen as just being there to have a good time. The men have perfect rights to go ... on these conventions and courses and conferences and leave their wives behind and screw around to their heart's content. But if a woman goes off and leaves her husband behind, or even if she's a single woman, and goes off and ever gets involved with a fellow unionist, and then that gets around, her credibility level is shot; she's not seen as serious; she's seen as a little plaything in the labour movement.'

Sexism and sex discrimination can be particularly strong in the informal culture of the union where women are *non-activist participants* (for instance, voting on contracts at ratification meetings) and *activist participants* (for instance, organizing votes against incumbent candidates). Variations in sexism are evident in many areas of participation – such as the willingness, ability, and ease with which women feel they can stand up and speak before a local union or labour council meeting, or a national convention, without being shouted down or cut off by male delegates. Yet another aspect is the role of informal socializing in union decision making. Women activists complain of important union decisions being made at bars after meetings or during conventions, and feel excluded because of a heavy macho atmosphere and the sexual treatment they receive from the brothers for daring to enter the bar area. One woman secretary of CUPW complained: 'The bar seems to be often where deals are made and where futures are made and where ... a lot of the decisions are made. There's a lot of carousing about in bars after the work is done, ... It's not to the benefit of women ... We get into this bar type of atmosphere where the men are all quite willing to make their deals and swap their stories and make their political plans, but the women in the bars are *seen* [by the men] as there for entertainment, ... because maybe they wanna get lucky, ... because maybe they can be picked up. [But in fact] they're there because that's where all the action is, that's where all the talk is going on, that's where all the decisions are made.' There can be a double sex discrimination here: discouragement from bar socializing by male unionists *and* by male spouses objecting to their partners socializing after hours instead of doing 'their' domestic work at home.

Women attending union courses, seminars, workshops, conferences, and conventions have been subjected to sexual harassment or assault by brothers attending the same courses. One PSAC woman official observed: 'Often sexual innuendo will occur ...; we've had in-residence training sessions, because you've got members staying at hotel accommodation, obviously away from their home environment, and we've had major problems where the courses are mixed, men and women, and we've had cases that have included sexual assault on the training sessions; a lot of women have been sexually harassed; it's just a big problem: the men tend to drink more heavily, and by way of drinking or whatever they seem to use that as an excuse for other kinds of behaviours that would be unacceptable in other environments.' Another woman union official reflected on her own personal experience with this type of behaviour:

'There's despicable cases of women being assaulted or raped in the labour movement. That has happened at the CLC schools and conventions ... where women have been sexually harassed or sexually assaulted or, in a couple of cases, actually raped by brothers ... There's not respect for women in the labour movement ... There is much sexual discrimination ... The CLC has not dealt at all effectively with it. They sent a task force around in 1989 investigating some of these horror stories from [labour] schools ... I myself was a victim in 1981 in ——. A brother tried to rape me. He came into my room when I was sleeping and I woke up and there he was! I remember afterwards I was just devastated, and thank goodness for tight blue jeans is about all I can say [chuckle] about this situation. He admitted it, but he was very cocky about it and said, 'Well, if I wanted to rape her, I would've raped her!' Actually, he was very drunk. The reaction of the CLC to this was to sit down with me and to say, 'This would be very bad publicity for us if this got out. So, you know, in the interest of the labour movement, this has never happened before; we're sure it'll never happen again. This was just this one case ...' Well, it's happened all the time! It happens at almost every [labour] school!

Without valid surveys, the extent of sexual harassment and assault in the labour movement is difficult to determine. Many unions are making concerted efforts through educational programs and punitive sanctions to cope with this issue. While sexism may discourage some women from becoming *activist* and gaining access to *official positions*, other women fight back and collectively push for programs, educational literature, workshops, training courses, constitutional changes, and other measures designed to reduce the intensity of sexism in order to better facilitate their general participation in unions and access to union office.

To combat sexual harassment, women in unions have put most of their efforts into developing contract language to cover cases where the victim is a union member and the harasser is a manager, supervisor, or employer. Co-worker harassment – where both the victim and her harasser are members of the same or different unions – is a more difficult issue. It occurs where a union has organized either a public- or private-sector workplace, or where the union itself is the workplace. Women who complain against a union brother are sometimes seen as scabs, anti-union, or undermining union solidarity. (Are women supposed to put up with harassment just because the harasser is a union brother rather than an employer, manager, or supervisor?) There have been some collective successes. After trying unsuccessfully several times, the Women's Caucus of the Ontario Public Service

Employees Union (OPSEU) succeeded in 1982 in having the convention pass a constitutional amendment 'that included freedom from 'sexual harassment' as a right of all members.'[5] Because of women's political and educational work, some unions have put in place programs to combat sexual harassment among union staff. In 1986, the Canadian Union of Public Employees (CUPE), in cooperation with the Administrative and Technical Staff Union, Canadian Staff Union, and the Office and Professional Employees' International Union, set up an Employee Assistance Committee and a program called 'Let's Talk' to develop procedures among union staff for dealing with personal and sexual harassment, and to encourage a more comfortable, hospitable working atmosphere in its union offices.[6] A statement against harassment is now read at the beginning of a number of CUPE schools and conferences. The Ontario Federation of Labour has developed a sexual-harassment policy that's included in every workshop kit – such as health and safety – that, according to one Steelworker official, 'states quite clearly: you don't do it; if you do it you get sent home, simple as that.'

Since 1984 PSAC women have employed a *separate organizing* tactic in setting up women-only training courses to *empower* themselves in dealing with sexual harassment. On this and other sex/gender issues, a *different* course for both women and men called Men and Women Talking has been set up. One PSAC activist explains the rationale for the two courses: 'If the objective of the [women-only] course is to *empower* women, then we need to develop a safe environment for women to do that in. If you're dealing with a whole bunch of issues, like sexual harassment, affirmative action, equal pay, child care, ... you don't want to spend a lot of time discussing the validity of those issues ... There was resistance [from men] ... The reason we have it for women-only is because, in a group of 20 women sharing their experiences, there are going to be women who have been sexually harassed ... The identification of the problem is a much easier task to accomplish when, within a group in a safe environment, people bring [up] their experiences. Having identified the problems, you can move much more quickly with strategies ... To help overcome some of the resistance to this course, we offered a weekend course for men and women to talk about women's issues, but, to be frank about it, it was a bit of getting them [the men] off our backs. It was a compromise ... Let's give them their weekend course.' The PSAC has also set up a national sexual harassment coordinating committee consisting of female staff officers or sexual-harassment stewards who do educational work on this issue, hear complaints, and advise members on how to deal with it. Its constitution now provides for the suspension of any member for sexual harassment. In one case, a ranking male officer, who was harassing a female member in a PSAC course, had his union membership privileges suspended for five years – which means that he does not have the right to hold office in the union, to be at membership meetings, or to vote on contracts or strike action.

One of the unions with the most activist programs against sexual harassment is the Canadian Auto Workers (CAW). In 1988, after the women's committee held a number of forums on harassment, the CAW National Executive Board adopted a policy against different types of harassment – such as sex, race, sexual preference, disability, and religion – with specific actions to be taken for transgression. Defining sexual harassment as 'any unwanted attention of a sexual nature such as remarks about appearance or personal life, offensive written or visual actions like graffiti or degrading pictures, physical contact of any kind, or sexual demands,' it asked that its policy statement be posted on union bulletin boards and published in local union newspapers. The board was concerned that co-worker harassment 'creates a climate of intolerance and division among the membership,' erodes 'our unity and strength' and weakens 'our effectiveness at the bargaining table or on a picket line.'[8] Thus, the CAW portrayed co-worker harassment as impairing the functioning of the union in general. After Marc Lepine, shouting 'I want the women – you're all a bunch of feminists', massacred fourteen female engineering students in Montreal on 6 December 1989, the CAW and other unions strengthened their campaigns against violence against women.[9] This horrible tragedy stimulated greater discussions of the linkages among co-worker harassment, violence between union members, and violence against their spouses and partners by union brothers in their personal relations at home. The 1991 CAW Women's Conference stated: 'Violence against women is a union issue ... Many of our [women] members are now in violent or dangerous personal situations ... Many men in our union, as in society, are abusers and batterers ... As a union, part of our role is to break this silence on the issue of violence against women ... The labour movement has many resources and strengths that can help women struggle against sexism and violence in our society.'[10]

The efforts to *empower* women by eradicating sexism are only one way of breaking down impediments to the exercise of women's leadership in the rank and file and among union officials. A different strategy – one manifested much more directly among official union positions – is the struggle to institute affirmative action, or designated positions for women, especially at executive levels in national unions, the CLC, and provincial federations of labour.[11] Victories in the fight against sexism aid the struggle for affirmative action: a reduced intensity of sexism should make men (and women) more open to designated positions. Yet, to some extent, a reduced level of sexism lessens the need for specially designated positions for women. But because sexism in the labour movement is so deeply ingrained and resistant to quick solutions, and despite the positive gains made so far, affirmative action continues to be a pressing political strategy in order to increase the numbers of women officials. In dealing with the *disempowering* effects of sexism, it is a way of *empowering* or *re-empowering* women.

AFFIRMATIVE ACTION

There has been little noticeable improvement in the representation of women on the national executive boards of unions, although there has been greater improvement at the regional and local levels. Although the absolute numbers of women on national executive boards have increased, this change has not kept pace with the increases in the numbers of women joining unions. During the early 1980s, the gender gap – the percentage difference in women between executive boards and the rank and file – did not narrow significantly, and in some unions widened. Among all unions, in 1979 women constituted 29 per cent of members and 21 per cent of executive boards; in 1981 women made up 31 per cent of members and 16 per cent of the boards; by 1985, women formed 36 per cent of members and 19 per cent of the boards. So the gender gap widened in this period – from 8 per cent in 1979 to 15 per cent in 1981 to 17 per cent in 1985. Among non-government national unions based in Canada, in 1979 women made up 42 per cent of members and 30 per cent of national executive boards; by 1985, women constituted 47 per cent of members but only 22 per cent of boards – a widening of the gender gap from 12 to 25 per cent.[12] Partly because of the persistence – indeed worsening – of the gender gap (which, in turn, is rooted in the continuation of sexism discussed above), during the early 1980s activist women among both the rank and file and in official positions, especially at the local and regional levels, using the strategy of *separate organizing* (discussed above and by Linda Briskin in chapter 4), pushed for designated executive positions for women – commonly known as affirmative action slots. Collective political strategizing was done through women's committees and caucuses, which educated union members on systemic sex discrimination that women faced and the importance of affirmative action to rectify it. They lobbied for votes among female and male delegates to labour conventions in support of constitutional changes creating one or more designated positions for women on executive boards. As a result, affirmative-action positions are now in place at the national level in several unions, in several provincial federations of labour, and in the CLC. The constitutional changes provided for the nomination and election of women to the designated positions. Depending on the labour organization, women's committees and caucuses have more or less power in selecting the women candidates to stand for election to these positions. The women candidates usually become part of the executive slate nominated at conventions, and are voted upon by all delegates, both male and female.

Women in the Ontario Federation of Labour (OFL) led the struggle to set up affirmative action in the labour movement and the workplace. In 1981 and 1982, the OFL women's committee held a think tank and a conference, 'Our Fair Share: Affirmative Action and Women,' attended by over 170 delegates. The committee consolidated the ideas from this conference and formulated actions for 1982–3.[13] They established coalitions with community groups. Nine public forums calling for mandatory affirmative action were held across Ontario in Toronto, London, Sarnia, Guelph, Kingston, Ottawa, Hamilton, Sudbury, and Sault Ste Marie.[14] A different member of the women's committee took responsibility for meeting with community groups in each of these communities. Educational material was distributed within and outside the labour movement.[15] In 1982 the OFL convention adopted the women's committee policy statement on affirmative action, and the following year set aside five of twenty-one vice-presidential positions for women. In 1984, the OFL women's committee submitted to the Ontario government a report consolidating over one hundred submissions to the public forums, and urged it to institute mandatory affirmative action in the workplace by setting up committees consisting of equal numbers of labour and management, with a representation of women proportional to their numbers in the workplace.[16] In 1987 the OFL expanded its executive board by two positions, and required that one be filled by a visible minority. It also increased the number of women and visible-minority persons filling staff positions. By 1989, women filled four of the nine program staff positions (one a visible minority), and seven of the eleven field staff positions (one a visible minority). One native woman occupied an administrative position.[17]

There are several important points to make about the OFL women's affirmative-action campaign. The OFL was the first labour federation to set up designated positions for women. As one staff woman at the OFL said: 'We were the first labour body in North America to do that. We were the lead. We took it on.' The driving force for the campaign came *collectively* from women in the OFL, especially on the Women's and Human Rights committees. Starting from a base in *separate organizing*, the campaign built outwards through coalitions with union and non-union community groups across Ontario, and took the form of educationals and lobbying the Government and its MPPs. Most important, the OFL definition of affirmative action was not narrowly restricted to establishing mandatory affirmative-action positions for women, but was widened, 'spelling out actions to help break down the systemic barriers women face, including access to jobs, skills training, equal pay for work of equal value, child care and protection from sexual harassment.'[18] Thus, the OFL women integrated affirmative action in the internal structures of the labour movement and in the workplace. One of the women who sat on the OFL women's committee and was involved in the campaign for affirmative action stated that 'we had to look at ourselves internally. You can't call for affirmative action measures [in the workplace] without cleaning up your own house first. And that's what the federation did.'

Taking its cue from Ontario, in 1984 the CLC added six vice-presidential positions for women only. This was a response to the small number of women who had ever held executive positions in the Congress. Before 1984, the number of executive positions held by women could be counted on one hand – such as Hugette Plamondon, the first woman elected in 1956 from the meat packers in Montreal, Nadine Hunt from Saskatchewan, and Grace Hartmann and Shirley Carr from CUPE in Ontario.

There were two suggestions in the CLC as to how affirmative action could be put into place. One was to have six men step aside and designate their positions as for women only. This meant that these men would have to give up power, which was a hard pill to swallow. As a CUPE activist in New Brunswick put it: 'It became more than the token stuff. You're now talking power things when you get into the affirmative action stuff within the executives ... People were getting a basis of power. And when you started talking about how you dealt with women's leadership within locals or within affiliates, you're really getting into power discussions. At the local union level, what we saw was a lot of backlash to that and I think that at the CLC level, you saw maybe some sense of nervousness.' To alleviate this nervousness and to reduce the chance of a backlash, a second mechanism was put in place. This was the creation of six *additional* vice-presidential positions as affirmative-action slots on the CLC executive to be filled by women from the largest unions. While this procedure avoided a direct power confrontation on gender grounds, the question still remains as to why the men on the executive agreed to create any positions specifically designated for women only. A CUPW official suggests a reason: 'Putting women in the affirmative-action positions is a very hard thing for some of them [men] to accept ... The only reason why they did it was because it was becoming blatantly obvious to the membership and to the employers and to the country as a whole that these ... executive councils ... were predominated by men and were sexist ... They had to bring in affirmative action ... mostly to save their own neck, or to give the appearance of equality.'

There was widespread support among CLC affiliates and delegates for the *principle* of affirmative action. As one CUPE delegate said, 'I'll never forget the CLC convention. There was [chuckle] two of us who opposed the affirmative-action resolution. It was just like horror in the hall [chuckle]. How dare these women stand up and oppose this.' However, there was some dissatisfaction over how it was *implemented*. There was a perception among some women activists that the creation of the affirmative-action positions at the 1984 CLC convention had a suspicious air of manipulation by the old male guard. One CUPW woman official recalled her experience at the convention:

I found it a farce in that once the affirmative-action positions ... were accepted as a constitutional change ..., the old boys, as I call them, or the slate, immediately filled them with women who they had hand-picked months earlier. They immediately had election material, glossy printed election material and pins and T-shirts ..., coming out on the floor for these six hand-picked women. The women at the convention never had a chance to put forward anyone they may have wanted ... or even to discuss the situation. Once we were given the six women, immediately who the women would be was taken away from us ... These women were all hand-picked by their union bosses. So ... what are these women doing there? They haven't even cleaned out the sexist language within the CLC in its own constitution. At least we know they're not representative of women. They had no real claims of working on women's behalf before and certainly they were women, however, that the old boys could manipulate and who were sure to uphold the very strong slate system within the CLC ... To this day that slate system and the way that the women are picked remains the same within the CLC.

This opinion, however, was not universally shared. Others believe there has been an evolution among the women sitting on the CLC executive towards greater independence and assertiveness, especially with the coming on to the Council of women either as federation presidents (Barb Byers from Saskatchewan, Susan Hart-Kulbaba from Manitoba) or as national union presidents (Judy Darcy from CUPE). One of the women from the CLC executive looks back on this evolution:

[At first in 1984] one or two of them [in the affirmative-action positions] were very outspoken but their leader was there; it was very difficult for them to take a different position than their leader ... I witnessed them being told what to say rather than what they felt like saying ... No man can deny that they did that. I watched it, my colleagues watched it, and we talked about it. So there's no question! ... I'm the leader and I voted this way, ... that's where the sister voted, she voted the same way, even though it may not have been what she would likely have done. Now I think we're over that. Over the years we have progressed. ... There's such a change in the women that we have on the council now ... because they are not afraid of anything. Mind you, they don't vote against their leader, but they speak out on every subject and they will voice their opinions if it is, in fact, against some of the stuff that's been going on. They're really very active now. So I can see we're working towards an era where we may not have to have those seats anymore.

Women in the Alberta Federation of Labour (AFL) learned from the weakness in the CLC affirmative-action mechanism, and sought to improve on it by removing, as much as possible, male control over the selection of candidates. In 1985, the AFL convention passed a constitutional amendment setting up four affirmative-action slots for women, one a vice-president-at-large and the other three council members-at-large. At each convention, the women's caucus ('an informal mechanism organized by the women's committee but part of the formal convention agenda') elects the women for the four positions; they then become part of the convention slate which is voted on by the delegates. In theory, a woman could run against the women's caucus' candidates; in practice, it has never happened.[19] This suggests that the women's caucus has some influence over filling the affirmative-action positions. One woman official reflected on this difference between the CLC and AFL: 'I was very active on the [AFL] women's committee in assuring that the women's caucus would choose our executive council affirmative-action positions rather than like with the CLC where women had no say in who would be the women representing them.'

Although there was strong convention support for the constitutional change, affirmative action in Alberta was not won without a struggle, especially from the fire-fighters, who adamantly opposed it. Another PSAC woman recalls the struggle: 'I was one of probably five women that were struggling for about six years to change that constitution, and finally convinced the men that they needed to support us at the microphones if we were going to pass this by-law change to the constitution ... The men were very much against it and we tried for two years to have them at least agree to bring it to the convention, and each time it would be defeated in the executive council, so it never got to the convention floor. Then we finally, in the third year, got them to agree to take it to the convention floor.'

In 1991, there were twenty-three positions on the executive of the New Brunswick Federation of Labour – the president, secretary-treasurer, ten area vice-presidents, and eight heads of labour councils, plus an affirmative-action slot. Of these, only four are women – one is president of a labour council, and the other three are area vice-presidents, one with special responsibility for women's issues. There are a number of standing and ad hoc committees, each with nine members, one from each labour council plus a vice-president in charge of the committee. Women make up an average 33 per cent of the committees, although some, such as the women's, are all women, while others, such as education and environment, are all male. There was initially not much support, and some hostility, among the men for setting up an affirmative-action position on the executive. As in the cases of Ontario and Alberta, the women's committee had to develop a very methodical strategy at labour conventions to win them over. One woman from the Office and Professional Employees International Union (OPEIU) involved in the struggle looks back on their tactics: 'Each member of the [women's] committee had taken the issue, and we had found ... eight reasons why we needed an affirmative-action position ... Each member targeted on one reason ... Everybody went to the mike ... and we were able to educate the delegates on the reasons ... why we needed it and got their total support. But before that resolution came up, [there was] a lot of talk on the convention floor. You heard, 'Oh Jesus, I hear —— wants a goddamn job for herself.' Well, I never ran for the job. I didn't want the job. Or I heard, 'The women got their [women's] committee, now they want another goddamn job.' ... Yet the thing passed almost unanimous.'

Besides the provincial federations of labour and the CLC, a number of unions have set up affirmative-action positions on their national executives. The Canada Employment and Immigration Union (CEIU) component of the Public Service Alliance of Canada (PSAC) has three affirmative-action positions for women who are national vice-presidents for western, central, and eastern Canada. Since 1984, the Energy and Chemical Workers Union (ECWU) has had one affirmative-action position on its national executive board. The CAW has reserved three positions on its twelve-member National Executive Board – two for women and one for a visible minority. Yet other labour organizations – such as the Saskatchewan and Nova Scotia Federations of Labour, and the United Food and Commercial Workers Union, the United Steelworkers of America, and the Canadian Union of Postal Workers – have not moved to institute affirmative action. In each case, the reasons are different, ranging from women's lack of mobilization on this issue to resistance from men.

Although there is widespread support for the *principle* of affirmative action, some women in the labour movement have been dissatisfied over how it has been *implemented*, as previously noted. There is a sentiment among several activists among both the rank and file and union officials, especially outside the national executive boards, that the male establishment – the old boys' network – has retained too much control over the selection of the women for these positions, especially through convention slates. As a result, there has been concern expressed over the kinds of women nominated and elected to affirmative-action positions: are they competent as union officials and activist leaders? are they too beholden to the men who put them there? do they fight for women's issues?[20] are those women from industrial unions selected for these positions less militant than the ones from public-sector labour organizations? In terms of the meaning of union leadership, as outlined above, several of the women who were interviewed expressed concern over whether the women elected to the designated positions were *informal activist leaders* recruited from the *rank and file*, or were 'parachuted' in from other *formal union positions* where they were not particularly known to be activists. There was also concern expressed over whether the women, as they move into affirmative-action positions, undergo a conservative transformation, or continue to maintain their militancy and fight for feminist and democratic rank-and-file issues. In addition, why have all the women in the CLC affirmative-action positions been white until the 1992 constitutional change that added two slots for visible-minority persons (those initially elected were a woman and a man)? Do racism and sexism reinforce one another, or do they operate independently?

Despite these concerns, it cannot be emphasized strongly enough that affirmative action is a way of opening up official positions that might otherwise have remained closed to women, especially for visible-minority women. Thus, it is a way by which women can *empower* themselves. The kinds of women recruited into executive positions through affirmative action are likely to be *grass-roots, rank-and-file activists*; the men who move into senior executive positions are more likely to be seasoned veterans from the middle ranks of *union hierarchies*. A woman from the Alberta Union of Provincial Employees observed: 'There's probably more women that are new to the labour movement coming on to the executive councils through these affirmative-action positions than there is any new men coming on – new [in the sense that they] have not sat on the executive of their union forever ... I was [just] a member of my union and I sat on the executive council [of the federation] and some of the other women were [just] members of their union, not a business rep, business agent, union rep, [or] executive member of their union. So by putting women on, they were putting the grass roots on.' As the women in these positions gain leadership experience and move into other positions, there should be a 'gender ripple effect' of increasing the proportion of women on union executives and in other senior positions.

CONCLUSIONS

The survival and growth of a vibrant and healthy labour movement depends on nurturing *activism* within the *rank and file*, among *union officials*, and in women's *separate organizing*. Since feminism today is the most creative energy within the labour movement, the future of trade unions depends to a great extent on the flowering of feminism within its ranks. There are three hallmarks in this blossoming – *empowering, mobilizing, and democratizing.* If sexism continues unchecked, women will not be empowered to become rank-and-file activists or leaders holding union office. But women's self-mobilization, especially through separate organizing in women's committees, helps to democratize union structures, which opens them up to innovative programs, such as campaigns against co-worker sexual harassment and assault. These then help to reduce the intensity of sexism, which pays dividends to the labour movement by involving more women members on an activist level in everyday union affairs, as well as encouraging non-union women and non-activist union women to participate more fully in trade-union committees and programs. Similarly, the campaign for affirmative action is constructed on, and in turn strengthens, the triple foundation of democracy, empowerment, and mobilization. As a democratic mechanism, affirmative action opens up previously closed executive positions to under-represented sections of the rank and file – women, visible minorities, and the disabled. This act of enhancing the representation of marginal sections of the labour movement, made possible through the mobilization of women's *separate organizations*, deepens the democratization of union structures, and empowers previously marginal sections of the labour movement. The struggles against sexism and for affirmative action are thus simultaneously women's issues and classic trade-union issues. A healthy and vibrant labour movement and trade-union feminism depend on the success of such campaigns.

NOTES

I am grateful to Linda Briskin, the participants in the Women and Trades Unions Workshop, and to Carol Reed, Pamela Sugiman, Marie Tigkos, Don Wells, Jerry White, and the anonymous reviewers for their helpful comments on earlier drafts of this paper. Thanks are also due to Lilian

Baskott, Karen Bertelsen, Liz Crozier-Organ, and Marlene Loke for interview transcriptions, and to Jenny Blain, Marj Brown, Lynn Bueckert, Sue Calhoun, Cheryl Jahn, Carol Read, Patricia Sadoway, Dorothy Stewart, Jane Stinson, Sharon Tamaro, and Cliff White for data collection. Funding was received by the author and Jerry White from the Social Sciences and Humanities Research Council of Canada (grant no. 482-89-0020). I accept responsibility for the weakness of this paper, which others mentioned here should not have to bear.

1 However, women have been very prominent historically in the leadership of some unions (e.g., nurses) and in particular labour disputes (e.g., among garment workers and telephone operators).

2 Should full- and part-time staff be considered leaders, officials, or employees of the union? Constitutionally they are to follow the directions of elected officials. Yet in several labour organizations they wield considerable informal power in deciding on policies and in collective-bargaining and grievance procedures.

3 See especially Miriam Edelson, 'Challenging Unions: Feminist Process and Democracy in the Labour Movement' (Ottawa: Canadian Research Institute for the Advancement of Women 1987); and Linda Briskin, 'Women, Unions and Leadership,' *Canadian Dimension*, Jan./Feb. 1990, 38–41.

4 SORWUC, a feminist union active in banking and other service sectors in British Columbia during the 1970s, combined direct democracy (e.g., members voting on all union policies) with a disdain for bureaucracy, patriarchy, and business unionism.

5 Debbie Field, 'Coercion or Male Culture: A New Look at Co-Worker Harassment,' in Linda Briskin and Lynda Yanz, eds, Union Sisters: Women in the Labour Movement (Toronto: Women's Press 1983), 156

6 CUPE, 'Awareness Policy and Process (CUPE and Its Staff Unions)' (1988)

7 CUPE, Equal Opportunities Department, *Harassment Awareness Kit* (1991), 26–7

8 CAW, Robert White, 'Harassment in the Workplace,' *Letter No. 7* (10 June 1988); CAW Women's Conference, *Women Moving Ahead* (7–10 Sept. 1988), Port Elgin, Ont. The CAW also produced a video on harassment, 'Call Me Sister, Call Me Brother.'

9 The deeply ingrained nature of sexism in the labour movement is suggested by the number of complaints the central CAW leadership received from the local level about such an initiative.

10 CAW Family Education Centre, *Breaking the Silence of Violence*

Against Women, Report of CAW Women's Conference (11–14 Aug. 1991), Port Elgin, Ont.
11 Briskin 38–9
12 Based on an analysis of data collected by Statistics Canada under the Corporations and Labour Unions Returns Act. Space limitations do not permit a more detailed discussion of these data.
13 OFL, *Officers' Reports* (1982), 8, 24
14 OFL, *Officers' Reports* (1983), 3, 7
15 OFL, *Officers' Reports* (1983), 21
16 OFL, *Making up the Difference: Ontario Women Speak Out*, Brief to the Government of Ontario on the Results of the Ontario Federation of Labour Campaign on Women and Affirmative Action (1984) (compiled by Shelly Acheson and Janis Sarra), 42; OFL, *Officers' Reports* (1984), 5, 24
17 Letter, Carrol Anne Sceviour, Human Rights Director (Women's Issues), to Carol Phillips, Canadian Auto Workers, 18 Oct. 1989
18 OFL Women's Committee, *Affirmative Action: How We Got Started* (no date)
19 Carol Reed, Edmonton. Personal correspondence, June 12 1992
20 In affirmative action, Briskin states, 'there is no guarantee that a woman, by virtue of her sex, will have progressive politics on women's issues.' Briskin 38

6

Women Working for Unions: Female Staff and the Politics of Transformation

JANE STINSON and
PENNI RICHMOND

The purpose of this paper is to discuss the experience of women who work full-time as union staff: an aspect which has not received much attention in the literature on women and unions. Broadening the discussion to include this neglected element is itself a reflection of the inroads made by women into unions. As increasing numbers of women have come to work in this capacity within the union movement, the need for change in union practices, structures, and expectations relating to its full-time staff has become more apparent.

Unions, formed by working people to provide a collective structure to fight more effectively for their interests, are meant to function democratically, including the membership in collectively determining policy and direction, and electing leaders to implement them. While unions rely upon the voluntary activism of their members, they have evolved into organizations which are heavily dependent upon staff to service members, to organize, to educate, to research, and to carry out union policy. All this gives staff a significant degree of power, which, depending upon how it is used, can advance or impede a union's democratic mission.

The ability of staff to move towards representative democracy or, instead, to resist change and accrue power cannot be separated from the fact that the majority of them are still white men, and that their network has functioned to hire and to privilege those men while excluding others.

Except in clerical and administrative occupational categories, women are under-represented in staff positions, just as they are in elected positions. It is important to understand how and why this is so, in order to determine what changes are required to enable more women to work full-time for the union as staff, and to recognize the changes in union practices with respect to women that result from such participation.

The analysis presented here is informed primarily by personal experience. The authors have been involved in trade-union work for well over a decade. We began as union activists and moved to full-time, specialist union staff jobs at the national level. Much of our experience has been in public-sector unions with a high proportion of female members. We have also been involved to differing degrees in the women's movement outside unions. In writing this article, we circulated a draft to over a dozen other women who work as union staff. The comments of these women, employed as both specialists and field staff representatives working for public- and private-sector unions in different parts of the country, captured a broader range of opinions and experiences.

They expressed a tremendous emotional reaction to having their experience articulated, and encouraged us to speak out even more forcefully about the problems women staff encounter and the need for change. These women share with us the premise that unions are essential in organizing to fight against the exploitation of workers generally and to improve conditions for women workers specifically. Like us, they are committed to working for unions. But at the same time many of us are angry, hurt, and frustrated by some of our experiences both as union activists and as staff. This was eloquently expressed by one long-time woman staff member who wrote: 'When I think about my own experiences in the [union] I remember vividly some of the more horrendous incidents and I am angry at how I was hurt for being a woman in that environment; yet I know that I grew and developed in that work tremendously and women in the [union] were organizing in the workplace and in the union. Exciting gains were being made. It was thrilling and rewarding. But hard nonetheless. I loved it and hated it.'[1]

In writing this paper we had to struggle with self-censorship that arose from our loyalty to the movement and fear of a backlash for speaking out. We are acutely aware of living in a society whose dominant forces are hostile to unions, one in which employers will use any criticism of unions to undermine their credibility with union members or the public, and one in which some male trade unionists make life difficult for women who challenge the status quo. Nevertheless, we believe that the issues and questions raised here are essential for unions to address in order to strengthen all of us for the struggles which lie ahead.

We begin by looking at where women are located as staff within the union structure, distinguishing between clerical, specialist, and field representatives. Differences in the role of staff between various unions as well as prevailing and alternative models for union work are then explored. From there we identify problems encountered by women working as union staff, changes which have taken place, as well as those still required, and the importance of these changes to the future of the union movement.

WOMEN AS STAFF WITHIN UNIONS

The employment patterns of unions differ little from other organizations when it comes to occupational segregation on the basis of sex. The vast majority of women working for unions are employed as clerical workers. Staff representatives account for the majority of non-clerical union employees. They are on the front line working with local unions, often assisting with grievances or appeals and local union bargaining, possibly doing educational work, organizing local union involvement in campaigns on particular issues, assisting with union organizing itself, and working on a variety of other projects. Historically, very few women have been employed in these positions, although women are starting to make important inroads into this area of work. The most significant changes in the number and proportion of women union staff seems to be occurring in what we call specialist positions, which are primarily, although not exclusively, located in head offices. This category includes technical specialists in education, communications, research, health and safety, legislation, grievances and arbitration, human rights and race relations, as well as women's programs.

Women as Clerical Workers

It is important to explore the concentration of women in clerical and administrative positions within unions. Why are unions no different in this regard, despite their own policies and criticisms of other employers? Clearly, patriarchal views and attitudes which seriously underestimate women's abilities and potential too often influence hiring decisions in unions, much like other organizations. A traditional, 'natural' division of labour arises, in which support roles are perceived as female, women are reluctant to apply for 'male' jobs, and men do not seek admittance to 'female' occupational ghettos where power and privilege are all but absent.

Linked to this is 'business unionism' – hierarchical, authoritarian, and non-inclusive – which perpetuates divisions of labour by discouraging participatory, collective approaches to organizing and carrying out union work. It is resistant to challenging and reorganizing an occupational hierarchy which does not value and involve those at the 'lower end.'

Within this context, it is not surprising that there has been little mobility for female clerical workers into specialist or staff rep positions. Women in these positions may not be perceived as possessing the necessary qualifications. In addition, as an employer the union does not consider the creation of training or bridging positions its responsibility or a priority. There is also pressure to fill staff rep positions from the membership. Fortunately, some unions are beginning to analyse and remove discriminatory aspects of their own staffing practices. Pressure for change is primarily coming from predominantly female unions, and the membership itself, to implement internal employment-equity programs for the many who have previously been excluded.

Opportunities for clerical-staff mobility may be greater with regard to staff rep positions in the field than with specialist positions. This is because the structure of representatives' servicing work in the field provides more opportunity for clerical workers to be involved in reps' work. Because reps are often out of the office, clerical workers in the field may play a liaison and communication role for local union activists unable to get in touch with their servicing representative. Some staff reps may encourage the clerical staff's interests and abilities in this way (although all too many do not). As well, some clerical workers are interested in understanding and trying to be a part of the staff rep's work, whereas others are not or are discouraged from such involvement.

So, in the absence of affirmative-action/employment-equity procedures, mobility for clerical workers has depended partly on the expectations and desires of both the staff rep and the clerical worker and on the union's willingness to value and recognize clerical work experience. Mobility for clerical workers, especially into field staff positions, also depends on the strength of competition from union members who are also seeking those jobs. As an employer, the union must wrestle with decisions in hiring and promotion which involve balancing internal gender equity against opening up staff positions to the union's membership.

Women as Representatives and Specialists

Few unions publish a comprehensive breakdown of their employees by sex or race. This makes it difficult to know to what extent women are making inroads into non-traditional jobs in unions as specialist staff and field representatives. A selective survey of some of the major national unions, conducted for this article, sketches a partial picture.[2]

The extent to which women have gained entry in the position of staff rep varies widely from union to union. Based on those from which we were able to get this information, the involvement of women ranged from a low of 6 per cent in the Canadian Auto Workers[3] to a high of about 40 per cent in the Eastern Canada Council of the Office and Professional Employees International Union (OPEIU).[4] It is noteworthy that the proportion of all female members also is low in the CAW, estimated at around 20 per cent,[5] and is much higher for OPEIU, almost 70 per cent.[6] For other unions the proportion of female reps fell between these extremes. For example, women account for about one-quarter of the field reps in both the Canadian Union of Public Employees (CUPE)[7] and the Public Service Alliance of Canada (PSAC),[8] whose membership in both cases is approximately half female. And in the former Communication Workers of Canada (CWC; now part of CEP, the Communication, Energy and Paper workers Union), with a 40 per cent female membership, about one-third of the representatives are female.[9]

Although a more comprehensive survey is required, these few examples are indicative of the current situation. None of these unions has achieved a male/female staff ratio which reflects the proportional balance of its membership. Not surprisingly, it seems that the proportion of female staff reps is lower in unions with a predominantly male membership, although there is no consistent relationship between the proportion of female members and female staff reps. A political commitment on the part of the union membership and leaders appears to be an influential factor in hiring women into staff rep positions. For example, the national executive boards of both the OPEIU and the former CWC have had since the mid-eighties a commitment to hiring women, which has been formalized as union policy.[10] CUPE also adopted an affirmative- action measure in 1984 which was designed to increase the number of women in field staff positions. It established a requirement for half of those selected to participate in the internal staff training program to be women. Owing to budget constraints the training program was suspended after a few years, but was reinstated again with this requirement in 1992.[11] The Public Service Alliance of Canada has also made an effort to hire more female staff reps over the past few years, and now is bound by a resolution passed at the 1991 national convention calling for employment equity in the union's hiring.[12]

Other important factors which influence the ratio of male/female staff are the number of positions and the degree of turnover. For example, the Eastern Canada Council of the OPEIU has only eighteen staff-rep positions and the CWC had about thirty, whereas CUPE has over two hundred. In assessing proportional representation we recognize that percentage can be deceiving, since it requires a smaller number of women to replace outgoing male reps to alter significantly the gender balance in unions with a smaller staff.

It appears that women have made greater advances in being hired into specialist positions than into staff-rep ones. In the Canadian Auto Workers (CAW), for example, women now account for over two-thirds of the specialist staff at the head office.[13] And in the national office of the Canadian Union of Public Employees, women account for about half of the membership of the in-house union representing specialist and senior administrative staff.[14] Women make up about one-third of the membership of a comparable in-house union in the Public Service Alliance of Canada.[15]

A number of factors may explain why women are more likely to be found in these positions than as staff representatives. One is perception of qualifications. Women may be perceived as being more qualified for specialist than for staff-rep positions because they have acquired the requisite training from external sources such as a university, a specialized training program, or another workplace. To be perceived as qualified for a staff-rep position, by contrast, one is often expected to have been active in the union hierarchy over many years. Systemic discrimination can weed women out at this stage, or

when hiring is done: in the absence of affirmative-action requirements, for example, there can be a differing degree of openness to
hiring women among those responsible for staffing positions in
various sections of the union. Women may not be perceived to be up
to the long hours and confrontational work (for example, in dealing
with management, negotiating, handling grievances) which a staff-rep
position is considered to require. The lengthy process of 'lay apprenticeship'[16] for such a position, not to mention the demands of the
position itself, may be more difficult for many women to achieve,
given family commitments or a desire for a more balanced lifestyle.

THE CONTRADICTIONS OF UNION WORK

General research on women in non-traditional occupations has found
that they often face a discriminatory and hostile environment where
they are considered unsuited for certain jobs, for example those
which require leadership, decisiveness, or physical strength, or where
they may be considered unacceptable to clients who will disregard
their judgment or authority.[17] Similar problems have been identified
for women in trade-union work. For example, a study of women in
full-time union positions in England found that two-thirds
experienced a lack of acceptance; they felt they had to fight harder to
gain the same respect as men in similar situations. This problem was
most acute for those servicing a predominantly male membership and
also for those who were younger and less experienced. As well, just
over half of the women reported sexual harassment from both union
members and colleagues. The incidence of general sexual discrimination was even more widespread. The authors concluded that
the common experience of sexual discrimination for the majority of
women full-time officers was a factor which likely discouraged
women from entering or encouraged them to leave this occupation.[18]

Similar problems have been noted in Canada. The lack of
acceptance reported by female staff may range from being ignored to
outright hostility, causing women to feel either that they don't 'fit in'
or are definitely not wanted. As well, it often causes women to work
harder in order to be listened to, respected, and able to accomplish
their goals. Passive resistance and a simple inability to 'get it' may
explain why women's concerns are considered to be outside the 'main
business' of the union or why few resources are allocated to dealing
with them. However, some women also encounter more open forms

of hostile resistance which may take the form of repeated demeaning and belittling comments, ostracism by other unionists, and sexual harassment.

Consider the treatment of one woman who was hired as a staff rep after working as a secretary in the same union office for many years. A male colleague yelled angrily at her that she should not have been given the job when there were many men who had applied (despite the fact that she had more seniority than any of them and was more qualified). Another male staff rep spread malicious rumours about her with both co-workers and members in the locals she was assigned to service. Her locals were told not to expect too much from her since she was 'only a secretary.' She was discounted not only through the undervaluation of her skills as a secretary but also because her years of union experience were within the union for which she was employed. This wasn't considered 'real union' experience, just as her job wasn't considered valuable work experience.[19] Another woman, who works in a predominantly male union, told us that some locals made it clear they did not want to be 'serviced by' a woman rep; as a result she felt silenced and tested all the time.[20]

In a few recent cases women staff, collectively and individually, have filed sexual- harassment complaints in response to a poisoned work environment consisting of sexist jokes, belittling comments, frequent criticism, false accusations, lesbian-baiting for hugging another woman, and repeated efforts to undermine their credibility. It is encouraging to see that these cases have been treated seriously by the unions for whom these women worked. Thorough investigations were undertaken by outside experts, reports were filed, and disciplinary action was taken against those found guilty of sexual harassment. Follow-up action included education sessions for the staff on sexual harassment and gender equity as well as the hiring of more women. It is noteworthy that both of these unions have women elected to national leadership positions.

It is true that not all women staff experience treatment this extreme, and also that some male colleagues provide invaluable cooperation and support. If it weren't for the sense of collectivity and support that exists among many women, and for the support of some male co-workers, fewer women would stay in union work.

But why does this resistance to women exist within unions? Essentially, union culture, practices, and structures continue to be male-dominated. Some men may be afraid of losing their power within the movement and therefore oppose equality for women. They may fear that as women become more active they will eventually displace them from current or future elected and staff positions which provide recognition, privilege, authority and, in some cases, large salaries and extensive benefits. In addition, increasing the number of women involved may generate more questions and challenges to these men, including their assumptions about what should be priorities for the union and how the union should function.

Fear of change more than a conscious resistance may also be at work. Men may be confused by changing gender relations and uncertain about how to act. As a result they favour the stability and predictability of tradition. They feel threatened by the changes proposed by feminists and may strongly oppose them.

In addition to the problems described above, the expectations, responsibilities, and hours of work discourage women from union work. Union work is 'greedy work.'[21] It has the potential to be all-consuming, especially when the union relies so heavily on the voluntary contribution of time during evenings and weekends by union activists. For many union staff work is not just any job, but a vocation. The union can easily become one's primary life, replete with a family of union 'brothers' and 'sisters,' most of whom do not have the privilege of being paid for many hours of union activism weekly. Union work can be very contradictory. It can be exhilarating, with the positive rewards of seeing workers come together, resolve problems, and move forwards toward greater justice and equality; but it can also deny time for involvements outside work and create conditions for serious health problems such as burn-out.

Historically, union staff jobs have been held primarily by men who were either single or had a wife who looked after the home and family. In the past, male union staff may not have experienced much conflict between their work demands and home responsibilities if their wives accepted being a 'union widow.' But this conflict is much greater today both for men who want to or are pressured to take on a more active role at home and for women whose spouses are not prepared to be the primary homemaker. Moreover, for women, a double standard still applies: while men receive social encouragement for challenging traditional gender roles, women who do so by committing themselves fully to their union work risk not only loss of relationships, guilt, and isolation, but also social disapproval.

It is still common for many union staff to regularly work fifty to sixty hours a week, and sometimes more. The long hours, frequent evening and weekend work, travel, and pressure of many union jobs takes a toll on the personal lives of both men and women. Two recent surveys of union staff found that the workload, long hours, and stress created serious problems for them. In one survey over 80 per cent of the respondents complained that the workload was so great that they were getting sick from it. One in five respondents indicated that they either were on the edge of burn-out or already felt burned out.[22] The lack of family time was the most frequently reported problem for staff in one union,[23] and this was echoed by the staff of another: the biggest impact of their job, they noted, was the lack of time for their family or self. Their personal life was sandwiched between the demands of their job and, indeed, they felt that it was expected that they would not have much time for social or family life. A number of staff also pointed to the contradiction between what the union preached for its members and what its own practice was.[24]

One woman wrote to us that she 'would not still be working for the Union if I had to work as a Servicing Representative. Fortunately, I had the chance to get a job as Equal Opportunities Representative which is very interesting and challenging, but not as time-consuming as a Servicing Rep ... I have two young children and am not prepared to sacrifice my family for the sake of my work. The future for women as Union Reps is bleak unless there is a recognition of their domestic and personal needs. This is also an issue for men as their health is also suffering from the insane demands placed on Union Rep's.'[25]

Male staff are also starting to express the conflict they feel between their work and home demands. At a training session on gender equity for the field staff of a large public-sector union, one male participant eloquently described the tension he felt between the long hours required to do a good job as a staff rep and the awareness that, therefore, he was not taking on an equal role or responsibility at home. Another male rep admitted that it was only once his wife went away for six months on a temporary work assignment and he was left responsibility for running the household and looking after the kids that he developed a real appreciation for how difficult she must find his frequent absence.[26] These anecdotes indicate that significant changes may be occurring particularly among the younger male staff, who have a stronger desire to be more involved in parenting and who have spouses who are also committed to their paid work or activism.

There appears to be a convergence between the feelings of men and women about balancing union work and personal life, but there are still important differences in their working reality. Even if the amount of working time spent by male and female staff is the same, one should also consider how that time is being spent. For example, women at a staff training session thought they spent less time socializing during working hours and were forced to work harder and use their work time more efficiently than their male colleagues since their double day meant they had less time to play with.[27]

DO WOMEN MAKE A DIFFERENCE TO UNION WORK?

Research suggests that women in non-traditional jobs often have a different approach to work than their male counterparts. One recent study of 204 women in ten different male-dominated occupations identified four major ways in which women approached their work differently than men. These included
- a service orientation to clients, which involved listening carefully to others and emphasizing cooperation over conflict;
- a nurturant approach to co-workers, such as expressing caring feelings, mixing fun and work, respecting and valuing differences, and encouraging men to change;
- an insistence upon a balanced lifestyle which revolved primarily around women's efforts to balance competing demands from their paid work and family obligations; and
- an attraction to using power differently than men did. Power was not seen as a means of control over others but as a means of ensuring a fair distribution of resources and helping people get control over their own lives.[28]

There is some evidence of these differences between male and female union staff. But it would be a gross oversimplification to suggest that these characteristics universally distinguished women from men. Not all women adopt these principles and act in this way. Also, some men share elements of this approach. To the extent that many women do have a different approach, it is not due to certain innately female characteristics; rather different approaches between men and women may be explained more by women's structural position within society and the social construction of gender differences.

A British study of union staff[29] discovered significant differences between men and women in aspects of their work which corroborate these findings. For example, female staff gave a higher priority to involving women in the union, as was indicated by more time being spent by women staff in organizing women workers, involving them more in union activities, and promoting their specific interests.[30] The authors also suggested that women staff were more prepared to 'widen the scope of collective bargaining to embrace questions such as sexual politics at the workplace and the integration of women's paid and domestic work.'[31] This tendency was demonstrated by the higher priority women attached to child care, maternity leave and measures to combat sexual harassment as collective-bargaining priorities. In contrast, male staff were more concerned about low pay, an important but also more traditional, economic issue. The study considered these women 'agents of transformation' who were highly committed to using their position to address the specific needs of women workers through organizing and negotiations.[32]

There are indications that many Canadian female staff also have an approach to union work that differs from that of their male counterparts, reflected in what the women consider priorities and how they, particularly as field staff, relate to members. For example, one female servicing representative told us of how she put more effort into negotiating paid maternity leave and making sure that women had good benefit-plan coverage than had the previous male rep who serviced those locals. This change was warmly received by the female members, who were happy to have a representative who 'really understood our issues.'[33] In this case, the female rep strongly believed in economic independence for women and that women workers should not be dependent on a husband for a good benefit plan. This attitude was in contrast to her predecessor's, who believed that these women did not need benefits because they were married, assuming that their husbands should provide for them.

Another female staff person saw differences between organizers in their approach. The biggest difference she noted was with regard to sexual harassment. Women organizers were the only ones to receive complaints of sexual harassment during an organizing campaign, perhaps because they would raise sexual harassment as the type of problem the union could help them with, whereas few of the male organizers would give this as an example. As a woman she was more sensitive to the problems women had in attending meetings because of child care and to difficulties with their husbands about signing union cards. In addition to the secrecy normally maintained around the employer during an organizing drive, many women also wanted to keep their union activities from their husbands. Signing a union card was seen for some women 'not as being about joining the union per se, but about exercising independence' from a husband as well. Their lack of confidence in taking on a leadership role in an organizing drive was also more likely to be discussed with a female organizer who was working with union members.[34]

The different approach of many women to working with union members is in strong contrast to the traditional approach. The dominant model for the role of union staff is that of 'servicing' the members, – the staff looks after the members' needs. Members rely on staff to fulfil the role of expert and authority figure, to be the white knight charging in to rescue the weak local when it needs help. Rather than fostering a more participatory and inclusive decision-making approach which aims to develop skills, confidence, and abilities, members are told what to do. This reliance on the staff for guidance in decision making is a way of exerting control over the local union. In this situation, it is hard to draw the line between technical and political advice – an example of how staff exert a strong informal authority or power within unions.

The very presence of female staff can make an organizational difference. At the most basic level, women in staff positions provide important role models. Seeing women in union jobs helps other women to identify with the union and possibly see themselves in such a role. The fact that most staff are men conveys an implicit message to women that they would not be suited for a staff job.

By giving encouragement to some members and not to others, staff reps especially influence who becomes involved in the union. Staff often play a mentoring role in developing local leadership and in some cases acting as a gatekeeper – facilitating or discouraging the possibilities for a union job. White women, and also women and men from visible minorities, are less likely to be mentored unless they conform to expectations of their appropriate role and place.

Changing this dominant conception of the role of staff is difficult. Some women who try find they have to overcome resistance from some of their colleagues, who don't believe things can or should be done differently, and also initially from members who have been told by former staff that certain areas of responsibility were 'none of their business' and who believe the staff should do it for them.[35]

A FEMINIST ALTERNATIVE

Yet feminist members, leaders, and staff have been advocating an alternative approach to unionism for many years. Most of the emphasis has been on changing the nature of elected leadership positions,[36] but much of this approach should apply to the role of staff as well.

A feminist alternative approach for union activity involves democratizing and humanizing unions as well as shifting the emphasis from business unionism to social unionism.[37] Democratization is pushed forward by the greater importance many women attach to the process of how things are done rather than to the traditional (patriarchal) emphasis on results. Women's experience of being excluded or undervalued may explain the greater importance we attach to reaching out to involve others, to being inclusive, and to gaining and sharing knowledge and developing women's skills and confidence.

This alternative approach also challenges the traditional business-unionist approach which narrowly focuses on improving wages and benefits, by pushing for a form of 'social unionism' which recognizes that union members' lives are not limited to their paid jobs alone. Women have been responsible for pressing unions to address a broader range of issues of importance to female members' lives such as child care, reproductive choice, violence against women, and even the division of domestic labour. In this way feminist women have been an important force in getting unions to go beyond an exclusive concern with events in the workplace. This influence has led to union involvement in coalitions with the community – women's organizations, churches, organizations of aboriginal peoples, and visible minorities, and other popular sector groups – on a range of issues.

Women's involvement in unions also creates demands for humanizing union work. This aspect has been described as 'recognizing the importance of how people feel about what they are doing, whether they feel listened to, respected and rewarded for their efforts.'[38] Such humanization also involves a transformation of personal interaction within the union, which means inviting differing points of view, validating each other's experiences, and working together collectively to achieve goals, whether in a local executive, a negotiating team, or a committee. Many female staff particularly object to the long hours of work, often in the evenings and on weekends and out of town, which make it very difficult to sustain family or other meaningful personal relations outside of work.

Some women staff have been organizing to change the conditions of their own employment.While a number of unions and labour centrals have had policies and informal guidelines for increasing the numbers of women on staff (CAW, the former CWC, for example), it has only been in the past couple of years that the political commitment to developing comprehensive, inclusive affirmative-action plans and measures has been won. As mentioned earlier, both PSAC and CUPE are currently involved in this process, which in each case includes joint committees of management and unions and, in the case of CUPE, representatives of disadvantaged groups as well. At its last convention, CAW also passed a resolution which calls for affirmative-action plans for staff as well as for members.

These actions will be precedent setting in identifying discriminatory practices throughout union structures, setting goals and timetables, and developing a full range of flexible workplace options.

It will mean initiating a serious ongoing campaign to identify and enlist women to take on these responsible roles within the movement. And it means developing an inclusive, representative approach, one which ensures that all women – women of colour, women with disabilities, lesbians, and aboriginal women, as well as able-bodied, white straight women – are part of the process.

AREAS OF CHANGE

Anti-Harassment Procedures: Clearly, labour must demonstrate and must be seen to demonstrate a commitment to eradicating harassment in-house as well as in the workplaces of its members. Over the past two years, there has been concerted action within numerous affiliates and central labour bodies to develop and revise anti-harassment policies for their employees and members who attend union functions. Care has been given to the development of accessible, expeditious complaint procedures and redress mechanisms, and of serious penalties for offenders. In addition, anti-harassment training sessions have been conducted at the national and regional level with senior staff, elected union officers, instructors, and members by unions themselves, and by central labour bodies. Staff within CUPE, CWC, CLC, and PSAC have been involved in training sessions to combat racism, sexism, and equality issues generally. While some of these sessions have had mixed results, there is a sense that the commitment to ongoing training of this nature is firm.

Changing the Greedy Culture of Union Work: Considering the degree of work stress identified by men and women staff, and the need to work in an environment which recognizes and supports family and personal responsibilities, it is clear that the all-consuming culture of union work must be addressed. Yet work flexibility, including shorter and variable hours of work, fair family- leave entitlements, and child-care support remain controversial – or invisible – issues in many unions.

Some significant gains have been made through collective bargaining in addressing this major problem. For example, in 1981, PSAC (CULE) staff went on strike to win a 35-hour work week, with lieu time or overtime paid for additional hours. (It is useful to remember that union staff contracts have traditionally contained no hours of work, reflecting the philosophy that one must be on call whenever needed, regardless.) It is true, to be sure, that staff may not be able to take all of the time owed in the PSAC agreement, but this is, nevertheless, an important measure in having the employer recognize and compensate long hours. It could, in fact, be one factor in forcing the union to re-assess the structures and demands of the work itself.

In many contracts, parental-leave provisions have been brought into line with recent changes to the Unemployment Insurance entitlements; or improved upon. For example, CAW staff currently receive six months' leave at full pay (not UI) and 6 months at 75 per cent for maternity leave; parental leave has now been negotiated for an 18-week period, again with full pay. Benefits are paid by the employer throughout this period, and seniority accrues. Other staff unions – within PSAC, OFL, CUPE, CWC – have negotiated the UI standards for length of leave, but top-up of 93 per cent is provided. CUPE staff are entitled to a further two years' unpaid leave of absence to prolong maternity or adoption leave. PSAC staff receive five days' paid-family responsibility leave and leave without pay for up to one year for the care and nurturing of children under school age.

OPEIU Local 343 (OFL) staff have bargained child-care costs of $30 per child per week, and an additional $40 for overnight out-of-town work or $10 for evening meetings. CULE (PSAC reps) have gained child-care costs to be covered in full when staff is out of town on employer-sponsored training. While these gains may seem minimal in the light of child-care costs, they are generally hard to win and set a precedent which challenges the notion that staff, knowing what the job entails when they are hired, should either cope or not work in the job.

OPEIU-343 has also bargained a $450 annual health-enhancement provision, which covers health-club memberships, massage therapy, and so on, as well as $300 for counselling in addition to what is provided under health-insurance benefits.

CUPE, PSAC, and OPEIU-343 have also gained an inclusive definition of 'spouse' as the one to whom one is legally married or with whom one is living regardless of sex; all benefits are thus available to all staff and partners, lesbian, gay, or straight.

One final and quite significant trend is the joint bargaining of staff unions; in CUPE, PSAC, and OPEIU-343 (OFL), for example, clerical and administrative bargaining units, staff representatives, and specialist units bargain together through most of the process.

All the changes above have occurred through a political process which has included women staff mobilizing around their own interests, and with their male co-workers on some issues; women staff working closely with an increasingly organized and militant rank-and-file base; and both activists and women staff pushing for and receiving leadership support, particularly from women officers. There is a long way still to go. There is also a sense of collective power which builds, victory upon victory.

CONCLUSION

While female staff can make a difference, they alone cannot bring about significant change. Their efforts should ideally be part of a three-point configuration, with pressure for change also coming from the membership and political leaders.

As is evident from this paper, discriminatory employment practices and attitudes have hardly been eradicated from the union movement. Yet it is critical that the collective strength and agency of women staff not be forgotten in our examination of our working experience. While progress has been sluggish and faltering, it is, none the less, being made, and recent trends indicate a speed-up in some areas.

The ability for female union staff to make a difference depends on a number of conditions. In part, this process begins at an individual level, to the extent they support feminist goals or seek to alter a traditional model of union work. But it also depends on the specific climate and broader context within which they are working.

For example, a staff woman who wants to try to alter traditional practices and priorities is unlikely to have much success if she is working within an extremely hostile environment, one which is not tolerant of or strongly resists an alternative, feminist approach. This underlines the importance of developing a strong base of feminist organizing within the female union membership (or at minimum, a small supportive network where she can seek refuge and revitalization). These women can make use of the democratic structures and practices of the union, for example to organize for resolutions to be passed at conventions, and require specific measures to be adopted to address women's needs and concerns, which create pressure on the political leadership for bringing about change. Female staff can play an important role in facilitating this development by encouraging women to become active and working to demystify the political process.

In addition to the strength of feminist organizing at and by the membership base, support from the political leadership, especially at the very top, is also crucial. Political leaders have an official authority, and therefore greater potential authority, to bring about change which exceeds that of staff. They are the ones who ultimately determine the priorities of the union and how scarce resources will be allocated.

In many ways, the importance of the feminist project within unions goes beyond women activists, staff, and leaders to the future of the movement itself. Within the context of grass-roots demands for democracy, equality, and increased participation; and of massive workplace restructuring, including polarization along class, race, and gender lines, the labour movement is faced with significant challenges. These challenges consist of the ability to make the union relevant to and representative of the membership, mobilize the membership in general, work closely and cooperatively with the community, and organize the unorganized.

Many of the criticisms and proposed solutions coming from feminist union activists, regardless of their roles in the labour movement, are directly relevant to the movement's ability to grapple successfully and progressively with these challenges. Women staff members, however, from our specific location in the movement, are an increasingly significant force for change and can make an important contribution as agents of transformation.

NOTES

1 Personal correspondence received 5 May 1992
2 More comprehensive data is available in J. White's book *Sisters and Solidarity: Women and Unions in Canada* (Toronto: Thompson Educational Publishing 1993).
3 Calculated from CAW staff seniority list, 1 May 1992
4 Personal communication with Simon Berlin, representative, Eastern Canada Council, OPEIU
5 CAW affirmative-action policy statement adopted September 1991
6 'OPEIU Statistics and Structure,' 12 Apr. 1991
7 Calculated from 'Male and Female Representation within CUPE,' Equal Opportunities Department, December 1990
8 Personal communication with Anne McKnight, senior education representative, Public Service Alliance of Canada
9 Personal Communication with Trish Blackstaffe, assistant to the president, Communication Workers of Canada
10 Personal communication with Simon Berlin and Trish Blackstaffe
11 'Trainee Rep Program Restarts,' CUPE *Leader*, Jan./Feb. 1992: 6
12 Personal communication with Anne McKnight
13 Calculated from CAW staff seniority list, 1 May 1992
14 Calculated from CUPE seniority list as at 31 Dec. 1991
15 Based on personal communication with Anne McKnight
16 Edmund Heery and John Kelly, ' "A Cracking Job for a Woman" – A Profile of Women Trade Union Officers,' *Industrial Relations Journal* 20, no. 3 (1989): 196
17 A. Spencer and D. Podmore, eds, *In a Man's World: Essays on Women in Male-Dominated Professions* (Tavistock 1987), cited in Heery and Kelly 196; K.S. Koziara and D.A. Pierson, 'The Lack of Female Union Leaders: A Look at Some Reasons,' *Monthly Labor Review* 104, no. 5 (1981): 30–2
18 Heery and Kelly 197–9
19 Personal communication, 11 May 1992
20 Personal communication, 21 Apr. 1992
21 L.A. Coser, *Greedy Institutions: Patterns of Undivided Commitment* (Free Press 1974), cited in Heery and Kelly, 192
22 Survey of CWC staff on stress prepared for 1991 annual staff training session
23 G. Lowe, 'CUPE Staff Workload Study: Report,' submitted to the Joint Project Management Committee, 25 Sept. 1990, 8

24 Survey of CWC staff on stress
25 Personal correspondence, 30 Apr. 1992
26 Personal communication, 6 Nov. 1991
27 Personal communication, 6 Nov. 1991
28 Patricia Lunneborg, *Women Changing Work* (New York: Bergin and Garvey 1990), xviii
29 This study uses the term 'full-time officers' since it does not distinguish between full-time political leaders and employed staff.
30 Heery and Kelly, 'A Cracking Job'
31 E. Heery and J. Kelly 'Do Female Representatives Make a Difference? Women Full-time Officials and Trade Union Work,' *Work, Employment and Society* 2, no. 4 (1988): 503
32 Heery and Kelly, 'A Cracking Job,' 201
33 Personal communication, 11 May 1992
34 Personal communication, 13 May 1992
35 Personal communication, 11 May 1992
36 See, for example, Linda Briskin, 'Women, Unions and Leadership,' *Canadian Dimension*, Jan./Feb. 1990, 38–41, and Miriam Edelson, 'Challenging Unions: Feminist Process and Democracy in the Labour Movement' (Ottawa: Canadian Research Institute for the Advancement of Women 1987)
37 Jamie Kass, Speech given to the CUPE Ontario Division Women's Conference, April 1990
38 Kass 4

7

Black Women Speak Out: Racism and Unions

RONNIE LEAH

The relationship between race and gender within the labour movement is seriously under-researched. Through interviews with three Black women unionists, this paper will begin this critical, much needed exploration.[1] It will map out five broad themes that have emerged in these interviews. The first section will look at the state of organizing around race, and to some degree around the intersection of race and gender, that has taken place in the past decade in Ontario. The next section examines the extent to which women of colour must shape their own struggles and to what extent they must reach out to other groups in an attempt to find support for their goals. The third theme is the nature of racism within the labour movement, and the fourth and closely related theme concerns the type of Black leadership that best serves to maintain the independence and critical stance of those who lack power by virtue of both their race and gender. The final theme is the relationship between the organizing efforts of Black and white women within the labour movement.

Interviews with June Veecock, director of human rights and race relations for the Ontario Federation of Labour (OFL), were conducted in October 1988 and October 1992. Yvonne Bobb, president of Local 520 of the Ontario Public Service Employees Union (OPSEU), was interviewed in May 1989 and November 1992. Since these interviews took place three-and-a-half to four years apart they offer a valuable opportunity to assess whether these two women feel there has been significant progress on the treatment of race within the labour movement in the past three to four years. Muriel Collins, an executive member of Local 79 of the Canadian Union of Public Employees

(CUPE) and chair of CUPE's National Women's Committee, was interviewed in December 1991 and again in November 1992.

As Carty notes, 'Black women's experiences are historically and institutionally structured in ways that are different from those who are not Black and female.'[2] When studying the issue of race, and especially the intersection of race and gender, care must be taken to acknowledge that race is experienced by Black, immigrant, Aboriginal, and Asian women in unique ways. In this paper the three women interviewed are primarily talking about the experience of being Black within the union movement. There are, of course, some obvious patterns in racist behaviour, but generalizations and universalistic assumptions about how all women of colour experience racism obscure the diversity of women's experience and oppression.

At the same time that racism is a unique experience, it is also clear that race and gender cannot be separated. A good example of how sexism and racism merge is in the area of sexual harassment. In the *Colgate Palmolive* case that recently came before the Ontario Human Rights Commission, a Black woman experienced what could be called a 'race specific' form of sexual harassment. For example, pornography was placed in her locker depicting sexually explicit acts between Black women and white men.[3] 'This woman at Colgate Palmolive,' notes June Veecock, 'experienced both racism and sexism. I am convinced that her experiences as a Black woman exacerbated the sexism.' In many ways this example demonstrates how a woman of colour can be singled out for harassment around race as well as gender, thereby reinforcing and intensifying feelings of isolation from her male as well as her white female co-workers.

ORGANIZING AROUND RACE

All three women interviewed said they remain impatient with the slow rate of change. In Muriel Collins's words: 'They tell us, "your time hasn't come yet." I've been here over thirty years – when is it my time?' Yet, despite their frustration with the pace of change, to varying degrees each woman feels that some progress had been made in the past decade. The most positive sign is that the issue of racism is now 'more visible' within the labour movement as a whole and that, as Yvonne Bobb comments, it has become an 'accepted fact that it [racism] is now on the agenda – that it is a legitimate union issue.' She feels that a lot has happened in the past ten years and that more activists, 'people like myself,' are now speaking out about racism within the union movement. 'Yes, there have been some changes. But there is still a long way to go.' In this section some of the activities of several large labour organizations will be examined in order to assess the type of changes that have taken place in the past decade.

The OFL's stand against racism began in 1981 with endorsement of a 'Racism Hurts Everyone' campaign. Shortly thereafter, the federation appointed a human rights director for race relations, a position currently held by June Veecock. It was the first labour federation to establish affirmative-action seats for women in 1983 and, later, a seat for visible-minority workers. The OFL's April 1986 conference, Building the Participation of Workers of Colour in Our Unions, served as an impetus for anti-racist work in the Ontario labour movement and encouraged organizing by Black unionists. A series of forums on racism across the province in 1988 moved the question of racism higher on labour's agenda. In recent years the OFL has adopted a policy of zero tolerance to sexual, racial, and personal harassment, and the OFL policy paper, *Challenging Harassment*, was unanimously adopted by delegates to the 1991 annual convention.

CUPE has also taken concrete steps to mobilize workers of colour within its ranks. Following its 1987 national convention, which directed the union to take immediate action to develop a 'vigorous anti-racism campaign,' CUPE endorsed the Rainbow Committee,[4] and appointed its first anti-racism coordinator, Harminder S. Magon, in April 1991. The committee's 1991 report encouraged consultation with racial-minority workers within CUPE 'in order to give them a voice in the union.' The committee included twelve members plus the coordinator; it has now achieved gender parity and has taken steps towards better regional and ethnic representation.

In Muriel Collins's assessment, although it has been a struggle by workers of colour to get the Rainbow Committee, this development reflects her observation that there has been some progress in the past decade. 'We got up on the convention floor in 1986 to fight for the Rainbow Committee,' she comments, 'and we made a difference; somebody listened. People are more receptive now – they've seen the results of our work. The Rainbow Committee in CUPE is able to get something moving ... Our mandate is to attain equal opportunity within CUPE at all levels.'

CUPE has taken a lead in developing an internal affirmative-action program recommending structural changes for both staff and leadership. Indicative of CUPE's commitment to affirmative action for women of colour, the union has appointed Muriel Collins and an Aboriginal woman, Lois Hill, as co-chairs of the Ontario Division Women's Committee. In September 1991 the CAW-Canada (National Automobile, Aerospace and Agricultural Implement Workers Union of Canada) passed a similar policy which calls for mandatory measures to achieve internal affirmative action for women and minority workers. Noting that growing numbers of women and visible minorities are coming into the CAW, this initiative sets forth a plan for increased representation at the national and local levels, and for hiring which reflects the gender and racial make-up of the membership. At a 1992 Canadian Council meeting, CAW President Buzz Hargrove appointed staff member Hassan Yussuf, 'a well known human rights activist,' to coordinate the union's fight against racism.[5] The Ontario Public Service Employees Union (OPSEU) recently added an elected provincial human-rights committee to its constitution similar to the union's long-standing women's committee.

In terms of the process by which change has taken place, those interviewed thought that organizations which were open to addressing issues of gender were also more receptive to demands about race equality. Further, organizing around racism has in some ways paralleled organizing around gender. For a long time labour struggles against racism and sexism proceeded in two separate and sequential spheres. The 1970s saw the emergence of a trade-union women's movement and the formation of women's committees and support for activism around women's rights. In the 1980s, workers of colour began to organize against racism, which led to the formation of human-rights committees and the development of anti-racist policies.[6]

In recent years unified labour strategies have begun to emerge that simultaneously address both sexism and racism. The educational work around racist and sexual harassment, as well as employment equity, has played an important role in the convergence of these issues. For example, in 1987 the OFL's Women's Committee and Human Rights Committee jointly developed the Federation's *Statement on Equal Action in Employment*, which highlighted the connections between racism and sexism; in 1991 these two committees co-sponsored a forum on 'Making Employment Equity Happen' at the OFL convention.[7]

In CUPE, establishment of the union's Anti-Racism Office in April

1991 has helped facilitate the integration of race and gender issues. For example, the office's anti-racism coordinator, Harminder Magon, officially attended CUPE's 1991 Ontario Division Women's Conference, 'Equality Now,' in order to reinforce the union's support for dealing with issues relating to equality, discrimination, harassment, and racism. Similarly, the 1991 Ontario Division Human Rights Conference, 'Employment Equity – CUPE's Response to Sexism and Discrimination in the Workplace,' linked together sexism and other forms of discrimination. The April 1992 CUPE Ontario Women's Conference, 'Equality into Action,' also included a focus on disabled women, Aboriginal women and women, from racial minorities. The Equal Opportunities Department and the Anti-Racism Office have also been working closely together on developing strategies for 'mandatory, jointly negotiated, workplace affirmative action programs' for the target groups.[8]

The policy development in the CAW also indicates a clear convergence of the issues of race and gender in recent years. For instance, the CAW policy, 'Harassment in the Workplace,' was adopted by the National Executive Board on 10 June 1988. It called for the creation of a 'workplace environment free from harassment,' targets both sexual harassment and racial harassment, and outlines detailed complaint procedures. The union also produced a video in 1988, 'Call Me Sister, Call Me Brother,' based on interviews with CAW members concerning sexual and racial harassment in the workplace. According to Peggy Nash, assistant to the president responsible for human rights and women's programs,[9] the caw has recently established several educational programs on harassment in order to better implement these policies, including a three-day training program for handling harassment complaints.

In 1987 the CAW negotiated a Human Rights Training Program with General Motors, which provides for three hours of instruction for all employees (both union and management). This joint GM-CAW program provides the CAW with an innovative starting point for educating workers on human rights. In 1988, CAW implemented a comprehensive human-rights course which targeted the rank-and-file membership for education on racism and sexism, since the union has highlighted these areas of discrimination as critical for labour solidarity. Human-rights courses are aimed at the dominant group of white males, explains Nash, enabling them 'to understand the rules and policies of the CAW, to be sensitized to the needs of other groups, and to understand that diversity is a good thing.' In 1992 the CAW established two courses for women and workers of colour for which a concerted and successful effort was made to attract women of colour. These courses were developed with a local union advisory committee which, as Nash points out, included women of colour. The courses took a new approach to union education in order 'to reach beyond the traditional leadership of white men,' and so that 'disadvantaged groups within the union' could 'build their own networks, formulate their own demands and develop their own strategies.'

Although the coming together of race and gender was applauded by all three women, June Veecock expresses strong concern about the convergence of these issues. She points out that race has become the priority in her activism and she feels that there is a danger that 'when you lump it all together in the context of human rights ... sometimes the racism gets lost.' This point will be returned to when separate organizing is looked at in the next section of this paper. Indeed, there is a need to focus solely on race and to work out strategies for fighting racism which are at the top of the agenda; yet as we shall see, there is also the necessity of reaching out to integrate race with initiatives around such issues as gender, sexual orientation, and poverty.

Despite their basic belief that there appears to have been some progress on the issue of racism, the interviewees still remain sceptical. June Veecock, perhaps the most pessimistic, argues that the situation is still 'abysmal' despite the greater awareness about racism which is demonstrated by the growing number of union policies on racism. She contends that 'there are a lot of rhetorical statements about policies, but these policies are not always translated into action on the shop-floor.' It appears that change is reflected mainly at the policy level, while there is limited success in implementing these anti-racist policies at the grass-roots level.

This concern about national policies not being implemented at the local level is echoed by Muriel Collins, who describes the process of organizing a human-rights committee for Local 79, the large Toronto local of CUPE: 'We had to push for a Human Rights Committee. The union didn't see the need for it. It took a lot of persuasion to establish a task force for this committee.' Thus, even when the union establishes central policies and committees which address issues of racism and sexism there remains the fundamental problem of implementation 'on the ground.' Collins concludes: 'We've come a long way. The issues are being addressed in CUPE National, also the

Ontario Region. At the local level, the issues are not being addressed the way we want ... In my local [79] it has changed. Now it must shift in other locals.' The CAW's progressive human-rights policies at the national level are not always reflected in the union locals. Delegates to a June 1992 CAW human-rights conference identified the secondary local union leadership as the 'number one obstacle to solving racism within the union.'[10]

Similar doubts about how policy gets implemented are raised over the related issue of the effectiveness of education – often assumed to be one of the main mechanisms of policy implementation. Peggy Nash of the CAW, for instance, has expressed concern about the shortcomings of some human-rights courses. 'They are based on the traditional male model of education ... [where] people get lectured to; they don't get a chance to really talk through their feelings.'

Much more fundamental than the issue of educational techniques, however, are concerns about the effectiveness of human-rights education in changing workers' actual practices of discrimination. Sherene Razack, a woman of colour who has trained union staffers on human-rights issues, notes that 'everyone knows the rhetoric now,' but there is 'very strong resistance' to real change. She feels that there have been only cosmetic changes – that trade unionists 'get it right during the course but not in reality.' According to Razack, education alone does not challenge racism if there is not organizing around power.[11]

SEPARATE ORGANIZING

The question of separate organizing was raised by all three women and each agrees that some form of autonomous organizing is necessary. One reason for the need to have separate organizing around race was expressed earlier by June Veecock; her concern was that when issues are brought together 'sometimes racism gets lost.' Another reason behind the need for separate organizing is suggested by Yvonne Bobb, who emphasizes the importance of groups fighting their own battles: 'Nobody is going to do this for you. It's your struggle, you have to do it for yourself ... Other women are saying, ' "I can fight for you just as good as you can fight for yourself." What I am saying is that people can understand it, they can sympathize with you, but they don't live it.' Muriel Collins echoes a similar chord: 'To bring the Black sisters along, we have to meet and talk ... We have to come forward and do things for ourselves.'

The mid to late 1980s was a period during which groups representing workers of colour expanded rapidly. In 1986, Yvonne Bobb recalls, Black workers came together and formed the Ontario Coalition of Black Trade Unionists (OCBTU), 'as a result of the racism that existed in the union movement.' The OCBTU has provided non-white workers with a base for further anti-racist organizing and a small core group continues to function as a collective. According to Bobb, president of OCBTU, the coalition is reviewing its work with the aim of developing a national focus. They are also looking at ways of involving non–trade unionists, particularly women. As Bobb explains: 'There's a whole group of women that are excluded because they are not unionized.'

June Veecock feels that the OCBTU faces some problems in its work, given the powerlessness experienced by Black workers and their 'fear of a backlash in their own unions if they are known to be active.' Yet she notes that there are signs that autonomous organizing is getting stronger. For example, the Organization of Black Tradesmen and Tradeswomen of Ontario, the Association of Black Law Enforcement Officers, and the Black Canadian and Caribbean Workers Association have recently been formed. Black nurses in the Toronto area are also organizing against systemic racism in the hospitals with support from the Congress of Black Women. In addition, Black workers have organized in caucuses within the labour movement. In the OFL, Black caucuses have been organized for the annual conventions since 1985, and they have mobilized to push for greater representation in the Federation. Muriel Collins notes that 'there was a Black Caucus at the 1991 OFL Convention. It was extremely good.' According to June Veecock, organizing by the caucus and the OCBTU contributed to the successful push for two seats for visible minorities on the CLC executive. Yvonne Bobb also points out that Black caucuses have been organized at CLC conventions, and at the 1992 convention Black women held their own workshop.

Although there is clear evidence that Black unionists in Canada are organizing around their own aspirations and making links with organizations devoted to a similar agenda, such as the Coalition of Black Trade Unionists in the United States, there are also some signs that their concerns are being integrated with those of other groups. Women and workers of colour are joining coalition groups such as the Employment Equity Coalition. Muriel Collins sees this coming together as a positive and inevitable process. 'As time goes by,' she notes, 'everyone comes together. We really want to get in line with other coalitions and women's groups out there. We all have to work together instead of thinking of our autonomy. The more of us there are, the more power we have, the better we can work for equality. We have to work together: unions, public and private sector, community groups. It must be combined.'

Despite this trend towards some integration, there appears to be a degree of tension perceived by those interviewed between Black and white women activists within the labour movement. As will be discussed in the last section, this is partly rooted in bitter personal experiences and partly based on what several of the women describe as the racist patterns and reactions of some white women activists.

THE NATURE OF RACISM WITHIN THE TRADE UNION MOVEMENT

A unifying theme of all the interviews with these three women is that racism exists as much within the labour movement as in the workplace. Each recounted stories of the racism they have experienced throughout their working lives. Muriel Collins, for example, recalls how in 1976, she was 'one of the first Black women hired in an all-white home for the aged ... in essence the message was "You're Black, we don't want you here." It was hard.' June Veecock explains how racism, since it is primarily based on visual distinctions, is different from other forms of 'discrimination'. She describes how people will equate anti-Semitism or discrimination against the Irish with racism against visible minorities and maintains 'it's just not the same.' Once non-visible immigrants 'have established themselves, once they've paid their dues, they're no longer new immigrants.' People of colour, however, some in Canada for four and five generations, 'still get asked where they're from ... If you're a person of colour you're from somewhere, you couldn't possibly come from here. And so you are always perceived as an outsider.'

When comparing racism within the labour movement and in the workforce generally, the women agreed that the union movement often reflects racism in the broader society, and this can be a difficult problem to confront. They identified several forms of racism. June Veecock noted that the lack of representation on union committees and the lack of employment opportunities in staff positions are serious problems for workers of colour.

Two of those interviewed stressed that for women of colour who have emigrated from another country, the insistence on Canadian work experience hurts one's chances of advancement not only in the labour market, but also in the labour movement. The treatment of their non-Canadian accents exacerbates the problem. As Yvonne Bobb notes, 'You also are discredited because you have an accent ... People say, "Oh Yvonne you don't communicate well." It's not that I don't communicate well, it's because I have a dialect, I have an accent and I do it differently. So I'm accused of not communicating well.' Muriel Collins echoes this point: 'It's a question of accent. If you don't have a Canadianized accent, you're not acceptable.'

Another form of racism which those interviewed described was discrimination based not just on colour of skin, but on the shade of one's skin. As Yvonne Bobb notes, all minority workers of colour do not experience racism equally and she sees the phenomenon as 'sort of like a caste system ... "that one is lighter, that one is darker" if you understand what I'm trying to say.' June Veecock also points out that 'racism has everything to do with colour.' She describes a system of discrimination that operates even in the Caribbean where 'we too have light skinned Blacks, and we have Blacks with straight hair and we have very dark Blacks and those are degrees of privilege ... and the lighter the skin and the straighter the hair, you're allowed a little more than the woman or man that has darker skin.' For Veecock this represents a 'hierarchy of oppression' that can cause serious problems in implementing both internal affirmative-action programs as well as employment-equity legislation. She admits the issue is 'very awkward' to discuss, but suggests that given the reality of this hierarchy, people can be selected for a job or counted in equity statistics who have 'very, very light skin [and] straight hair ...' To help avoid this problem she suggests that some type of 'sub-categories' be employed so that everyone gets represented.

Each of the women interviewed feels that Black women experience 'more intense' or 'greater' racism than other workers of colour. Some of this feeling is likely rooted in the fact that they are 'doubly disadvantaged' by race and gender; however, distinctions about the shade of one's skin may also play a role in this perception.

LEADERSHIP

Since each of the three women interviewed has worked her way up to a position of leadership in the union structure from the rank and file, the issue of leadership came up often. They all feel that this is a critical time for organizing around race and that strong and innovative leadership is needed. One of the most frequent issues raised was how can Black women avoid co-optation into the white male union structures even as they gain leadership positions through affirmative-action policies? It can be argued that increasing the numerical representation of women and workers of colour into elected positions on the OFL, the CLC, and other labour federations will not by itself lead to changes in union power structures unless leadership is part of a larger strategy of grass-roots organizing by these groups.[12] There is also a concern about how these representatives should be elected. For example, the struggle for affirmative-action positions in the CLC raises questions about whether visible-minority representatives to the executive board should be elected by caucus at the convention or elected by the large affiliates. Even if representatives are elected by caucus, Veecock notes, the large affiliates can dominate the affirmative-action seats because they are in a position to send large contingents of visible-minority workers to the convention. If elected by the affiliates, representatives are unlikely to go against their unions. 'Your union is picking up your cost,' comments Veecock, 'so of course you are going to be very concerned about that.' The question is whether the people elected will represent workers of colour as a specific interest group when their loyalty may be to their affiliates. As a result, Veecock concludes that the main way to organize against racism is at the grass-roots level. Having a person of colour sitting on the executive board does not necessarily guarantee representation of rank-and-file workers' interests.

Yvonne Bobb raises another concern about the nature of leadership – that unions are more likely to support workers of colour who are 'politically acceptable' to the dominant power relations and who do not challenge the union hierarchy. A similar issue is raised in this book by Carl Cuneo (in chapter 5): 'The danger is that, by becoming formal union officials, women (as well as men) may – but not necessarily – buy into the formal, bureaucratic, and patriarchal conceptions of authority held by union managers, and hence demobilize themselves.' Yvonne Bobb also warns about this potential. She argues that when a Black person is elected to a position she or he is essentially silenced. 'You can't get on the floor and organize the rank and file. You are stopped dead.' 'When women get into power,' continues Bobb, 'they become part of the system ... They may be very good people, but once they're up there, they're isolated, they take on the strategies of the institution.' Like Veecock's, her solution is to stay as close as possible to the rank-and-file movement – to stay 'radicalized.'

These women have demonstrated their leadership on the issue of racism in different ways. June Veecock, for example, sees her main task as fighting to remove barriers to the employment and participation of women of colour in the labour movement. Muriel Collins noted that her personal goal is to be seen as a 'concerned' leader. 'You can't stay in the union office. Black women have to see that you care. They have to see that someone takes action ... I go out and meet with people, talk with them, get their concerns, go into the trenches ... The important thing is the people on the shop floor, to maintain contact with them ... [We] need to be accountable to the rank and file.' Yet, as several of the women pointed out, differences in power between leaders and their constituencies can lead to isolation, distrust, and even accusations that the leaders have 'sold out.' This is particularly difficult at a personal level because, since there are so few Black women union leaders, they face great pressures and stress in their jobs.

RELATIONSHIPS WITH WHITE WOMEN

Throughout the interviews there were numerous references to Black women being 'disillusioned' with the mainstream, largely white, women's movement and there emerged a common perception that there was little support from white women activists for either individual women of colour or for the issue of racism. June Veecock thinks this partially has to do with the fact that 'women who have struggled with women's issues seem to think that if we start addressing racism in a serious way, then we will be moving away from the traditional women's issues, that this will dilute or overshadow the struggle for women ... Black women are recognizing that we have a struggle within the women's movement.' Yvonne Bobb makes a similar point: 'If women isolate minority women who speak up ... it's going to create a struggle within a struggle ... Progressive women have to recognize that there is a struggle. And it's a women's struggle; racism is a women's struggle.'

Yet, in spite of the insistence that the focus on racism would not 'dilute or overshadow' the struggle for women, June Veecock feels that activists have to get their priorities straight. She describes attending the Gloria Steinem breakfast sponsored by a feminist lobby group[13] and thinking to herself, 'It is becoming increasingly difficult for me to locate myself as equally in the struggle against sexism ... I feel compelled to fight racism. I can't always give sexism the same attention.' Later in the interview Veecock emphasized that this is a view which is still being debated by women of colour. This debate around race and gender is likely to be a serious challenge for both white and non-white women in unions.

Each of the women had stories that demonstrate how white women had not been as supportive of them individually, or for their organizing efforts around racism, as they would have expected from other feminists. Yet these examples were sometimes counterbalanced with instances where some white women had expressed a great degree of solidarity and support. For example, Yvonne Bobb describes the lack of support she received from white union women when she decided to run for the executive board of OPSEU. 'I was told my time was not yet.' However, Bobb also describes a white woman in OPSEU who, several years earlier, had 'stepped aside' so Bobb could run for the presidency of the women's caucus. 'We have remained good friends ... I visit her house, she visits mine ... [She] has been my mentor ... and I respect her.' Bobb feels that this woman did something few white women are prepared to do. She argues that white women 'should know, because they have been victimized ... [Yet] they are doing exactly the same thing to Black women.' She feels that white women must 'reassess where feminism has brought women,' and 'reconsider their treatment of women of colour ... Are we [white women] doing what society has done to us ... Are we doing the same to Black women?' Bobb also calls for white union women to come to terms with their own racism: 'Let's deal with the issue. What is it that threatens you, that causes you not to accept my credentials, my skills, my concerns, my issues? That's the debate that has to happen. Why you are feeling threatened?'

CONCLUSION

In this paper several emerging trends in the Ontario labour movement have been highlighted: union initiatives on race and gender and the convergence of these initiatives; the issue of autonomous organizing; the persistent, if sometimes subtle, nature of racism within the labour movement; the question of what type of leadership is needed to mobilize Black women to become active in their unions; and, finally, the critical issue of the relationship of Black women's organizing to often parallel organizing done by white women. Since only three, however prominent, Ontario Black women unionists were interviewed for this paper, the observations have to be seen as exploratory. Each of the themes that have emerged in the interview data deserves further study. It is especially important to do research outside of Ontario to ascertain whether these developments in one province are similar to those in other regions. More detailed analysis is also needed about these issues so the labour movement is able to develop more effective strategies for organizing against racism and sexism. What are the most effective models of change and how can the many obstacles be overcome?

The trends highlighted by these interviews also suggest that a great number of challenges lie ahead to achieve a fully integrated, representative labour movement. Perhaps the most critical challenge facing women in unions is to find more viable ways to work together. The assessment made by Black women unionists that they feel excluded from the organizing initiatives of white women and that white women in the labour movement have not been supportive of their Black sisters' organizing around racism must be seriously addressed.

NOTES

1 I would like to thank Yvonne Bobb, Muriel Collins, and June Veecock for generously sharing their time and their understanding with me. I would also like to thank Linda Briskin for her helpful editorial suggestions, and I would particularly like to thank Patricia McDermott for her generous and helpful editorial assistance.

2 Linda Carty, 'Black Women in Academia: A Statement from the Periphery,' in Hirmani Bannerji et al., Unsettling Relations (Toronto: Women's Press 1991), 16

3 This case was discussed by lawyer Mary Cornish during her presentation at the CRIAW Conference on 14 November 1992 in Toronto. Cornish Advocates represented the complainant at the Human Rights Commission and the Workers' Compensation Board between 1986 and 1991.

4 Formally known as the National Working Committee on Racism, Discrimination and Employment Equity

5 John MacLennan, 'CAW Fights Racism,' *Canadian Dimension* 26, no. 7 (October 1992): 16

6 These developments are detailed in Ronnie Leah's 'Organizing for Daycare,' in R. Argue, C. Gannage, and D.W. Livingstone, eds, *Working People and Hard Times* (Toronto: Garamond 1987) 260–73; and Ronnie Leah, 'Linking the Struggles: Racism, Feminism and the Union Movement,' in J. Vorst et al., eds, *Race, Class, Gender: Bonds and Barriers* (Toronto: Garamond 1989), 166–95.

7 Reported in the OFL Women's Committee's *Women's Rights Bulletin* (January 1992).

8 The term 'target groups' refers to the four groups designated under both federal and provincial legislation, namely: disabled people, women, Aboriginal people, and visible-minority groups.

9 Peggy Nash made these comments during an interview with the author on 13 November 1992.

10 MacLennan, 'CAW Fights Racism,' 12

11 Sherene Razack's comments were made in response to an earlier version of this paper presented to the Canadian Women's Studies Association, Learned Societies Conference, Charlottetown, June 1992.

12 Linda Briskin, 'Women, Unions and Leadership,' *Canadian Dimension* 24, no. 1 (Jan./Feb. 1990): 34–41, has made a similar argument with regards to women's organizing in unions.

13 The Legal Education and Action Fund's (LEAF) annual Person's Day breakfast

8

Unionism and Feminism in the Canadian Auto Workers Union, 1961–1992

PAMELA H. SUGIMAN

GENDERED POLITICS IN THE UAW[1]

In the past, the United Auto Workers (UAW) International Union was widely-regarded as a highly democratic organization that stood at the forefront of struggles for social justice. Recently, the Canadian Auto Workers Union (formerly the UAW Canadian Region) has attained a similarly impressive record on social activism and democratic process. However, when we consider the politics of gender, we begin to see a more complex and contradictory history. In the past, the UAW upheld a gendered vision of social justice. UAW leaders adopted a narrow definition of unionism that advanced the general principles of democracy, equality, and worker unity, yet failed to question blatant sex-based inequalities in employment, union, family, and the community. They thereby reinforced divisions that employers had established long before the union was formed.

Assuming the existence and legitimacy of a male-breadwinner family, UAW leaders, for instance, negotiated contracts that contained sex-specific job classifications and set inferior wage rates for women workers. In 1961, a wage agreement between UAW Local 222 and General Motors (hereafter GM) in Oshawa set the hiring rate for a male assembler at $2.16 an hour, while it established a hiring rate for a female assembler at $1.87. Likewise, the contract stipulated that a male bench hand start at a rate of $2.07, compared to $1.87 for a female bench hand.

Collective agreements also upheld sex-based non-interchangeable seniority groups. In 1961, the Local Seniority Agreement between GM (Oshawa) and Local 222 stated that 'the seniority rights of men, women and boys shall be exercised only in separate seniority classifications and shall not be interchangeable.' Furthermore, paragraph 62(7) of the GM Master Agreement read, 'It is understood that female employees cannot make application for jobs vacated by male employees or vice versa.' Thus, while the seniority principle ensured that employers lay off workers in the reverse order in which they were hired, sex-based seniority groups meant that the rule operated only within a sex category.

After standing without serious challenge for over two decades, these sex-based clauses came into question in the mid-1960s. During the 1960s, General Motors, one of the largest auto manufacturers in southern Ontario, restructured its operations. While many workers were affected by the reorganization, most male employees could retain their jobs by transferring from one department to another. Given sex-based job classifications and restricted seniority rights, however, women could only move into a limited number of jobs. Indeed, after restructuring, only one female department would remain in the Oshawa plant, the wire and harness. The transfer of the female-dominated cutting and sewing departments from Oshawa to GM's Windsor plant thus resulted in the loss of an overwhelming proportion of the female workforce. Between 1965 and 1967, 300 to 400 female jobs had been eliminated.[2] By 1968, women with seniority dating back to 1962 had been laid off for fifteen months, while GM continued to hire male employees.[3]

These practices angered many female employees. Driven by this anger, a small group of about seven outspoken and politically astute women from UAW Local 222 decided to confront sex discrimination collectively in both the industry and their union. 'We kept fighting this and saying that this isn't right,' reported union activist and GM employee Bev McCloskey. However, both their employers and most union officials ignored the women's protests. In fact, in response to their protests, the president of Local 222 bluntly rejoined, 'Why don't they [laid-off women auto workers] go to Toronto and get a job?' When McCloskey proposed that the women 'bump' lower-seniority men on the assembly line, the chairman of the union bargaining committee quipped that 'he wouldn't want his wife hanging off a welder in the body shop.'

Frustrated by the indifference and, at times, resistance of some male unionists, the women looked beyond the established perspective of their union. While these women based their struggle for gender equality on the basic tenets of industrial unionism – the seniority principle and the right to grieve discriminatory treatment as dues-paying unionists – they also drew on ideas about women's rights in society. They expanded their vision of social justice and gained a greater sense of efficacy. In redefining patriarchal unionism with a sensitivity to gender politics, women workers began to theorize the links between the various bases of social inequality.

The women also drew on methods of mobilization that were typical of the women's movement in the 1960s and 1970s. Such strategies included consciousness-raising, recognizing the political implications of 'personal' issues, and self-empowerment through separate organizing.[4] At annual UAW International women's conferences, female delegates participated in mock union locals, assessed shop-floor strategies for confronting discrimination, and learned about the UAW grievance procedure, policies, and legislation affecting women employees. Inspired by the American women they met at these conferences, on 18 September 1968, the women from Local 222 also formed an official women's committee. Committee members identified women workers' problems and on the basis of this knowledge, they made recommendations to the local union executive board. In addition, they promoted women's union citizenship and furthered their technical understanding of UAW procedures. Some women, in fact, saw the committee as 'a training ground for future jobs in the union.' Most important, the committee provided women workers with an arena in which they could identify issues, vent frustrations, and realize their common predicament.

The committee's most consequential struggle, however, was legislative. Recognizing that the Ontario Human Rights Code, 1961–2, prohibited discrimination on the basis of colour, race, creed, and national origin, but not sex, the Women's Committee launched an organized campaign to amend the Act. The legislative amendment in fact became the committee's central and defining goal. In pursuing this goal, the women from Local 222 aligned themselves with middle-class feminists in academic and artistic circles. Although they formed an especially strong bond with women in the left-leaning New Democratic Party, more broad-based and non-partisan groups such as the Voice of Women also became part of their network.[5]

After participating in numerous protest marches, letter-writing campaigns, and lobbying efforts in the provincial legislature, the women were successful. In the spring of 1970, the minister of labour declared that Bill 83 to amend the Ontario Human Rights Code was to have its final reading in the Legislature, and he personally invited the Women's Committee members to attend. In December 1970 the bill became law. And insofar as legislation supersedes collective agreements, unions and employers in Ontario were consequently forced to eliminate all sex-based provisions in contracts.

REDEFINING THE UAW AGENDA

In the decade following this breakthrough, the UAW International and, on a lesser scale, the Canadian Region office fervently publicized the union's prominent stand on women's rights. Indeed, the union's record is impressive. The UAW Canadian Region held its first women workers' conference in 1964, long before the Ontario Federation of Labour or the Canadian Labour Congress had even established women's agencies. In addition, in 1970 the union created a Canadian Women's Department to co-ordinate activities for the promotion of gender equality.

Through the union, women workers also advocated equal pay for work of equal value,[6] access to the male-dominated skilled trades,[7] establishment of a UAW women's scholarship program,[8] the elimination of protective legislation for women,[9] sexual harassment policies, fair pensions for women,[10] and improved maternity-leave provisions.[11]

At the April 1970 UAW Constitutional Convention, women workers called for 'full equality now.' These few words accurately describe their agenda throughout the decade. Recognizing that they were affected not only by what happened in the workplace, but also by social arrangements within private households and in the community, they began to challenge gender inequality in its various forms. For instance, at the Canadian UAW Women's Conference in 1971, delegate Peggy Buchanan declared, 'If we could bring equality into the home where men would share the housework and care of the children, it would allow women to fulfill career potentials and make the men something besides just breadwinners to their children.'[12]

'Women all over the world are experiencing a new consciousness of their rights, status, and of themselves as persons,' declared Caroline Davis, director of the UAW-CIO Women's Department, before the Ninth Annual Canadian Women's Conference in 1972. She cited women's efforts to establish paid child care as a prime example of this change.[13] In addition to promoting the child's welfare, some women unionists advocated child care for women's own well-being. Furthermore, they criticized day-care schemes that overlooked the needs of factory employees who worked rotating shifts.[14] These women long 'fought for babysitting in the workplace,' recalled Betty Murray. 'They wanted some kind of a system where they could bring their kids to work and not be worried. They could go down there at lunch time and see how they are ... They fought and fought for that.'

Some UAW women also put birth control and women's reproductive rights on their agenda.[15] Pat Creighton recalled sitting in Ottawa in a committee room during their campaign for equal rights. A female physician got up and 'said if that Pill was meant for men, it still wouldn't be on the market. They'd still be testing it ... that was another side effect from the Women's Committee ... It just branched out! And the women started thinking, it wasn't just in the workplace that they were abusing us.'

In May 1970, the Local 222 Women's Committee publicized the 'abortion caravan' that was travelling across Canada, advocating the legalization of abortion.[16] Maurie Shorten, chair of the original Local 222 Women's Committee, even established an abortion referral service. For fifteen years, she ran an advertisement in the local union newspaper for a doctor in Buffalo who ran a legal clinic. Abortions were then illegal in Oshawa.

The UAW also stepped up its campaign for women's rights through the legal process.[17] In addition to employment standards, women promoted more egalitarian marriage and divorce legislation[18] and more stringent laws regarding the abuse of women and children.[19] Some members of the Local 222 Women's Committee were personally involved in efforts to aid battered women. They also helped establish a local rape crisis centre and drug and alcohol treatment programs for women. These were not traditional UAW concerns.

'The women's revolution will be a mistake, if we just make it from our own standpoint,' declared Olga Madar. 'We must open doors of opportunity for families to participate ... We do not agree with every tenet of different women's groups, but we must work together on basic principles.'[20]

While only a minority of women were activists, the others were not untouched by the politics of the women's movement. 'Union-wise' feminists had educated and politicized their female co-workers in various ways and degrees. Even women who clung to conventional beliefs and arrangements modified their outlook and actions in light of radical new ideas. In many women, elements of feminism co-existed (uneasily) with patriarchal ideologies.

FEMINISM IN A PATRIARCHAL FRAMEWORK

These policy statements and demands, however, must be assessed in a wider context. While impressive, they were often inconsistent with the practices and sentiments of many (male) union leaders at both the national and local levels, as well as the majority of rank-and-file members. While women unionists undoubtedly expanded labour's agenda, they did not fundamentally transform the union. Even after they won equal contract rights and legal recourse to challenge sex discrimination, women remained on the periphery of union affairs. For example, throughout the 1970s and 1980s, there were still proportionately few women in union office. Pressured by American UAW Executive Board member Olga Madar, in 1968 George Burt, UAW director in Canada, recommended that the union improve female representation on staff and hire a woman researcher in Canada.[21] However, later in the year, Dennis McDermott, Burt's successor, maintained that he would not appoint staff on the basis of gender, religion, or ethnic background. 'In my view,' he stated, 'there should be no essential difference in the treatment or the aspirations or the activity of a person in the labour movement because of sex differences ... I do not believe a strictly female suffragette-type movement within the trade union structure is the answer.[22]

Not to be deterred, female unionists repeatedly lobbied UAW leaders to appoint women to the union's international staff,[23] regional office,[24] International Executive Board, and District Council. Some women even suggested that the union implement affirmative action to ensure female representation on local union executive boards.[25]

Between 1970 and 1977, the number of women in the UAW Canadian Region rose from roughly 10,000 to 14,500.[26] Yet during these years, delegates to women's conferences and meetings observed that most instructors were men,[27] there were no female 'Local Union Discussion Leaders,'[28] UAW leader Dennis McDermott was often absent from these forums, and his substitute speakers seldom discussed women workers' specific concerns.[29]

In 1973, less than 5 per cent of the female membership in Canada (60 out of 13,153) held office in their local union, there were 10 women out of roughly 200 District Council delegates, and in the

Toronto area there were only 14 women out of a total of 274 persons on collective-bargaining committees. In addition, out of a total of 900 UAW representatives, only 17 were women.[30] Some women participated in union standing committees, but they were concentrated in consumer affairs, recreation, and women's committees.[31] And while two females were appointed to the Canadian UAW staff in 1976,[32] few women had assumed decision-making positions.[33]

Some women claimed that they did not encounter resistance from men in their union locals, but seasoned activists also warned delegates against being 'too optimistic.' 'Some locals don't even tell the members about the Women's Department Conference,' said one woman.[34] Moreover, a delegate to the 1974 Canadian Women's Conference called the UAW a 'highly male organized group who generally like the status quo' and find women to be 'unacceptable speakers at their meetings.' A number of women also claimed that they simply could not win union office. According to GM worker Pat Creighton, 'There's always been one or two women on the slate, but they're never up there in the position of power ... That's the way it's been. That's why you don't see women in the union hall ... It's an old boys' club.' Bev McCloskey echoed this sentiment, noting that there are 'not enough jobs to go around so the guys have got to keep them.' In her view, the only way women could achieve proportionate representation in elected union office is through affirmative action.

In short, insofar as the legal-contractual changes of 1970 did not immediately alter the union, women workers had to wage their struggles in a masculinized context. This strategy involved many contradictions and women activists handled the resulting tensions in three central ways. They tended to promote strict 'equality' as opposed to differential treatment based on sex. Many women rejected 'feminist' beliefs and denied any affiliation with the women's-rights movement. And, some women expressed ambivalence about separate organizing through local-union women's committees.

'That was the concept back in those days – equal rather than preferential,' explained a CAW national representative. This was the philosophy of the old industrial unionism. Although they undoubtedly recognized that there were sex-based conflicts within the union membership and acknowledged women's distinct problems and interests, most union leaders and members maintained that the tenets of industrial unionism, alone, would eliminate gender-based inequalities. Women's experiences, however, had demonstrated that the general principles of equity and democracy, alone, could not achieve this end in a framework of systemic inequality. The seniority principle, democratic rule, and equal application of the collective agreement did not take into account women's subordinate position in society and their historically restricted status in industry.

Yet, when presented with a choice between workplace equality and gender-specific treatment based on difference in situation, most women accepted the dichotomy and strongly advocated the former. The women's gender consciousness was tempered by a keen awareness that their union brothers distrusted and resented the distinct status of a minority group. Auto worker Rose Taylor accurately captured this philosophy in stating, 'The union's more for equality. They won't split up men and women's issues. They're all union issues.' Unionists were reluctant to say, 'The women they have this issue and the men have that issue.' They preferred to say, 'We all have this issue.'

Consequently, throughout the 1970s and 1980s, many women tried to prove that their goals were identical to those of men in the labour movement. This concern likely prompted a UAW member to tell women's conference delegates in 1973 that, in order to get women on the Canadian UAW staff, they must form a coalition with men. 'Women's problems are men's problems,' she stated emphatically. 'You should have specifically invited men here so you could show them that women's problems are men's problems.'[35] At a 1977 women's conference, a group of delegates similarly stated that women had taken on too many 'symbolic issues,' such as changing the name of the 'Workmen's' Compensation Board in British Columbia to 'Worker's' Compensation. 'We should consider men allies, not antagonize them,' these women argued.[36]

This perspective also led women to accept the same terms of employment as men, and abandon references to sex-based differences. For example, when women gained equal seniority rights, GM management decided to remove the stove and refrigerator from their lunch room. Managers reasoned that because men and women had equal rights under the contract, they should receive identical treatment men with respect to breaks and facilities. Local 222 Women's Committee chair May Partridge agreed with this view, stating, 'If this is in the interests of equality then I say we have a half-hour lunch break as the rest of GM.'[37] Likewise, in reference to legislation that forced companies to either let women leave work five minutes before midnight or provide them with transportation, Partridge argued that such a 'privilege' was undesirable if women wanted to achieve equality and the respect of their brothers.

Most UAW leaders upheld the notion that 'differential' treatment was 'preferential' treatment or 'privilege.' If women want to 'lead' in the workplace and the union, they had better 'take off the gloves and lace,' advised a prominent union official. Gordon Wilson, then UAW education director in Canada, told a delegation of women unionists that they must 'assert' themselves. 'Don't look to be patronized, get in there and fight,' he advised.[38] Conference delegates repeatedly stated that women 'aren't aggressive enough.' 'If women respected themselves as much as men respect themselves, they wouldn't have any problems,' said one worker. Similarly, American, Caroline Davis told her Canadian sisters that 'timidity' shows a lack of self-respect. She added that 'men don't lack this respect toward themselves or other men.'[39] These comments were part of a pragmatic response to the women's situation, but they were also gender-biased. They championed an approach, a cultural style, that white men had long used in their struggles with management.

In March 1971, the Local 222 Women's Committee reported that although the 'general feeling ... is that Bill 83 [to amend the Ontario Human Rights Act] protects only females,' 'This is not the case. It is legislated to encompass both sexes ... As one of the girls ... stated, "we are not trying to beat you, just join you." '[40] Throughout these years, women repeated old ideas that they must be accepted as 'UAW members instead of female members' (my emphasis).[41] One worker explained: The problems for a man who is widowed with children, is [sic] the same problems [as for] a woman widowed or divorced or left with children. It's the same problem for a man or a woman ... Any problem that arises in the shop – it will be a problem for men and women.'[42]

In this restrictive context, most women furthermore denied that they held 'feminist' ideas and loyalties. While they had drawn on some of the principles and strategies of the women's movement and allied themselves with self-proclaimed feminists in the community, many women activists in the UAW declared that they were not feminists. 'You had a couple on there that were feminists,' [said a former member of the Local 222 Women's Committee]. But other than that, no. It was just that we wanted equal rights ... The only involvement I ever had was through the union, trying to get the women in ...

Other women's movements, no. I'd never been active in them. Some of them I don't believe in.' Another Women's Committee member asserted: 'That word feminist doesn't sit with me the way it should. I believe that every human being has a right to choices. But nothing to do with male or female.' Given feminism's bad name, these denials at first seem unimportant, especially because they blatantly contradict the women's actions. However, on close inspection, their need to dissociate themselves from the popular concept of 'feminism' and espouse an alternative ideology is telling. Throughout the 1970s, and less noticeably in the late 1960s, women auto workers distinguished between 'equal rights' and 'feminism.' They furthermore promoted a goal of 'equality' as opposed to 'liberation.' May Partridge skilfully explained this distinction in a poem entitled 'Liberation – no ... equality – yes.'

We elected a committee
With one aim in mind
To equalize the contract
The solution we must find
In all the daily papers
Others worked toward the end
Of 'Liberating' women
By Eliminating men
This was not the purpose
WE gave up leisure time
But 'Eliminating' language
That kept us in a bind
. . . .
The law's been passed, accepted,
by this giant called G.M.
Our fight is far from over
Till we educate the men
We know our design is different
On this point we'll agree
We're not asking 'LIBERATION'
Just 'EQUALITY.'[43]

Female auto workers moved carefully and somewhat ambivalently between conventional womanhood, patriarchal unionism, and a working-class feminism or feminist unionism.[44]

Just as they formally dissociated themselves from the feminism of the women's-rights movement, women unionists questioned the future of local women's committees. This scepticism was rooted in both a lingering fear that they would be penalized for waging a separate struggle from their union 'brothers' and an understanding that they might become ghettoized within the union structure. Without secure access to UAW resources, women's concerns could easily be subsumed in the general labour struggle.[45] Thus, some women argued that they should become active in 'mainstream' union affairs and not isolate themselves in their own group.

Upholding this belief, GM worker Pat Creighton firmly contended that, after 1970, the Local Women's Committee 'should have died.' 'It should have been put to rest,' she said, then you would sit as equal partners. But by givin' them the women's committee we were never an equal partner ... Just take a little jaunt in the [union] hall and ask them ... when was the last time a female sat on the Executive?' Creighton believed that 'things pertaining to women didn't come up' at the general membership meetings because they were left to the Women's Committee.

Indeed, some women unionists suggested renaming the committees 'workers' councils' and calling the Women's Conference the 'Labour Equality Conference.'[46] After much debate, however, delegates to the UAW Women's Conference in 1977 decided that such a change would defeat their purpose. Members of the Canadian UAW Women's Advisory Committee argued that women should use the Women's Committee as a 'vehicle' to sustain their 'own identity' and by renaming it they would be 'letting down' the female membership.[47] In defence of the Women's Committee, an Ann Bailey wrote:

You want to know what we do
We are trying not to wear a man's shoe
We are standing up for women's rights
To bring your problems to the light

No longer shall we sit back –
To feel that as women we all lack –
The ability to work and take a stand –
Shoulder to shoulder with a man –
All we want is an even share
You may find we make a good pair.[48]

Furthermore, shortly after their success in 1970, many original members resigned from the Local 222 Women's Committee. These women believed that they had achieved their most important goal, equality of opportunity under the contract. Pat Creighton recalled: 'I said, "Uh uh, not this girl." It's like General Motors and the union saying, 'Now you girls, you've got the Women's Committee. Now be content with that." ' Auto worker Fay Bender also left the Women's Committee after the legislation was passed. Like Creighton, Bender felt that her job on the Committee was done. She was not sure what it did after 1970. In 1972, there were reports that the members met every month but it was 'totally stagnant.'[49]

REDEFINING 'EQUALITY' IN THE CAW: AN ALLIANCE OF FEMINISM AND UNIONISM

With equal seniority rights, long-standing female auto workers have been able to retain their jobs in a rapidly contracting labour market. Throughout the 1970s, 1980s, and early 1990s, however, auto employers did not hire substantially more women. Consequently, small pockets of females currently work in departments that remain male-dominated. As women were dispersed in these masculine work settings, they lost their own distinctive work culture of past years. The unity that existed among women who were concentrated in female departments such as the sewing room and the wire and harness, has disappeared at General Motors. In some ways, job desegregation eroded the strong gender identity, women's culture, and sense of sisterhood that was nurtured in exclusively female departments. This unity ultimately provided a base for women's political mobilization. Consequently, it is not surprising that after the original women's committee members stepped down, a new group of women did not enthusiastically take up where the original activists left off.

The early struggles of women unionists, however, have paved the way for subsequent change. In 1984 and 1987 respectively, CAW representatives negotiated an affirmative-action program with the Big Three auto makers, as well as three hours of company-paid human-rights training for all GM employees. In addition, in 1992 the union began leadership training programs for women and visible-minority members. The union also holds an annual national women's conference and a human-rights conference.

Although many individual union members and local-level leaders have been active in struggles for gender equality, most of these recent policy measures were initiated and implemented at the national level by CAW staff. Staff representatives have tended to introduce such measures slowly and cautiously in order to avoid a backlash and even their outright rejection by union locals. Union locals, in general, have not been pushing the agenda for equality. The CAW is still a patriarchal institution that needs to foster a greater understanding of the politics of gender and race among the majority of its membership.

Feminism and unionism co-exist uneasily in the labour movement. For working-class women, the union represents a viable vehicle for achieving social change. It is an important reference point and resource. Feminist unionists have promoted a greater inclusiveness of the union membership and they have expanded labour's agenda. However, women have had to wage their struggles within a masculine context. They have therefore tried to combine conventional union principles with ideas about women's rights in a way that makes sense to them and is acceptable and legitimate to working-class men. In short, these women have developed a feminist unionism – a type of unionism that has been shaped by relations between men and women, as well as between employers and workers.

NOTES

1 Some of the following discussion, originally appeared in Pamela Sugiman, ' "That Wall's Comin' Down"': Gendered Strategies of Worker Resistance in the UAW Canadian Region,' *Canadian Journal of Sociology* 17, no. 1 (Winter 1992): 1–27.
2 Public Archives of Canada (PAC), MG 28, I 119, Acc. 83/215, Vol.16, File: 'General Motors – Windsor'; Interview with Beverly McCloskey, 1990; Interview with Maurie Shorten, 1990
3 PAC, MG 28, I 119, Acc. 81/081, Box 52, File: 'Local 222 Correspondence,' Bev McCloskey to Caroline Davis, 25 Oct. 1968
4 For a discussion of strategies used by the women's movement in Canada, see Nancy Adamson, Linda Briskin, and Margaret McPhail, *Feminist Organizing for Change* (Toronto: Oxford University Press 1988).
5 The Voice of Women was founded in July 1960, in an effort to 'unite women in concern for the future of the world.' By the fall of 1961, it had a membership of 5000. Although the Voice of Women was primarily a peace organization, it addressed a number of issues, such as

biculturalism, women's health and safety, and the legalization of the distribution of birth-control information (Adamson, Briskin, and McPhail 39).

6 For example, Archives of Labor and Urban Affairs (hereafter ALUA), UAW Women's Department: Lillian Hatcher Collection, Box 20, File: 20-30, 'Conventions and resolutions, 1968–73,' 'Resolution re' Working Women, 20–27 March 1964

7 For example, PAC, MG 28, I 119, Acc. 88/324, Box 67, File: 'Women's Advisory Council, 1970–82,' Summary, 15th Annual UAW Canadian Women's Conference, 8–10 Sept. 1978

8 For example, PAC, MG 28, I 119, Acc. 86/472, Box 4, File: UAW Women's Department, Summary of the Tenth Annual Canadian Women Workers' Conference, 14–16 Sept. 1973

9 For example, PAC, MG 28, I 119, Acc. 81/081, Box 51, File: 'Local 27 Correspondence,' Resolution, 'Women in the Canadian Region'; CAW, 'Resolutions,' in *Proceedings, Twenty-third UAW Constitutional Convention,* 23–28 Apr. 1972

10 For example, Julia Majka, 'Women and Pensions,' *UAW Local 199 News* 14, no. 7 (June 1979), 3

11 For example, PAC, MG 28, I 119, Acc. 83/215, Box 8, File: 'General Motors Negotiations, 1964,' GM Settlement Gains, Insurance and Health Care Improvements, 1964.

12 PAC, MG 28, I 119, Acc. 88/324, Box 67, File: Canadian UAW Council Women's Committee, 1972–81, Proceedings of the Eighth Annual Canadian Women's Conference, 16–17 Oct. 1971

13 For example, PAC, MG 28, I 119, Acc. 83/215, Box 12, File: Toronto Office – Education Department, January 1971–December 1973, Summary of the Ninth Annual Canadian Women Workers' Conference, 22–24 Sept. 1972

14 For example, PAC, MG 28, I 119, Acc. 86/472, Box 4, File: UAW Women's Department, Summary of the Tenth Annual Canadian Women Workers' Conference, 14–16 Sept. 1973

15 For example, ALUA, UAW Women's Auxiliaries – Series III Collection, Box 10, File: 10-11, 'Canadian Region, 1955–76,' Agenda, UAW Canadian Women's Conference, 9–10 Sept. 1967.

16 May Partridge, 'Women's Committee Report,' *The Oshaworker* 28, no. 9 (7 May 1970), 8

17 For example, delegates to the 1970 Canadian UAW Women's Conference reviewed current provincial legislation, such as laws regarding separate wage scales and job classifications. In addition, they argued that protec-

tive legislation conflicts with equal opportunity. PAC, MG 28, I 119, Acc. 81/081, Box 46, File: 'Allen Schroeder,' Summary of the Seventh UAW Canadian Women's Conference, 26–27 Sept. 1970; PAC, MG 28, I 119, Acc. 83/215, Box 12, File: 'Toronto Office – Education Department, January 1971–December 1973,' Summary of the Ninth Annual UAW Women's Conference, 22–24 Sept. 1972

18 For example, ALUA, UAW Women's Auxiliaries – Series III Collection, Box 10, File: 10-11, 'Canadian Region, 1955–76,' Agenda, UAW Canadian Women's Conference, 9–10 Sept. 1967

19 'How Can We Help You?' *UAW Local 199 News* 14, no. 8 (Oct.–Nov. 1979), 10

20 PAC, MG 28, I 119, Acc. 88/324, Box 67, File: 'Canadian UAW Council Women's Committee, 1972–81,' Proceedings of the Eighth Annual Canadian Women's Conference, 16–17 Oct. 1971

21 ALUA, UAW Canadian Region – General Files Collection, Box 25, File: 3, 'International Union, Research Department, 1968,' George Burt to Carrol Coburn, 13 Feb. 1968

22 ALUA, UAW Canadian Region – Officers' Files Collection, Box 54, File: 6, 'Dennis McDermott, Regional Director, October 1968,' Dennis McDermott to Lee Chiodo, 4 Oct. 1968; ibid., UAW Canadian Region – Series III Collection, Box 73, File: 7, Canadian UAW Council, 1968, Minutes of the UAW Canadian Council, 14–15 Sept. 1968

23 For example, ALUA, UAW Canadian Region – Locals Collection, Box 91, File: 1, Local 222, Oshawa, 1966, Abe Taylor to Olga Madar, 28 Sept. 1966

24 PAC, MG 28, I 119, Acc. 86/472, Box 4, File: UAW Women's Department, Summary of the Tenth Annual Canadian Women Workers' Conference, 14–16 Sept. 1973

25 PAC, MG 28, I 119, Acc. 81/081, Box 46, File: 'Allen Schroeder,' Allen Schroeder to Delegates to the UAW Women's Conference, 3 Nov. 1970

26 PAC, MG 28, I 119, Acc. 88/324, Box 65, File: 'E. Johnston,' inter-office communication re: 'Women Membership in UAW,' 11 May 1977

27 Interview with Maurie Shorten, 1990

28 PAC, MG 28, I 119, Acc. 81/081, Box 51, File: Fourteenth Annual UAW Canadian Region Women's Conference, Summary of the Fourteenth Annual Canadian Women Workers' Conference, 16–18 Sept. 1977

29 For example, PAC, MG 28, I 119, Acc. 88/324, Box 67, File: 'Canadian UAW Council Women's Committee, 1972–81,' Summary of the Eighth Annual Canadian Women's Conference, 16–17 Oct. 1971

30 PAC, MG 28, I 119, Acc. 86/472, Box 4, File: UAW Women's Department,

Proceedings of the Tenth Annual Canadian Women Workers' Conference, 14–16 Sept. 1973

31 Ibid., Summary of the Eleventh Annual Canadian UAW Women Workers' Conference, 13–15 Sept. 1974

32 PAC, MG 28, I 119, Acc. 81/081, Box 51, File: Fourteenth Annual Canadian Region UAW Women's Conference, Summary of the Fourteenth Annual Canadian Women's Conference, 16–18 Sept. 1977.

33 Even in 1991, there were no women on the GM Master Bargaining Committee and only one woman sits on a local GM bargaining committee. This is Pat Baker from the GM Trim plant in Windsor, where women in General Motors are concentrated.

34 PAC, MG 28, I 119, Acc. 88/324, Box 67, File: Canadian UAW Council Women's Committee, 1972–81, Proceedings of the Eighth Annual Canadian Women's Conference, 16–17 Oct. 1971

35 PAC, MG 28, I 119, Acc. 86/472, Box 4, File: UAW Women's Department, Summary of the Tenth Annual Canadian Women Workers' Conference, 14–16 Sept. 1973

36 PAC, MG 28, I 119, Acc. 81/081, Box 51, File: Fourteenth Annual Canadian Region UAW Women's Conference, Summary of the Fourteenth Annual Canadian Women Workers' Conference, 16–18 Sept. 1977

37 May Partridge, 'Women's Committee Report,' The Oshaworker 29, no. 8 (15 Apr. 1971), 8

38 PAC, MG 28, I 119, Acc. 86/472, Box 4, File: UAW Women's Department, Summary of the Tenth Annual Canadian Women Workers' Conference, 14–16 Sept. 1973

39 PAC, MG 28, I 119, Acc. 83/215, Box 12, File: Toronto Office – Education Department, January 1971–December 1973, Summary of the Ninth Annual Canadian Women Workers' Conference, 22–24 Sept. 1972

40 May Partridge, 'Women's Committee Report,' The Oshaworker 29, no. 5, (4 March 1971), 3, 5

41 CAW, Proceedings, Twentieth UAW Constitutional Convention, 16–21 May 1966

42 PAC, MG 28, I 119, Acc. 86/472, Box 4, File: UAW Women's Department, Summary of the Eleventh Annual Canadian UAW Women Workers' Conference, 13–15 Sept. 1974

43 May Partridge, 'Liberation – no ... Equality – yes,' The Oshaworker 29, no. 4 (18 Feb. 1971), 2

44 For a discussion of working-class feminism, see Heather Jon Maroney, 'Feminism at Work,' in Juliet Mitchell and Ann Oakley, eds, What Is Feminism (New York: Pantheon Books 1986), 101–26.

45 See Linda Briskin, 'Union Women and Separate Organizing,' chapter 4 in this volume.
46 PAC, MG 28, I 119, Acc. 86/472, Box 4, File: UAW Women's Department, Proceedings of the Thirteenth Annual Women's Conference, 17–19 Sept. 1976
47 PAC, MG 28, I 119, Acc. 81/081, Box 51, File: Fourteenth Annual Canadian Region UAW Women's Conference, Summary of the Fourteenth Annual Canadian UAW Women Workers' Conference, 16–18 Sept. 1977
48 Ann Bailey 'Women's Committee,' mimeo, n.d.
49 May Partridge, 'Women's Committee Report,' The Oshaworker 30, no. 5 (6 April 1972), 7

PART III
UNIONS AND WOMEN WORKERS

9

Patterns of Unionization[1]

JULIE WHITE

It has often been noted that a large number of women have joined unions since the 1960s, the figure rising from 250,000 in 1962 to one-and-a-half million by 1989. Since women have been joining unions more rapidly than men, the percentage of women out of the total number of union members has also increased consistently over the same period, from 16 per cent to 39 per cent.[2] However, these positive figures hide a more negative and problematic side of the situation.

The speed at which women have been joining unions has slowed dramatically since the 1970s. Throughout the 1960s and 1970s the pace of unionization among women was sufficient to more than match the increasing number of women joining the labour force. As a result, the proportion of paid women workers belonging to trade unions rose from 16 per cent in 1966 to 28 per cent by 1983. However, since 1983 there has been a relatively low growth in the number of women union members, and the rate of unionization for women has not increased, but has remained stagnant at around 28 to 29 per cent.

Among men, the unionization rate has fluctuated more than for women, but the overall trend has been a decline since the 1960s. The combined impact of the decline in male unionization and the stagnation for women has meant that the overall rate of unionization for both sexes has fallen from 35 per cent in 1983 to 33 per cent by 1987, with only a partial recovery to 34 per cent by 1989. Thus, while women continue to unionize and to do so at a faster rate than men, it may be of little comfort to find that their influence is expanding in a labour movement that is stagnant or declining.

Women continue to belong to unions less often than men, although the gap has narrowed considerably. In 1976, 39 per cent of men were unionized, compared with 21 per cent of women, a gap of 18 per centage points. By 1989, the figures were 38 per cent and 29 per cent, a gap of 9 percentage points.

This paper will examine the most recent trends in the patterns of unionization, both generally and specifically among women. The relatively new Labour Market Activity Survey (LMAS) provides far more precise information than was previously available, and the following discussion is an initial look at what we might learn about union organizing from this data. The analysis is based upon unpublished data from the LMAS for 1989; a description of this data and its use in this paper is provided in the appendix to this chapter.

The LMAS data confirms some past research, but also gives some unexpected results, indicating that the relationship between women and unions is more complex than was previously understood.

TRENDS IN UNIONIZATION

The massive unionization among public-sector workers in the 1960s and 1970s has left public administration and education/health services as the two industries with the highest percentages of unionized workers. With rates of unionization at 70 per cent and 67 per cent respectively in 1989, these industries are often referred to as 'saturated' as far as union membership is concerned, implying that little further unionization is possible. (See table 1.)

As rates of unionization in the public sector stabilized in the 1980s, organizing in other industrial sectors did not increase, leading to the stagnation in union membership outlined above. In particular, attempts to organize in the department stores of the trade industry and in the banks of the finance industry have met with almost total failure.[3] The three industrial sectors with the lowest rates of unionization – trade at 15 per cent, finance at 12 per cent, and personal/business services at just over 11 per cent – have not been penetrated to any degree by union organization.

Manufacturing has a relatively long tradition of unionization, but although the rate of unionization is above average at 45 per cent, still the majority of workers in this industry are not unionized. Meanwhile, shifts in the composition of the labour force are working to erode union membership in manufacturing, where jobs are being lost, and union members with them.[4] This change is partly the result of

TABLE 1
Rate of unionization, by sex, by industry, 1989 (percentage)

Industry	Overall rate of unionization	Unionization of women	Unionization of men
Public adminstration	70.4	68.2	72.0
Education/health/ welfare/services	66.9	65.1	71.8
Transportation/ communication/utilities	60.2	57.1	61.5
Manufacturing	45.3	33.2	50.1
Trade	15.2	12.8	17.5
Finance	12.4	11.7	13.8
Personal/business services	11.5	10.4	13.1
Non-agricultural primary	34.8	18.1	37.9
Construction	34.3	12.2	38.7
Agriculture	10.6	10.9	10.4
All industries	37.9	34.2	41.3

technology making human involvement redundant, and partly the result of increased competitiveness, including most recently free trade, pressing businesses into bankruptcy or out of the country.

Service industries are no longer just growing faster than goods-producing industries; between 1981 and 1986 *all* new jobs created were in the service industries.[5] Many of these new jobs are in the industrial sectors with the lowest rates of unionization.

There is a shift in employment taking place not only between industries, but also within industries. In general, middle-wage jobs are being lost and there is an increase in both lower- and higher-paid work, a polarization between the 'good jobs' and the 'bad jobs,' as the Economic Council of Canada has called them.[6] Moreover, a large percentage of new jobs are non-standard, that is, part-time, temporary, small-scale self-employment, generally low paid and insecure types of work. Between 1981 and 1986, half of all new jobs created were these non-standard types of jobs, the hardest to unionize.[7] However, the shift to the higher-paid 'good' jobs also involves a loss of union members, since administrative and technical jobs are not highly unionized.

While the gap in the rates of unionization of men and women has narrowed over the years, there continues to be a substantial difference.

According to the LMAS data, in 1989 34 per cent of women workers were unionized, compared with 41 per cent of men.[8] As table 1 shows, in every industrial sector women are less organized than men, although the gap is most pronounced in manufacturing. The differential rates of unionization for men and women within industries provides the major reason for the lower rate of unionization among women.

Why are the workers in certain industries, or certain types of jobs, less unionized than others, and how does this difference apply to women? Four factors will be examined here: small workplaces; workers employed in part-time and part-year jobs; lack of organization of women in clerical occupations; and employer opposition.

SIZE OF WORKPLACE

Size of workplace has a profound impact upon the rate of unionization. The policy of labour-relations boards to certify by individual workplace makes the costs of organizing small workplaces prohibitive, particularly when any form of employer opposition drags out the legal delays and expenses. The overall rate of unionization was 38 per cent in 1989, but in firms with fewer than 20 workers only 13 per cent of workers belonged to unions. As table 2 shows, the percentage of unionization rises in step as the size of firm increases, so that 32 per cent of workers were unionized in firms with 20–99 workers, 50 per cent in firms of 100–499 workers, and finally 56 per cent of workers belonged to unions in firms with more than 500 workers.

This situation would be of little significance if few workers were employed in small firms, but 28 per cent of all workers are employed in the smallest workplaces of fewer than 20 workers. Almost half (49 per cent) of all workers are employed in workplaces with fewer than 100 workers.

How does the lack of unionization in small workplaces relate to the different rates of unionization by industry? As one would expect, industries with a low rate of unionization have a large percentage of small workplaces. For example, in personal/business services, with a unionization rate of less than 12 per cent, fully 70 per cent of workers are in firms with fewer than 100 workers, and in trade, where only 15 per cent of the workers are unionized, the figure is 60 per cent. The reverse also holds true. Public administration, education/health services, transportation, and manufacturing are all indus-

TABLE 2
Rate of unionization and distribution of workers, by sex, by size of firm, 1989
(percentage)

Size of firm	Rate of unionization	Distribution of all workers	Distribution of women workers	Distribution of men workers
0–19	12.6	27.9	30.8	25.3
20–99	32.1	20.9	20.0	21.7
100–499	50.1	15.6	14.6	16.5
500+	55.9	35.6	34.7	36.5
All firms	37.9	100.0	100.0	100.0

tries with relatively high rates of unionization (45–70 per cent), and the majority of the jobs in these industries, between 63 and 71 per cent of them, are concentrated in firms with over 100 workers.

However, the finance industry is an exception, since it has a low rate of unionization (12 per cent), and yet the majority of the workers are employed in large workplaces. Sixty-one per cent of the workers in this industry are found in workplaces with more than 100 workers, and over half (51 per cent) are employed in the largest firms with more than 500 workers. There has been a focus of attention upon the real difficulty of organizing small bank branches, but in fact the majority of jobs in finance are in large offices. While the size of workplace may explain part of the difficulty of organizing bank branches, it does not explain why the majority of workers in the larger workplaces within the finance industry remain non-unionized.

With regard to the impact of the size of firm on the unionization of women, the LMAS data provides much more extensive information than was previously available. In the past I examined data from just the manufacturing industry, which showed that more women than men worked in small workplaces. I suggested that this pattern might hold true for other industries, and if so the size of workplace would have a significant impact not just on unionization, but also upon the differential rates of unionization by sex.[9]

In fact, the LMAS data show that manufacturing is the only sector where women are clearly and consistently concentrated into the smaller workplaces, and where men dominate the larger-sized firms. In personal/business services and in education/health services women are also disproportionately found in small workplaces, although the trend is not so pronounced. However, in other industries the differ-

TABLE 3
Distribution of workers by size of firm, by sex, by industry, 1989 (percentage)

	0–19		20–99		100–499		500+	
	Women	Men	Women	Men	Women	Men	Women	Men
Public administration	14.8	10.7	14.2	17.5	11.9	16.2	59.1	55.6
Education/health/ welfare services	20.1	12.6	18.1	18.1	21.3	23.8	40.4	45.5
Transportation/ communication/ utilities	15.8	15.1	9.9	15.0	9.2	13.5	65.5	56.4
Manufacturing	16.8	12.0	28.4	21.5	22.7	23.1	32.1	43.3
Trade	41.7	37.3	17.7	24.2	10.0	12.6	30.5	25.9
Finance	23.6	20.0	15.7	18.0	9.3	12.2	51.3	49.7
Personal/business services	48.5	36.5	25.4	27.0	10.6	14.6	15.4	21.9
Non-agricultural primary	31.8	25.1	17.4	20.9	15.3	12.8	35.5	41.2
Construction	59.6	52.1	23.5	27.2	8.8	10.4	8.1	9.9
Agriculture	73.7	75.8	16.2	11.0	7.5	8.6	2.6	4.5
All industries	30.8	25.3	20.0	21.7	14.6	16.5	34.7	36.5

ences by sex in terms of size of firm are either negligible or inconsistent. (See table 3.)

Looking at all industries combined, there is overall a significant difference in the proportion of men and women only in the smallest workplaces, with fewer than twenty workers. In these firms are employed almost 31 per cent of women workers, compared with 25 per cent of men. This difference would have a negative impact on the rate of unionization among women, since only 13 per cent of workers in these firms are organized. However, it is also true that slightly more men than women are employed in workplaces of 20–99 workers, which have rate of unionization of 32 per cent, somewhat below the average. In the larger firms there are slightly more men than women, but the differences are very small (table 2).

PART-TIME AND PART-YEAR WORK

Part-time and temporary workers are harder to organize than full-time permanent employees, because it is often more difficult to identify them and make contact given their work schedules, and because of their increased vulnerability to intimidation and employer opposition, since these workers often have less job security than full-time workers. In Ontario the practice of separating full- and part-time workers into separate bargaining units has not helped the process of organizing part-time workers, and in several civil-service jurisdictions casual workers are prohibited from joining unions.

The LMAS data allows us to examine the rates of unionization for both part-time and part-year workers. Part-time workers are employed for less than thirty hours per week, while part-year workers are employed full-time but for less than twelve months (see the appendix for fuller definitions). While the overall proportion of workers who belong to unions is 38 per cent, the rate falls to only 27 per cent among part-time workers and to 21 per cent among workers employed part-year. For part-time workers who also worked less than twelve months, the rate of unionization drops drastically to just 12 per cent.

These non-standard types of employment form a major segment of the labour market. Nineteen per cent of all workers are employed part-time and a further 10 per cent are employed full-time but only for part of the year. Thus, the total number of workers in these non-standard types of jobs, and therefore with low rates of unionization, constitutes 30 per cent of all workers. Almost one out of every three workers in 1989 was employed part-time or part-year.

As table 4 shows, there is a heavy concentration of part-time work in personal/business services, trade, and education/health services. Part-year work is more evenly distributed, although again personal/business services has a relatively high per centage. In fact it is the primary, construction, and agriculture sectors which have very high percentages of part-year workers (23 to 31 per cent), to be expected given the seasonal nature of these three industries.

When both part-time and part-year work are combined, the results are more startling. Personal/business services has a remarkable 44 per cent of its workers in these non-standard types of employment. Trade is not far behind at 37 per cent. Certainly these high rates of part-time and part-year employment help to account for the low rates of unionization in these two industries. However, the finance industry again proves to be an exception, with a low rate of unionization and also a below-average level of non-standard jobs (19 per cent). It is

TABLE 4

Percentage of workers employed part-time and part-year, by sex, by industry, 1989

Industry	Part-time workers	Part-year workers	Part-time and part-year workers	Women, part-time and part-year	Men, part-time and part-year
Public administration	10.1	9.4	19.5	25.0	15.3
Education/health/ welfare services	28.4	3.9	32.3	37.0	19.7
Transportation/ communication/ utilities	12.0	7.2	19.2	25.0	16.9
Manufacturing	5.2	9.2	14.3	21.6	11.4
Trade	27.8	8.8	36.6	47.2	26.5
Finance	14.1	4.9	19.0	21.4	14.1
Personal/business services	30.3	13.4	43.7	47.6	38.2
Non-agricultural primary	5.4	23.3	28.7	47.7	25.2
Construction	8.9	27.5	36.4	45.8	35.0
Agriculture	22.3	31.4	53.7	56.8	51.7
All industries	19.2	10.3	29.5	37.3	22.6

perhaps surprising to find that education/health services also has a high proportion of non-standard employment at 32 per cent of its workforce, despite its high rate of unionization.

How do these non-standard types of employment affect women? The low rate of unionization among part-time workers is important, because 70 per cent of part-time workers are women. The lack of unionization of part-time workers therefore helps to explain the lower rate of unionization among women. However, this relationship does not hold for part-year workers, who are more often men than women. Nine per cent of women are employed part-year, compared with 12 per cent of men. As noted above, there is a concentration of part-year work in the seasonal work of agriculture, other primary industries, and construction, all male-dominated sectors.

However, when both part-time and part-year workers are combined, the larger number of part-time workers and the very heavy concentration of women in part-time work produces a concentration of women in these non-standard jobs overall. Thirty-seven per cent of women hold either part-time or part-year jobs, compared with 23 per cent of men.

Does the presence of part-year and part-time workers help to explain some of the differential in rates of unionization between men and women within industries? As table 4 shows, in all industrial sectors women more often hold part-year and part-time jobs than do men, so this difference would have an impact on women's lower rate of unionization in every sector. In two industries there is a particularly strong concentration of women into non-standard jobs. In trade 47 per cent of women are employed part-time or part-year compared with only 27 per cent of men, and in education/health services the figure is 37 per cent of women compared with 20 per cent of men.

To summarize this section, part-time and part-year employment is found in all industries, although especially in personal/business services, trade, and education/health services. Women are disproportionately represented in these non-standard types of employment, and are more often concentrated into these jobs in all industries. As with small workplaces, non-standard employment poses a real challenge to the union movement. While there are legal and strategic reasons why it is more difficult to unionize part-time and part-year workers, none the less they form close to one-third of all paid workers.

CLERICAL WORKERS AND UNIONIZATION

Another possible explanation for the different rates of unionization by sex is that within industries men and women occupy different occupational groups. It is particularly important to consider clerical work in some detail, since almost one-third (32 per cent) of all women in paid jobs are clerical workers, compared with only 7 per cent of men. There are two-and-one-quarter million clerical workers and 80 per cent of them are women. If unions are unable or unwilling to organize clerical workers within an industry, even where other workers are unionized, this will have a negative impact upon the rate of unionization among women.

Clerical work cuts right across industrial categories, since clerical workers are found in all industrial sectors. The LMAS data allows us to look at clerical workers, broken down by different industries. (See table 5.)

TABLE 5
Rate of unionization of clerical workers, by industry, 1989 (percentage)

Industry	Overall rate of unionization	Rate of unionization of clerical workers
Public administration	70.4	72.0
Education/health/welfare services	66.9	47.9
Transportation/ communication/utilities	60.2	68.5
Manufacturing	45.3	26.2
Trade	15.2	18.8
Finance	12.4	14.2
Personal/business services	11.5	11.7
Non-agricultural primary	34.8	14.6
Construction	34.3	10.3
Agriculture	10.6	2.0
All industries	37.9	31.8

In the three industries where the overall rates of unionization are low (trade, personal/business service, and finance), it is not surprising to find that the same is true for clerical workers within those industries. There is little distinction between clerical and other workers, since the rate of unionization for all is very low.

In the four industries with relatively high levels of unionization, the situation varies. The transportation industry is unusual because clerical jobs are more highly organized than the industry in general (69 per cent compared with 60 per cent). This is probably due to the high rate of unionization among communication workers, particularly postal workers, who are included in this data as clerical workers. In public administration, unionization of clerical workers is also slightly higher than that of other workers, attributable to the high level of unionization among clerical workers employed by the federal and provincial governments.

However, in the other predominantly public-sector industry, education/health services, unionization of clerical workers is only 48 per cent, compared with 67 per cent for the sector overall. In manufacturing, the unionization of clerical workers is also much lower than the general rate of unionization, with only 26 per cent of clerical workers organized, compared with the overall rate of 45 per cent. The lack of unionization among clerical workers would help to explain the lower rate of unionization of women than men in these two industries.

EMPLOYER OPPOSITION

Unionization normally entails more leverage for workers in obtaining improved pay and conditions of work, more control and more protection in the workplace. Employers therefore have every reason to oppose organizing campaigns, particularly in industrial sectors that are generally non-unionized. In the 1930s and 1940s employers in manufacturing and mines staunchly refused to recognize industrial unions, and the resulting disruptions ultimately produced legislation to regulate labour relations. More recently, the successful opposition of employers in the finance and trade industries has been well documented. The banks in particular have demonstrated their ability to avoid unionization, being powerful organizations with huge resources, an unshakeable ideological opposition, and a readiness to violate the law as necessary.[10]

There is a clear difference with regard to employer opposition between the private and public sectors. In the public sector the opposition has been less virulent, in part because governments are more constrained to obey the law. While many restrictions are placed upon the rights of public-sector workers, basic certification has been far easier to obtain in the public sector than in many private-sector industries.

Obtaining information on the rate of unionization by public/private sector is somewhat difficult, because it cuts across the regularly tabulated industries. However, for 1986 the calculations were made from the LMAS data. In that year the overall rate of unionization was 34 per cent. However, the difference between the private and public sectors was dramatic – unionization in the private sector was only 26 per cent, while in the public sector over 71 per cent of jobs were unionized.

Employer opposition is often most effective in small workplaces where workers are placed in a close relationship to management and it is more difficult to resist intimidation. Likewise part-time and part-year workers are particularly vulnerable when they do not have any security of employment. These factors combine to create an effective barrier to organizing efforts.

In the current economic context, employers are stressing the necessity of controlling labour costs to meet international competition, and are moving to increase their use of various forms of cheap labour, including women, part-time, and casual workers. Opposition is intense to any attempts to improve the pay and conditions of the lowest-paid workers, whether by unionization or by legislation. In Ontario, employer resistance to equal-pay legislation in the private sector was intense,[11] and the business reactions to suggested changes in labour-relations legislation have been remarkably virulent.

CONCLUSION

It is apparent from the above analysis that size of workplace, part-year and part-time work, and employer opposition have a critical effect, both upon the rate of unionization in general and upon the rate of unionization among women in particular. The combined impact is dramatic. While 38 per cent of all jobs were unionized in 1989, the rate of unionization for full-time, full-year jobs in the largest workplaces of over 500 workers stood at 62 per cent. However, it is clear that these patterns vary from one industry to another, and it is important to analyse the situation by industrial sector in order to understand the rates of unionization both generally and for women.

Attempts to organize in personal/business services and trade will continue to be hampered by the large percentage of non-standard work and small work-places in those industries. The negative impact of these factors in these two industries is particularly important, given that between them they employ over one-third of all workers (34 per cent), and 40 per cent of all women workers.

The third industry that is virtually non-unionized is the smaller finance industry, where just over 5 per cent of all workers are employed. The evidence in this paper suggests that we need to look again at the finance industry, given that the majority of jobs are in large workplaces of more than 500 workers and that the workers are primarily full-time and full-year. Moreover, women in finance are not particularly concentrated into either non-standard work or small workplaces.

In the traditionally male-dominated and relatively well-organized manufacturing industry, there remain significant numbers of workers employed in small workplaces and on a part-time and part-year basis. Women are particularly negatively affected because of their disproportionate presence in these small workplaces and non-standard forms of employment. As well, clerical jobs are predominantly non-union, to the detriment of unionization among women in this industry.

In the so-called saturated public-sector industries, non-unionized workers replicate the characteristics of the less-organized industries. Education/health services gives particular cause for concern, since it provides employment for a much larger percentage of the workforce than does public administration (17 compared with 8 per cent), and over one-quarter of all women workers are employed in this sector. Although the unionization rate is 67 per cent, there are still 693,000 unorganized workers in that industry, more than in the poorly organized finance industry. In this industry, women's jobs are disproportionately part-year and part-time, more women than men work in small workplaces, and clerical workers are relatively poorly organized. Of the unorganized workers in education/health services, 60 per cent are in workplaces with fewer than 100 workers, 42 per cent are part-time or part-year workers, and 77 per cent are women.

Theoretically of course, none of the factors outlined in this paper should have an impact upon the fundamental right of workers to join a union, a right supposedly guaranteed under the law. However, the certification procedure based on individual workplaces, the legal restrictions and delays, and the violations by employers all contribute to withholding the protection of union membership.

The union movement in Canada desperately needs what has been called a 'fourth wave' of unionization. Craft workers began unionizing in the 1800s, industrial workers in the goods-producing sectors organized primarily in the 1930s and 1940s, and public-sector workers followed suit in the 1960s and early 1970s. Now there has to be organizing in the private service-producing sectors with traditionally low rates of unionization, as well as increased attention to the non-unionized in other industries.

[margin annotation: waves of unionization.]

Other contributors to this collection discuss the changes necessary to achieve this new wave of organization. In particular, Judy Fudge analyses the need for a fundamentally different legal framework that would permit bargaining among groupings of small workplaces by sector or by region, and the challenges this poses to the union movement. Changes will be required not only in legislation, but also in the union movement itself. Pat Armstrong discusses the need for union methods and organization based upon the particular relations and conditions of women's work, suggesting that strategies derived from the industrial-union model have not always served the interests of groups such as nurses. Pat McDermott describes the differences in picket-line activity between construction workers and women sales clerks at Eaton's.

The union movement is certainly aware of the need to respond to the new conditions. The loss in union membership in the early 1980s and the dismal rate of unionization south of the border have galvanized some unions into a renewed focus upon organizing the unorganized. More part-time workers have been organized in recent years,[12] some unions have undertaken internal structural assessments and mergers, and increasingly the union movement is responding to the needs of women, immigrants, and workers of colour. The success of these and future changes in maintaining a healthy and vibrant union movement in Canada remains to be seen.

NOTES

1 This article is based upon material obtained for Julie White, *Sisters and Solidarity: Women and Unions in Canada* (Toronto: Thompson Educational Publishing 1993).

2 Statistics Canada, 'Corporations and Labour Unions Returns Act, Part II – Labour Unions,' Cat: 71-202 (Ottawa 1966–89). All data in this introductory section is drawn from this source, although information on the proportion of paid workers unionized is unpublished for earlier years.

3 Bank Book Collective, *An Account to Settle: The Story of the United Bank Workers (SORWUC)* (Vancouver: Press Gang Publishers 1979); Rosemary Warskett, 'Bank Worker Unionization and the Law,' *Studies in Political Economy* 25 (Spring 1988); Anne Forrest, 'Organizing Eaton's: Do the Old Laws Still Work?' *Windsor Yearbook of Access to Justice* 8 (1988)

4 J. Myles, G. Picot, and T. Wannell, 'Wages and Jobs in the 1980s: Changing Youth Wages and the Declining Middle,' Statistics Canada Labour Market Activity Survey Analytical Studies (July 1988), 35

5 Myles et al. 2

6 Economic Council of Canada, 'Good Jobs, Bad Jobs: Employment in the Service Economy' (Ottawa 1990)

7 Economic Council of Canada 12

8 The CALURA data used in the introduction (see note 2) shows 29 per cent of women and 38 per cent of men belonging to unions. The LMAS figures for the same year are 34 per cent and 41 per cent respectively.

The CALURA data is used in the introduction because the LMAS is too recent to allow for historical analysis.

9 Julie White, *Women and Unions* (Ottawa: Canadian Advisory Council on the Status of Women 1980), 46–50
10 White 45; Bank Book Collective; Warskett
11 Carl Cuneo, *Pay Equity: The Labour-Feminist Challenge* (Toronto: Oxford University Press 1990)
12 Heather A. Clemenson, 'Unionization and Women in the Service Sector,' Statistics Canada *Perspectives* (Autumn 1989), 35

APPENDIX: THE LABOUR MARKET ACTIVITY SURVEY

Since 1986 Statistics Canada has carried out the Labour Market Activity Survey (LMAS). A questionnaire is attached to the monthly Labour Force Survey in January of each year, and obtains information on all the jobs held by a respondent in the previous year. It asks whether the job was unionized or non-unionized, and this information can be analysed by detailed industrial and occupational categories, by sex, by size of firm, and by part-time and full-time work, among many other factors. It provides material for a far more detailed analysis of unionization by sex than information previously available through the Corporations and Labour Unions Returns Act (CALURA).

For the purposes of this paper, the most recent data available was for 1989, and was selected on the basis of the last job held by each worker in the year. For people working in December that job would be included; for people who had stopped working prior to December, but had worked during the year, the most recent previous job would be included. Thus, only one job for each worker is included, and yet the scope of the data is broader than the snapshot of one month provided by the Monthly Labour Force Survey, which includes only workers employed in that month.

Part-time workers are defined in the standard way for Statistics Canada as workers employed for less than thirty hours per week. Included here are workers employed part-time on both a full- or part-year basis.

'Part-year workers' refers to workers who were employed full-time but whose jobs lasted for less than twelve months, either because the job both started and ended in 1989, or because the job ended in 1989 but had not lasted a full twelve months. This is not necessarily a sample of only casual or temporary work, because it includes workers who may have quit or been fired from jobs that were ostensibly permanent positions. However, it is a much closer approximation to looking at temporary employment than any other data available.

Owing to space limitations three industrial sectors are included in the tables but excluded from the detailed textual analysis – construction, agriculture, and non-agricultural primary. All three have unique patterns of unionization for structural, legal, and historical reasons, and all three of these industries together included only 3.5 per cent of all employed women in 1989.

10

Collective Bargaining and Women's Workplace Concerns

PRADEEP KUMAR

The serious labour-market plight of working women is a major challenge facing the Canadian labour movement. Economic and social equity, inside and outside the workplace, is labour's vision and goal.[1] Trade unions, throughout their history, have fought for equality for women and other disadvantaged groups through both the legislative and collective-bargaining processes. However, while significant progress has been made in both the legislative and collective-bargaining spheres, marked inequalities in income and employment opportunities based on gender still persist. The working environment for women remains insecure and stressful, characterized by frequent harassment and violence, insufficient protection against discrimination and unsafe work, and inadequate provisions for child care, family-related leaves, and flexible work schedules. There appears to be a widespread consensus within the Canadian labour movement that unions need to escalate their efforts towards labour-market equality, safe and harassment-free work environments, and policies and practices to make it easier for women to balance more effectively their work and family life.[2] The suggested program of action includes legislative and political action, a high priority for issues of concern to women in collective-bargaining negotiations, and the increased participation and representation of women in unions to ensure a gender perspective, paying specific attention to the needs and situation of women, in all union decision-making processes. Unions in Canada are also beginning to realize that the historical reliance on protective legislation is not enough, and that collective bargaining is a more effective tool for achieving economic and social equality at the workplace and for improving the work environment.

This paper examines (1) Canadian unions' collective-bargaining agenda to meet women's workplace concerns and (2) the provisions in major collective agreements relating to key issues of specific concern to women, and the extent to which these provisions exceed legislative norms of equality and/or assist women in effectively enjoying their legal rights. The purpose of this examination is to review the gains made for women through collective bargaining and to discuss the future potential of the collective-bargaining institution to meet women's workplace concerns and expectations. The analysis underscores the importance of a fuller involvement of women in the union decision-making processes through changes in union structures to empower women, that is, to facilitate their participation in the collective-bargaining process and strengthen women's presence and influence within the union.

The paper is organized into three sections. The first describes the unions' collective-bargaining agenda, based on the bargaining goals and priorities of major unions and independent associations of nurses and teachers. These include four major public-sector unions – the Canadian Union of Public Employees, the National Union of Public and General Employees, the Public Service Alliance of Canada, and the Service Employees International Union; four large private-sector unions – the United Food and Commercial Workers, the Canadian Auto Workers, the United Steel Workers of America, and the Communications and Electrical Workers of Canada;[3] and associations/unions of teachers and nurses. The eight unions, all affiliated with Canada's major labour federation, the Canadian Labour Congress, and the two groups of independent professional associations account for almost one-half of the total union membership and over 70 per cent of all women union members in Canada. Their collective bargaining agenda and programs of action, therefore, are representative of union efforts on behalf of women. The second section examines the outcomes of collective-bargaining to assess the relative success of union efforts in incorporating women's concerns into collective agreements, in particular their efforts to strengthen legislative norms of equality. The final section summarizes the gains made by women through collective bargaining, and discusses the importance of fully integrating women in union decision-making structures to make collective bargaining an effective tool for meeting women's workplace concerns.

UNION BARGAINING GOALS AND AGENDA

A review of the policy statements of the Canadian Labour Congress and the major public- and private-sector unions, as well as associations' policies and programs,[4] indicate that the persistent labour-market inequities and related social and workplace problems facing working women are high on the Canadian labour movement's priority list for collective bargaining. Key issues of universal concern relate to unequal access the to labour market, work environment, and work arrangements including pay- and employment-equity mechanisms, part-time worker rights, child-care facilities, maternity and paternity leaves and related provisions for coping with conflicting demands of paid work and family responsibilities, violence against women and workplace harassment, and job security and health-and-safety protection against the growing diffusion of new technology. The review of union literature also suggests that while most unions believe that collective bargaining is 'one of the fundamental and most effective tools for creating equality,' and that 'collective bargaining must not only conform with equality legislation but it must clearly lead the law,' they also emphasize that collective bargaining is only a limited-purpose institution, particularly in the context of Canada's adversarial industrial-relations system. The practice of collective bargaining is based on the multiple interests of different groups where the pursuit of the goals of one group is made difficult by the interests of other groups. Since 'collective bargaining is, by definition, an institution designed to achieve a balance among a number of conflicting goals' and interests,[5] a potential gap between union bargaining objectives and the actual collective-bargaining outcomes is inevitable. Improvements in wages and benefits traditionally take precedence over changes in work environment. The attainment of the goals of a group of workers also depends on their political influence within the union. Because of the low participation of women in the negotiating process it is not surprising that, in many workplaces, 'women's issues are still the first to be dropped at the bargaining table.'[6] The effectiveness of collective bargaining on women's issues is further hindered by employers' inability to accept women's realities, and their reluctance to fully accept unions and collective bargaining as legitimate institutions. Unions in their agenda, therefore, emphasize that collective bargaining on women's issues needs to be supplemented by progressive changes in labour and social legislation, education programs, and political action to build women's presence and influence in unions and workplaces.

The collective-bargaining agenda of individual unions varies depending on their industry jurisdiction, their growth strategy, the gender composition of their rank and file, the nature of the employers they bargain with, the decision-making mechanisms, and the degree of women's presence in the union leadership and staff. The emphasis on particular issues also differs markedly. For example, public-sector unions with a predominantly white-collar female membership have placed a heavy emphasis on pay- and employment-equity measures, provisions to deal with sexual harassment, advance notice and consultation on technological change, protection against the health-and-safety hazards of prolonged working on video display terminals (VDTs), and family-related leaves. Private-sector unions, whose membership and leadership is largely male, have been slow to pursue women's issues and have focused mainly on work-environment improvements. They have treated equality as a social and economic goal rather than as a gender issue. Their recent focus on employment equity, harassment, and work and family issues follows the decline of membership in traditional jurisdictions and the expanding potential of union organization among women. The bargaining priorities of professional associations, by contrast, have traditionally included professional-development issues and job-security concerns. Their emphasis on employment equity, extended maternity, paternity, and family-related leaves, prorated benefits for part-time workers, and more recently a healthy and safe working environment free from harassment is a product of a changing work environment in the education and health areas.

A greater part of the collective-bargaining agenda of unions in Canada seeks to strengthen and, wherever possible, expand upon legislative protection and norms of equality. Collective-bargaining provisions are also meant to provide women with more cost-effective and speedy means of using their legal rights and benefits. Canada has an extensive array of protective labour-market and social legislation dealing with issues of concern to women.[7] Equality rights, including the promotion of affirmative-action programs, are also protected by the Canadian constitution.[8] Unions in their policy statements and programs of action contend that the legislative protections are inadequate, in some cases non-existent, and need to be expanded through collective-agreement provisions. For example, to date employment equity is only legislated in the federal jurisdiction. Moreover, the federal legislation only requires the reporting of workforce data and the achievement of goals, and does not provide effective penalties or sanctions against inaction. Pay-equity legislation does not cover private-sector workers except in Ontario, and many groups (such as child-care workers) are not covered where comparisons cannot be made in the absence of male-dominated jobs. There is very little legal protection against technological change. Only four jurisdictions (federal, Manitoba, Saskatchewan, and British Columbia) provide for advance notice of change. However, legal provisions are generally quite weak. The length of notice required is often short, and the legislation includes a number of 'opting-out' provisions.[9] The legislation also does not afford sufficient protection against health-and-safety hazards related to prolonged work on video display terminals. While there are legislated standards for maternity, paternity, and adoption leave, and partial earnings replacement is available through unemployment-insurance programs, family-responsibility leaves are not mandated in any jurisdiction except Quebec.[10] Similarly, while harassment is banned in all jurisdictions, human-rights violations are, generally, treated on the basis of complaints and the resolution processes are protracted and expensive.[11] Worker security, pay and employment equity, and family-related leaves are, therefore, a collective-bargaining priority for most unions. Unions believe that improvements in work environment and employment opportunities are more effective when programs are designed, implemented, monitored, and assessed jointly by unions and management.

Almost all unions in Canada have policy statements and a collective-bargaining agenda on women's workplace concerns. A number of public- and private-sector unions have set up women's conferences and committees to formulate a gender perspective on collective-bargaining goals and strategies and to guide the union in furthering the status of women inside and outside the workplace. Of the eight public- and private-sector unions studied, the two public-sector ones – the Canadian Union of Public Employees (CUPE) and the National Union of Public and General Employees (NUPGE) – appear to have the most detailed policies and programs of action on women's issues. CUPE, the largest union in Canada with a total membership of over 400,000 of whom 52 per cent are women, has a comprehensive strategy and program of action on legislative reforms, collective bargaining, and educational courses. Programs are coordinated by the Department of Equal Opportunities set up by the National Executive Board in 1987. The program formulation and policy implementation is guided by the National Women's Taskforce, established in 1979 by a convention resolution, and a network of women's/equal-opportunities committees at the local level. The union's legislative and collective-bargaining strategies are included in its *Equal Opportunities Policy Statements*, a binder on equal-opportunities resolutions, various information kits on major issues (such as sexual harassment, part-time work, job sharing, parental leave), pamphlets (for instance, on affirmative action and pay-equity myths), proceedings of the National Women's Conference, and *The Facts*, a bi-monthly union publication.

The National Union of Public and General Employees,[12] the second-largest union in Canada with a membership of over 300,000, of whom 56 per cent are women, similarly has an integrated and well-defined strategy, programs, and policies on equality issues pertaining to women, including model agreement clauses and an affirmative-action policy to enhance women's presence in union structures and activities. The NUPGE pamphlet *Bargaining for Equality*, first published in 1982, is the most popular and widely used guide to negotiating contract clauses on equality issues in both the public and private sectors. The guide includes a discussion of collective-bargaining strategies, the rationale for key contract clauses of interest to women workers, and examples of representative agreement provisions. The booklet advocates collective-agreement clauses on (1) paid time-off to attend union meetings, in view of the dual role of women as workers and home-makers; (2) protection against discrimination through a no-discrimination clause to reinforce existing human-rights legislation and to allow pursual of human-rights violations through the grievance/arbitration process; (3) retention of seniority for women on maternity leave; (4) flexible hours of work; (5) leave of absence for illness within a family or for medical and dental appointments, marriage, divorce, and domestic emergency; (6) maternity, adoption, and paternity leave, with provision for 'topping up' of benefits provided under unemployment-insurance legislation; (7) employer-subsidized child care facilities; (8) sexual harassment, preferably a separate clause with specific procedures for investigation and resolution; (9) technological-change impacts on jobs and workplace health and safety, including protection from the ergonomic hazards and possible radiation effects of video display terminals, particularly on pregnant employees; (10) equal pay for work of equal value, with provisions for union participation in the formulation and implementation of job evaluation systems; (11) affirmative-action or employment-equity programs to remove systemic barriers to equality and improve the economic status of women and other disadvantaged groups; (12) prorated wages and benefits for part-time workers.

While CUPE and NUPGE have an integrated collective-bargaining strategy and program of action, unions such as the United Food and Commercial Workers, Canadian Auto Workers, and United Steelworkers have been focusing on selected issues of concern to women. For example, the United Food and Commercial Workers, the largest private-sector union in Canada with a membership of nearly 180,000, of whom 47 per cent are women, has recently formulated a strategy emphasizing legislation, negotiations, and education on the 'challenges of coping with family, work and union responsibilities.' The union's bargaining agenda includes employer-subsidized child-care facilities, maternity and parental leave, leave for family responsibilities, caring for elderly or disabled relatives, reduced work week with full pay, variable work arrangements, easing the problems of injured workers in family life, coping with stress, protection of social programs, and awareness of changing family roles.

The Canadian Auto Workers Union (CAW), with a membership of over 173,000, of whom 20 per cent are women, has emphasized employment-equity and work-environment issues in its collective-bargaining pursuits. With a growing women's membership, the union collective-bargaining agenda on women's issues has expanded in the past few years. The recent CAW convention adopted a comprehensive affirmative-action program which included an integrated program of action on collective bargaining, education, and legislative action on women's issues as well as a policy of 'fair representation and inclusion' of women in union structures and activities. The union prides itself on its achievements at the collective-bargaining table in the areas of child care and employment equity. It was the first union in the private sector to negotiate subsidized child care in 1984 with the Big Three auto makers (General Motors, Ford, and Chrysler) and secure funds to build an on-site child care centre in Windsor, Ontario. The union has also negotiated no-discrimination clauses, human-rights training, and employment-equity provisions with the auto makers. Its employment-equity program at General Motors won an award from the Ontario government in 1987 for its ground-breaking work and for recognizing the need to ensure fair and equitable treatment for employees. The union also has an extensive education program to train women activists and stewards.

The United Steelworkers of America, with a membership of over 160,000, of whom 13 per cent are women, has similarly placed work-environment issues, including sexual and racial harassment and employment equity,[13] high on its collective-bargaining and educational agenda. District 6 of the United Steelworkers has been particularly active in developing collective-bargaining demands and contract language on equity, harassment, and work/family-related issues, promoting the formulation of women's committees at the local union level, and in conducting educational programs to enhance women's leadership, communication and collective-bargaining skills. The Working Together and Women of Steel development courses, recently introduced by the District to 'help women break through some of the barriers' are examples of the union's recent proactive initiatives on women's issues. These initiatives, according to the union, are helping women to acquire skills to address issues of equality, negotiate issues of concern to women, and change union structures that have inhibited participation of women in the collective-bargaining process. The union is also encouraging the establishment of joint labour-management committees at the plant level to look at issues of restructuring and training that include employment-equity goals. Usually, these kinds of committees meet outside of collective bargaining, incorporating any letters of understanding or schedules into the collective agreement.'[14]

The nurses' and teachers' unions have also become active on harassment-free-environment and employment-equity issues, pursuing them at the collective-bargaining table. The two groups account for nearly 377,000 women union members, nearly one-quarter of the total female union membership in Canada. The Canadian Teachers' Federation (CTF),[15] a national organization of thirteen provincial and territorial teachers' associations with a total membership of about 230,000, has formulated policies dealing with discrimination and gender stereotyping, affirmative action, equal access to opportunities, child care, sexual harassment, pornography, and parental leave. The collective-bargaining agendas of the Federation of Women Teachers' Associations of Ontario (35,500 members), incorporated in its model collective agreement, and of the Ontario Secondary School Teachers' Federation are examples of the growing sensitivity of teachers unions to women's problems. Among the issues identified by the Federation of Women Teachers' Association are class size, preparation time, the use of seniority in redundancy and lay-off decisions and its accrual during maternity and extended parental leave, the rights of part-time teachers, and affirmative action. Similarly, the Ontario Secondary School Teachers' Federation has adopted statements on affirmative action, sexual harassment, and the probationary and contract employment of teachers for the purposes of collective bargaining.

Although their primary focus is still professional development and related issues, nurses' unions and associations have become aggressive in negotiating matters relating to pay and employment equity, pensions, part-time workers' rights, family-related leaves and a harassment-free work environment. For example, the Ontario Nurses' Association (ONA), with a predominantly female membership of over 52,000, has recently adopted a statement on workplace harassment which states that 'it is the right of all of its members to work in a healthy and safe work environment free from harassment, and it is the responsibility of management to ensure that workplace is free from harassment.' Almost all ONA collective agreements include a no-discrimination clause to facilitate the filing of grievances relating to harassment. The association has also successfully negotiated paid maternity leave including retention of seniority during the leave period, personal leave, and the right to refuse work on VDTs.[16] Similarly, the British Columbia Nurses' Union (membership 21,000) has actively pursued women's concerns through a collective-bargaining agenda that includes demands for work-site-child care facilities, employee assistance programs, leaves for family illness, effective occupational health-and-safety standards and their joint monitoring, and policies to address workplace violence and harassment. The Federation of Quebec Nurses, the largest organized women's group in Quebec with a membership of over 41,500 women, is advancing at the collective-bargaining table such women's concerns as workplace violence, sexual and racial harassment, and programs and policies to better balance work and family lives. The union has recently negotiated a comprehensive contract with the Quebec Hospital Association providing for expanded maternity, paternity, and other family-related leave provisions.

The preceding analysis of the bargaining goals and priorities of major Canadian unions and associations suggests that unions in Canada are becoming increasingly sensitive to women's workplace concerns. The growing awareness of women's serious labour-market plight is partly a defensive response to the increasing disenchantment with union policies and programs.[17] The increased attention to women's issues also reflects Canadian unions' proactive strategy to reassess their bargaining priorities and organizational structures, and to look beyond traditional methods and approaches to consider more effective ways to enhance their appeal to a large pool of unorganized women workers and to provide better services to members.

COLLECTIVE-AGREEMENT PROVISIONS ON KEY WOMEN'S ISSUES

Table 1 (pages 218–19) provides an empirical perspective on the frequency of collective-agreement provisions on key issues of concern to women. The figures are a rough measure of the success of union efforts at the collective-bargaining table. Two categories of issues are highlighted; one relating to a healthy, secure, and safe working environment and the other pertaining to equal rights and benefits afforded to women workers. Among the key work-environment-related issues are discrimination, sexual harassment, the right to refuse unsafe work, health-and-safety aspects of video display terminals, contracting-out restriction protections against technological change, and flexibility in hours of work. Equal rights and benefits cover equal pay for work of equal value, participation in job evaluation, part-time worker-rights, affirmative-action programs, family-related leaves, seniority retention during maternity leave, day-care facilities and opportunities for training, work sharing, and job sharing. The analysis applies to all agreements covering five hundred or more employees 'in-force' as of January 1991. The national database, maintained by Labour Canada, consists of 1002 collective agreements covering over two million employees, almost one-half of all workers in Canada covered by collective agreements.

It is important to note the major limitations of the data in table 1. First, they only cover 'major' agreements and exclude small labour contracts covering fewer than five hundred workers. Since a majority of women work in small and medium-sized establishments, data may not provide a true perspective on collective-bargaining gains made for women. The exclusion of bargaining units of fewer than five hundred workers may also overstate the success of union efforts since large bargaining units tend to exercise greater bargaining power than small units. Second, the analysis is based on the quantity rather than the quality of collective-agreement clauses. This is an important limitation since collective agreement clauses vary markedly in their content. For example, in the case of sexual harassment, while one agreement may simply state that 'the union and employer recognize the right of employees to work in an environment free from harassment,' another may clearly define harassment and provide specific procedures for investigation and resolution.[18] Similarly, employment equity clauses vary considerably. Some simply express the union and management desire to establish an affirmative-action program. Others provide detailed guidelines, timetables and specific measures for recruitment, trainings and communications.[19] Finally, although collective-agreement provisions are a good indicator of the relative success of union efforts on the collective-bargaining table, they do not always reflect how hard unions have fought. The union's ability to negotiate a collective-agreement provision is constrained by the attitudes of employers, among other factors. If an employer categorically rejects proposed contract language, there is usually little that a union can do, short of strike action, to persuade the employer. Even in the case of strike action, the union may have to drop certain contract demands as a compromise to resolve the dispute. There is no systematic information available on how hard unions fight for women's issues on the collective-bargaining table or on how frequently contract proposals of concern to women are withdrawn because of other union priorities or strong employer opposition. Laurell Ritchie,[20] in her analysis of employer responses to collective-bargaining initiatives on women's issues, cites many examples of employer resistance to collective-agreement provisions on such issues as sexual harassment, prorated benefits for part-time workers, protection against technological change, and on-site child-care facilities. Usual employer responses on sexual-harassment clauses include: 'existing statutes (human-rights codes) provide appropriate mechanisms so contract language is unnecessary; there is no need to 'superimpose another procedure'; 'the character of the collective agreement would be destroyed if it became a repository for issues, of human rights, safety, health etc'; the provision 'would impose an unnecessary burden on the administration of the agreement, in terms of cost, complexity and delay.' Similarly, provisions on child care are opposed on the ground that 'costs of on-site child care are prohibitive' or that 'it is a matter of social policy, not employer responsibility.' Ritchie also

TABLE 1

Collective-agreement provisions on issues of concern to women in major collective agreements, 1991

	Collective agreements		Employees covered	
	Number	Percentage	Number (in thousand)	Percentage
Total	1002	100.0	2081.6	100.0
Work-environment related				
Anti-discrimination	512	51.1	1376.1	66.1
Sexual harassment	258	25.7	948.3	45.6
Unsafe work – Right to refuse	181	18.1	280.1	13.5
Work on video display terminals				
Additional rest period	47	4.7	129.8	6.2
Re-assignment to other work	156	15.6	645.6	31.0
Special eye examination	56	5.6	143.4	6.9
Quality of working life	129	12.9	255.8	12.3
Contracting out – Restrictions	400	39.9	927.5	44.6
Flexible hours of work				
Compressed work week	152	15.2	418.6	20.1
Right to vary hours	91	9.1	296.5	14.2
Overtime – Right to refuse	308	30.7	657.2	31.6
Technological-change protection				
Advance notice	530	52.9	1234.1	59.3
Training or retraining	466	46.5	1162.9	55.9
Employment guarantee	108	10.8	247.4	11.9
Equal-rights and benefits related				
Equal pay for work of equal value	74	7.4	393.8	18.9
Participation in job evaluation				
Bipartite	149	14.9	381.6	18.3
Union participation	313	31.2	604.4	29.0
Part-time workers' rights				
Health-and-welfare benefits	238	23.8	757.8	36.4
Holidays	266	26.5	921.7	44.3
Hours-of-work limits	242	24.2	771.1	37.0
Part-time to full-time ratio	14	1.4	39.6	1.9
Pensions	53	5.3	132.6	6.4
Prorated benefits	87	8.7	219.6	10.5
Seniority	281	28.0	842.5	40.5
Severance pay	104	10.4	490.0	23.5
Sick leave	270	26.9	876.2	42.1
Vacation	282	28.1	956.1	46.0

TABLE 1 *(concluded)*

	Collective agreements		Employees covered	
	Number	Percentage	Number (in thousand)	Percentage
Affirmative-action programs	52	5.2	180.0	8.6
Family-related leave – paid				
Adoption leave	138	13.8	538.4	25.9
Illness-in-family leave	270	26.9	686.3	33.0
Marriage leave	195	19.5	798.0	38.3
Maternity leave	374	37.3	1069.8	51.4
Parental leave (extended)	6	0.6	11.7	0.6
Paternity leave (extended)	2	0.2	1.3	0.1
Personal-reasons leave	82	8.2	127.8	6.1
Seniority retention during maternity leave	531	53.0	1293.1	62.1
Childcare facilities	22	2.2	71.1	3.4
Training				
On-the job (fully paid)	274	27.3	745.5	35.8
Outside courses (fully paid)	65	6.5	185.2	8.9
Work sharing	18	1.8	21.1	1.1
Job sharing	66	6.6	103.1	5.0

Source: Labour Canada, Bureau of Labour Information (unpublished)

points out that out that 'employers are usually part of business networks that discourage individual members from breaking new ground that establishes a precedent for others in the same type of enterprise.'

The data in table 1 suggest that, judging by the frequency of collective-agreement clauses, union efforts to achieve labour-market equality for women through collective bargaining have had a mixed success. On work-environment-related issues, figures show that, whereas a majority of employees are covered by clauses relating to no-discrimination on grounds of sex and to advance notice and training or retraining in the event of technological change, the progress on other key issues of concern to women has been slow. Less than one-half of the workers in major agreements are covered by sexual-harassment clauses – a key workplace protection sought by women. Contracting-out restrictions for job security are found in only 40 per cent of agreements affecting less than a million workers, 45 per cent of the total. Health-and-safety protection remains inadequate. Quality-of-work-life provisions (such as joint committees to improve work environment, job rotation programs, and availability of counselling services) are minimal, available in only one out of eight collective agreements. Flexible work schedules are still uncommon; only 14 per cent of the workers have a right to vary hours, only one in five has a compressed work week, and fewer than one in three enjoys the right to refuse overtime.

The progress on equal pay and benefits and related issues has been similarly slow. Collective-agreement provisions on child-care facilities are almost non-existent, found in only 22 of the 1002 agreements and covering only 71,000 workers, 3.4 per cent of the over two million workers in major bargaining units. They are largely in the auto industry and the federal and provincial public services. Only 7 per cent of the agreements, covering 19 per cent of all employees, have equal-pay-for-equal value provisions; however, almost one-half of the agreements do provide for union-management committees and/or explicit union participation in the implementation of job-evaluation systems. Affirmative-action programs have been negotiated in only 5 per cent of the agreements and cover fewer than 10 per cent of the total employees. Equal rights for part-time workers are still elusive for a majority of workers. Fewer than 10 per cent of the agreements provide for prorated benefits, only 27–8 per cent of the contracts have provisions for seniority, sick leave, vacation, and holidays, and barely 5 per cent of the agreements stipulate pension benefits for part-time workers. Only 24 per cent of the agreements provide health-and-welfare benefits and just 10 per cent make provision for severance pay. Only a handful of agreements have limits on the use of part-time employment through set ratios of part-time to full-time workers.

Figures show that work and family-responsibility-related leaves are getting increased attention in collective agreements. A majority of employees in major bargaining units are entitled to paid maternity and paternity leave, providing benefits over and above those available through the unemployment-insurance program. However, only between one-quarter and fewer than one-half of the employees are covered by paid adoption leave, marriage leave, and leave for illness in the family. Only a handful of the agreements make provision for extended parental and paternity leave or leave for personal reasons. Similarly, slightly over one-quarter of all agreements, affecting one-third of the total employees in bargaining units, contain provisions for fully paid on-the-job training, and only 6.5 per cent of the agreements covering fewer than 10 per cent of the employees provide for paid training through outside courses. Work sharing and job sharing are still relatively new programs found in very few agreements; work-sharing provisions exist in only 18 agreements and job sharing is provided in 66 contracts. The two programs cover only about 6 per cent of the total employees in major bargaining units.

The data in table 1 imply that, overall, collective bargaining has been slow to respond to women's issues. Moreover, it appears that collective-bargaining gains have been largely confined to areas where legislative standards have been mandated. Thus, while unions have succeeded in winning clauses against discrimination or for maternity and paternity leaves, they have been unable to make much headway on such key issues of concern to women as child-care facilities, affirmative action, equal rights for part-time workers, and family responsibility leaves – areas where legislation has been either non-existent or limited. The lack of visible success on these issues can be attributed to both employers' resistance, reflecting their inability to accept women's reality in the workplace, and the apparent failure on the part of unions to pursue vigorously the collective-bargaining route to equality. However, it can be argued that since women's issues did not receive widespread attention until recently, and unions have had to work very hard to transform the attitudes of their own members and employers, union achievements have been significant, particularly over the past few years.

A similar analysis of contract provisions of special interest to women workers was undertaken by Laurell Ritchie in 1987, in a paper commissioned for the Institute on Women and Work, City of Toronto.[21] The analysis covered 950 agreements and 2.1 million employees, using the same Labour Canada database. A comparison of her results with the data in table 1 suggests that indeed unions in the past four years have made significant progress on women's issues through collective bargaining. For example, between 1987 and 1991, no-discrimination clauses in major agreements have increased from 376 to 512, with a more than 37 per-cent increase in employee coverage, from 1 million to 1.38 million. The incidence of clauses on sexual harassment has gone up substantially, from 95 (affecting 539,000 employees) to 258 (948,000 employees). Affirmative action clauses have almost quadrupled from 13 to 52, with employee coverage rising from 48,750 to 180,000. Equal-pay-for-work-of-equal-value provisions have more than doubled. Union participation and the contractual right to file grievances on job evaluation or classification systems has similarly increased. Provisions for childcare facilities have risen from 14 to 22, covering almost twice the number of workers in 1991 (71,100) than in 1987 (40,880). There also has been a noticeable increase in collective-agreement clauses on retention of seniority during maternity leave and on rights for part-time workers. Seniority-retention clauses have shown a 45 per cent increase, from 367 to 531, with employee coverage expanding from 888,000 in 1987 to 1.3 million in 1991. Significantly more part-time workers now get health-and-welfare benefits, holidays, sick leave, and severance pay, but there has been very little change in regard to pension entitlement and prorated benefits. Perhaps the most marked progress has been in the area of paid leaves for family-related purposes, particularly with respect to maternity leave, adoption leave, leave for family illness, and paternity leave. However, very little progress is evident on paid extended parental leave and paternity leave. The progress, therefore, has been slow, but significant. An important aspect of the collective-bargaining gains is that they exceed and strengthen legislated standards. As Ritchie has pointed out: 'While in many instances a minority of the approximately 2 million workers covered by the agreements have actually won the provisions referred to, the fact remains that each and every one of the provisions are in excess of what is currently provided for in employment standards and other legislation which unorganized workers must rely upon.'[22]

Her observations are as valid today as they were in 1987. Moreover, the aggregate figures understate the significant achievements made by individual unions in a number of jurisdictions and in large bargaining units. An analysis of current collective-agreement provisions on issues of interest to women by sector, union, jurisdiction, and size of bargaining units showed that the incidence of clauses varies markedly.[23] For example, the public sector is far ahead of the private sector on the frequency of clauses (and the number of employees covered) on equal pay for work of equal value, flexible work schedule and hours, paid family-related leaves, part-time worker rights, job sharing, sexual harassment, affirmative action, no-discrimination clauses incorporating both the human-rights code and one or more prohibited grounds for discrimination, day-care facilities, and health-and-safety protections relating to the use of VDTs. The private-sector contracts have a greater incidence of clauses on the right to refuse overtime, work sharing, contracting-out restrictions, training (both on-the-job and through outside courses), technological-change provisions and quality of work life. Similarly, the analysis revealed that the incidence of clauses on women's issues was much higher in larger bargaining units (consisting of 1000 and more workers) than in smaller units (covering 500–999 workers). The relatively greater success of unions in the public sector and in larger bargaining units appears to be related to different employer attitudes, the higher percentage of women in the public sector, and the significantly greater bargaining strength of unions. The provisions also vary by jurisdiction, with a greater incidence of clauses of special interest to women in multi-provincial agreements, and in Quebec and Ontario.

Differences between unions are equally noteworthy, reflecting varying collective-bargaining priorities on issues of concern to women, bargaining power, and the degree of women's involvement in union structures, activities, and programs. For example, the incidence of collective-agreement clauses and employee coverage on no-discrimination and sexual-harassment clauses is significantly higher in public-sector unions and among nurses and teachers than in private-sector unions. Public-sector union contracts also have a significantly higher frequency of clauses on retention of seniority during maternity leave, flexible working hours, day-care facilities, equal pay for work of equal value and union participation in job-evaluation systems, part-time-worker rights, and family-related leaves. The relatively greater success of public-sector-union efforts is related to the dominant position of women in their membership and in union leadership and staff positions, leading to a greater priority given to women's issues at the collective-bargaining table. The private-sector unions, by contrast, appear to have done better in negotiating quality-of-work-life programs (incorporating joint committees to improve the overall work environment, job rotation, employee assistance and counselling services, or health and recreation facilities), contracting-out restrictions, advance notice and training in the event of technological change, affirmative-action programs, and general and on-the-job training. The growing importance of these clauses in the private sector is related to the increasing emphasis on flexibility and work reorganization. Except for affirmative-action programs, the provisions are of equal benefit to men and women. In light of the fact that women constitute a small percentage of private-sector-union membership, collective-bargaining gains made for women in the area of affirmative action and training are indeed significant. As one union official has noted, 'without the female membership base in many workplaces, negotiation of women's issues is much more difficult.'[24]

CONCLUSIONS

The Canadian labour movement, in recent years, has placed a high priority on collective bargaining for achieving labour-market equality for women and improving their work environment. The new strategy is based on the premise that the historical reliance on the legislative process has not been sufficient. Collective bargaining is viewed as a more effective tool for a fundamental and progressive change, in both leading social and labour-market legislation and ensuring its effective implementation through the incorporation of clauses of special interest to women in collective agreements.

A review of the collective-bargaining agendas of major public and private unions and of independent teachers' and nurses' associations and an analysis of the frequency of collective-agreement provisions on selected issues suggest that while women have made significant gains through the collective-bargaining process in many areas, the progress has been agonizingly slow and varied, in many cases inadequate and unsatisfactory, and at times leading to questions about the seriousness of the unions' commitment to gender issues. Areas of serious concern to women not dealt with adequately through collective bargaining include sexual harassment in the workplace, affirmative action, child-care facilities, equal rights and benefits for part-time workers, training and retraining for job mobility and advancement, and flexible work schedules and leaves for a better balance between work and family responsibilities.

A key reason why collective bargaining has been slow to respond to women's issues is the apparent lack of urgency on the part of many unions to integrate women fully into union decision-making structures, programs, and activities. Women, despite their growing numbers in the workforce and in the union rank and file, have very little presence in union structures[25] and therefore wield only marginal influence on the union decision-making process. They face many obstacles, both external and internal, and structural barriers that limit their participation and involvement.[26]

Women's participation and representation in the union decision-making process is viewed as a key indicator of the unions' commitment to women's concerns. Analyses of women's situation and union attainments in the collective-bargaining and legislative arena, in Canada and abroad, have clearly shown that unions in which women are highly represented are more likely to succeed with corporations and governments in achieving a broad range of equality rights and opportunities and support programs for a better balance between work and family responsibilities.[27] However, despite the increased awareness of the need for a greater involvement of women in union decision-making structures, unions have only paid lip-service to this cause. The conclusion reached by a recent CLC paper, *Empowering Union Women: Toward the Year 2000*, is instructive: 'We need to develop a more women-centered union perspective, a feminist perspective; one which will become part of the dominant outlook for the trade union movement, if we hope to be successful at involving more women and strengthening the labour movement as a whole ... It should not simply mean trying to get more women to participate in the union as it is. Instead, it should mean that by recognizing women's different reality the unions must change and adapt to encourage and assist more women to get involved.'

The CLC paper outlines the progress made through the establishment of women's committees, conferences, equal-opportunity staff, and special positions for women on executive boards. These committees appear to have made significant contributions towards (1) challenging overtly sexist attitudes, (2) a greater awareness of the discrimination women face, (3) improvements at the bargaining table, (4) the involvement of women in unions, and (5) the formulation of a number of important policies. However, as the CLC paper notes, while 'women's committees and conferences have played a vital role in providing a forum for education, discussion and organizing, these forums are rarely integrated into the decision-making structures.' The paper suggests many measures to promote women's union involvement, including measures to overcome women's double day and sexism, and to build leadership, provide paid time for union work, and revise union practices and structures.[28]

There appears to be a growing realization within the Canadian labour movement that a gender perspective through increased women's involvement and representation in the union decision-making process is necessary for the effectiveness of collective bargaining and legislative action on women's issues. The Canadian Labour Congress, various provincial federations of labour and a number of major public- and private-sector unions have recently initiated reviews and assessments of the obstacles facing women and the special measures required to promote and strengthen women's participation in all spheres of union life. Serious questions are being asked about the need to change union practices, structures, and environments to facilitate women's greater participation in union activities. 'Internal equality' has become a high-priority goal of the Canadian labour movement. Many unions and federations have taken important proactive steps to change union policies and structures, and to increase and modify their educational programs to build women's leadership and bargaining skills and to remove the obstacles women face.[29] The efficacy and future potential of collective bargaining as an effective tool for achieving equality for women is dependent on how successful unions are in integrating women fully into union decision-making structures and programs. Increased participation of women in collective-bargaining processes is the only way that women can exploit fully the potential of collective bargaining to achieve equality and ensure a safe, healthy, secure, and productive work environment.

NOTES

The author is grateful to Linda Briskin, Sue Milling, Luise Czernenko, Heather-Jane Robertson, David Boys, Michael Lewis, Kathy Runnings, Rosemary Warskett, Penni Richmond, participants of the York University Research Seminar on 'Women and Unions,' and two anonymous reviewers for their helpful comments and suggestions on an earlier draft of this paper. The author also thanks the research staff members of CUPE, NUPGE, SEIU, PSAC, UFCW, USWA, CAW, CWC, the Canadian Teachers' Federation, the Ontario Nurses' Association, the BC Nurses' Union, and the Quebec Federation of Nurses for providing valuable information, and to David Arrowsmith for his research assistance. The School of Graduate Studies and Research, Queen's University, kindly provided financial assistance for the study.

1 See Canadian Labour Congress, *Social Policy Statement*, adopted at the 19th Constitutional Convention (Ottawa 1992), and *A New Decade: Our Future*, Document no. 14, 19th Constitutional Convention (Ottawa 1990).
2 Canadian Labour Congress, *A New Decade: Our Future* and *Violence Against Women Policy Statement* (Ottawa 1992).
3 The Communications and Electrical Workers of Canada merged in November 1992 with the Energy and Chemical Workers Union and the Canadian Paper Workers Union to form the Communications, Energy and Paper Workers Union. The new union is the fourth-largest private-sector union in Canada, with a membership of 145,000.

4 Canadian Labour Congress, *A New Decade, Social Policy Statement,* and *Violence Against Women Policy Statement;* Canadian Union of Public Employees, *Equal Opportunities Policy Statement* (Ottawa 1991); National Union of Public and General Employees, *Bargaining for Equality* (Ottawa 1982), *Negotiating Employment Equity* (Ottawa 1990), and *Opening the Door to the Future,* Futures Committee Report to the 1990 Convention (Ottawa 1990); Public Service Alliance of Canada, *Collective Bargaining Demands: PSAC–Treasury Board Negotiations 1991* (Ottawa 1991); Service Employees International Union, *Resolutions on Women in the Workforce, Work and Family and Other Issues* (Washington 1991); United Food and Commercial Workers, *Balancing Work and Family Responsibilities* (Toronto 1991); United Steelworkers of America, *Canadian Policy and Bargaining Conference Papers* (Toronto 1992), *Women of Steel Development Course* (Toronto USWA District 6 and Ontario Women's Directorate, July 1991), and *National Policy Conference Papers* (Toronto: USWA District 6 1992); Canadian Auto Workers, *Building Our Union: Solidarity in Diversity: Canadian Auto Workers Affirmative Action Plan* (North York, Ont. 1991) and *A New Decade – Challenging the Corporate Agenda: Our Response,* Report to the National Convention (North York, Ont. 1990); Communications and Electrical Workers of Canada, *Policy Statements on Women Workers* (Ottawa 1991); Canadian Teachers' Federation, *CTF: Its Objectives and Policy* (Ottawa 1990) and *Women and Education* (Ottawa: n.d.); British Columbia Nurses' Union, *Policy Manual* (Burnaby, BC: n.d.); Fédération des Infirmières et des Infirmiers du Québec, *Themes: Document for Consultation,* 2nd Biennial Congress (Montreal 1991); Federation of Women Teachers Association of Ontario, *Bargaining for Women in the 1990s* (Toronto: n.d.); Ontario Nurses' Association, *Statement on Problems in the Workplace* (Toronto 1991); Ontario Secondary School Teachers' Federation, *Handbook: 1989–90* (Toronto 1989).
5 Thomas A. Kochan and Harry Katz, *Collective Bargaining and Industrial Relations,* 2nd ed. (Homewood, Ill.: Irwin 1988), 6–10
6 Ontario Federation of Labour, *Taking Stock and Moving Forward: Union Women in the 1990s* (Toronto 1990), 28
7 See Pradeep Kumar, Mary Lou Coates, and David Arrowsmith, *Canadian Labour Relations: An Information Manual* (Kingston, Ont.: Industrial Relations Centre, Queen's University 1991), 71–218
8 Section 15(1) of the Constitution defines guaranteed equality rights. Section 15(2) deals with affirmative-action programs and states that

subsection (1) does not preclude any law, program, or activity that has as its objective the amelioration of conditions of disadvantaged individuals or groups, including those that are disadvantaged because of race, national or ethnic origin, colour, religion, sex, age, or mental or physical disability (Kumar, Coates, and Arrowsmith 3).

9 Economic Council of Canada, *Innovations and Jobs in Canada* (Ottawa: Supply and Services Canada 1987), 113–14

10 Monica Townson Associates, *Leave for Employees with Family Responsibilities* (Ottawa: Women's Bureau, Labour Canada 1988), 83

11 See Ajun P. Aggarwal, *Sexual Harassment in the Workplace*, 2nd ed., (Toronto: Butterworth 1992), and Ontario Human Rights Code Review Taskforce, *Getting Human Rights Enforced Effectively: An Issue Paper* (Toronto: Ontario Human Rights Commission 1992).

12 NUPGE consists of thirteen component unions – nine provincial public-service employees' unions, two unions of brewery workers, the Ontario Liquor Board Employees' Union, and the Health Sciences Association of British Columbia. While component unions negotiate independently, general collective-bargaining goals and strategies are formulated nationally through a national convention. A national collective-bargaining advisory committee, consisting of the chief negotiators of component unions, coordinates bargaining activities.

13 The union is a pioneer in negotiating a first collective agreement in 1991 (with Placer Dome Inc.) providing for an employment-equity plan for the hiring, promotion, and training of First Nation employees.

14 Comments by Sue Milling, staff representative, USWA National Office in a communication to the author

15 The CTF, it should be noted, does not bargain directly. Organizations affiliated with the Federation follow their own agendas for collective bargaining. CTF's role is to provide information and education. It holds an annual seminar on women and education for representatives of its provincial and territorial organizations to raise their awareness of women's concerns and help them in formulating collective-bargaining demands.

16 See Pradeep Kumar and Lynn Acri, 'Unions' Collective Bargaining Agenda on Women's Issues: The Ontario Experience,' *Relations industrielles* 47, no. 4.

17 See, for example, Canadian Union of Public Employees, *Shaping Our Future: Report of the Commission on Structure and Services* (Ottawa 1991). The report noted that during the consultation process 'the Commission was reminded on numerous occasions of CUPE's commitment

to equality for all members and of the need to reflect that commitment in the union's structures and service delivery. The Commission found there is a concern – particularly among women, members of racial minorities, aboriginal people, people with disabilities, gays and lesbians – that the union needs to do more to counter discrimination in the workplace, in our union and in Canadian society more generally' (10).

18 Aggarwal 369–73
19 Kumar and Acri 635
20 Laurell Ritchie, 'Women Workers and Labour Organizations,' paper commissioned for the Institute on Women and Work, City of Toronto, November 1987 (mimeographed), 57–74
21 Ibid. 53–6
22 Ibid. 56
23 Data are available from the author on request.
24 Sue Milling, USWA, in a communication to the author
25 There is no readily available information on women's representation in union leadership and staff positions. The surveys conducted by the Quebec Federation of Labour (QFL) and the National Union of Public and General Employees (NUPGE) in 1989 and the data on the status of women in the Canadian Union of Public Employees reported by Ritchie in 1987 suggest that, while there has been a marked increase over time, women continue to be under-represented in executive and staff positions as well as in negotiating and grievance committees. See Quebec Federation of Labour, *Report of the Committee on Access to Equality* (Montreal 1989); National Union of Public and General Employees, *Affirmative Action Survey* (Ottawa 1989); and Ritchie 94. The QFL survey revealed that, while women had achieved proportional representation on local union executive boards, they were poorly or less well represented on committees dealing with negotiations, grievances, and health and safety, and at conventions, on general councils, on advisory committees, and on staff. The survey found that women are less involved as shop stewards and business representatives. Similar findings were reported by the NUPGE survey. The survey concluded that women are usually under-represented on bargaining committees even among the bargaining units with a high percentage of women members.
26 See Quebec Federation of Labour Report and Canadian Labour Congress, *Empowering Union Women: Toward the Year 2000* (Ottawa: CLC Women's Bureau 1990), 17–22.
27 See Alice Cook, 'Women and Minorities,' in *State of the Unions*, George Strauss et al., eds (Madison, Wis.: Industrial Relations Research

Association 1991), 237–57, and 'International Comparisons: Problems and Research in the Industrialized World,' in *Working Women: Past, Present and Future*, Karen Shall Cross Koziara et al., eds (Washington: Bureau of National Affairs 1987), 332–73; Ruth Needleman and Lucretia Tanner, 'Women in Unions: Current Issues,' in *Working Women*, 187–224; Susan C. Eaton, *Women Workers, Unions and Industrial Sectors in North America* (Geneva: International Labour Office 1992); Anne Treblicock, 'Strategies for Strengthening Women's Participation in Trade Union Leadership,' *International Labour Review* 130, no. 4; European Trade Union Institute, *Positive Action for Women in Western Europe* (Brussels 1989); Canadian Labour Congress, *Empowering Women*, and B.C. Government Employee's Union, *White Paper on Women in the BCGEU* (Burnaby, BC: 1991).

28 Canadian Labour Congress, *Empowering Women*, 24–31

29 Prominent among these are affirmative-action programs initiated by CUPE, various components of NUPGE, CAW, the Steelworkers, and the Communication Workers. Also active in this regard are the Ontario Federation of Labour, the Quebec Federation of Labour, and the Canadian Labour Congress. The new CLC structure, adopted at its 1992 convention, following the Report of the Task Force on the Role and Structure of the CLC, includes six 'gender affirmative-action members' designated by the six largest affiliates on its 46-member executive council, and two gender affirmative-action representatives on its 16-member executive committee. The actual number of women on the executive council currently is 13.

11

The Gendered Dimension of Labour Law: Why Women Need Inclusive Unionism and Broader-based Bargaining

JUDY FUDGE

Labour-relations institutions are central to any mode of regulating unequal social relations. Similarly, the appropriate roles of men and women workers, trade unions, and collective bargaining constitute key elements within a social formation. Thus, it is important to examine how labour-relations law and institutions have influenced the uneven structure of trade-union representation in Canada in general and the unionization rate of women workers in particular.

THE FEMINIZATION OF LABOUR AND THE BREAKDOWN OF NORMS

Since the recession of the mid-1970s most industrial economies have undergone a profound process of economic restructuring. The recession marked a shift from the use of labour-intensive to capital-intensive forms of production. The goods-producing sector contracted as the service sector expanded. Large numbers of women entered the expanding sectors of clerical, sales, and personal/business service work. Part-time and temporary work increased, fed by the rising female participation rate. Union protection declined. Differences became more pronounced between the masses of women working in the feminized sectors of the economy and the few who found increased opportunities for success in business and the professions. In these ways the transformation of the female labour force was central to capitalist restructuring and the reconfiguration of the working class in advanced industrialized economies.[1] Moreover, the feminization of the labour force was matched by a complementary feminization of the labour market – the increase in jobs typically associated with women; jobs that are part-time, temporary, poorly paid, unorganized, and insecure.[2]

One effect of this process of restructuring has been to render visible the norms or assumptions of the standard employment relationship. According to Muckenberger, 'the selective function of [the standard employment relationship] has probably always existed, and was one reason why it was always a normative, partly fictitious, reference model rather than an empirical pattern of employment.'[3] Gendered assumptions about the appropriate role of women in the labour market served to make the selective function of the standard employment relationship invisible at worst and unproblematic at best.

The two-fold process of feminization of the labour force and labour market has begun to reveal the gendered assumptions upon which Canadian labour-market policy is based. The feminization of labour not only threatens our norm of the male worker with a dependent family, it threatens our norm of collective bargaining as the most suitable means of improving the terms and conditions of employment.

In addition to the increase in non-standard forms of employment there appears to be a structural shift to small workplaces. In 1985, nearly 84 per cent of all of Ontario's registered businesses had fewer than ten employees.[4] However, it is important not to confuse small workplaces with small employers. Many large employers, like banks and trust companies, to identify two obvious examples, consist of comparatively small workplaces.

Capital's extension of these forms of organizing labour (the growth in non-standard employment) and production, whether it is services or goods (the proliferation of small workplaces), severely tests the capacity of unions to extend collective bargaining to the unorganized. The existing framework of labour-relations law is ill-suited for organizing both workers in non-standard forms of employment and workers in small workplaces – many of whom are women.

Collective bargaining has never taken hold in any general way in Canada beyond certain sectors characterized by the absence of competition. Unionized workers employed in competitive sectors, although they received the benefits of union protection through seniority arrangements and grievance arbitration, have not received wages and benefits which are comparable to unionized workers in the non-competitive sectors.[5] Moreover, the majority of women employed in female-dominated occupations and workplaces outside of the public sector have not had the benefit of collective bargaining. And while it is true that unionization significantly increases women's wages, unionized women workers still receive lower wages than their male counterparts. From the beginning, collective-bargaining legislation has not worked for the majority of workers in this country.

This evaluation of the limitations in the Canadian collective-bargaining law and practice suggests two questions which must be addressed: first, why is it that collective-bargaining law has failed to provide trade unions with the means to organize half of the working population in Canada, and second, why has this fact not resulted in a demand for the wholesale revision of the structure of labour-relations legislation?

THE SIGNIFICANCE OF THE BARGAINING STRUCTURE ON WOMEN'S UNIONIZATION

Bargaining-Unit Determination

Under Canadian collective-bargaining law, employees and unions cannot simply determine the bargaining constituency for the purpose of forcing an employer to recognize and bargain with the collectivity. In exchange for the legal obligation which requires employers to recognize unions for the purpose of collective bargaining, unions gave up whatever ability they had to determine their formal bargaining structures. Unions are not permitted to exercise industrial sanctions to force employers to recognize them; instead, labour-relations boards were granted the exclusive authority to certify a union which represented a group of employees defined by the board as an appropriate bargaining unit. The bargaining unit defines the constituency of employees from which a union must obtain majority support in order to be certified as the exclusive bargaining agent of those employees for collective-bargaining purposes. It also defines the group of employees which can engage in collective action for the purpose of collective bargaining. The certification process is controlled by the board, and requires a union to sign up a majority of employees in a unit as members. Once the union has received sufficient support, it can apply to the board for certification. At that time, the board will inquire as to whether the unit of employees organized by the union is appropriate for the purpose of collective bargaining. If the board so finds, the union is certified and can then compel the employer to meet with it for the purpose of concluding a collective agreement.

During the period that the union is seeking to sign up members, employers are prohibited from engaging in a number of unfair labour practices which, by and large, cover interference with lawful trade-union activity.

The bargaining unit is the basic structural feature in Canadian labour-relations law. Under Canadian collective-bargaining law, labour-relations boards have the exclusive authority to determine the appropriate bargaining unit. Although labour-relations legislation provides some guidance as to what constitutes an appropriate bargaining unit in certain situations – for craft workers or professional employees, for example – this is the exception rather than the rule. Boards across Canada have developed well-established policies on what constitutes an appropriate bargaining unit. It is useful, therefore, to examine in detail the policies of a specific board in order to unearth the assumptions upon which bargaining-unit determination rests.[6]

Community of Interest

The Ontario Labour Relations Board, for example, has developed a number of criteria to guide its discretion in determining the appropriate bargaining unit. These include community of interest among the employees, practice or history of collective bargaining, desirability of separating white- and blue-collar employees, aversion to the fragmentation of a unit, agreement of the parties, desires of the employees, organizational structure of the employee, and traditional methods of union organization.[7] But the most important criterion that the board looks to is the community of interest of the employees. The tests to determine community of interest include the following:

1 nature of work performed
2 conditions of employment
3 skills of employees
4 administration
5 geographic circumstances
6 functional coherence and interdependence

What is significant about these criteria is the extent to which they reflect the initial production decisions of the employer about how to organize production, where to organize production, what to produce, and the kinds of employees and skills needed in the production process. Thus, bargaining-unit structure in Ontario replicates the employer's initial decision about how to organize production, rather than the employees' choices about who to associate and bargain with.[8]

The Ontario Labour Relations Board's bargaining-unit policy results in a highly fragmented structure of bargaining. The single-employer, single-location unit is the cornerstone of board policy, despite the existence of some exceptions. Moreover, the fragmentation of bargaining structure in Canada extends beyond the single-employer, single-location unit to reflect some broader occupational distinctions. Since the board defines a bargaining unit in terms of occupational classes rather than individuals, standard units have emerged. The Ontario board's policy regarding standard units reflects its understanding of employees' community of interest. Although a factual determination of the appropriate bargaining unit must be made in each case, the board is loath to depart from its previous determinations of appropriate bargaining units.

Standard units defined by the Ontario board include a standard production unit and a standard office unit. The separation of office employees from production employees, except where the office employees are located in or next to the plant, is a well-entrenched policy. Moreover, the Ontario board has a policy of separating part-time and students workers from full-time workers at the request of either the employer or the union. Inside and outside municipal employees will generally be separated into different units by the board. Homeworkers have been excluded from a unit of production workers employed in a factory in the garment industry. These are just a few of the Ontario board's standard units.

The board's policy regarding standard units entrenches an artificially narrow conception of workers' common interests which is based upon the employer's initial production decisions. While it is true that there are many interests which may conflict within a workplace, there are also many commonalities. As Forrest notes:

Wages are a powerful unifying force. From the employee's point of view, the elimination of wage differentials between locations or between full- and part-time workers may be more than equitable, it is a practical means of combatting the employer strategy of whipsawing [one group of workers off another]. Sources of tension within a workforce are many and are not limited to those institutionalized by the board's practices. Office workers may have demands unique to their situation, but so do women, immigrant, skilled, and senior groups, though none is recognized as a distinguishable bargaining constituency by the board.[9]

Gender Bias in Bargaining-Unit Determination

The criteria the board employs for determining workers' community of interest are gender-biased. The nature of work performed by men and women differs, as do the skills they are required to exercise in their jobs.[10] Since men and women generally are employed to perform dissimilar jobs, their conditions of employment differ. Thus, it is not surprising that standard occupational units reflect and reinforce the gendered occupational structure of the labour market. Office workers, most of whom are women, will in the vast majority of cases be separated into different bargaining units than manufacturing, construction, and non-agricultural primary workers, most of whom are men, employed by the same employer. This is also the case for part-time workers and homeworkers, most of whom are women. Moreover, since women are often employed in female-dominated establishments, the policy of defining the appropriate bargaining unit in terms of a single location and a single employer reflects existing gender biases in the labour market. The gendered segregation of bargaining units, in turn, reinforces the perception that male-dominated and female-dominated units have different communities of interests. Thus, the result of the board's standard-unit policy has been a bargaining structure which is deeply fragmented along gender lines.

Fragmentation and Its Impact on Union Power

Another result of the Ontario board's standard-bargaining-unit policy is a pronounced tendency towards certifying very small bargaining units. According to the 1989–90 Annual Report of the Ontario Labour Relations Board: 'Small units continue to be the predominant pattern of unionizing efforts through the certification process in 1989–90. The average size of the bargaining units in the 573 applications that were certified was 30 employees, the same as in 1988–89. Units in construction certifications averaged 7 employees, the same as in 1988–89; and in non-construction certifications they averaged 41 employees, compared with 40 in 1988–89. Eighty-two percent of the total certifications involved units of fewer than 40 employees, and 42 percent applied to units of fewer than 10 employees.' In general, the board policy of small units favours the employer's interest in limiting the scope and impact of collective bargaining to small groups of employees.

In part, the Ontario board's policy bias in favour of small units can also be explained in terms of its decision to facilitate organizing in certain sectors. Initially, the board's standard unit in the retail and service sector was one comprising all the locations of an employer in a defined geographic area, typically a municipality.[11] However, in the mid-1970s the realities of organizing fast-food restaurants and trust companies had shaken the board's confidence in this approach, since multi-establishment units are harder to organize. Recognizing the right to self-organization as a primary theme of the Ontario *Labour Relations Act*, the board said it would lean towards the bargaining structure which facilitates organization, with the result that a single establishment certificate is now common in these sectors.

But the problem with this approach to bargaining-unit determination in the case of small workplaces is that there is no necessary correlation between a bargaining-unit structure which facilitates organization and one which results in viable collective bargaining; in fact, the opposite is true. Outside of the construction industry, which has a legislated broader-based bargaining structure, it is extremely difficult for a small unit to obtain a first collective agreement. This is because the bargaining unit not only might determine the success of the certification application, but also affects the bargaining power of the union and the point of balance it creates with that of the employer. Small units of employees simply do not have much bargaining power unless the sector is highly unionized or the workers in the unit hold a monopoly over necessary skills, as is the case in the construction industry.

Between 1976 and 1986, only 50 per cent of all certified bargaining units secured a first collective agreement.[12] While the incidence of bargaining failure was higher in those situations where the employer interfered, almost half of the units without first agreements encountered no petition and laid no unfair-labour-practice complaint.[13] The failure of a bargaining unit to secure a first agreement results from the overwhelming power advantage of the employer. In every jurisdiction with the exception of Quebec, employers are free to hire replacement workers to keep their operations running during a strike. Moreover, unions are prohibited from engaging in secondary or sympathy action which might bring greater pressure to bear against the employer. Employers, by contrast, can mobilize the productive, organizational, and financial capacity of the entire firm to defeat a strike.

Informal Broader-Based Bargaining Structures

It is important to note, however, that the formal bargaining structure which is established by the bargaining-unit determination process does not necessarily determine the actual form in which bargaining takes place in specific sectors or industries. Several unions have developed informal bargaining structures which are designed to mediate and modify the fragmentation which results from the formal bargaining unit structure. For example, the Canadian Auto Workers (CAW) bargains master agreements for several of their large plants and employers which link bargaining on behalf of office workers, who are predominantly female, to that of workers in the plants, the majority of whom are men, as a way of securing decent wages and benefits for the former. Usually a master agreement will include a number of plants as a way to prevent employers from pitting plant against plant to whipsaw down the terms and conditions provided by collective agreements. Another method of rectifying the chaotic process of bargaining which results from a fragmented formal structure is pattern bargaining, where one or two 'key' bargains form the basis of settlements throughout the industry.

Despite the opportunity to modify the formal bargaining structure through voluntary agreement, more centralized, informal bargaining structures remain the exception rather than the norm.[14] This is because any deviation from the formal structure depends upon the voluntary and mutual agreement of the parties. Unions are prohibited from using their collective power to force employers to bargain on a basis that departs from the unit described in their certificate.

Voluntary broader-based bargaining structures tend to be limited to dominant sectors in the economy where employers are in a monopolistic or oligopolistic position, such as automobile manufacturing. Since the dominant firms in these sectors are male-dominated, the benefits of informal bargaining structures have tended to be confined to male workers; however, on occasion, where office and production workers are represented by the same union, master agreements have benefited the former. Moreover, because informal broader-based bargaining structures depend on the existence of market conditions which make such structures acceptable to both employers and unions, they are unstable. Increased competition through industrial restructuring undermines the oligopolistic or monopoly conditions which are necessary for employers to agree to adopt or maintain centralized bargaining structures.

This is precisely what happened in the Canadian meat-packing industry in the mid-1980s, when, as Forrest recounts, the national meat-packers wanted out of their industry-wide agreements.[15] When the United Food and Commercial Workers Union insisted on retaining its centralized bargaining structure, Burns, a national meat-packer, charged it with failing to bargain in good faith. Labour-relations boards in Alberta, Manitoba, and Ontario upheld Burns's complaints, and the union was forced to give up the industry-wide bargaining structure it had established in the 1940s.

The major problem with informal, broader-based bargaining structures is that a union cannot insist on them in the face of employer opposition. Once market conditions change to the extent that employers no longer perceive their benefit, these structures can be eroded. Since unions will then only be entitled to rely on the muscle of single-employer, single-location bargaining units, it is possible that employers will succeed in playing bargaining units off one another in order to whipsaw down collective agreements. While Canadian manufacturers, unlike their American counterparts, have not as yet mounted an assault on existing informal broader-based bargaining structures, the long-term viability of these forms of bargaining is threatened by the current political emphasis on increased industrial competition.[16] To prevent further fragmentation, what is needed is formal, and legally enforceable, broader-based bargaining structures.

THE SYMBIOTIC RELATIONSHIP BETWEEN BARGAINING-UNIT
STRUCTURE AND TRADE-UNION ORGANIZING STRATEGIES

There have been some limited proposals for modifications to the fragmented bargaining structure which predominates in Canada. Some commentators sympathetic to unions have called for the consolidation of small bargaining units of the same employer in order to jump up the bargaining clout of single-location units in the retail and banking sectors.[17] This would help women workers in particular. In addition, proposals for a designated small-workplace sector to facilitate organizing and bargaining for workers located in small work-places have been endorsed by organized labour.[18] But in the main, organized labour appears to be suspicious of broader-based bargaining.

Part of the suspicion of broader-based bargaining structures is no doubt due to the fact some such schemes have been introduced in the past by governments at the behest of employers or, at least, on their behalf. A variation on broader-based bargaining through an accreditation system was legislatively imposed in the construction industry to limit the power of the craft-based construction unions which were obtaining fairly hefty wage increases in the 1970s.[19] But it is important to recognize that the power of construction unions resides in their monopoly over skilled labour and in the nature of the industry. A fragmented structure lends itself to whipsawing by unions in these kinds of situations. Thus, the system of broader-based bargaining in the construction industry was designed to undermine the power of trade unions. In addition, the British Columbia labour board's policy of favouring large, encompassing bargaining units resulted in a number of failed attempts by unions to achieve certification.[20] In Nova Scotia, it is clear that the 'Michelin Bill' was designed to ensure that Michelin could operate in a union-free environment.[21] The legislation applied to situations where an employer had a number of plants in geographically distinct areas in the province and required a union to obtain a majority of the total number of workers at the employer's plants in order to be certified. These examples provide some basis for organized labour's suspicion of broader-based bargaining structures, as such structures tend to be imposed at the behest of employers and not on behalf of unions.

But the labour movement's legitimate suspicion of broader-based bargaining structures which have been introduced either to constrain union bargaining power or to make organizing more difficult is not a sufficient explanation of its failure to consider more inclusive unionism and broader-based structures. The main reason that unions have not called for a radical revision to the bargaining-unit determination process which deeply fragments collective bargaining can be found in the institutions which regulate labour relations.

The bargaining-unit determination and certification process vests exclusive representation rights in the union which signs up a majority of employees in what has come to be considered a standard unit. This process can easily lead to inter-union rivalry as different unions race to obtain majority support. To avoid inter-union warfare over which union should represent a particular group of workers, unions have drawn jurisdictional lines. Unions with a history of organizing particular groups of workers in specific sectors have come to believe that they have a right to represent these groups. To protect these jurisdictional rights, unions have entered into voluntary agreements within the labour movement to ensure that union jurisdictional boundaries are respected. To give these voluntary jurisdictional boundaries some clout, unions have formed central organizations with other like-minded unions. These central trade-union congresses and federations are vested with the authority, through their constitutions, to police jurisdictional boundaries and thereby prevent one union affiliate from raiding workers in another's organizational territory.

But the effectiveness of this method of preventing jurisdictional rivalries is complicated by the fact that in Canada and Quebec there are rival trade-union centrals. This rivalry stems from the historical, political, and strategic differences between unions.[22] Unions with competing social, economic, and political visions have formed different central organizations on the basis that their vision best addresses the needs of working people. Unions affiliated to different centrals often seek to assert jurisdiction over the same groups of workers. For this reason, inter-union rivalry is a not infrequent feature of the Canadian and Quebec labour landscape. Moreover, even within one central organization affiliates may, and sometimes do, assert jurisdiction over the same group of workers, particularly where there is an attempt to organize workers located in sectors or employment situations that have not previously been organized. The fact that central organizations are weak in relation to their affiliates undermines the capacity of the labour movement to resolve jurisdictional battles.[23]

For this reason, the resolution of jurisdictional battles and inter-union rivalry has devolved to labour-relations boards through their control over the certification and decertification processes. Since the prize of exclusive representation rights goes to the first union which signs up the majority of employees in a proposed bargaining unit, unions tend to accept, rather than challenge, the labour-relations boards' standard units. Because union are unwilling to take the risk of proposing new bargaining-unit structures, those structures which emerged during the major organizing drives from the 1940s through the 1960s (when only a few, unsuccessful, attempts were made to organize female-dominated sectors and occupations) are frozen in labour-board policy. In this way, the institutional structures of unions reflect the labour-relations boards' policies regarding standard units. In fact, the boards' standard bargaining units create a profound incentive against the development of innovative organizing structures by trade unions. Barriers are built into the labour-relations system which inhibit the extension of unionization and collective bargaining to workers in small workplaces in competitive sectors and workers in non-standard forms of employment. The symbiotic relationship between labour-board bargaining-unit policy and trade-union structure helps to explain why unionization has not been extended to women workers in the private sector.

In this context, the real social, economic, and political objectives of unions are downplayed in organizing drives. In order to persuade a group of workers to sign up with it rather than a rival, a union must offer tangible benefits to the potential members. Thus, the ability both to secure higher wages and benefits and provide contract-administration services for its members becomes the union's primary selling point at the expense of its broader social and political agenda. Unions which depart either from this form of 'responsible' unionism, the primary concern of which is to secure sectoral economic gains for their members, or standard units which replicate a narrow, and gendered, understanding of workers' community of interests run the risk of not being certified. Accordingly, their capacity to maintain a membership base and struggle for their broader social and political objectives will be undermined. In this way, the legal institution of exclusive representation, majority rule, and bargaining-unit determination encourages what Annunziato calls commodity unionism and discourages other forms of unionism.[24]

Inter-union rivalry, in turn, militates against the development of broader-based bargaining as each union seeks to secure the best deal for its members, rather than engage in a form of coordinated bargaining which might flatten the distribution of wages and benefits across the units in a sector.[25] Although there are some examples of coordinated bargaining by unions which represent the same categories of workers in a particular sector, these tend to be the exception rather than the rule. Moreover, because the boards ultimately resolve jurisdictional disputes in concrete organizing drives, there is no sustained pressure within the labour movement to come up with an effective mechanism for resolving jurisdictional disputes. This symbiotic relationship between the central elements in labour-relations law, on the one hand, and trade-union structures and organizational strategies, on the other, tends to reproduce within both the labour movement and the collective-bargaining structure an atomized, competitive market which is fragmented along gender lines.

INCLUSIVE UNIONISM AND BROADER-BASED BARGAINING
STRUCTURES

Systems of labour-market regulation can be characterized along the dimension of whether employment conditions are regulated on a national or industry-wide basis or on a firm or workplace basis. Canadian labour relations is situated at the latter, fragmented end of the spectrum. While this form of organization probably gives unions more control over the labour process, thereby enabling them to secure better terms and conditions for their members, a consequence of a fragmented structure is 'to expose the remaining parts of the employment system to unregulated terms and conditions of employment.'[26] The structural bias in Canadian collective bargaining legislation towards narrow, economistic forms of unionism results in an extremely precarious secondary labour market. Not only does this bias mean that the workers in the bottom half of the labour market, many of whom are women, derive either little or no benefit from collective bargaining, it also undermines the possibility of broader political support for policies which support unionism.

The profound fragmentation reproduced by Canadian collective legislation has not served women well. Moreover, the growth in both non-standard forms of employment and small workplaces undermines the capacity of the labour movement to halt the steady decline in union membership density. Reforms which simply tinker with the existing collective-bargaining regime may slow down this decline, but they will not reverse it. What we need to do is reconsider the structural elements of Canadian labour-relations law which influence trade-union strategies.

But before we can meet this challenge, it will be necessary to persuade a labour movement which has lived with, and been shaped by, the existing legislative regime that the dominant model must be revised. Unionized workers in the mass-production, non-agricultural-primary, and the transportation sectors have done well by the system that was designed for them in the first place.[27] The fragmented bargaining structure of Canadian labour relations has not inhibited the ability of industrial unions to secure for their members a family wage. However, there is evidence based upon international comparisons of different forms of unionization and bargaining which suggests that the gains for these workers have come at the expense of workers who are employed in the competitive, secondary labour market. The gap between the wages and benefits of unionized workers and the unorganized is greater in countries with fragmented bargaining structures than it is in those countries characterized by more centralized bargaining systems.[28] Moreover, the evidence suggests that the reason for this gap is that, in contrast to fragmented bargaining schemes, centralized bargaining regimes result in a better social wage for all workers.

Our norms of collective-bargaining law and the standard worker no longer meet the reality of a restructured labour market. Women's labour-market participation rate is approaching that of men's. The conventional understanding that men work for wages which are adequate to support dependent wives and children is being undermined as increasingly households have to rely on at least two wage-earners to maintain the standard of living which they became accustomed to in the 1970s.[29] Moreover, it is likely that with the growth in non-standard forms of employment more men will be performing jobs that historically have been associated with women. But rather than responding to the strains on the existing institutional arrangements for regulating labour relations and the hegemonic paradigm associated with it with nostalgia for the past, it is essential to treat this period of instability as presenting an opportunity to reconceive both labour-market policy and trade-union strategy. As Mahon has indicated, the 'labour market will always have a structure, just as the business firm will have a structure. The issue is what the new structure will look like and how existing institutions can be changed in order to create it.'[30]

What is needed is the development of new forms of broader-based bargaining and inclusive unionism which do not replicate and reinforce the deeply fragmented, gendered, and hierarchical labour market which currently exists. While it is likely that employers will strongly resist such strategies, there is nothing new in this. In Canada, employers have long fought union organization and collective bargaining, accepting the presence of trade unions only when it was politically unfeasible to do otherwise. In the past, alternative models of unionism have existed which challenged the narrow economism which results from an institutional structure which reinforces workplace, regional, and occupational divisions. The histories of the One Big Union and the Workers Unity League, which sought to organize workers on a broader basis, attest to this fact. The Service, Office and Retail Union of Canada, which sought to implement a feminist form of unionization designed specifically for female-dominated sectors and occupations, is another example of an alternative form of unionism. But even though each of these organizations was ultimately unsuccessful in developing lasting representative institutions in the face of opposition from employers, the state and, sadly, the labour movement, their legacy in challenging conventional understandings and institutional arrangements should not be ignored.

The labour movements in Canada and Quebec urgently need to address their internal rivalries if they are going to survive during this period of economic restructuring. Union mergers, consolidated bargaining initiated by councils of unions which organize workers in specific sectors, associate-membership status for the households of trade-union members, representation of unemployed workers, and community-based unions are possible avenues for addressing union fragmentation and rivalry. While such representational forms will not be achieved without a struggle within the labour movement, it simply is not possible to ignore this challenge if organized labour is to be revitalized in order to confront capital's renewed offensive.

Similarly, it is imperative for unions in Canada to break out of the constraints of narrow economism by linking the demands of their members with the concerns both of unorganized workers and of social movements such as women's, anti-racism, and anti-poverty organizations. And while it is important to be realistic about the difficulty of this task, there already exists some encouraging examples. Both the International Ladies' Garment Workers Union and the Victoria Labour Council have implemented initiatives which seek to obtain the benefits of employment-standards legislation for unorganized workers.[31] In addition, the solidarity pacts entered into by the Canadian Union of Postal Workers and the Public Service Alliance of Canada with a range of progressive social movements during their 1991 strikes are important beginnings of a broader political strategy. These strategies not only disrupt the barriers between unorganized workers and the labour movement, they reforge the connection between economics and politics which liberal-capitalist democracies have so long sought to obscure. Only by developing a popular front both within the labour movement and between other social movements will it be possible to make the international links needed to fight global capitalism.

Until the labour movement begins to embrace inclusive forms of unionism it will not be possible to address the fragmented structure of Canadian collective bargaining. According to Standing, 'unless communal unionism develops in place of craft or industrial unions, protection of vulnerable groups will be partial at best and easily circumvented. Male-dominated trade unions must fully incorporate women and struggle for 'women's issues' at least as strongly as for others; otherwise their collective strength will continue to dissipate.'[32]

Broader-based bargaining structures will not simply be a gift from the state; rather state-sanctioned institutional arrangements which facilitate broader bargaining will only result from a political vision which challenges the inequality and subordination inscribed in the status quo. Central to this political vision must be a determination both to broaden and democratize trade-union representative institutions and to eradicate gender inequalities in the home and labour market. What is needed is a shift away from a trickle-down labour-market policy to a strategy which is designed to improve the wages and conditions of workers, many of whom are women, at the bottom. Inclusive unionism and broader-based bargaining are necessary not only if women workers are to enjoy trade-union representation; they are necessary for the survival of a strong and effective union movement for men workers as well.

NOTES

1 Monica Boyd, Mary Ann Mulvihill, and John Myles, 'Gender, Power and Postindustrialism,' *Canadian Review of Sociology and Anthropology* 28, no. 4 (1991) 407; Kathyrn Ward, ed., *Women Workers and Global Restructuring* (Ithaca: ILR Press 1990); Jane Jenson, Elisabeth Hagen, and Ceallaigh Reddy, eds, *Feminization of the Labor Force* (New York: Oxford University Press 1988)

2 Guy Standing, 'Global Feminization through Flexible Labor,' *World Development* 17 (1989): 1079

3 Ulrich Muckenberger, 'Non-Standard Forms of Work and the Role of Changes in Labour and Social Security Regulation,' *International Journal of the Sociology of Law* 17 (1989): 386

4 Urban Dimensions Group, Inc., *Growth of the Contingent Workforce*

in Ontario: Structural Trends, Statistical Dimensions and Policy Implications (Toronto: Ontario Women's Directorate 1989), 27–8

5 John O'Grady, 'Beyond the Wagner Act, What Then?' in Daniel Drache, ed., *Getting on Track: Social Democratic Strategies for Ontario* (Montreal and Kingston: McGill-Queen's University Press 1991), 155–6

6 While there are some variations in the bargaining-unit determination policies of labour-relations boards across Canada, generally the policies are similar to those developed and administered by the Ontario board.

7 Jeffrey Sack and C. Michael Mitchell, *Ontario Labour Relations Law and Practice* (Toronto: Butterworth 1985), 137–8

8 I owe this insight to Harry Glasbeek.

9 Anne Forrest, 'Bargaining Units and Bargaining Power,' *Relations industrielles* 41, no. 4 (1986): 846

10 Joan Acker, 'Class, Gender and the Relations of Distribution,' *Signs* 13 (1988): 481–2

11 Sack and Mitchell 143

12 Laurell Ritchie, *Women Workers and Labour Organizations* (Toronto: Institute on Women and Work, City of Toronto 1987), 107

13 Forrest, 'Bargaining Units and Bargaining Power,' 840, citing Ontario Labour Relations Board data for the fiscal years 1970/71 to 1980/91

14 John C. Anderson, 'The Structure of Collective Bargaining,' in Morely Gunderson and John C. Anderson, eds, *Union Management Relations in Canada* (Don Mills: Addison-Wesley 1982), 173–95; Robert J. Davies, 'The Structure of Collective Bargaining in Canada,' in W. Craig Riddell, ed., *Canadian Labour Relations* (Toronto: University of Toronto Press 1986), 211–56

15 Anne Forrest, 'The Rise and Fall of National Bargaining in the Canadian Meat-Packing Industry,' *Relations industrielles* 44, no. 2 (1989): 393

16 Broader-based bargaining in the automobile industry has been under threat in the United States since the recession of the early 1980s. The recent dispute at the Caterpillar heavy-machinery plant in Peoria, Illinois, resulted in a large, and likely permanent, tear in pattern bargaining in the heavy-machinery industry. Moroever, in 1992 Loblaws announced its intention to break pattern bargaining in the retail-food sector.

17 Forrest, 'Bargaining Units and Bargaining Power,' 848–9; Rosemary Warskett, 'Bank Worker Unionization and the Law,' *Studies in Political Economy* 25 (Spring 1988): 66

18 O'Grady 164

19 Joseph B. Rose, 'Mandatory Bargaining Structures: What Are the Consequences?' in Geoff England, ed., *Essays in Labour Relations Law* (Toronto: CCH 1986), 25

20 John Baigent, 'Protecting the Right to Organize,' in Joseph M. Weiler and Peter A. Gall, eds, *The Labour Code of British Columbia in the 1980s* (Calgary: Carswell 1984), 45–62; Rod Germaine, 'The Structure of Bargaining Under the Labour Code,' in Weiler and Gall 77–98

21 Daniel Drache and Harry Glasbeek, *The Changing Workplace: Reshaping Canada's Industrial Relations System* (Toronto: James Lorimer 1992)

22 Education Committees of the CSN and CEQ, *The History of the Labour Movement in Quebec* (Montreal: Black Rose 1987); Bryan D. Palmer, *Working Class Experience* (Toronto: Butterworth 1983); Craig Heron, *The Canadian Labour Movement* (Toronto: James Lorimer 1989); Desmond Morton with Terry Copp, *Working People* (Ottawa: Deneau 1984)

23 Carla Lipseg-Mumme, 'Canadian and American Unions Respond to Economic Crisis,' *Journal of Industrial Relations* 31, no. 2 (1989): 229

24 Frank R. Annunziato, 'Commodity Unionism,' *Rethinking Marxism* 3, no. 2 (1990): 9

25 Anderson 187

26 Jill Rubery, 'Women and Recession: A Comparative Perspective,' in Jill Rubery, ed., *Women and Recession* (London: Routledge and Kegan Paul 1988), 271

27 Judy Fudge, 'Voluntarism and Compulsion: The Canadian Federal Government's Intervention in Collective Bargaining from 1900 to 1946,' Oxford University, D.Phil. thesis, 1988, chap. 5

28 Jelle Visser, *In Search of Inclusive Unionism*, Bulletin of Comparative Labour Relations no. 18 (Deventer, Netherlands: Kluwer 1990); OECD *Employment Outlook 1991*, 118–19

29 Geoffrey York 'Family life: Not enough money, too much stress,' Toronto *Globe and Mail*, 3 Jan. 1992, A1–A5

30 Rianne Mahon, 'From Fordism to ?: New Technology, Labour Markets and Unions,' *Economic and Industrial Democracy* 8, no. 2 (1987): 5

31 The ILGWU has organized a local of homeworkers and part of its mandate is to ensure minimum standards for them until it can represent them for collective-bargaining purposes. The Victoria Labour Council acts as an agent for unorganized workers in employment-standards cases in order to protect the workers' anonymity.

32 Standing 1194

12

Can a Disappearing Pie Be Shared Equally?: Unions, Women, and Wage 'Fairness'

ROSEMARY WARSKETT

'So what do we want? Fairness ... Pay Equity, because half our members are women working in undervalued jobs.'[1]

Equal pay for work of equal value is currently the leading union strategy to raise women's pay and close the wage gap. Many researchers, however, have pointed out the limited impact of the policy – low wages are still a reality for most women in Canada.[2] This situation can only worsen given the present economic crisis and the restructuring of the workplace, both of which are undermining many of the wage gains won by women in recent years.

My argument is that we need a more comprehensive approach to the problem of women's unequal pay, based on a union agenda of wage and work solidarity. In such a difficult economic period as this, equality for workers must be about 'sharing the austerity' with those who have been marginal to the policies and practices of the labour movement – women, minority groups, and the unemployed.[3] This is an approach that would place the equality of all workers as 'main business' at the negotiating table and integrate the issue of equal pay with other strategies directed at the economy and the state. The problem, however, is where to begin. Such an approach must start with an assessment of the unions' definition of what constitutes 'fair' wages, and of the practices that flow from this norm, and a redefinition of what is fair for women and men.

In this chapter I will explore how unions historically have defined 'fair' wages, and the way in which, in the present context, this definition works in contradiction to strategies to promote women's wage equality. I conclude the chapter with a discussion of how to resolve this contradiction through building a union agenda that will represent the interests of all workers and in so doing will strengthen the union movement's capacity to challenge the threats to the livelihood of all working people posed by global capitalism.

UNIONS AND FAIR WAGES POLICIES

There has been an assumption within union ranks that unionization is the means to achieve 'fair' wages for all workers. While there is substantial evidence that working under a union contract generally results in better wages for both women and men, this does not necessarily mean union women are placed in a fairer wage position in relation to union men.[4] Despite the fact that unionized workers receive higher wages,[5] the question of whether unions actually reduce gendered wage inequality remains open. One of the problems here has been that the empirical work is insufficiently disaggregated to distinguish which unions and which policies are more successful in reducing wage inequality. In any case, any empirical result stills needs to be related to an analysis of 'fair' wage setting for all workers. In this way we will be able to understand how these practices have benefited men to a greater degree than women.

Consider then what 'fairness' constitutes. Fair wages, a fair deal, fair comparisons, a fair day's work for a fair day's pay have long been popular union slogans. Defining and measuring fairness is not neutral, however. What is considered fair for one group of workers is not necessarily fair for another group. Unions define wage fairness in a particular fashion, bound up with conventions and practices which frequently operate to legitimize and perpetuate an income hierarchy that is not egalitarian.[6] Such a hierachy exists not only between certain groups of male workers but in general between men and women, white and non-white. Indeed, in a recent study on wages, race, and gender, it was found that for all classes 'white men have the highest income, followed by non-white men; non-white women have the lowest income, although only marginally lower than white women.'[7] More important, as shown in another study, what was considered in the past to be a fair and just wage for men was invariably considered to be more than a just wage for women.[8] These studies point to a need to identify precisely how, despite the application of equal value, the union movement's definition of 'fair' wages has resulted in a wide variety of practices that attenuate increases in real wages for women and continue to reproduce wage inequality between men and women.

We can identify three approaches to the 'fair' distribution of wages taken by parts of the Canadian labour movement during its more than one hundred and fifty years of existence. These are based respectively on wages for skills, wages for living, and wages for the family head. All three approaches had a negative effect on the wages of women.

Wages for skills historically placed emphasis on the craft or profession of workers and therefore on job content. The wage demanded is thus relative to the skills required to perform the duties of the job. At the turn of the century, from the standpoint of craft workers, women and newly arrived immigrants were considered to be 'dilutees,' that is, low-waged labour who potentially could be used by management to undermine craft skills. For the most part, this perspective led to women and immigrant workers being excluded from craft jobs and the union brotherhoods, resulting in occupational segregation into lower-valued jobs.

We can see the continuation of this tradition, somewhat weakened, in equal pay for equal work. This type of wage demand is explicitly based on skills and job content. It is a normal practice of unions to make comparisons between their members' skills and those of higher-paid, equally qualified workers.[9] Applying equal pay for equal work in this manner, however, only ensures that the pay of women's jobs such as clerical work is compared with other clerical work in other firms (mostly non-unionized) or public sectors. This approach results in pattern or comparison bargaining that simply perpetuates the lower pay of clerical workers and of women generally. The same can be said for most female-dominated jobs such as secretaries, librarians, nurses, and data processors.

Often operating in contradiction to the 'fairness' of paying for skills is the second approach to a 'fair' wage distribution, that stresses the need for all workers to earn a living wage. This approach embraces the simple philosophy that everyone has to pay the same price for a loaf of bread. The dominant demand then becomes that the wages of the lowest paid be at a living minimum. But this concept of fairness also operates against women because of the assumption that women are secondary wage earners, dependent on men to provide for living costs. A living wage that is below subsistence level is considered 'fair' for women because of their subordinate status in the family unit.

Also, liberal-democratic societies promote a hierarchical definition of fairness that conflicts with the principle of equality, but is in accord with equal opportunity. These societies accept that it is 'fair' for some to have higher living standards than others. The more 'meritorious,' employed in work of a higher status, are thought to have earned and thus deserve this higher standard. Again, in this sense, women 'lose out' because their work generally is socially constructed to be of lower status and lower value.

Linked to the concept of a living wage is the third approach, where in 'fairness' consists of the family head earning enough to provide for all members of the family. It is assumed that the head will be, of course, male. The brotherhoods, like other sections of society, saw the home as women's proper place. Perceived exclusively as mothers and wives, rather than as co-workers, women were seen to be dependent on the male head of household.[10] Although craft unions advocated that women should stay in the home and men should earn a family income, the Trades and Labour Council (TLC) did adopt a policy of equal pay for equal work as early as 1914. This policy followed the general practice of many affiliate unions who used the equal-pay principle to protect them against 'dilutees,' especially during wartime conditions. Whether it was intentional or not, the policy contributed to keeping women out of male-dominated workplaces after the war because employers preferred to hire men.[11]

Although historically these three approaches have constituted the main policy philosophy for unions on the question of 'fair' pay, it does not mean that they opted entirely for one approach over another. Any one union's pay policy is frequently a combination of some or all of these approaches. Craft unions are noted, however, for their attempt to protect skill levels and higher rates of pay, whereas industrial unions are associated with egalitarian pay policies for mass-production workers.[12] Both kinds of unions and their memberships have historically taken the position that male workers should earn enough to support a family, and it is no coincidence that both have been traditionally male-dominated.

IMPLEMENTING THE NEW EQUALITY POLICIES:
CONTRADICTIONS AND CONSTRAINTS

Federal-government equal-opportunity initiatives, recommended by the Royal Commission on the Status of Women, began to be put in place at the end of the 1960s. These measures helped to raise the debate over women's unequal pay within the labour movement. This debate, together with heightened consciousness of women's union, labour-market, and household experience, mobilized union feminists who pushed policy making within the CLC in a new direction. In 1976, delegates to the eleventh constitutional conference of the Canadian Labour Congress seemed to make a historical move towards changing its policies and practices on equal pay when they accepted a statement on 'equality of opportunity and treatment of women workers.' While recognizing that women experienced discrimination and on average were paid less than men, the policy emphasized up-grading women's skills and vocational qualifications to allow them to compete equally with men. It also expressed the need to raise the lower average earnings of 'women possessing the same or similar qualifications or doing the same work or work of equal value.'[13] In other words, women should be paid equally when they have the same or a similar skill level as men. Unfortunately, the policy offered no criticism of the undervaluing of women's skills or the need of women and workers in general to earn a living wage despite their skill levels. In more than a decade since that policy statement, we can still ask to what extent do the present policies of the Canadian Labour Congress, and the practices of the affiliate unions, redefine what is fair and equitable. We need to question whether women's demand for 'fair' wages has been simply appended to the old practices, ones which in turn continue to reproduce lower pay for women. Have things really and fundamentally changed?

In 1984, the fifteenth constitutional convention did make a major change when it accepted a policy paper on women and affirmative action.[14] The policy made a direct attack on the practice and ideology of the family wage and 'the myth that men are the breadwinners.' It proposed a wide number of measures to bring up women's lower wages including bargaining for higher base rates and for across-the-board wage settlements, revaluing women's present skills through equal pay for work of equal value, and demanding opportunities to train for new skills in non-traditional jobs. Essentially it combined an emphasis on the need for women to earn a living wage, for employers to pay more for women's traditional skills, and for break-ing down the occupational segregation of women. A new definition of wage 'fairness' seemed to be in the making.

But policies need to be translated into practice if the condition of women is to change radically. There are a number of different reasons why change is not happening and why wage-setting practices within the CLC and affiliate unions continue to perpetuate women's lower pay in spite of the 1984 policy.

To begin with, policies directed at women are not integrated into policy making as a whole, leaving the 'main business' of unions unaltered. Although the policy on the need for social and economic reform passed at the CLC's 1990 convention does make an attempt to integrate women's fight for equality at a number of different levels into the program, nothing is said about traditional wage setting and other practices that continue to operate against women achieving equality.[15]

For example, at the same 1984 CLC convention that ratified the 'Women and Affirmative Action' policy discussed above, a campaign was initiated to promote job creation.[16] Its major thrust was an attempt to deal with growing unemployment by redistributing work through a reduction of hours of work with no cut in pay and the end of compulsory overtime. What is interesting was that no connection was made between this campaign and women's inequality and the fact 'that taking work as a whole – waged work and domestic labour – men work fewer hours than women and get much more pay.'[17] The campaign for a reduced working week did not recognize that both men and women need to earn a living wage and still have time and energy to do the household labour. The failure to make this connection between the two policies is symptomatic of the marginalization of union-movement policies and practices related to achieving equality for women.

There are serious consequences for the labour movement as a result of this marginalization. It means that the practice of pay equity and other attempts to raise women's pay frequently generate gender conflict and competition between those in female- and male-dominated groups. Such conflict means weakened unions and weakened solidarity. It also means that mainstream union practices and those designed to raise women's pay often work in contradiction to each other. Negotiations are a case in point. Pay-equity studies and bargaining often take place quite separately from other pay negotiations. Indeed, many union feminists supported separate pay-equity negotiations as a way of ensuring that the issue would be dealt with effectively.[18] The problem, however, is that other wage practices may negate the beneficial effects of re-evaluating women's work in a separate set of negotiations.

Percentage increases are one of the important ways in which pay gains for women are undermined. Since women are clustered in lower-paid jobs, percentage increases act to widen the wage gap between them and higher-paid workers who are frequently male. Despite the fact that for many years feminists in unions and in the community have called for decreasing differentials between workers as a way of narrowing the wage gap, this mode of thinking is far removed from the thinking of many union negotiators.

One reason for this is that in the 1970s, when high rates of inflation were recorded, many unions were engaged in Cost of Living Adjustment (COLA) disputes in an attempt to prevent erosion of wages for living. The demand for COLA had the effect of contributing to the present norm of demanding pay increases on a percentage basis. It should, however, be noted that where there are COLA formulas in collective agreements, they usually are translated into 'across-the-board' increases.[19] This is true for the Canadian Auto Workers' agreements with the large car manufacturers.

Some unions attempt to negotiate a combination of percentage plus across-the-board increases as a means of balancing the demands and needs of men and women members.[20] As the recession has deepened, however, it has become more and more difficult to negotiate this kind of compromise settlement. With low and often zero increases offered by the employer, union negotiators are reluctant to present this kind of settlement to the membership. They seek a general percentage offer that will be near the increase in the cost of living, so that real wages will be maintained. This was the argument given to Public Service Alliance of Canada (PSAC) women when the PSAC negotiated percentage increases in the 1988–9 round of bargaining.

Percentage increases are an important way in which workplace, gender hierarchies are reproduced. Many unions, especially those in the public sector, continue to make general pay demands on a percentage basis while pursuing equal pay for work of equal value for women members. This approach results in widening the wage gap between men and women at that same time that the union is demanding it be narrowed. Frequently union negotiators argue that there is no contradiction in this approach since equalization payments for women will bring them to the same level as the male comparator group or class. Although this argument has some merit, equalization payments are not rolled into the collective agreement and the women's rate of pay in the collective agreement stays at the lower rate and is used to compute pensions and other benefits.

But doing pay equity itself also leads to problematic practices as far as the achievement of wage equality between men and women is concerned. Equal pay for work of equal value (the basis of legislated pay equity) is, in effect, a demand by women to redefine the notion of wage 'fairness.' It is the demand 'for a fair wage that recognizes as valuable the caring, supporting, and nurturing aspects of many women-predominant jobs.'[21] Certainly the union movement's support for equal pay for work of equal value and legislated pay equity has in many cases led to success in raising union women's pay, particularly in the public sector, where legislation has played a leading role in initiating equal-pay studies and settlements. But there are limitations to this new concept of 'fairness' as a wage-setting practice based on the evaluation of job content and skills. One of the most significant is that it continues to reproduce large wage differentials and hierarchies.

Although 'doing' pay equity has often led to questions of how the wage hierarchy is constructed, it does not, as I remarked earlier, challenge the concept of hierarchy itself or in practice act to flatten it. Also, it does not question the occupational segregation of women or the quality of the jobs that many men and women engage in. It takes male wages and male skills as the standard norm and attempts to extend this standard to women, slotting some of them into the skill hierarchy at a higher level.[22] Women are segregated, in general, not only into lower-paid jobs but also into those supervised and controlled by others, generally men.[23] Thus, in practice, women's jobs will not often score highly through the job-evaluation process and their lower ranking in the job hierarchy is then only legitimized and confirmed by the pay-equity process.

Occasionally the successful application of pay equity has resulted in changes in the gender order that in turn threaten and shake up the hierarchy itself.[24] This is not only threatening to management but also to those unionists wishing to maintain the status quo or protect their relatively privileged place in the workplace. Fundamental questions remain also regarding the relationship between pay-equity studies and regular collective bargaining.[25] What will happen after the pay-equity exercise is over? Will male-dominated groups attempt to reassert traditional wage differentials through the collective-bargaining process? Without policies and practices that integrate pay equity into the main activities of unions and educate the membership into accepting women's wage equality as fundamental to achievement of 'fair' wages, traditional male-dominated wage practices will continue to assert themselves.

Measures to bring up the lower-paid jobs and flatten the wage hierarchy are traditionally a part of wage bargaining in industrial unions such as the United Steelworkers (USWA) and the Canadian Auto Workers (CAW). Women in general have not benefited from this tradition, however, since they are highly segregated from men occupationally and are grouped into different unions and bargaining groups.

Employment-equity strategies to break down occupational segregation in the industrial sector and increase the numbers of women in non-traditional jobs have met with mixed success. For example, the 'Women back into Stelco' campaign was formally supported at all levels by the USWA, but in the workplace and within the local union the women had to fight against sexual discrimination ranging from physical harassment to being typed as sandwich-makers during a strike.[26] When the recession bit hard in the early 1980s and all the women at Stelco were laid off because of lack of seniority, the union was unwilling or unable to find a solution to the traditional seniority list.[27] At present very few women are working at Stelco and this situation is unlikely to change given the present economic recession. A simily fate may also await the CAW's award-winning affirmative-action plan (1991) and the agreement with General Motors establishing local affirmative-action committees (1987). Growing layoffs in the auto industry may leave little room for the union to manoeuvre to encourage the hiring of women and break down occupational segregation.

Hiring women into non-traditional jobs is more complicated than it first appears, however. Take the case of Inco Ltd., where recently unionized office staff won a $200,000 pay-equity dispute and also negotiated company-wide seniority.[28] Shortly thereafter the company announced that the clerical workers, many of them women in their forties and fifties, must choose the job of mining or be laid off. The union's position was that while they were in favour of women engaging in mining it must not be a forced choice. Many men as well as women would find it intolerable to work in a mine, especially given the danger and difficulties of the job. Attempts to break down occupational segregation may result in resistance not only by men but also by women.

PRESENT ECONOMIC CONSTRAINTS

Unions are currently facing economic and political circumstances that make it even more difficult to achieve wage equality for women. The economic crisis is not only putting pressure on the mainstream practices of unions, but is also limiting the possibilities to implement policies for women. The current restructuring of work is weakening unions by creating competition between workers for scarce jobs and scarce resources. The fight to get women back into Steelco is a case in point. The beginnings of the current movement for equal pay arrived at approximately the same time that the 'fordist' economy of mass production and consumption was beginning to undergo profound changes as a result of economic crisis. Employment-equity policies can only be effective if there are jobs available for women and other target groups to take up.

There are powerful economic tendencies at work that are in the process of transforming the structure of industry and, as a consequence, the life of unions. The impact on workers as a result of these changes has been far-reaching and there appears to be no end in sight. The structure of production, employment, and technology have all changed radically over the last fifteen years.[29]

Global competitiveness became the slogan of business and neo-conservative governments during the 1980s. Along with trade harmonization (free trade), the requirements of international competition translated into a neo-conservative policy of 'flexible' labour markets. At the level of the manufacturing firm, global competition means increasing production with fewer workers through the introduction of new technology and new methods of flexibility in the production process. More and more, management is trying to reduce labour costs by a strategy of contracting-out and increased part-time employment, while intensifying work and extending hours of work for core workers.[30] Such a shakedown in the workplace and the consequent turbulent times for unions make it difficult to introduce novel wage and employment demands on behalf of women.

The relative weakness of Canadian manufacturing has been reinforced by global competition and the restructuring of capital, leading to an increase in service employment relative to manufacturing and resource industries. Almost 90 per cent of net job growth in the 1980s was in the private service sector, particularly in low-wage 'hamburger'-type jobs. Declining employment in primary and secondary sectors has had a dramatic effect on unionization. Between 1976 and 1986 union membership in mining and manufacturing declined from 83.2 to 66.4 per cent.[31]

The severe drop in blue-collar manufacturing and industrial jobs and the rapid expansion of marginal kinds of employment is resulting in even greater polarization between core and 'periphery' workers than previously. Traditional approaches to 'fair' wage demands are less workable than ever. Workers in the full-time, permanent, pensionable 'core' are, for the most part, male and white, while those on the 'periphery' include not only large numbers of women and youth, but also various ethnic and racial minorities. Data published by the Economic Council of Canada (1991) reveal that 36 per cent of women compared with 23 per cent of men were in part-time, short-term employment in 1988. Several researchers indicate that these changes are contributing to 'working poverty' among many women, especially those with dependent children.[32]

With the deepening of the economic crisis, neo-conservative governments, federal and provincial, have adopted more restrictive labour policies in an attempt to aid the faltering economy and make labour more productive and competitive. The public sector, the spearhead of unionized, better-paying jobs for women, is itself undergoing a crisis with privatization, contracting-out, and precarious forms of work. Recently, the federal and certain provincial governments have returned to the use of wage controls in order to lower wages. Recent cases of wage restraint in the public sector have a disproportionately larger effect on women than if applied to all sectors. Furthermore, since women are found in larger numbers at the bottom of the wage scale, they experience the controls more severely than higher-paid workers.

Given the current state of the economy and politics it is increasingly difficult to achieve equal-pay gains for women. The loss of manufacturing jobs and the increasing numbers of poor jobs in the service sector make the option of employment equity through affirmative-action measures less and less of a possibility. The current economic situation inevitably is increasing gendered and racial conflict over jobs and pay. In these circumstances it is even more crucial to devise a new set of policies and practices that will strengthen solidarity within the labour movement and make equality for all workers the top item on the agenda.

TOWARDS A NEW AGENDA OF WAGE AND WORK SOLIDARITY

I pointed out earlier that there were traditionally three approaches to pay within the Canadian labour movement: pay for skills, pay for living, and pay for the family head. Despite policy gains within the union movement, these approaches still have an impact on women's pay and their position both in the paid labour force and in the home.

Women still take most of the responsibility for domestic labour and this affects our capacity to undertake more responsibilities either in the workplace or in unions. The concept of the 'family wage' remains implicit within bargaining structures and practices, preventing women from being fully integrated into the system.[33] One of the major effects of the backlash against women and alternative movements in the 1990s is the reassertion that the home is women's proper sphere. Organizations such as the National Citizens' Coalition and REAL Women, while on the neo-conservative fringe, have contributed to keeping alive traditional attitudes against abortion rights, gay and lesbian rights, and women's full integration into economic and political structures. Fortunately, this picture is balanced by, first, (as noted earlier), the non-recognition by the CLC of the notion of a family wage and second, by the fact that even the most conservative union leaders now have to recognize changes that have taken place in Canadian society.[34]

Although being unionized unquestionably improves women's pay, we have seen that there is a wide range of economic and political factors working against women's full equality in the workplace and society generally. Despite union strategies women remain occupationally segregated into 'poor' jobs, and the continuing loss of 'good' jobs in manufacturing will add to the problem. Moreover, we saw that the two dominant union-policy approaches of pay for skills and pay for living often act in contradiction and are not integrated into a consistent approach that places the need to address women's inequality at the centre of union's 'main' business. The percentage of the income 'pie' going to workers is shrinking, making it more difficult for women to achieve wage equality.

What is needed is the development of policies and practices that promote solidarity between men and women and between workers of different races and ethnic backgrounds. Such an approach implies a conscious set of solidarity policies and practices that work to heal the division between men and women. Furthermore, they should be designed to overcome the contradiction between pay equity as a set of practices operating to maintain air inegalitarian wage hierarchy and wage solidarity, which focuses on increasing the wages of the lower paid for these reasons, a policy of wage and work solidarity should be placed at the top of the union movement's agenda, since it achieves both these objectives.

One of the best-documented examples of the wage-solidarity

approach is found at Canada Post among the inside workers, members of the Canadian Union of Postal Workers.[35] CUPW's opposition to the use of part-time workers and coders as a source of cheap labour, led the union to organize the part-timers and oppose the occupational segregation of coders from postal clerks. Both coders and part-timers were predominately women, but this fact did not lead to an exclusionary male union strategy. Julie White argues that it was the intent of CUPW to 'negotiate everyone in the bargaining unit into the same, single classification'[36] (and this was related to the union's philosophy of wage solidarity and equality). In general, a wage-solidarity approach should emphasize bringing up the wages of the lowest-paid to an acceptable living standard, flattening the hierarchy, and ensuring that gender bias is eliminated from the remaining pay differentials.

Solidaristic work is a demand currently being made by workers in LO (the union congress of blue-collar workers) in Sweden in an attempt to deal with the present economic realities they are facing.[37] One of the recurring themes of labour-process researchers relates to the de-skilling of work. It is argued that the continuing search by businesses to accumulate capital results in their need to increase production and reduce labour costs by separating out the execution of tasks from their conception. Fordism and its relations of production and consumption increased both production and the wages of male-dominated manufacturing workers at the same time as de-skilling work. The post-fordist economy of the 1980s and 1990s presents an entirely different situation, with the growing polarization between 'good' jobs and 'bad' jobs in terms of both skill levels and pay.

The demand for work solidarity is the demand for the requalification of work. 'Work organisation in the firm must be developed so that it can adjust to the growing knowledge and experience of all workers, not via "careerism" but through the development of work itself: a development that increases one's knowledge, broadens and deepens the range of tasks performed, and increases one's responsibility and authority.'[38] The demand for solidaristic work explicitly attacks the neo-conservative agenda of encouraging the development of a lower-wage economy polarized into many low-skilled, poorly paid jobs and fewer highly skilled, well-paid jobs.

Missing in LO's approach to solidaristic work is an understanding that work is cut through with gender and race relations and, as a consequence, women and workers of different races remain outside the demand for the requalification of work. There is also another sense in which gender relations are missing from the definition of solidaristic work – in terms of how we organize work in our communities and within our unions. If union women continue to have unequal responsibility for domestic work in the home and administrative work in their union locals, this in turn affects their potential to take on greater responsibilities in the union and the paid labour force. Work solidarity must, therefore, also be a policy in the home and in unions.

It is here that the demand for a shorter work week without losts of pay is key. It is mainly women who are part-time and casual workers. The equitable distribution of paid work would remove an important barrier to men's participation in domestic work, at the same time freeing women to take on greater responsibility in the paid labour force. The politics of equitable distribution of work also means a severe restriction on overtime (in order to create more jobs). These demands would benefit not only women in the paid labour force who work part-time and wish to increase their hours, but also the unemployed.

Solidaristic work and wages should, therefore, be demands that recognize gender and race differences and recognize that women and workers from minority groups have been excluded from the mainstream policies and practices. Union policies to equalize women's pay are at present a blend of a number of different initiatives, including the attempt to revalue women's work, raise the wages of the lowest-paid, and implement affirmative-action strategies to end women's occupational segregation. Wage and work solidarity – being a demand for quality jobs and quality pay for all working women and men – has the potential to combine with these various initiatives into a coherent whole.

Making these demands given the present economic crisis does not mean that they can be easily achieved, either in the short or long run. It is important, however, for the labour movement to make a start by changing its internal policies and practices with regards to wage 'fairness.' The end result of developing an internal policy of wage and work solidarity will be a set of internal practices that will build greater solidarity and strength. As a consequence, the union movement will develop a greater capacity to deal with those who have power to make economic and political decisions that affect the lives of all working women and men.

NOTES

1 Public Service Alliance of Canada, 'Who's Standing Up for Public Services' (PSAC Print Shop, August 1991)?' – a leaflet directed at the public just before the September 1991 strike in which one of the main demands was pay equity

2 See several chapters in Judy Fudge and Patricia McDermott, *Just Wages: A Feminist Assessment of Pay Equity* (Toronto: University of Toronto Press 1991).

3 The way in which union solidarity can act to marginalize women, the unemployed, and other sections of the working class is discussed in Rosemary Warskett, 'Defining Who We Are: Solidarity through Diversity in the Ontario Labour Movement,' in Colin Leys and Marguerite Mendell, eds, *Culture and Social Change* (Montreal: Black Rose Books 1992), 109–27.

4 It was found that after controlling for other determining factors the wage increase as a result of unionization is in the range of 10–25 per cent. Moreover, unions generally compress the wage structure. Morley Gunderson and W.Craig Riddell, *Labour Market Economics: Theory, Evidence and Policy in Canada* (Toronto: McGraw-Hill Ryerson 1988), chap. 16

5 In 1989, 29 per cent of women in the paid labour force were unionized, compared with 38 per cent of all male workers. What the wage benefits to being unionized and the lower rate of unionization among women indicate is the need to develop strategies for organising women and other lower-paid groups. Evidentially, this deserves more attention from the labour movement as a whole, but organizing activity can only come following research into problems of organizing the unorganized, such as the failure to unionize the financial and retail sectors, where large numbers of women are found.

6 Richard Hyman, *Social Values and Industrial Relations: A Study of Fairness and Equality* (Oxford: Basil Blackwell 1975), 232

7 Peter S. Li, 'Race and Gender as Bases of Class Fractions and Their Effects on Earnings,' *Canadian Review of Sociology and Anthropology* 29, no. 4 (1992): 501

8 Joan Acker 'Class, Gender, and the Relations of Distribution,' *Signs* 13, no. 3 (1988): 473–97

9 Alton W.J. Craig, *The System of Canadian Industrial Relations in Canada* (Scarborough: Prentice-Hall of Canada 1986)

10 Julie White, *Women in Unions* (Ottawa: Supply and Services Canada

1980), 16; Ruth Frager, 'No Proper Deal: Women Workers and the Canadian Labour Movement, 1870–1940,' in Linda Briskin and Lynda Yanz, eds, *Union Sisters: Women in the Labour Movement* (Toronto: Women's Press 1983), 60

11 Frager 52

12 These two union types should not be conceived in static terms. Both forms of unionism experienced dynamic change over the period of a century, in reaction to the restructuring of capital and the changing economic, political, and cultural environment of Canada and Quebec. Even in the case of craft unionism, in which the essence 'was to put up walls around each trade and keep out competition' (Craig Heron, *The Canadian Labour Movement: A Short History* [Toronto: James Lorimer 1989], 14), there were moments when that the narrow 'protection of the trade' conception was broadened to a more encompassing concept of the working class.

13 Canadian Labour Congress, 'Equality of Opportunity and Treatment for Women Workers,' policy statement approved by 11th Constitutional Convention (May 1976)

14 Canadian Labour Congress, 'Women and Affirmative Action,' policy statement approved by 15th Constitutional Convention (1984)

15 Canadian Labour Congress, 'A New Decade: Our Future,' policy statement approved 18th Constitutional Convention (May 1990)

16 Canadian Labour Congress, 'An Action Plan to Promote Jobs and Justice,' 15th Constitutional Convention document no. 29 (May 1984)

17 For a discussion of a redistribution of both waged and domestic work through the demand for shorter hours see Meg Luxton, 'Time for Myself: Women's Work and the "Fight for Shorter Hours," ' in Heather Jon Maroney and Meg Luxton, *Feminism and Political Economy: Women's Work, Women's Struggles* (Toronto: Methuen 1987), 167–78.

18 See Carl Cuneo, *Pay Equity: The Labour-Feminist Challenge* (Toronto: Oxford University Press 1990), 46

19 For example the Northern Telecom agreement with the Canadian Auto Workers' union provides for all employees, no matter what the wage gap. This means that in practice the COLA provision in this agreement narrows rather than widens the gap between low- and high-paid workers.

20 See, for example, Canadian Union of Public Employees, National Executive Board, 'A Coordinated National Strategy for CUPE Members on Pay Equity / Equal Pay for Work of Equal Value' (Ottawa: September 1986).

21 Joan Acker, 'Pay Equity in Sweden and Other Nordic Countries,' in Fudge and McDermott 252

22 See Rosemary Warskett, 'Wage Solidarity and Equal Value: Or Gender and Class in the Structuring of Work Place Hierarchies,' *Studies in Political Economy* 32 (Summer 1990): 55–83

23 Monica Boyd, Mary Ann Mulvihill, and John Myles, 'Gender, Power and Postindustrialism,' *Canadian Review of Sociology and Anthropology* 28, no. 4 (November 1991): 407–36

24 Joan Acker, *Doing Comparable Worth: Gender, Class, and Pay Equity* (Philadelpia: Temple University Press 1989)

25 Patricia McDermott, 'Pay Equity Challenge to Collective Bargaining in Ontario,' in Fudge and McDermott 122–37

26 Meg Luxton and June Corman, 'Getting to Work: The Challenge of the Women Back Into Stelco Campaign,' *Labour / Le Travail* 28 (Fall 1991)

27 See Jeffery Sack, Sandy Price, and Christine Deacon, eds, 'Seniority – Does It Conflict with Employment Equity?' *Lancaster's Employment Equity Reporter* 1, no. 9 (September 1992), for a discussion of 'the negotiated compromises that may have to be made between seniority rights and the goals of employment equity.'

28 *Globe and Mail*, 15 Dec. 1992, B4

29 Isa Bakker, 'Pay Equity in a Declining Economy: The Challenge Ahead,' in Fudge and McDermott 255

30 Gregory Albo, 'What Comes Next? Canadian Employment Policies after Fordism,' in Rianne Mahon, Jane Jenson, and Manfred Bienfeld, eds, *Production, Space, Identity: Canadian Political Economy Faces the Twenty-First Century* (Forthcoming 1993)

31 Statistics Canada, Corporations and Labour Unions Returns Act, *Annual Report, Part 11*, various years

32 See Morley Gunderson, Leon Muszynski, and Jennifer Keck, *Women and Labour Market Poverty* (Ottawa: Canadian Advisory Council on the Status of Women, June 1990)

33 Judy Fudge, in this volume

34 At a recent conference Clifford Evans, then Canadian director of the United Food and Commercial Workers stated that only one in six families fits the traditional pattern of a husband with a paid job and a wife at home (*Globe and Mail*, 21 Jan. 1992).

35 Julie White, *Male and Female: Women and the Canadian Union of Postal Workers* (Toronto: Thompson Educational Publishing 1990)

36 White, *Male and Female*, 79

37 Rianne Mahon, 'From Solidaristic Wages to Solidaristic Work: A Post-Fordist Historic Compromise for Sweden?' *Economic and Industrial Democracy: An International Journal* 12, no. 3 (August 1991): 295–325

38 Mahon, translated and quoted 309

13

Unions and Women's Occupational Health in Québec

KAREN MESSING and DONNA MERGLER

The ideology which has been used to support the sexual division of labour has had important consequences for occupational health. Male workers have been told that their superior strength has made them uniquely fit to undergo severe risks in such industries as mining, construction, metallurgy, and forestry. Women, in contrast, have been complimented on the patience and finesse which enable them to do routine repetitive tasks in cramped positions on assembly lines, without recognition of the associated health risks.[1]

Until recently, the presentation of men as the proud possessors of a monopoly on occupational risks has strongly coloured union prevention efforts, which have centred on gaining recognition for occupational accidents and illnesses in male preserves. Health-and-safety issues in women's jobs have been ignored, minimized, or looked at as specifically women's problems rather than health problems.[2]

When risks are perceived in certain jobs, the solution has often been to exclude women rather than to improve the job. Thus, barriers have been established by law and custom to the employment of women in jobs whose risks are dramatic and alarming. Also, women's health has been less important for unions and governments than making sure that women are fully available to fulfil their traditional social role as wife and mother; it is in this context that we must consider protectionist policies such as the exclusion of women from night work and from situations where foetuses may be endangered. It is also in this light that we can understand why traditional women's work in hospitals has been exempted from exclusionary practices regarding night work and work with radiation. Often, risks to health in traditional women's work have been received with incredulity, and women's complaints of unhealthy working conditions have often been diagnosed as 'hysteria.'[3]

Risks in women's jobs were described and denounced early in the century by such noted occupational-health physicians as Alice Hamilton and Harriet Harding,[4] and unions have supported some attempts to improve women's working conditions. A shorter work day in the United States and, more recently, various provisions of Québec's minimum labour standards were negotiated in response to the demands of women workers. However, women's occupational health has not been a priority for unions or governments.

Some feminist scientists have suggested that women's occupational health may not be properly defended by regulators and researchers because their conceptual categories have been formed in relation to traditional male occupational health problems.[5] Women have a specific biology and do paid and unpaid work whose characteristics differ from men's jobs; they undergo discrimination and harassment by virtue of their sex.[6] Their working conditions may therefore have specific risk factors and health effects, which may not be obvious without a paradigm shift.[7]

The authors, researchers in occupational health, have been involved in these debates both within and outside the union movement. We have participated in efforts to improve women's working conditions and health through an agreement signed in 1977 between the Université du Québec à Montréal and two major Québec unions, the CSN[8] and the FTQ.[9] (The agreement has recently been extended to include the CEQ.)[10] This 'protocole-UQAM-CSN-FTQ,' provides released time for teaching and university seed money for research.[11] It has enabled us to collaborate with the union women's committees on brochures on the protection of pregnant women, women's occcupational health, and health risks for women in non-traditional jobs; to carry out research in response to needs expressed by women workers; and to provide expert testimony in litigation involving women's occupational health.[12]

Basing ourselves on these experiences, we describe below three areas of study and intervention in women's occupational health and safety, and our perceptions of how they are being handled by the unions involved. We caution that our experiences do not necessarily provide a full picture of how unions have dealt with these questions, since we have not usually participated in making decisions.[13]

THE UNION CONTEXT IN OCCUPATIONAL HEALTH

Unions devote a large proportion of their resources in time and money to education and training around occupational-health issues, and to fighting for compensation for injured and ill workers. At the local level, health-and-safety issues are handled through committees elected by the union locals, where women's representation is blocked by the same obstacles which limit women's participation in unions generally.[14] By law, health-and-safety measures are administered in many companies by joint labour-management committees. These are, except in the most female-dominated unions, almost exclusively male. This male cast to union health-and-safety struggles has been reinforced by the Québec law on occupational safety and health, which gives priority for prevention funds to employment sectors with many compensated workers. Since many more men than women have suffered in the past from *recognized* occupational injuries and illnesses, fewer than 10 per cent of priority-sector workers are women. Hospitals, for example, are not included.

In contrast to the health-and-safety situation, no government-imposed regulations cover feminist issues. Equal-opportunity and equal-access programs, where they exist, are administered through employers' personnel or labour-relations offices. No joint union-management structures have been initiated by law; in fact, government officials responsible for administering equal-opportunity programs in the public sector often give the impression that they regard unions as major obstacles to full employment equity. For example, a recent government program offering funds to explore women's experience in reconciling family and professional responsibilities closely involved employers, but unions were excluded from the program and were not even mentioned in the booklet describing it.[15] Thus, government involvement in feminist issues in employment has tended to pose problems as women's issues and to blur differences between working women and management.

Within unions, women's issues are handled by women's committees ('comités de la condition féminine') or equal-opportunity committees ('comités d'accès à l'égalité'), almost exclusively composed of women. These have historically been concerned with maternity leave, day care, equal pay for work of equivalent value and, at the CSN, abortion rights. The committees have at various times had close contacts with women's groups, which have resulted in coalitions around labour standards, day care, and reproductive rights.

Traditionally, there has been little interaction between the male-dominated occupational-health-and-safety militants and those concerned with women's issues in any of the major Québec trade unions.[16] Women's committees are often outside the mainstream of union activity, because few women have sufficient time and energy to involve themselves both in women's committee affairs and union executives. However, in several areas, some interaction between the two groups in unions has been necessary in recent years. We describe three of these: precautionary reassignment and leave for pregnant women ('retrait préventif'); health problems of women in traditional jobs; and women's access to non-traditional (NT) jobs.

THREE CASES

Precautionary Reassigment and Leave for Pregnant and Breast-feeding Women

The 1979 public-sector collective agreement provided that pregnant or breast-feeding women whose jobs posed a risk for them or for their child were entitled to job reassignment without loss of benefits or, failing that, to fully paid leave. A similar clause was later included in the new law on occupational health and safety owing to pressure from unions and the Québec Council on the Status of Women, a government advisory board. Funding for the program came from the general workers' compensation fund, so as not to discourage individual employers from hiring women. It should be noted that the law does not oblige the employer to improve working conditions at the risky job site and thus constitutes an exception to the principle of 'elimination of risk at the source' underlying the rest of the law. Thus, some feminists had reservations about the law, considering it protectionist.

Since women were not thought to have hazardous working conditions, the program was not expected to attract many claims. For the first two years, the government did practically nothing to publicize it, and very little to provide guidelines for administrators. Unexpectedly, however, women applied for leave in large numbers, with one-third of pregnant workers taking advantage of the law in recent years.

An important consequence of both the original clause in the public-sector agreement and the protective-reassignment legislation was that union militants and staff involved in health and safety were required to think about pregnancy for the first time. Their first reaction was usually to call on the women's services of the unions to handle all questions of protective reassignment, but the overloaded women's services had to return the requests to regular staff. Thus, there has been a fair amount of interaction on this issue between union employers and members interested in women and those interested in health and safety, resulting in union-produced brochures on the procedures for obtaining protective reassignment, as well as many educational sessions on reproductive health in the workplace (in which the authors have participated).

In preparing and giving these sessions, unions and scientists had to clarify issues around protectionism and the extent to which working conditions should be changed for all workers. In theory, women with proper working conditions should be able to work almost to the end of their pregnancy, and take their maternity leave once the child is born so as to rest after childbirth and spend time with the child.[17] However, no list of proper working conditions for pregnant women has been included in the law or established by scientists. We do know that few working conditions are unsafe for pregnant women and completely safe for all other workers.[18] Thus, no sharp line can be drawn between an exposure dangerous for a fetus or breast-feeding infant and one which is dangerous for all workers.

For example, our information is clearly insufficient to decree safe levels of chemicals for pregnant or breast-feeding women. We will not reproduce here the debate on the validity of the exposure levels permitted in the workplace;[19] however, whatever validity they may have has been determined only for populations of healthy adult workers.

In many factories where there are chemical exposures, all pregnant women have been routinely given leave, since no reassignment to safe conditions is possible without cleaning up the whole workplace. However, the nervous system begins its development in the first few weeks of fetal development, and reassignment may come too late to be fully protective. Cleaning up the whole workplace may be the only real solution, especially since lead and organic solvents affect male reproductive cells as well.

Women's interest in precautionary leave led many who had not previously been involved in unions to attend their first union work-

shops. These women (admittedly not a random sample) were unequivocally in favour of the legislation, and very few worried about protectionism. For them, 'women's rights' were an abstract issue, while poor
working conditions and unreasonable employers were a daily reality.
Women workers were exposed to solvent fumes in a hockey-stick
factory, to violence in psychiatric hospitals, and to uncomfortable,
cramped positions on assembly lines. Hospital and factory workers
alike expressed repeatedly the feeling that their jobs left them
exhausted and weakened even when not pregnant and that pregnancy
at work was too great a burden to bear. It is hard to be against precautionary leave when so many women regard it as their only hope for
getting through a pregnancy in sound physical and financial health.

However, there has been unrelenting opposition to precautionary
leave, coming from employers, government, and even some union
sources. Opponents argue that the leave is a social benefit which has
nothing to do with working conditions and which amounts to an
extended maternity leave. The Health and Safety Commission opposes
many requests for precautionary reassignment on 'scientific' grounds,
invoking the uncertainty of calculations as to the risks for pregnant
and nursing women. This type of argument follows long-standing
traditions in the field of occupational health: before any risk is
accepted, unassailable scientific proof is necessary; the tiniest flaw in
available studies is underlined and used to deny the existence of risk.[20]

Unions have so far defended the law and protested vigorously when
restrictions have been imposed on its application. When the Health
and Safety Commission attempted to reduce women's access by
limiting the powers of the personal physician and by promulgating
unfounded guidelines concerning permissible exposures, the unions
fought the issue through the courts and won.[21] Feminists from the
community have formed a coalition in order to make sure the law is
not changed, and women's-committee representatives have been
active supporters of the coalition.[22]

Male union leaders have by and large enthusiastically supported
precautionary leave. In fact, union feminists have been forced on
occasion to restrain occupational-health activists who want to wrap
women in cotton for their entire pregnancy. Many non-feminists,
however, do not associate the need for leave with poor working
conditions. During educational sessions, male and female participants
often suggest that women should not work at all during pregnancy,
and this point is discussed with union representatives.

Some attention has been given to reproductive rights for male workers, but this has not been a major effort. In workshops, some men confuse our warnings of the adverse effects of their working conditions with insults to their potency, while others want to expand the law to protect men's ability to reproduce (often threatened by the same conditions that endanger pregnancy). Contradictions around this issue still cloud the discussions in the unions. There is increasing outside pressure to give precautionary leave under the same conditions as maternity leave (that is, paid for from general tax funds rather than employer contributions), as in the recently proposed federal legislation.[23] This solution becomes more attractive to union members as the Health and Safety Commssion increasingly restricts access to precautionary leave, forcing women to take unemployment benefits (for sick leave) instead.

Our thinking has evolved, influenced by interaction with union militants. Many feminists, particularly in the United States, uphold the position that even maternity leave is discriminatory against men.[24] However, studies have shown that in fact those women who have had access to precautionary leave are those with the harshest working conditions;[25] only the most hardened theoretician could want them to wait until similar protection was available for other workers. Our interventions in response to union requests have allowed us to understand the reasons for some tensions among union activists and among feminists. Real-life problems and the duty of unions to protect members and to support their attempts for better working conditions have led members to evolve quite divergent positions on these issues, and are resulting in constant evolution of the situation of women in unions.

With another member of our research group, Nicole Vézina, we have been able to observe how the unions view women's occupational health when pregnancy is not specifically involved.

Union-initiated Improvements in Working Conditions in Traditional Women's Jobs

Union thinking about occupational hazards has mainly responded to health problems in male-dominated industries; women's jobs are characterized by very different working conditions. Women in factories tend to work in relatively immobile positions, doing repetitive movements at a very fast pace. These are not the same physiological conditions as those found in the typical men's jobs, which may involve lifting heavy weights at widely spaced intervals. As mentioned above, women have fewer industrial accidents than men, and have been excluded from industries where risks are dramatically evident.

The more subtle nature of risks in traditional female jobs has led to delays in the recognition of these hazards. For example, women suffering from repetitive work at high speeds or from certain chemical exposures have been accused of hysteria, based on inadequate characterization of their working conditions.[26] Recently, however, unions have been successful in obtaining recognition for health problems associated with traditional women's jobs such as those of cashiers, sewing-machine operators, and micro-electronics workers.

One example has been the recent union struggle for improvement of cashiers' working conditions. Standing without moving for long periods is characteristic of many women's jobs in sales (cashiers, tellers, store clerks), in laboratories, and on factory assembly lines. This position exerts a demand on muscles, causing pain, and impedes blood circulation, causing swelling.[27] Since cashiers need to do a lot of stretching and reaching, employers have long maintained that such workers cannot accomplish their assigned tasks while sitting down. Nicole Vézina was asked by a grocery-store union to examine the worksite of a 41-year-old cashier who had back problems. The union gave a high priority to this case, because of its wide implications for many women workers, and findings presented to the Health and Safety Commission [28] eventually led to a decision requiring that cashiers be seated.[29] The impact of this decision has spread, and women working in supermarkets, department stores, and banks and on assembly lines are demanding, and in some instances obtaining, adequate seats. Although it took some effort to mobilize the union around this issue, it has since invested heavily in publicizing this decision, and in January 1992 held a colloquium for cashiers where the research was presented.

These and other union-inspired studies of the health effects of typical women's jobs have been helpful in combating the image of women with occupational health problems as weak people fussing about nothing. The increasing number of claims for musculo-skeletal problems among women doing repetitive work in factories and offices also seems to be stimulating government and union interest in these types of jobs.[30] The major obstacle to union action on health problems in traditional jobs seems to be indifference; it is sometimes hard to persuade union executives and even women workers that their problems are important. One union staff member carefully explained to us the difference between 'central' occupational health problems, such as accidents among construction workers, and 'peripheral' problems, such as stress in hospital workers. It seems that the long tradition of regarding women's health symptoms as being of 'hysterical' origin has not been entirely overcome.

A major obstacle to recognition of problems comes from the fact that standard setting has not always taken into account the working conditions found in women's jobs. Heat-exposure limits are a good case in point. When a hot workplace is mentioned, we picture men in foundries, glassworks, mines, and other jobs with a typically male pattern of physical exertion. In fact, heat-exposure standards have been based on studies of such industries, while the laboratory studies which justify heat-exposure levels have been carried out on young, healthy men.[31] This procedure has resulted in setting higher temperature limits for some women's traditional factory work than for men's.

Some years ago, we were contacted by union occupational-health-and-safety staff with a request from women laundry workers. These women, who operated semi-automated ironing and folding machines, suffered from symptoms similar to heat stress during the summer. Since the temperature at their worksite never exceeded the permissible values for 'light work,' occupational-health-and-safety inspectors refused to require the employer to make changes.

These women stood for most of the day, rapidly feeding laundered items (one item every three seconds) into the press or stacking the laundered items at the other end. Since this type of activity is very demanding for the cardiovascular system (as is heat exposure), we studied thermo-regulation of these workers in summer and in winter.

The results showed that these workers handled 1800 kilograms of laundry per day, their heart-rate profiles were similar to that of men working in mines, and medically recommended heart rates were exceeded 17.2 per cent of the time in winter and 46.2 per cent of the time in summer.[32] This study alerted us to fact that the definition of 'light work' used in setting temperature limits for workplaces in Québec may be applied inappropriately to women's jobs. There is, however, much work to be done before occupational health standards incorporate the characteristics of women's jobs.

Adjustment of standard-setting practices requires a paradigm shift in the way that the union movement and scientists look at occupational health.[33] In the current economic climate, when union members are having increasing difficulty in getting compensation for the most obvious traditional occupational health problems, we have not as yet had much success in persuading our union brothers and sisters to give a high priority to such epistemological changes.

In our research on women's traditional jobs, we have observed that women and men engaged in the struggle to improve women's working conditions must work hard to obtain recognition that a risk exists and that it is important to do something about it. Once the risk is recognized, union members easily support the idea that women should not have to cope with risk of physical injury in their jobs. However, women entering non-traditional occupations are expected to accept a high level of risk.

Adapting Non-Traditional Jobs to the Size, Shape, and Strength of Most Women

It has been calculated that in order for men and women to be distributed randomly across occupational categories, two-thirds of the total working population would have to change jobs.[34] In factories, there is a pronounced sexual division of labour, resulting in very different working conditions and salaries for women and men.[35] The reason traditionally given for the exclusion of women from non-traditional (NT) jobs in factories is women's inferior physical strength.[36] The average woman does differ physiologically from the average man, although there is considerable overlap between the characteristics of the two sexes. For several parameters involving size and strength, NT jobs require re-design before women can do them safely. Thus, when equal-opportunity legislation was passed in Québec, it appeared that, paradoxically, it might constitute a threat to women's jobs. In one textile factory, twenty-seven women were thrown out of work when the abolishing of sex-typed jobs obliged them to transfer to jobs requiring unaccustomed physical efforts.

After several problems arose, the women's committees asked whether women who try to enter NT jobs requiring physical strength might risk health problems and failure. They asked us to examine several NT jobs in order to suggest changes in their physical characteristics. We have studied several situations, including machine repair, mail sorting, and paint preparation.

The machine shop was integrated through intense efforts by Action travail des femmes, a feminist group. When a woman entered this shop, occupied by 1200 men and only two other women, she had more aches and pains than her colleagues, and eventually suffered a back injury. Many of these problems could be attributed not to inferior strength, but to the fact that she exerted her strength in unfavorable positions, because her workstation and tools were not adapted to her size. For example, the woman usually took longer than her male workmate to tighten bolts. However, when she used a longer wrench, she tightened the same bolts in less time than the man.[37] Similarly, in a package-sorting job, women's accident rate was much higher than men's, partly because smaller people had difficulties reaching over the conveyor belt.[38] In the lamp factory, a woman suffered from epicondylitis (tennis elbow) because of the large number of movements requiring tremendous grip strength, a parameter where sexual dimorphism is at a maximum.[39]

This area is quite thorny because of the necessity to protect women's access to NT jobs at the same time their health is safeguarded. Some feminists are reluctant to mention difficulties women may have, for fear that integration efforts will suffer. They fear that employers and colleagues will interpret the fact that some women have difficulties with some jobs to mean that women should not be allowed to enter NT jobs. In fact, many men take pride in the fact that their jobs are very hard and that not everyone can do them.

The most sensitive to these issues may be 'pioneers,' those who have struggled to gain access to NT jobs and are reluctant to complain about them. One electrician told us how a fellow-worker tried to expose her to severe electric shocks out of resentment at her presence in 'his' workplace. She nevertheless kept on working with this fellow for two months before requesting a transfer (*she* was transferred). She never involved the union in this problem, and has had no contact with the women's committee of her union central.

Other unionized women have told us that they have to fight very hard to hold onto their image and their tenuous place in the workplace and cannot afford to ask for the right-sized equipment or machinery. Women with such heroic attitudes do not always support efforts of university professors or women's committees to demonstrate that their jobs should be re-engineered so as to be made easier. However, our preliminary results show that when jobs are not re-engineered, tasks are either reallocated so that women end up doing different jobs from their male colleagues and thus earning their resentment, or, if they do the same tasks, women usually suffer more musculo-skeletal problems than their colleagues. The tension between protection of women's health and their jobs comes out strongly in this area, which requires careful maintenance of communication among the various union intervenors.

Union solidarity may also suffer if women must appeal to the employer for help against male co-workers, in the face of indifference from the union. One of the positive developments in this area has been the creation of operational alliances or at least dialogues between union women's groups ('comités de la condition féminine' or 'comités d'accès à l'égalité') and health-and-safety committees. Alliances between the two committees are not always easy, since women entering NT jobs and thereby incurring risk are thought by some to have brought it on themselves by being in the wrong place. Also, many NT workplaces do not have enough women workers to form a committee. Still, there are encouraging elements, such as the enormous health-and-safety representative (male) who refused to lift any weight that the women in his union could not lift, and the hospital union who supported a woman's access to a non-traditional job and also supported her grievance when she found the weights too heavy to lift. Another important positive factor has been the growing union activity around the question of sexual harassment, which has supported women entering non-traditional jobs. Unions now discuss both sexual and gender harassment, and have developed educational sessions and suggested union practices in these areas.

Union discussions around the occupational-health implications of equal-access programs have many relationships with older union debates regarding worker selection: Should the job fit the worker or vice versa? The fact that males in the workforce are ageing seems to be an effective argument in persuading health-and-safety officials that the job-design approach is increasingly relevant. However, the relationship between feminist groups and union organizations on this issue is not without problems. Unions have no way of influencing hiring directly, and have not usually been involved in efforts to hire women in non-traditional jobs. All-male unions may be quite unprepared for the arrival of the first women and fast action has sometimes been required on the part of women's committees in the unions in order to protect the rights of new women workers. Pressure from feminist groups from the outside acts as a stimulus to help integrate women workers, but may be used by management as a stick to beat the union as well. This area is extremely difficult for all intervenors, and meetings between feminists within the unions and members of health-and-safety committees have sometimes been extremely tense.

CONCLUSION

Several suggestions emerge for strategy. The first is that, unfortunately but unsurprisingly, it has been important to emphasize the advantages for men in the struggles around women's occupational health. For example, we have emphasized dangers to male reproduction when talking about pregnancy leave, and risks for smaller or older men when encouraging unions to request job re-design. Many of the problems first identified in women's jobs, such as stress and repetitive-strain injury, can be found in many men's jobs. In this way, collaboration between women's committees and health-and-safety committees may be facilitated.

However, we cannot ignore the resistance to male-female collaboration in the area of occupational health. Gut feelings such as pride in male strength and yearnings for protection among women are strongly felt during many discussions. Lately, owing to management's new ferocity, the terror of plant closing, fear of job loss, and consequent resentment of new women workers have joined the lengthening list of obstacles to introducing new ideas and practices.

Women's issues have not progressed evenly within unions. In some unions a plateau was reached quickly, while in others discussions around such issues as sexual harassment and pay equity have kept women's committees in contact with the membership. The public-sector negotiations, for a long time an important motor for the advancement of women's issues, may suffer from a recent renewal of government attacks and cuts. In order for these issues to be kept alive, coalitions with community-based women's groups need to be reinforced.

Coalitions between the labour movement and women's groups have an inspiring but chequered history in Québec. An idea of the extent of these links could be gleaned from the study of various mega-events issuing from the collaboration: the March 8 events which regularly attracted about 12,000 people in the early 1980s; the marches to support Chantal Daigle's right to abortion in 1990, attended by 3000–10,000 people; the March 1990 celebration of the fifty years of women's right to vote in Québec, attended by over 10,000 women. The power and resources of the labour movement have been important in initiating and supporting struggles for day care, reproductive rights, and access to employment. However, women's groups have sometimes denounced the slow pace of union gains in these areas, what they perceive as insufficient emphasis on these issues, and the sexist attitudes of some union leaders.

Lately, events around both March 8 and December 6 have tended to be organized separately by unions and women's groups. Feminists have occasionally joined with governments or employers in blaming union traditions such as seniority for halting the full integration of women into the labour market. Such practices have not endeared women's groups to union leaders, and it is sometimes difficult to get union approval for participation in coalitions. Yet contact with women's groups is an important source of strength and encouragement for feminists in the labour movement. It is a positive sign that a major reflection on the place of women in Québec society, the 29–31 May 1992 'Forum des femmes du Québec,' was organized by a federation of womens' groups, the Fédération des femmes du Québec, together with all the major trade unions.

In the current context, it may be hard for unions to adopt progressive stands, try new techniques, and create new coalitions. However, union membership is on the rise and the service sector, traditionally female, is growing at the expense of the manufactoring sector, traditionally male. In 1987, for example, four out of every five new members has been a woman.[40] Unions are therefore becoming aware that they must continue to break new ground in order that the health of all union members be protected.

NOTES

We acknowledge the participation of many members of CINBIOSE in the projects and discussions described above, as well as interesting talks with many union members Gregor Murray supplied us with information on Quebec unions. KM thanks the Social Sciences and Humanities Research Council of Canada for research support.

1 Karen Messing, 'Do Men and Women Have Different Jobs Because of Their Biological Differences?' in Greta Nemiroff, ed., *Women and Men: Interdisciplinary Writings on Gender* (Toronto: Fitzhenry and White-

side 1986); Donna Mergler, 'Les Effets des conditions de travail sur la santé des travailleuses: Rapport-synthèse,' in J-A. Bouchard, ed., *Les effets des conditions de travail sur la santé des travailleuses* (Montréal: Service de la condition féminine, Confédération des syndicats nationaux 1984), 215–28

2 Jeanne Stellman, *Women's Work, Women's Health* (New York: Pantheon 1977); Wendy Chavkin, *Double Exposure* (New York: Monthly Review Press 1984); Vilma Hunt, *Work and the Health of Women* (Boca Raton, Fla.: CRC Publishing 1978)

3 Carole Brabant, Donna Mergler, and Karen Messing, 'Va te faire soigner, ton usine est malade: La place de l'hystérie de masse dans la problématique de la santé des travailleuses,' *Santé mentale au Québec* 15 (1990): 181–204

4 Alice Hamilton, *Exploring the Dangerous Trades* (Boston: Little Brown 1943)

5 Jeanne Stellman and Mary Sue Henefin, *Office Work Can Be Dangerous for Your Health* (New York: Pantheon Books 1984); Karen Messing, *Occupational Health and Safety Concerns of Canadian Women* (Ottawa: Labour Canada 1991)

6 Pat Armstrong and Hugh Armstrong, *Theorizing Women's Work* (Toronto: Garamond Press 1990)

7 Karen Messing, Lucie Dumais, and Patrizia Romito, 'Prostitutes and Chimney Sweeps Both Have Problems: Toward Full Integration of the Two Sexes in the Study of Occupational Health,' *Social Science and Medicine* 36 (1992): 47–55

8 Confédération des syndicats nationaux, a Québec union with 200,000 members, about half of whom are women

9 Fédération des travailleuses et travailleurs du Québec, a Québec union with 350,000 members, about 30 per cent of whom are women

10 The Centrale de l'enseignement du Québec groups all of Québec's and primaty- secondary-school teachers, as well as some junior-college and university lecturers and professors and some support staff. It has a large majority of women members. Until recently, it has not been closely involved with health-and-safety issues.

11 Comité conjoint UQAM-CSN-FTQ, *Le protocole d'entente UQAM-CSN-FTQ: Sur la formation syndicale* (Services à la collectivité, Université du Québec à Montréal 1977); Comité conjoint UQAM-CSN-FTQ, *Le protocole UQAM-CSN-FTQ: 1976–1986. Bilan et perspectives* (Services à la collectivité, Université du Québec à Montréal 1988); Karen Messing, 'Putting Our Two Heads Together: A Mainly Women's Research

Group Looks at Women's Occupational Health,' in J. Wine and J. Ristock, *Feminist Activism in Canada: Bridging Academe and the Community* (Toronto: James Lorimer Press 1991; repr. in *National Women's Studies Association Journal* 3: 355–67)

12 The university also has an analogous agreement with women's groups, called Relais-femmes, about which information can be found in two reports: Université du Québec à Montréal, *Le protocole UQAM-Relais-femmes* (Services à la collectivité, Université du Québec à Montréal 1988) and *Bilan des activités 1987–88 et perspectives pour la prochaine année* (Services à la collectivité, Université du Québec à Montréal 1988).

In this context, we have furnished some expertise to the local women's health centre (Centre de santé des femmes) and to some groups involved with employment access such as Action-Travail des Femmes. We also work with predominantly male unions. These experiences are outside the scope of this chapter, and are described in two papers: Donna Mergler, 'Worker Participation in Occupational Health Research: Theory and Practice,' *International Journal of Health Services* 17 (1987): 151–167, and Karen Messing, 'Union-initiated Research on Genetic Effects of Workplace Agents,' *Alternatives: Perspectives on Technology, Environment and Society* 15 (1987): 15–18

13 It should be noted that we are also active union members, since the union representing the professors at our university is affiliated to the CSN. One of us was a member of the women's committee of the CSN from 1978–83 and is still a member of the equal-access committee of our local union. However, our perspective on the health-and-safety issues we discuss here is primarily derived from our experiences as resource people.

14 See Cuneo, chapter 5 in this volume.

15 The program entitled 'Programme d'action concertée sur la conciliation du travail et des responsabilités familiales,' is jointly sponsored by the Fonds FCAR and the Secrétariat de la condition féminine.

16 A major exception was the election of Monique Simard, head of the women's service, to a position of power in the CSN executive (1983–91), which was a statement about the importance of women's issues in negotiations in the public sector.

17 Karen Messing, 'Est-ce que les travailleuses enceintes sont protégées au Québec?' *Union médicale* 111 (1982): 1–6

18 Nancy Miller-Chenier, *Reproductive Hazards at Work* (Ottawa: Canadian Advisory Council on the Status of Women 1982)

19 Barry Castleman and Grace Ziem, 'Corporate Influence on Threshold Limit Values,' *American Journal of Industrial Medicine* 13 (1988): 531–59

20 'Environnement et santé: La santé au travail et les choix scientifiques,' in *L'avenir d'un monde fini: Jalons pour une éthique du développement durable*, Cahiers de recherche éthique no. 15 (Montréal: Editions Fides 1991), 107–10

21 Karen Messing, Abby Lippman, Claire Infante-Rivard, and Nicole Vézina, 'Les Nouvelles normes sur le retrait préventif de la travailleuse enceinte,' Report on the new government guidelines prepared at the request of the CSN, September 1988

22 The Coalition pour le maintien du droit au retrait préventif was initiated by feminist public-health workers who expressed concern when the government emitted directives restricting access to the law. They supported the union in its struggle to resist the guidelines, and are now mobilizing against recent attempts to change the law.

23 Marie-Claude Lortie, 'Les Travailleuses enceintes bientôt protégées par une loi fédérale,' *La Presse*, 29 Jan. 1992, B1

24 Lisa Vogel, 'Debating Difference: Feminism, Pregnancy and the Workplace,' *Feminist Studies* 16 (1990): 9–32

25 Geneviève Turcotte, 'How Pregnant Workers See Their Work, Its Risks and the Right to Precautionary Leave in Québec,' *Women and Health* 18 (1992): 79–96

26 Brabant et al. 181–204; Rosemarie Bowler and Donna Mergler, 'Stability of Psychological Impairment: 2-year Followup of Former Microelectronics Workers' Affective and Personality Disturbance,' *Women and Health* 18 (1992): 27–48

27 E.N. Corlett and R.P. Bishop, 'A Technique for Assessing Postural Discomfort,' *Ergonomics* 19 (1976): 175–82; R.L. Waterfield, 'The Effect of Posture on the Volume of the Leg,' *Journal of Physiology* 72 (1931): 131–6

28 Nicole Vézina and Julie Courville, 'Le Travail debout. Etude ergonomique du poste de caissière d'un supermarché' (Université du Québec à Montréal 1989), 98

29 Expert testimony for the employer's case against cashiers being seated was given by a former union activist, who had consistently supported anti-protectionist positions.

30 Laura Punnett, 'Soft Tissue Disorders in the Upper Limbs of Female Garment Workers,' *Scandinavian Journal of Work Environment and Health* 11 (1985): 417–25

31 Carole Brabant, 'Heat Exposure Limits: Equitable or Debatable,' *Women and Health* 18 (1992): 119–30

32 Carole Brabant, Sylvie Bédard, and Donna Mergler, 'Cardiac Strain among Women Workers in an Industrial Laundry,' *Ergonomics* 32 (1989): 615–28

33 Messing, Dumais, and Romito

34 Hélène David, 'Femmes et emploi: Le défi de l'égalité' (Québec: Presses de l'Université du Québec 1986)

35 K. Kauppinen-Toropainen, I. Kandolin, and E. Haavio-Manila, 'Sex Segregation of Work in Finland and the Quality of Women's Work,' *Journal of Organizational Behaviour* 9 (1988): 15–27; Donna Mergler, Carole Brabant, Nicole Vézina, and Karen Messing, 'The Weaker Sex? Men in Women's Working Conditions Report Similar Health Symptoms,' *Journal of Occupational Medicine* 29 (1987): 417–21

36 Joan S. Ward, 'Women at Work – Ergonomic Considerations,' *Ergonomics* 27 (1984): 475–79

37 Julie Courville, Nicole Vézina, and Karen Messing, 'Analysis of Work Activity of a Job in a Machine Shop Held by Ten Men and One Woman,' *International Journal of Industrial Ergonomics* 7 (1991): 163–74

38 Julie Courville, Nicole Vézina, and Karen Messing, 'Analyse des facteurs ergonomiques pouvant entraîner l'exclusion des femmes du tri des colis postaux,' *Le travail humain* 55 (1992): 119–34

39 Céline Chatigny, Ana Maria Seifert, Lucie Dumais, and Karen Messing, 'A Woman's Disease in a Man's Job: Chromosomes or Workshop Conditions? (submitted)

40 Statistics Canada, *Corporation and Labour Union Returns Act. Annual review* (1989), Catalog 71-202; Queen's University Industrial Relations Center, *Current Industrial Relations Scene in Canada* (Kingston: Queen's University Press 1990), 49

14

From the DEW Line: The Experience of Canadian Garment Workers

ARMINE YALNIZYAN

After more than a decade of economic restructuring and reframing political norms and values, labour markets throughout the industrialized world are in upheaval. The social consensus of the postwar period has dissipated, and with it the climate that legitimated the pursuit of such goals as full employment and stable, decent working conditions for all. As globalism and competitiveness become the dominant ethics, trade unions, especially in North America, are going through an unparalleled crisis. Are we witnessing the death of a social movement, or its painful metamorphosis?

A case study about garment workers in these times could strike some readers as charming but irrelevant history, an archaeological expedition into Canada's best-known, longest-lasting sunset industry. Nothing could be further from the truth. The dilemmas confronting garment workers now confront many other workers. As the same logic unfolds, creating strikingly similar 'adjustments' in sectors as diverse as food processing, automotive parts, and data entry, it is time to pay attention to the lessons that have been learned by these women over the last twenty years.

The Canadian garment industry can be seen as the DEW Line for labour-intensive sectors of the economy.[1] The story of how this sector has been transformed, and how the women working in it are responding to what is happening to them, may be the shape of changes to come for a growing number of workers in the global economy.

In telling the story, this article touches on the major challenges facing all unions today: the erosion of union representation; the growing precarious nature of being employed; the difficulties of servicing increasingly fragmented bargaining units; the rise of home-working and the challenges of organizing the new workplace; the importance and limitations of international links; and the difficult choices in allocating resources to both grass-roots struggles for workplace justice and overarching fights for legislative reform.

Of necessity garment workers, of which at least 80 per cent in Canada are women, find themselves on the front line of the battle to oppose the fragmentation of the workforce, developing different approaches to organizing, forging international alliances, and building a social movement. The new tactics being developed by these women raise questions all unions must eventually address because of the logic embedded in the emerging international economic order. How workers begin to cobble their response to these growing pressures will determine the viability of not only workplace-based collective strength but our ability to demand broader social change.

THE LEAKY SHIP: INDUSTRIAL REORGANIZATION AND THE DE-ORGANIZATION OF WORKERS

The drop in the rate of unionization in the Canadian garment industry is so stunning it's difficult to register: only 20 per cent of workers in the industry are organized today, compared with almost 80 per cent just thirty years ago.[2] What happened? Nothing short of the transformation of an entire industry owing to plant closures and restructuring. This decline has been intensified over the past three years as a result of continually liberalizing trade (and, more important, capital flows) through implementation of the Free Trade Agreement with the United States (FTA), changes in the General Agreement on Tariffs and Trade (GATT) and pressures flowing from the imminent North American Free Trade Agreement (NAFTA). Unions have simply been unable to overhaul their organizing strategies to address the new realities of an industry increasingly characterized by small and marginal employers that disappear and re-emerge literally overnight.

Strangely, the accelerated 'churn' in the market is accepted, even considered normal. It is part of a mind-set which has for almost twenty years assumed that clothing manufacturing in Canada was fated to become largely irrelevant as a source of jobs and wealth because of the pressure of low wages from so many points of the compass. While these pressures are real, the facts tell a different story: in 1980, almost three-quarters (73 per cent) of all manufactured goods, including clothing, bought in Canada were made here. By 1991, that percentage had dropped to just over half (56 per cent of manufactured goods and 55 per cent of clothing purchases were domestically produced).[3]

Since the clothing industry experienced the same decline as overall manufacturing, why is it portrayed as more dispensable to our economy? The answer may lie in the export figures: in 1980 exports represented just 1.3 per cent of total Canadian garment production, a figure that had grown to only 4.2 per cent by 1991. For the manufacturing sector taken as a whole, however, exports have become a critical segment of production, growing from 23 per cent to 43 per cent of total shipments over the same period.[4] The name of the game is the global market-place. Industries, such as garment manufacturing, that only service the domestic market are dismissed as being out of step with the times.

Who's Steering? Retailers Chart the Course

For the last few years, it seems that somebody has pressed the fast-forward button on change. Growing fall-out from implementation of the Free Trade Agreement with the United States, cross-border shopping, the recession, and cuts in people's disposable income have combined at the same time that American retailers – such as The Gap, Talbots, Nordstrom, Price Club, and The Limited – have begun establishing themselves in Canada. Many industry analysts believe that we have an oversupply of stores. Measured by any yardstick, there are more players trying to attract fewer consumer dollars. The lingering recession has made people more cost-conscious and the proliferation of discount houses, liquidation sales, and intense price competition between retailers has made shoppers accustomed to not paying full retail price. In order to survive, retailers are pressuring manufacturers to contain or cut costs like never before. This pressure sets up a vicious circle that is difficult to break. Ultimately it pits us, as consumers, against ourselves, as producers.

Fierce price competition also undoes loyalties and long-term relationships, facilitating further off-shore sourcing. Canadian retailers used to give preference to Canadian manufacturers not through formal policies but because of long-standing relationships. Such stability and security is a thing of the past. Everyone is looking for the best possible deal. A low-end Canadian retailing firm, Zellers, sums it up with its highly successful advertising campaign: 'Because the lowest price is the law.'

In an effort to comply with the 'law,' large Canadian retailers are increasingly moving to establish direct links with American suppliers. This is not surprising because American producers are bigger and can take advantage of longer production runs, benefiting from economies of scale because they are already geared to a much larger market than are Canadian producers. A powerful example of this trend was the Hudson's Bay Company's announcement that between 1992 and 1994 it would increase its purchases directly from the United States from 15 per cent level to 40 per cent.[5] The Bay is historically recognized as the most 'Canadian' department store. Founded in 1670, it operates 486 stores throughout Canada and is North America's 7th-largest department store, with sales of $5 billion in 1990. (The Bay also owns Zellers.) Similarly, the American retailer Sears Canada is considering making all its purchasing decisions from its U.S. head offices rather than having a separate Canadian buying office. As American retailers set up their chains in Canada to replace the retail outlets which are closing down here, they bring with them their own sourcing systems. These are based on American suppliers, but this does not translate into guaranteed American jobs. Over time more and more production has been taking place off-shore and is simply routed through the United States. As a result, Canadian manufacturers are losing out on new orders even though the number of retail outlets has not declined.

Pyramid Power: The New Shape of the Industry

Pushed by cut-throat price competition, retailers are breaking down the traditional patterns of production in the garment industry and replacing them with a new model. In the past, large manufacturing companies dominated a dual-economy industry which was also marked by many small family-run establishments. These companies had large workforces, usually coupled with a small in-house sales team which showed retailers the season's wares.

Now the industry is moving towards a 'pyramid' structure of production. In Ontario, the garment industry has become highly fragmented: 43 per cent of firms operate with one to four workers; only 23 per cent operate in establishments with more than twenty workers.[6] Manufacturers are increasingly unable to decide what they will produce. Instead large retailers and distributors, most often multinational companies, contract directly with manufacturers, telling them what styles and labels the stores will carry. The manufacturers merely operate as contractors, filling their own orders with a larger web of subcontractors and homeworkers. The giants of the industry – unlike the Fords, IBMs, or General Electrics of other sectors – are becoming invisible. They determine what is offered in the market-place but usually do not own production facilities and therefore do not directly confront workers. They are only recognizable by their label(s), but these continually change. By spinning vast webs of production and distribution through their networks of contractors, they avoid most of the risks of production. But their vast purchasing power gives them the ability to indirectly control at least the ceiling of wages and working conditions, there being no floor.

The role of the retailer has become the most significant development in driving the restructuring of the market-place in Canada, dictating where production will occur and under what working conditions. Retailers are demanding a faster turn-around time from placement of orders to deliveries, with heavy penalties meted on late deliveries. This is directly connected with the smaller inventories most retailers are holding.

As a result, production schedules are more erratic, affecting the predictability of work, and income, for those who still have jobs. In the past a manufacturer would have a relatively dependable volume of orders to be filled over the course of the season. Even with the occasional loss of a contract, a core of workers would be able to work on a series of standing orders. Now it has become more common to have to work overtime one week and be left with no work the next. The 'just-in-time' inventory system has created a 'just-in-time' model of the labour market. This new form of unemployment is all the more insidious since the periods of joblessness are often too short for workers to claim unemployment insurance. The sporadic work week means that workers no longer know how much they will make from week to week and that they will have to directly shoulder the impact and costs of fluctuations in demand. Since labour costs are a significant component of manufacturing garments, employers who are attempting to maintain their production in Canada tend to target wages as the first source of flexibility. In times like these, with so few job opportunities, it is easier to pressure workers into taking wage concessions and to pit worker against worker. If direct pressures to reduce hourly wage rates are not successful, more work can be contracted out and more homeworkers can be used.

Continuous price competition between contractors also leads to changing constellations of manufacturers. These suppliers generally subcontract to a number of producers, making it hard to target one large company, even through such mechanisms as strikes. Strikes have become increasingly hard to stage when even organized workplaces are replacing the more stable jobs with more precarious forms of work.[7]

The increasing fragmentation of the workforce in the garment industry is directly due to the emerging organization of the industry, one which is replacing factory production with literally thousands of women working from their homes for less than minimum wage and in poor working conditions. The best image for this new industrial structure is a pyramid. The top of the pyramid is dominated by a few large retailers. In Canada the Hudson's Bay Company, Eaton's, and Dylex control more than 40 per cent of the market. Armed with this control, retailers dictate to garment manufacturers when they want a garment, the exact time to produce it, and the price that will be paid for it. This year the Hudson's Bay Company even started to take garments on consignment. The next level down the pyramid from manufacturers consists of 'jobbers,' or contractors and subcontractors. Many garment manufacturers who are no longer able to operate factories work as jobbers, designing the garment, buying the fabric, and perhaps cutting the garment. These tend to be male-dominated occupations. They then contract the work out to other subcontractors, who in turn farm it out to individual homeworkers to finish the garment. Sewers are almost exclusively female. The pyramid structure not only consolidates power at the top, it fragments the bottom into tiny isolated units and drives this part of the economy, the part fed mostly by women, underground. This makes it extremely hard to establish clear and sufficiently long-term connections between workers to gear up strategies which could counteract, or at least make more visible, the further erosion of working conditions.

International Ladies Garment Workers' Union (ILGWU) research shows that homeworkers are mainly immigrant women, paid as little as $1.00 an hour and rarely more than $4.50.[8] Homeworkers do not get vacation pay, and their employers do not pay premiums for Unemployment Insurance or the Canada Pension Plan. They get no overtime pay and have no control over working conditions, often receiving an order on Friday that is due back on Monday. Some homeworkers are recent immigrants to the country and are employed through the informal social webs of ethnicity. But many, though not Canadian by birth, are experienced factory workers who were either laid off by their employers and offered contracted-out work or could not return to a factory after a maternity leave because they could not find decent child care that they could afford. Now they are doing the same work, sometimes for the same employer, for less money, out of their homes. The double day of factory work and family care becomes the endless, isolated day of homework and family care.[9]

THE RACE TO THE BOTTOM: LABOUR RELATIONS IN THE 1990s

In the spring of 1990 Prime Minister Brian Mulroney visited the Caribbean on a trade junket and announced the Caribbean Business Initiative, designed to enhance the economic development of the Caribbean basin. 'Outward processing' was the chief example that was put forth, harkening to the future by looking to the past. The Americans have had this arrangement (commonly known as the 807 program) with Mexico and the Caribbean nations for more than twenty years. The program has been used for electronics, such as TVs and stereos, and garments, that is, labour-intensive industries. In both industry sectors the labour-intensive part is the assembly of the good. These jobs are traditionally held by women.

Under the arrangement, garments are cut, bundled, and sent to the low-wage countries to be assembled and sewn there. The finished garments are then shipped back to the United States, with duty paid only on the labour component, not on the fabric or value of the garment. In the United States the label reads 'made in Mexico with U.S. components.' What has been saved for America is the traditional men's jobs.

This model of economic development has deep implications. The argument runs that, as part of aid packages to lesser-developed nations, we should send business, that is, employment. Implementation of this policy has resulted in the export of low-wage jobs but maintenance of the high-wage end of production. In the electronics and garment industries, this means exporting women's jobs and retaining men's jobs. For example, in the garment industry, the cutter is the best-paid job, a job held almost exclusively by men. There is one cutting job for every ten sewing jobs. Canadian unions drawing attention to this hypocrisy are cast as greedy and anti-aid/anti-development for poorer nations. As a model of organizing how things get produced, outward processing becomes an important divisive tool between male and female workers and, perhaps more important, between workers in one country and another.

But it does not take off-shore production to raise these same concerns of gender inequity in shouldering the costs of this period of restructuring. As we have seen above, the forces unleashed by the era of 'free' trade have greatly escalated the process of increasing downward pressure on workers in the garment industry and moving large parts of the industry, the sewing and final assembly, underground. Those most affected are immigrant women, without voice or representation.

By the late 1980s, imports had grown to 42 per cent of the domestic market for clothing. As negotiations for a free-trade agreement with the United States progressed, the central concern in the garment industry was the rapid dropping of tariff walls. This focus seemed to foster the development of a common analysis and an unlikely alliance between workers and employers in the garment industry. Both opposed further reductions of tariff barriers in the absence of an industrial strategy for a sector which has always been particularly vulnerable to cheap imports. Both agreed that Canada would be flooded with American-made garments, since producers in the United States, having a hard time competing with off-shore imports in their own country, would suddenly have a competitive advantage here owing to lower costs of production – primarily in the form of lower wages. It was clear that the low-end market would get massacred by competitors from the southern United States. But common wisdom has held that the fruits of free trade can be enjoyed in high-value-added, export-oriented, niche markets. So there was also a shared hope that some Canadian designers and manufacturers of high-end garments would be able to compete both at home and abroad. Workers in these niches felt relatively secure and ready to prove, along with their employers, that they were world-class.

Once the FTA was implemented, however, class interests no longer had the slightest appearance of converging. In assessing their ability to compete in the new economic reality, Canadian producers tended to either pursue a low-wage, mass-production strategy or get out of manufacturing altogether. Of course, the low-wage strategy is not unique to our relatively higher-waged Canadian market. The pressures facing garment workers here mirror exactly what workers are facing in the United States, Mexico, and South-East Asia, namely cost-containment in the face of mounting pressure from expanded free trade. Even though competitive forces mean the low-wage areas attract much of the work, these zones are not immune from further downward pressure on working conditions and wages. In fact, Mexico's garment industry is restructuring along the same lines as the Canadian industry with the rapid proliferation of contractors and homeworkers. Lean production systems depend on multi-tier wages and continental 'whipsawing,' where by concessions gained in one workplace are used to threaten workers elsewhere with a plant shutdown if they do not make their costs 'competitive.' It only takes one alternative site of production within the same company, at a subcontractor or abroad, to make this strategy work.[10]

BUILDING STRENGTH: THE SLOW DANCE OF SURVIVAL

If the chief pressure is low-wage competition, can Canadian workers slow down the erosion of their standard of living without pitting themselves against their American and Mexican sisters? Are there examples of cooperation and solidarity which suggest ways for labour to counterbalance the increasingly mobile nature of international capital? The Encuentro in Mexico City in October 1990 between Canadians and Mexicans was a meeting to discuss the limits and dangers of continental free trade. A handful of Canadians and Mexicans identified their common interests and the nature of the struggle. Solid personal connections were made, but limited resources have meant it has not been possible to produce a more lasting mechanism that could help a broad cross-section of workers in the two nations work more closely together. The future of the solidarity campaign rests in the hands of a tiny number of people.

However, the Encuentro did reinforce the adage, first coined by environmentalists, 'think globally, act locally.' It is relatively easy to forge international *symbols* of solidarity, such as joint statements or proposals for social charters, but hard to follow through with concrete support in our daily struggles.

The massive increase in capital's mobility over the last decade often reduces the debate on how to respond to a false polarization between protectionism versus international solidarity. The Encuentro underscored how false this schism is between protecting ourselves and building international links. Each local struggle can and must point out the broader process that is unfolding, drawing attention to what these forces mean to our sisters far away. How the ILGWU has begun to do this in Canada is another lesson in the importance of small, personal steps.

Doing Our Homework: New Models of Organizing

By 1991 the Ontario District of the ILGWU started to wonder if home-working and highly precarious forms of employment were becoming more the rule than the exception and decided to try to document the trends. Between 1987 and 1991, the official number of full- and part-time garment workers in the City of Toronto fell from 12,574 to 6520 workers.[11] At the same time, the union estimated that by 1991 there were about 4000 homeworkers in the downtown area. By provincial law, employers using homeworkers are bound to register their names, addresses, and wages paid with the Ontario Ministry of Labour, but this is yet another example of having a law that is essentially not enforced. As of 1991, the ministry had fewer than seventy registered homeworkers. This listing reflected the make-up of union member-ship in factories, showing that more than 60 per cent of these workers are Chinese or Vietnamese – a reasonable finding given that the garment industry is concentrated in the cosmopolitan Greater Toronto area.

Based on this knowledge, the union put an ad in Chinese newspa-pers saying they would pay $10 to interview homeworkers. They established a Homeworker Hotline service, giving workers a chance to ask questions and get help. They put out a pamphlet in Chinese and Vietnamese describing workers' rights, put the Hotline's number on it, and distributed the pamphlets in community centres that serve the Chinese as well as pool halls and gambling halls, where many of the Chinese and Vietnamese men in Toronto gather. This effort generated the first thirty people that were interviewed for a study undertaken by the union.[12] The researcher was a Chinese-speaking woman trained as a social worker in Hong Kong. She did not just conduct the interviews and write the report, but also counselled and slowly developed a relationship with these women. One of these Chinese homeworkers was deaf and had never learned sign language so was unable to communicate. She was earning roughly $1 an hour.

The researcher put her in touch with the Canadian Hearing Society, dramatically changing her life.

In a sense, the process of conducting this study was a first crack at organizing these workers, though that was not its focus. Its purpose was looking for natural ways to build links among these workers. Part of that link was the organizer, and the painstakingly slow, labour-intensive building of trust between her and these workers. The turning-point for this organizing campaign came when, a few months after the study was completed, the organizer held a tea party for the interviewees to discuss the possibility of organizing a homeworkers' association. Of the original thirty, only two people came. By the end of the month, five women had joined the Homeworkers' Association. Six weeks later, there were fifteen. By the sixth month of organizing, thirty-five homeworkers had joined the association.

Shortly after the tea party, the union organized (and heavily subsidized) a Saturday bus trip to a sugar bush. It rented a school bus and sold tickets, with reduced rates for members of the association. Chinese-speaking homeworkers brought their children, husbands, friends, and other relatives. People had to come to the union office to buy tickets in advance and to catch the bus, so the office and its staff became familiar as a facility and a location. One month later another trip was organized, this time to Niagara Falls for the Blossom Festival. Through word of mouth, as well as community-service announcements on TV and in Chinese newspapers, two busloads were filled. On both occasions, the organizer let people know about the association and what it could do for them, but in a social setting.

This is a far cry from traditional organizing, where hundreds of members may sign cards within a week. The mechanics of this process are also a departure from tradition. The most successful avenue for organizing thus far has been social day-trips. These women are isolated in their homes, often with young children, with little money and less knowledge about places to explore in their adopted country. Day outings provide an opportunity for these new immigrants to experience an outing with those they most trust, their family.

This type of organizing is built on trust and acceptance and for this reason is heavily reliant on both personal contact and word-of-mouth communication. This approach has created a situation where husbands of the homeworkers working in garages or auto-parts plants or Chinese restaurants are also beginning to show interest in joining the association. The first members were restaurant workers, and if enough workers in one restaurant get interested the union can engage in traditional organizing so these associate members can become full union members. The 'accidental' links between precarious sectors are not surprising. Places offering precarious employment commonly use immigrant labour. Since there is an informal network among immigrant workers in each cultural circle, once it has been tapped communication becomes easier.

It is not yet clear if this slow, incremental process works differently in different language, ethnic, and cultural groups. At this point there are bi-weekly social events such as summer picnics at the Island, cherry-picking, and visiting the African Lion Safari. Sports and play events for the children will, it is hoped, bridge some of the differences and permit, through their families, the forging of meaningful and long-term connections between people.

The Homeworkers' Association: Half a Union or More?

The Homeworkers' Association was charterd under the ILGWU's Local 12 in February 1992 and organizing the homeworkers began in April. Since the Ontario Labour Relations Board does not permit a bargaining unit of only one worker, there is no formal certificate for the local and the union has no legal right to bargain collectively on behalf of these women. But the union has started to provide other services, such as advocacy at the provincial Employment Standards branch. In such cases the union acts as the worker's agent, shielding homeworkers who file a complaint regarding some violation of the Employment Standards Act. For example, the ILGWU recently launched an anonymous complaint for a woman who had completed thirty hours of work one week for an employer and earned only $115, far below Ontario's minimum wage.

The association has organized activities every Saturday, so that every two weeks there is a social event and on alternating weeks there are legal seminars providing information on employment rights, landlord-tenant issues, unemployment insurance, severance pay, and divorce counselling. Educational seminars are being planned for associate members: how to fill out income-tax forms, since homeworkers are officially self-employed; how to work with immigration lawyers, since so many homeworkers wish to bring their families to Canada; and how to maintain their sewing machines.

The ILGWU also refers homeworkers to the Apparel-Textile Action

Centre (ATAC), a joint project between four sponsor groups: ILGWU Ontario, the Amalgamated Clothing and Textile Workers, the Chinese Garment Workers' Association, and Women Working With Immigrant Women. This grouping has received federal funding from the Industrial Adjustment Service to run an ongoing labour-adjustment centre for organized and non-union apparel and textile workers. ATAC provides counselling and referral to Canada Employment Centres for training and assistance with Unemployment Insurance forms. It is also now running a full-time government-sponsored language-training program out of the union office, offering basic and intermediate-level English courses. There are participants from four plant closures, including one non-union plant closure, as well as homeworkers who registered through the Homeworkers' Association. In all, the union sponsors six English-as-a-Second-Language courses, four of which are full-time and two run on the weekend, providing opportunities for ninety people.

It should be noted that there is concern and some resentment about the push to organize homeworkers. Union members are worried that by organizing homeworkers, the union appears to be condoning their use. The only response to that argument is that as long as minimum standards (in wages, hours, and working conditions) are being so dramatically undercut within the same city limits, unions will continue to experience enormous pressure to engage in concession bargaining on standards. The point of organizing homeworkers is to build up their standards and narrow the gap; however, it may be that the only meaningful way of reducing the gap between unionized, factory-based workers and homeworkers is through legislative change that will permit broader-based bargaining.

Partly in response to these concerns, the ILGWU Ontario spearheaded the formation of the Coalition for Fair Wages and Working Conditions for Homeworkers in 1991. This campaign brought together worker advocacy groups, legal clinics, the women's movement, and the church in order to press for legislative reforms, including a new framework for organizing. A key recommendation of the brief they prepared was to change the definition of employer in the Labour Relations Act. The goal was to make the principal contractor (owner of the label) accountable for a certain minimum standard of working conditions for all employees working on that contractor's products at any point in the subcontracting chain. Under current legislation only the immediate employer, not the original contractor, can be held responsible for violating minimum standards.

A NEW WORKPLACE, A NEW POLITICS – A NEW UNION STRUCTURE?

The workplace of the future is at once more fragmented and more connected than in the past. Long-term trends have made an increasingly polarized labour market grow more reliant on low-wage job growth, about the only place where jobs *are* being created at all.[13] The low-wage sector of the economy is also more marked by substandard and precarious forms of work, characterized by high turnover, language and cultural barriers, fear of reprisal for reporting flagrant violations of rights, and little information about those rights in the first place. Building channels of communication is that much harder when only 20 per cent of the factory-based workforce is organized and where it is not unusual for there to be fifteen different ethnic and linguistic groups in one garment factory alone.

Unions have not historically reached out to these sectors. The traditional approach is to go after a large group of workers in one plant, sign them up and apply for certification. But if the workplace of the future is more typified by small, diverse, highly mobile locations, it will not be possible to tie organization to the production facility. Instead, organization must focus on the workers themselves and their communities. This approach goes back to the origins of organizing as a social movement, organizing that is grounded in a sense of community. This is the basis of the ILGWU's organizing efforts with those at the bottom of the pyramid.

Unions representing low-wage workers, such as in the garment industry, operate with small budgets since dues reflect income earned. These unions do not only have to absorb the costs of organizing workers and negotiating and maintaining collective agreements in industries which are typified by many small workplaces and high turnover. Since low-waged industries tend to hire from immigrant populations, effective representation must also include such basic services as the proper translation of contracts and materials to inform members of their rights and of local campaigns. Paradoxically, the unions with the smallest revenues are the ones confronted with disproportionately large demands on their budgets. Because these demands are all legitimate and because they cannot all be met, members inevitably end up feeling under- or mis-represented.

Overcoming the barriers inherent in the low-wage sector requires a continuous infusion of money to establish and maintain links among workers. In the case of organizing homeworkers, this effort cannot be financed by the workers themselves. It costs $12 a year to join Local 12. Since the association does not generate enough dues to pay for staff, and the other ILGWU locals are in no position to subsidize this venture, the union had to find new funding to hire a full-time Chinese-speaking woman to organize homeworkers. Thus far, the union has raised money from the provincial government as well as from its head office in New York. Now it is looking at fund-raising from major unions and community organizations in the Toronto district. The ad hoc nature of financing this project raises concerns about its long-term sustainability and the way in which unions work together. The conundrum is this: organizing the low-wage sector requires enormous resources and is a task that cannot be self-financed by those who will benefit. It will have to be subsidized by union members who can pay more dues. Can traditional unions dominated by well-paid, primarily white male workers adapt themselves to co-exist with poorly paid, primarily immigrant and female workers, without hostility and without subsuming these other interests?

International or Not: What Is the Best Structure for Unions?

The challenge the low-wage sector presents to the labour movement echoes another long-standing tension, that between affiliates within an international union. There are structural limitations within an international union when one partner is big and the other little. In the case of garment workers, this dynamic has resulted in a serious threat to the very viability of their unions in Canada. The seriousness of the situation is typified by the type, timing, and amount of support offered to the Canadian locals by their international offices during the free-trade fight. Even though American headquarters passed resolutions opposing the FTA, this was not followed by organizing or by any real educational, financial, or strategic help for 'our' struggle. The reason for the lack of solidarity and support was simple. The proposed FTA did not seriously affect American workers and actually seemed a benefit as jobs would start to flow south of the border, creating a potential source of new members in the United States.

The fight against free trade launched by the Canadian locals of garment unions was necessarily scaled down because there was no up-front promise of support from their head offices. By the time some limited resources were allocated to the fight, the agreement had been signed and the Canadian federal election was over. To add insult to injury, resources were allocated by head office soon after to develop an export strategy for American-made clothes in the Canadian market. This project was staved off only after loud protest from the Canadian affiliates.

Does the answer lie in separating from the international structure? The answer is not simple because separation alone, even if achievable, would not address the second important issue, that of the neccessity of union merger. Unions thinking of separation face an almost impossible task. First, international union constitutions are clearly designed to discourage such enterprises. For example, one constitution stipulates that, regardless of the size of the membership, if more than seven members vote against the motion to leave the international, the application is null and void. Should that hurdle be surmounted, there are other obstacles. Assets such as bank accounts, property, and even office chairs immediately revert to being the property of the international should a local or region leave.

Even if separation occurred, few Canadian locals or regions would be well positioned to survive. There are three trade unions operating in the garment sector in Canada. The luxury of duplicated resources when every union faces the same constraints is no longer affordable. But discussions for merger have been going on for twenty-five years and each time the old argument is revived with no resolution: who will be king?

If the question of who will end up representing those in the merged structure seems intractable, the issue of resources remains another giant stumbling block. In a country as big as Canada, maintaining connections with members from British Columbia to Quebec is an expensive proposition. Decisions about where to hold a national conference and how to divide travel costs when all regions are cash-strapped inevitably cause conflict among delegates. More significantly, lack of resources can and does force cancellations of critical national forums such as conventions and strategy sessions.

Rebuilding the House of Labour

Working for progressive change both at home and abroad requires that each link in the chain is strong. If unions are so constrained that they must evaluate if it is possible or desirable to take the time and expense to talk to each other in Canada, how can enduring connections be made with workers in other parts of the global economy?

The prerequisite for building a movement which can challenge the corporate agenda is resources.

Union consolidation in the garment industry emerges as a key long-term strategy to be pursued, but not just for this sector. Bringing together the infrastructure of workers' representation across all sectors and across the nation would provide weaker unions with better access to business information on a sectoral basis, legal know-how, better educational programs, and larger research capacities. That would translate into less undercutting of the bargaining gains of stronger unions. Pooling resources creates a mechanism for identifying trends and tactics, coordinating strategies of resistance, and developing alternative proposals for economic development. There are obvious rewards of bringing together workers in different plants or countries of the same multinational company to share information on organizing and bargaining tactics. The challenge is to find the most appropriate mechanisms.

Perhaps the best we can offer to one another are the lessons and limited successes from our own local struggles and experiments. The existence of a relatively sympathetic government in Ontario may make it more possible to push for legislated protection of homeworkers here. If this occurs, it makes it that much more probable in another jurisdiction.

CONCLUSION: MAKING THE LINKS

The massive increase in capital's mobility over the last decade has made visible the comment that 'everything that is solid melts into air.' As the speed of change becomes dizzying in our daily lives, the debate on how to respond often gets reduced to protectionism versus international solidarity.

The garment industry has been undergoing massive restructuring for the last twenty years on a global scale. This process has taught garment workers many lessons: first, how important international solidarity is and how difficult it is; second, that the schism between protecting ourselves and building links is a false division. In fact, buying into this either/or mentality ignores the nature and significance of the small, disparate victories required to build a strong international movement which demands economic justice.

The experience of the ILGWU over the last few years raises many questions. Is it better to be employed under substandard working conditions than to organize and ultimately shut the factory down? Should union resources be targeted on organizing workers in such a highly fragmented industry? Or should they be targeted at the top of the pyramid, for example, fighting for better legal definitions of who is the employer? Should resources be deployed to push for the enforcement of existing employment standards? Or to create a different regulatory climate?

For more than a decade the industrialized nations have conducted the social experiment which unleashed capital, allegedly for the purposes of creating greater wealth for everyone. The 'hands off the private sector' mentality has resulted in the growing polarization of society, the gradual erosion of the legitimacy of public goods, and the dominant fetish for short-run profits. In the early 1990s, there is an almost palpable sense that things are out of control.

The return to an unregulated market has some irreversible consequences. While each company makes its own 'rational' economic micro-decision, the effect at the macro-economic level will be to destroy Canadian industry – the garment industry being but one classic example. There is an urgent need to challenge this incredible economic myopia, to think in a broader, long-term context.

Because they represent workers in many different worksites and geographic locations, labour unions are just as well positioned as banks and multinational companies to see the trends which are developing. The difference is in their vantage-point. Union staff and community workers must reveal the broader, global implications of the latest consolidation of capital that is under way for each community and workplace struggle. Unless the economic vision imbedded in the FTA, the NAFTA, and the GATT is challenged, workers' strengths and rights will continue to be eroded no matter where they live. Communities all over the world need to urge governments to re-regulate the economy. With entrenchment of economic bad times, it will become easier for activists to make visible the way in which 'free' trade promotes a tension between us as consumers and as producers. As more people begin to recognize that this dynamic is not sustainable in the long run, legitimate space will be created for demanding such policies as legislation which ensures that we can produce a significant share of what we consume in the sectors we believe are key to our economy.[14] Even small victories such as obtaining procurement policies which support national or local suppliers can be used to demand similar changes in other jurisdictions. Given the pressures we are facing and the nature of changes being sought, Canadian unions will only be able to survive in a way that is meaningful to their members if they move towards consolidation in sectoral clusters within one national union. Consolidation would counteract the problem of inadequate resources for individual unions and would coordinate our fight-back struggles. Sectoral components would give the larger structure direction and shape. These components would make international connections more representative, while the consolidated structure would be able to offer a level of resources that could transform international connections beyond the symbolic into something powerful, constructive, and concrete.

The task which faces garment workers is the same task that others face, and it is immense: we must find enduring and relevant ways of linking ourselves as consumers, as producers, and as citizens in the world. This case study offers one perspective on the economic terrain that is being created and the steps that might help negotiate and redirect its shape.

NOTES

The author would like to thank members of the various coalitions working in Toronto to promote justice for garments workers, in particular activists within the International Ladies Garment Workers' Union. Their stories, views, and hopes for the future are the inspiration for this piece.

1 In 1955 the American and Canadian governments installed the DEW Line, a Distant Early Warning network of radar stations strung in a line across the Arctic Circle, designed to provide early warning of an aerial attack on the territories of Canada and the United States by Soviet missiles coming over the North Pole. I thank Laurell Ritchie of the Canadian Auto Workers, Local 40, for this compelling analogy.
2 Estimates from the International Ladies Garment Workers' Union, Ontario division
3 Statistics on total manufacturing come from the Canadian Manufacturers' Association, Year End Review and 1992 Economic Outlook, 19 Dec. 1991. These figures are compiled from Statistics Canada data. Statistics on the clothing industry come from Statistics Canada catalogue no. 65-207. (Unpublished) estimates for 1991 are provided by the Textile, Clothing and Footwear Directorate of Industry, Science and Technology Canada.

4 Canadian Manufacturers' Association, *The Agressive Economy: Competing to Win* (Toronto: CMA, June 1992), 45

5 As cited in *DNR*, a men's-apparel trade magazine, in November 1991: 'Within three years Hudson's Bay plans to buy 40 percent of its corporate merchandise mix within the U.S. ... HBC required any sourcing between the two countries be done on a "direct basis" without the intervention of agents, licensees or Canadian subsidiaries ... The primary reason behind HBC's unprecedented move to increase U.S. sourcing is the impending free trade agreement between the two countries.' Tariffs will begin to be lowered next year and will be completely eliminated by 1998.

6 Statistics Canada, unpublished figures produced for the ILGWU

7 James Parrot, 'Fashioning an Industrial Strategy for Garment Workers,' *Labour Research Review #19* 11, no. 1 (Spring 1992): 55–67

8 The statutory minimum wage in Ontario by the end of 1992 was $6.35. Even high-profile designer labels, such as Alfred Sung, Lida Baday, and Jones New York rely on home-based garment workers. For example an Alfred Sung jacket that sells for $375 earns the sewer $4.00. Virginia Galt, 'Protection for home-based workers promised,' *Globe and Mail*, 2 Oct. 1992

9 Homeworkers' Coalition Backgrounder no. 1 (1992), prepared for the Clean Clothes Campaign, which seeks fair wages and working conditions for homeworkers

10 Kim Moody and Mary McGinn, *Unions and Free Trade: Solidarity and Competition* (Detroit: Labour Notes 1992), 15

11 *Annual Employment Surveys*, Metropolitan Toronto Planning Department, 1991

12 Homeworkers' Coalition, *Fair Wages and Working Conditions for Homeworkers*, Brief to the Government of Ontario (Toronto: ILGWU Ontario District, December 1991)

13 Economic Council of Canada, *Good Jobs, Bad Jobs* (Ottawa: Minister of Supply and Services Canada 1990)

14 This is the basic principle behind such content legislation as the Canadian Auto Pact, drafted in the 1960s and arguably one of the key levers to promoting economic growth and prosperity in this country during the postwar period. Such policy options are precluded by implementation of the NAFTA.

15

Professions, Unions, or What?: Learning from Nurses

PAT ARMSTRONG

This article is more about ideas than about evidence; more about raising issues than about providing answers. It focuses on nurses, but uses them as a particular example of larger issues. It argues that the emerging service economy and the new structures and management strategies within the service sector require new methods of collective organizing, ones that reflect the concerns and conditions of the women who make up the majority of the service labour force.

THE CONTEXT

In the early years of this century the majority of workers were employed in the primary and secondary sectors and most of the workers were men. And since the early years of this century, there have been three main kinds of workplace organizations designed to defend collective interests. While they have overlapping concerns and often similar strategies, professional associations, craft unions, and industrial unions each reflect and address particular relations and conditions of work. Each has been developed primarily by and for men. Each has been altered through struggles with particular employers and through applications to particular workplaces, but the three basic models remain evident today. As women entered the labour force, they adopted these models for their own purposes, albeit in their own altered forms.

Today, most workers are employed in the service sector and most of the service-sector workers are women. In many workplaces, management is moving away from hierarchical, obviously authoritarian, highly centralized structures towards decentralized, flattened hierarchies and team structures based on commitment.

Although the workplace has become increasingly feminized and the work is being transformed, there has not been a correspondingly dramatic change in workplace organizations. Of course, unions and professional organizations have been quite conscious of the need to adjust strategies to accommodate changes in work. They have been quick to point out the dangers of new managerial approaches, new technologies, new ownership patterns, and new locations for work. As Judy Fudge[1] points out, they have begun to explore alternative regulations that would address the problems created by the decentralization of the workplace and the privatization of services. Such organizations have also been deeply embroiled in debates about how education and training programs can be redesigned to reflect better the needs of both workers and workplaces.

And certainly the male-centredness of unions and professional associations has received considerable attention. Some women have responded to the male dominance by organizing their own associations. Other women have developed a variety of strategies to make their presence felt in all three kinds of organizations. They have challenged the exclusion of women from the seats of power within these groups. They have successfully demanded that 'women's issues' such as child care, maternity leave, and part-time work be included in the agenda. They continue to push for a restructuring of decision-making to better suit women's ways of participating.

But what has not been evident is a fundamental rethinking, akin to the kind that took place with the rise of industrial unions, that develops new structures and strategies to address not only new conditions and relations of work but also the concerns of a predominately female labour force. Many of these service jobs involve different relations, different skills, different kinds of discipline, different kinds of decision making, and different kinds of workers from those predominant when the current models for organizing were developed. Nursing provides an example of women adopting and adjusting the male models of professional organizations and of industrial unions. It also provides an example of the increasing inadequacy of these models for current conditions.

WHAT'S IN A PROFESSION?

It is not surprising that nurses initially formed professional organizations to represent their interests or that many belong to professional organizations today. The medical doctors who provide nurses with their most immediate model of a professional association are by far the most powerful group within the health-care system. Medical doctors not only determine who can and cannot practise medicine; they also have an enormous say in who else can do what to whom in terms of testing, treatment, and care. As well, they have considerable influence in establishing the shape of health-care policy in this country. These doctors are generally held in high esteem and have average incomes at least three times that of nurses. Equally important, they claim a sense of vocation, a commitment to ethics and to people that fits well with nursing aims.

For doctors, and for many social scientists, this privileged position is explained and justified by the nature and relations of medical work as well as by the capacities of the practitioners. Abraham Flexner, author of a report credited with contributing greatly to the establishment of the scientific paradigm as the basis for North American medical schools, set out several criteria that distinguish a profession from other jobs.[2] Professions, he claimed,[3] are basically intellectual disciplines, taught in educational institutions, based on a body of knowledge that is practical rather than theoretical, organized internally, and motivated by altruism. Nurses, according to Flexner, do not meet these criteria because 'the responsibility of the trained nurse is neither original or final.'[4]

Since Flexner developed this list in the early part of the century, social scientists have offered variations on this theme. Friedson, for example, maintained that a profession requires a legal monopoly, control of how knowledge is both produced and applied and a code of ethics or something similar that demonstrates the profession can be trusted.[5]

Following this approach, many nurses have assumed that the way to improve nurses' position is to conform to these criteria for a profession. In the late-nineteenth century, the first specialized 'training' school for nurses was opened and was followed, a quarter of a century later, by the establishment of the first professional association. The Canadian National Association of Trained Nurses (CNATN) sought to encourage 'mutual understanding and unity among nurses in Canada,' elevate 'the standards of education and promotion of a high standard of professional honor and establish a code of ethics.'[6]

About the same time as the national association was being organized, nurses began to struggle with provincial governments for another professional attribute, the legislative regulation of nursing.

The first mandatory regulation was not introduced until 1953, however, and four provinces still do not have such legislation.[7] The successor to the CNATN, the Canadian Nurses' Association does provide tests for the registration of nurses and thus in effect determines who can call oneself a registered nurse.

The Canadian Nurses' Association (CNA) also pushed to make nursing education more an intellectual than an apprenticeship experience. The organization wanted schools devoted to 'the education of the nurse, not as it is under the present system, to lessening the cost of nursing in the hospitals.'[8] In other words, nursing students would no longer provide a free labour force, but would instead spend more time in formal education. It was not until the late 1950s, however, that the association was successful in transferring nursing education from hospitals to colleges and universities. Since the early 1980s, the CNA has adopted a policy of making a university degree the minimum requirement by the turn of the century and has worked hard to develop graduate programs in nursing.[9] The theory is that a general education base will make nursing both more like other professions and more independent. 'When the profession's goal [is] of having all practitioners entering the field of nursing graduate from university programs in nursing, it is likely that the monitoring function will no longer be necessary.'[10]

With the movement to university education and the development of graduate programs, nurses will meet most of the criteria applied to a profession. They will have a professional association, a code of ethics, a virtual monopoly on practice, an intellectual preparation, and control of how knowledge is applied. 'While nursing is advancing in defining its own body of knowledge, nursing research has not progressed to the extent that one could state yet that nursing has explicitly defined its own body of knowledge through research.'[11] The Canadian Nurses' Association is committed to meeting this one remaining criterion on Flexner's list.

After almost a century of working towards meeting these professional criteria, nurses remain far behind medical doctors in terms of power, prestige, independence, and pay. Flexner would maintain that this difference reflects the nature of nurses' responsibility, but many social scientists would claim that it reflects a failure to understand the basis of the doctors' position. As Johnson argues in *Professions and Power*,[12] the assumption that a profession's position follows inevitably from its members' capacities or work 'falls into the error of accepting the professionals' own definitions of themselves.' For him, professions are more about class, power, and historical circumstance than they are about the attributes of work or the practitioner.

A particular group of medical doctors – allopathic practioners – formed a professional organization in order to establish a monopoly long before there was much efficacy in their treatment. These men used their class ties to gain legislative regulation of practice before there was any complex body of knowledge to transmit and in order to establish the educational credentialling process. Their long struggle for power was as much about protecting the interests of a specific group of men as it was about protecting the public from ill-prepared practitioners. University education was as much about the exclusion of other classes as it was about applying proven standards of treatment. Until this century, patients were at least as well off with an apprenticed homeopath as they were with a university-educated, allopathic physician, but the Canadian Medical Association won its monopoly long before its members' methods proved effective.[13]

Like the craft guilds in existence at the end of the nineteenth century, the professional organizations were a means of protecting the collective interests of independent entrepreneurs and of establishing standards. In contrast to craft guilds, however, professions moved to provide training primarily through universities rather than apprenticeship programs, and professionals worked with people rather than materials. Doctors have been able to influence the development of health care, both in terms of how it is structured and who does what where, mainly because they were the first to gain power and because they retained their class ties with those in power. Unlike craft members, the majority also retained their private practices.

Johnson's critique of traditional approaches emphasized class, struggle, and historical circumstance. What it left out was sex.[14] The doctors who won those early struggles to achieve dominance for allopathic practitioners were men. These men used their power to prevent women from carrying on traditional practices such as midwifery and to exclude women from the required university programs.[15] At the same time, they worked to ensure that nurses would conform to the 'I see and am silent code' and remain handmaids to doctors.[16]

These men not only determined whether and how women participated; they also established the basic tenets of the medical system.

Medicine was to be based on a scientific paradigm with a considerable amount of specialization, organized in a hierarchical fashion with doctors on the top, and focused on treatment rather than care. 'In effect, medicine needed to be seen as a masculine profession and distanced from the unorthodox female practice of home medicine'[17] and the emphasis on care.

Nursing is based on alternative principles. Most nurses do general-duty work, they frequently work in teams, do a wide variety of tasks, often simultaneously, and they focus on care. But following the professional model, some nurses have sought to improve their position by making nursing work more like medical work. There has been an increasing emphasis on nursing as a career, on specialized training, and on nursing administration courses intended to prepare nurses for places closer to the top of the hierarchy.[18] And nursing graduate programs 'are engaged in advancing the scientific basis of nursing.'[19]

Adopting the male professional model has not served to gain for nurses the power, pay, or prestige of doctors because doctors' power, pay, and prestige did not result exclusively from the nature of their work or their skills. Rather, the nature of the work and the value attached to their skills developed to a large extent as a result of their power. And doctors used this power to exclude women and subordinate nurses. Conforming to the criteria listed for professions, then, is unlikely to improve nurses' position significantly and may mean abandoning the traditionally female commitment to care and interdependence.

DO UNIONS FILL THE BILL?

Jensen's research on the collective bargaining of nurses[20] led her to conclude that nurses had a number of other reasons for initially choosing to form professional associations rather than unions. They had 'difficulty identifying with the male-dominated, working-class, labour union movement' and, as women, felt uncomfortable with the adversarial nature of labour relations. They saw aggressive bargaining as unprofessional and feared unionization would lead to strikes. They were also concerned that management nurses would be ineligible for union membership. These management nurses would then be both unprotected and separated from other nurses.

There are at least two additional reasons for looking to professions.

Until the Second World War many nurses did private- duty work. As a 1897 article in the *Toronto Star* indicated, 'nurses work up a practice in much the same fashion and character as physicians.'[21] Like physicians, they did not have a common employer with whom to negotiate. Unwilling to be at the mercy of those who hired them but unable to form unions effectively, nurses came together in a professional organization in order to establish collective rights. Equally significant was the professional sense of vocation combined with a commitment to service and to people, a commitment that was much less relevant to unions in the primary and secondary sectors, given the nature of the work.

It was professional associations then, rather than unions, that began to bargain with employers as more and more nurses became employees. By the 1940s, the Canadian Nurses' Association supported collective bargaining but insisted that the bargaining agent should be the professional association and that there be no strikes.[22] The options for the various provincial associations were limited by both the labour laws that would not enforce their claims and their own rejection of more militant action. While this bargaining process led to some significant gains for nurses, not all employers followed the recommendations of the employment-relations committees that met with the associations. The limitations of an approach based on the assumption of shared understanding with management, combined with an organizing drive on the part of unions, good economic times, and the women's movement, encouraged many nurses to reconsider their stand on unions and strikes.[23]

The real turning-point came in the early 1970s with 'the Saskatchewan ruling.' The Service Employees International Union successfully argued that the Saskatchewan Registered Nurses' Association could not act as a union because it had a board of directors that included management nurses. The Supreme Court ruled against the appeal by the Canadian Nurses' Association, arguing that the involvement of nurse managers in the bargaining process constituted a conflict of interest.[24] From this point on, new unions emerged to handle the collective-bargaining functions. These unions were organized with impressive speed, primarily because the base had already been laid by the professional organizations. Today, 80 per cent of Canadian nurses are subject to collective agreements.[25]

As Jensen points out,[26] workplace organization to defend collective interests led to considerable gains for nurses. Wages, benefits, hours, and job security all improved enormously and seniority was recognized. Nurses won the right to have some say in working conditions, communications with employers improved, and the processing of complaints was formalized through grievance procedures. Women also won the right to keep their jobs after they married.

Because many of these victories were won before the Saskatchewan ruling, it is not easy to separate out those gains that can be attributed to unions and those that can be attributed to the professional associations. The difficulty is compounded by the fact that professional organizations continue to exist and to represent many nurses. With the exception of Quebec, these associations are still the primary organization in Canada for management nurses. And professional organizations continue to play a central role in lobbying for changes to the health-care policy that sets the overall conditions for nursing work,[27] as well as in determining the standards of practice for most nurses.

That professional associations continue to exist alongside unions may be seen as a simple vestige of a former time, as a misguided attempt to gain prestige, or as a source of conflict with unions and a limit on their power. From any of these perspectives, the solution to the problem of overlapping functions would be to eliminate professional associations entirely, to have a state-appointed body determine standards and disciplinary measures, and to allow-lower level management nurses to form separate unions.

But the continuation of professional associations can also be seen as an indication of the problems union organizations have in addressing the full range of conditions nurses face. Their existence suggests that there are issues and tensions not considered in traditional union practices or in current labour law. Many of the problems nurses had with unionization have either disappeared or been resolved. Most nurses are now employees rather than independent practitioners, most have formed their own female-dominated unions, and most have been willing to contemplate strike action.[28]

However, many nurses remained concerned about the nature of the bargaining process, about the regulation of professional conduct, and about the exclusion of management nurses, especially when such exclusion is used by administrators to divide nurses from each other. Many also remained concerned about retaining the particular character of nursing work, about ethics, and about a commitment to care.

THE NEED FOR NEW STRUCTURES

Neither union nor professional models neatly fit nurses' needs. And this is true for an increasing number of women workers. There are several reasons for this lack of fit. First, the social relations involved in nursing and other service work are significantly different from those in the industrial sector, where unions first developed, and from those of male professionals. This difference, in turn, is related to the nature of the work and to the fact that it is mainly women's work. The concerns of nurses are very much related to the kind of work women do and the kind of structures they work within. Second, there is a vocational commitment that not only has to be acknowledged but also must be structured into work relations. Third, questions of discipline, skill, hiring, and evaluation are different from both those in the industrial sector and those in traditional male professions such as law and medicine. Fourth, decision making is more complex. What follows is designed to indicate why these issues must be addressed as we rethink the structures and practices of collective organizations.

Much of current labour law and of union practice reflects the relations on the shop floor. In the industrial sector there is a relatively clear division between bosses and workers and a relatively antagonistic relationship between the two. The primary motive for employers is profit, and for employees, better wages and working conditions. Their interests clearly diverge and employees have little possibility of becoming owners. Even though supervisors usually emerge from the ranks, their obvious job is to direct and control those below them and it is extremely unlikely that the supervisor will return to the shop floor.

Not surprisingly, then, labour laws and union strategies have been designed to clearly separate management and worker rights. Employees have fought to get grievance procedures to protect workers against bosses and to define tasks very clearly. Workers have struggled to make seniority rather than merit or skill the basis for promotion and job security. Discipline, qualifications, and evaluation have been defined as primarily management concerns. Moreover, unions have been justifiably suspicious of worker involvement in decision making, arguing that this is mainly a means of co-opting workers and their ideas.

The relations in much of the service sector are more complex. They are complicated by the fact that much of the work is done in the public sector and much of the work involves people, not products. In these sectors, there are four, rather than two, major players. Furthermore, many of the employees often have very different work histories and work relations from those in the industrial sector.

At the top of the hierarchy, making many of the decisions, are senior administrators. At least some of these administrators have begun as providers of services. Moreover, in the public sector there are often a variety of structures that formally at least allow employees some input into decision making. Senior administrators in the public sector increasingly act like senior managers in other sectors, however, especially as cost cutting instead of service becomes the primary concern. Increasingly, they are educated as administrators, not as service providers, and those who have been practitioners rarely return to their earlier work. The difference, then, between these bosses and those in the industrial sector may be primarily at the level of discourse. They may justify their actions on the basis of professional and service concerns and may make claims about identifying with employees as well as about collective decision making that may not be evident in daily practices. Yet some differences between these types of managers remain.

While the differences among managers may be small and shrinking, the difference at lower managerial levels remains quite significant. The junior managers in hospitals are usually from the ranks and many will return to the ranks. Their power over other workers is likely to be limited both by the rotation aspect of the work and by pressure from other workers, as well as by formal structures that make decision making more collegial. In hospital wards, many nurses become unit managers for the night, only to be replaced by a colleague next day. Even when they are managers, they often work in teams with other nurses. Here, too, there are growing pressures that push these junior managers to act more like managers in industrial organizations and less like colleagues who share similar concerns. These pressures come from both managerial strategies at the upper levels and from union practices.

Like those in the industrial sector, organizations in the service sector have large numbers of people who are not in managerial positions. However, in many of these workplaces, the bulk of the employees are in the middle, not at the bottom, of the hierarchy. Many are required to have extensive years of schooling and see themselves as professionals. In hospitals, nurses form the majority of the workforce. The organizational hierarchy is shaped more like a barrel than like the pyramid characteristic of most industries. Many of the workers at the middle have considerable influence on the work of those below them, without in any formal sense being bosses or managers. Moreover, many have been involved in decision-making structures within the organization, although this involvement has not consistently meant the power to decide.

While the industrial sector produces things, the service sector relates to people. This difference means there are critical additional players who must be taken into account in work relations. One of the factors that makes professional organizations both attractive and seen as necessary is the fact that people, not products, are at stake. And many of those who work in the service sector do so without close supervision. Unlike unions, professional organizations claim to protect not just their members but also the non-members they serve and to discipline members who fail to follow a code of ethics.

The rapidly expanding, and female-dominated, service sector has much in common with nursing work. For many of the other women who work in the health-care sector, in community and social service, and in schools or universities, there are not only bosses and workers but also clients, students, or patients as well as lower-level managers who switch back and forth between service provision and managerial work. While the character of the managerial work may be increasingly like that in other workplaces, significant differences continue to influence how work is done and how decisions are made. Moreover, jobs in other service areas also involve interaction with people. A growing number require extensive years of formal education and the independent application of knowledge to variable conditions, have non-pyramidal structures, and are based on team work. Thus, they too will share many of these work relations, relations that are different from those in industrial sectors.

A second basis for rethinking collective organization is what could be called a sense of vocation, to use a very old-fashioned term. Nurses are certainly not the only group that sees their work as a matter of commitment to helping others but, in their case, this quality is often what we think of first when we think of the work. Nursing work, like much of women's work, is about caring, about interaction with others, about an involvement that goes well beyond specified tasks or monetary arrangements. This caring, this part in helping people get better, is often what nurses see as the most important and rewarding aspect of their work.

There is no question that this commitment to care has often served as a basis for the exploitation of nurses, among other women. Nurses were carefully taught to put this commitment above material concerns such as pay or holidays, above concerns about physicians' competence or power, and above concerns about conditions of work. The structure of the organizations in which they worked served to reinforce this commitment. At the same time, those in charge employed a variety of strategies designed to prevent women from developing alternatives or from rebelling. Especially in the early years, professional associations too made commitment the priority and disciplined nurses who failed to do so, in the process too often replicating rather than challenging the oppressive nature of the work.

There is no question that union perspectives helped enormously in overcoming the worst aspects of these carefully taught and strongly held beliefs. But the struggle for better pay, benefits, and hours, along with the struggle for the right to say no and to define jobs, has also fit with the emphasis on tasks and the development of formulas for care. Collective agreements have frequently reinforced a tendency to reduce the work to a series of operations, subject to technical procedures and closer supervision. Too often, these agreements make it more and more difficult to care and more and more difficult to have a say over the work.

This is not to suggest that unions have been unaware of the process, that they have not won important victories, or that they have had many alternatives. Certainly the structure of the work and the power of managers are responsible for much of the problem, especially in the face of cut-backs and new managerial strategies. Nor is it to suggest that professional associations have been much help in dealing with these issues. Indeed, in stressing specialization, university degrees, and scientific paradigms, these professional associations may be taking nurses a long way from caring. Rather, it is to argue that the union model, even as altered by nurses, can reinforce a tendency towards making nursing work like male factory work and thus help reduce the significance of the vocation and commitment which has been important to women in their work for so long . By following the male professional model, nurses' professional organizations have frequently had a similar effect.

This is not a problem exclusive to nurses, or even to professional women. Large numbers of women are directly or indirectly involved in providing services to people, in jobs that involve interaction with others, in jobs that involve care. For many of the women in White's study of mainly non-medical hospital workers, 'the care-giving aspects of work were the "glue" that held them to the job. There were few comments on wages and many on the changes in the labour process.'[29] Many men in the study felt the commitment argument was simply a way of preventing protest or of getting more work done. Few valued the intrinsic rewards associated with caring. The union underestimated the power of women's commitment and did not foresee that women were more willing to go on strike about changes that would affect patients than they were about changes that threatened their pay. We could dismiss this outlook as mere false consciousness on the part of the women, reflecting traditional views of women's natural capacities, and assume that most will begin to think like men once their jobs become more like those of men. Or we could take this commitment and defend the best parts; we could use it as the basis for preventing women's work from becoming more like men's and for restructuring our collective organizations. We could even use it to make men's work more like that of women.

The notion of vocation is also related to how we approach questions of discipline, skill, and evaluation. The essence of professional work is the application of knowledge to variable situations. Indeed, variability is inevitable when dealing with people as most professionals, and many women, do. And this has traditionally meant that those doing the work have considerable autonomy. This autonomy in turn has been justified in terms of acquired skills identified through a formal procedure such as licensing, of a commitment to helping people made explicit in a code of ethics, and of a disciplinary procedure designed to ensure that the code is followed. All of these aspects have been largely controlled by colleagues in the same field.

There have, of course, been many problems with these processes. Some professions have used their licensing powers to limit access in ways that have little to do with acquired skills or capacities. Acceptance into the profession may have at least as much to do with sex, race, and class as it does with knowledge. Codes of ethics are frequently ignored and professional associations may seldom enforce their codes, and rarely evaluate or discipline members. Conversely, members may be disciplined in ways that pay little attention to the constraints of their working conditions or individual rights. Consequently, those who use the services and some of the members of the profession may be protected more in theory than in practice.

Union approaches to such questions, however, can be equally

problematic for those who deal with people. The standard practice is to make discipline, hiring, and evaluation a management right. Under the labour laws, union rights have been primarily restricted to defending members according to defined procedural rules. Workers can object to the way management proceeds by initiating a grievance, but not to the rights themselves. Management rights are a large and residual category. Union approaches reflect and address the relations in an industrial setting. When applied to other workplaces, they can serve to reinforce the tendency to separate conception from execution and can help transform political issues into technical processes far beyond the control and comprehension of the members.

Unwilling to give up the advantages of either approach, nurses have tried to solve the conflict between traditional professional control and traditional union practices by dividing up the work. In most provinces, the professional association does the evaluation, licensing, and disciplining while unions use the grievance procedures to protect individual rights in the workplaces and provide defence for members called before their professional association. But this approach too has significant disadvantages.

There are major problems with the professional discipline process. 'The tendency of any professional association is to view and judge the professional employee's conduct in isolation from the particular work place and working context. In other words, the panel tends to look only at the conduct in question on the one hand, and the applicable standards on the other.'[30] These panels leave the workplace unchanged. Moreover, employers are increasingly complaining to the associations and all complaints are pursued. The nurses who are accused as a result can suffer considerable losses, even if they are exonerated. However, the professional organizations do help maintain members' autonomy and do allow individuals served by the membership a place to seek redress. Colleagues, rather than the employer, are the judges of appropriate behaviour in certain areas.

Although the nurses' unions can influence workplace conditions, they cannot discipline or evaluate members. If the disciplinary process were to be confined to the workplace, nurses are unlikely to have much say in the process. They would be limited to providing a defence for their members, given the current legislation. Under such conditions, the employer would set the standards and rules of conduct, as well as evaluate performance. Issues would primarily be handled through the formal grievance process. For unions, the question is not, have professional standards been broken, but have employees' rights been violated. Unions can protect the rights of patients in general through influencing things like working conditions, but they can do little for individuals who have been badly served by their members.

Here, too, we could dismiss the professional organizations' concern with accreditation, evaluation, and discipline as unfair, outdated, and élitist. We could argue that colleagues have no business evaluating members and that this should be left to the employer. If we go this route, however, we are again encouraging a move towards an industrial model, where workers' possibilities are severely limited. We could instead learn some lessons about how to prevent a further erosion of autonomy and how to extend the best aspects of these practices to other workers. Or better yet, we could figure out new ways of providing autonomy while defending the collective rights of both workers and clients, students and patients.

Part of the evaluation and accreditation issue is the question of skill. Professions have traditionally argued that there are significant skill differences among individuals. According to this perspective, individuals should be hired, promoted, paid, and fired on the basis of credentials and merit. Skills are important in job satisfaction and in personal development. The problem, of course, is that merit and skill are not objectively determined criteria. Much depends on who gets to define the terms and far too often they have been defined by a dominant male élite. Women's skills, especially their caring skills, have rarely been highly valued and are often seen as natural capacities inherited at birth. Moreover, as nurses can attest, skill distinctions have frequently been used as a means of dividing members from each other.

Unions have traditionally argued that employers should base distinctions among workers primarily on seniority. From this perspective, a nurse is a nurse is a nurse and if any jobs are available, they should go to the most senior nurse. While this may help ensure jobs for members and eliminate the problem of defining the terms, it also opens the way for an intensification of labour. In nursing, this has already happened with the introduction of floating assignments, a system which allows employers to assign nurses anywhere in the hospital depending on need.

In the case of skills, then, we have to develop a more sophisticated strategy that recognizes skills, but one that does this in the least discriminatory and the most collective manner, and in ways that recognize women's skills. Difference need not mean inequity. Indeed, treating people the same way can well mean inequity. Skills have long given people a sense of satisfaction in their work and have limited employers' powers. We need to recognize, and use, this fact in our strategies.

In each of these areas, the question of who decides is critical. Professions have traditionally argued that a group of relatively equal colleagues should decide. Many of the institutions that employ professionals have long assumed their participation in a wide range of areas. The actual powers of individual professionals have varied enormously, but the principle of collegial control has a long tradition. However, this control is being challenged by the increasingly bureaucratic structures and the new managerial styles.

In the past, industrial union officials seldom participated in decision making, nor did their members. Increasingly, union officials are involved in a wide range of committees within their organizations and workers without official positions in the union are increasingly invited to participate. Many unionists and theorists have been justifiably suspicious of such invitations to participate, arguing that this is a strategy to co-opt and divide workers from each other.

We could reject these overtures as co-option and demand that decisions be made by our unions negotiating with those on top of the hierarchy. Or we could use them to develop more genuinely democratic decision making within a broader range of workplaces. The different relations, the sense of vocation, and the questions of skill, discipline, evaluation, and decision making that are increasing factors in women's service work cry out for new ways to represent and shape women's concerns. New workplace structures and managerial strategies are forcing us to respond, and we need to do this with new structures and strategies.

CONCLUSION

Women's best jobs in the service sector are becoming increasingly like those in the industrial sector at the same time as more and more women take on service work. Unions have made significant gains for women and have developed some innovative ways of addressing their concerns. But many union strategies have served to reinforce, rather than combat, these tendencies towards loss of skill and loss of power. They do so because we primarily follow a model for collective action based on relations and conditions in the industrial sector and because we are constrained by outmoded labour legislation.

To combat these tendencies, and to participate fully in the radical restructuring currently under way, we need to develop a vision of what constitutes good workplace relations, good conditions of work, and good work. At the same time, we need to rethink fundamentally our structures and strategies for workplace organizing. Otherwise, we will not be able to provide alternatives to the bifurcation into good and bad jobs that is on the workplace agenda.

This does not mean abandoning the traditional commitment of unions to equity and the struggle for workplace control. Nor does it mean rejecting what we have done in the past. Indeed, unions and professional organizations have laid the groundwork for, and begun the process of, the kind of radical change I am arguing we need. Professions have gone a long way in demonstrating the possibilities for collegial participation, for individual rights, and for influencing public policy. Unions have developed critical strategies for achieving equity, protecting collective rights, and improving conditions of work and pay. Women's organizations in the broader community suggest some alternative models that grow out of feminist concerns and practices. But we need a more coherent strategy based on a recognition of the particular relations and conditions of women's work.

NOTES

1 Judy Fudge, chapter 11 in this volume
2 Bernard Blishen, *Doctors in Canada* (Ottawa: Minister of Supply and Services 1991), 18
3 Janet Kerr, 'Professionalization in Canadian Nursing,' in Janet Kerr and Janetta MacPhail, eds, *Canadian Nursing Issues and Perspective* (Toronto: McGraw-Hill Ryerson 1988), 28
4 Quoted in Kerr 28
5 Eliot Freidson, 'Dominant Professions, Bureaucracy and Client Services,' in W.R. Rosengren and M. Lefton, eds, *Organizations and Clients* (Columbus, Ohio: Merril 1970), 20–35
6 Helen Mussallem, 'The Changing Role of the Canadian Nurses' Association in the Development of Nursing in Canada' in Kerr and MacPhail 401, and Phyllis Jensen, 'The Changing Role of Nurses' Unions,' in Alice Baumgart and Jennice Larsen, eds, *Canadian Nursing Faces the Future* (Toronto: C.V. Mosby), 460

7 Kerr, 'Professionalization'

8 Quoted in Mussallem 403

9 Janetta MacPhail, 'The Role of the Canadian Nurses' Association,' in Kerr adn MacPhail 33

10 Kerr 33

11 Janetta MacPhail, 'The Professional Image: Impact and Strategies for Change,' in Kerr and MacPhail 53

12 Terence Johnson, *Professions and Power* (London: MacMillan 1972)

13 David Naylor, *Private Practice Public Payment* (Montreal: McGill-Queen's University Press 1986)

14 Pat Armstrong and Hugh Armstrong, 'Sex and the Professions,' *Journal of Canadian Studies* 27, no. 1 (1992): 118–35

15 Veronica Stron-Boag, 'Canada's Women Doctors: Feminism Constrained,' in S.E.D. Shortt, ed., *Medicine in Canadian Society* (Montreal: McGill-Queen's University Press 1981)

16 Judi Coburn, ' "I See and Am Silent": A Short History of Nursing in Ontario 1850–1930,' in Jo Acton et al., eds, *Women at Work; Ontario 1850–1930* (Toronto: Women's Press 1974)

17 Carol Barnes, 'The Professions and an Ethic of Care,' in Carol Barnes et al., eds, *Women's Caring: Feminist Perspectives on Social Welfare* (Toronto: McClelland and Stewart 1991), 50

18 MacPhail, 'The Role of the Canadian Nurses' Association' and 'The Professional Image'

19 Kerr, 'Professionalization'

20 Jensen 460–3

21 'How Nurses Live,' *Toronto Star*, 11 March 1897; repr. 16 Jan 1992

22 Janet Kerr, 'The Emergence of Nursing Unions as a Social Force in Canada,' in Kerr and MacPhail 212

23 Jensen 463 and Kerr, 'Emergence,' 213

24 Kerr, 'Emergence,' 212

25 Eleanor Adaskin, 'Organized Political Action: Lobbying by Nurses' Associations,' in Baumgart and Larsen 477

26 'The Changing Role' 462, 464

27 Adaskin, 'Organized Political Action'

28 Judith Hibberd, 'Organized Political Action: The Labor Struggle in Alberta,' in Baumgart and Larsen

29 Jerry White, *Hospital Strike* (Toronto: Thompson 1990), 44

30 Catherine Wedge address to the BCNU convention (Vancouver: BCNU 1991), 4

PART IV
STUDYING WOMEN AND UNIONS

16

A View from Outside the Whale: The Treatment of Women and Unions in Industrial Relations

ANNE FORREST

As a discipline, industrial relations has never been very interested in the experiences of women, as workers or as trade unionists. The centre of attention has long been occupied by men. The workers, the organizers, the strikers: all have been men. One looks in vain for the contributions of women: their organizing drives, their strikes are 'missing' from the history books. Of women, we learn mostly that they were cheap, unskilled labour; potential strikebreakers who threatened to take away men's jobs.

That women, today, are clearly at the centre of the union movement – organizing and striking in their thousands – has done little to change their marginal place in the discipline. At best, industrial-relations scholars are mildly curious about the new subjects of collective bargaining – maternity/paternity leave, child care, flex time, and pay equity – the so-called women's issues that forward-looking unions are advised to take up. But attention is limited. For the most part, the journals and texts remain stubbornly silent on the subject of women and unions. The 'malestream' of academic industrial relations continues on as before, if not entirely oblivious to the presence of women, then certainly unaware that their presence (or absence) makes much of a difference.

It is from studies of men, their work and their unions, that the discipline has taken its shape. Of central concern are the growth and development of these unions. How collective bargaining institutionalizes and regulates industrial conflict is a perennial theme of academic research and writing. The task of the scholar, Dunlop[1] argued, was to explain 'why particular rules are established in particular industrial-relations systems and how and why they change in response to changes affecting the system.' Theoretical constructs like 'job regulation' and the 'web of rules' underscore the extent to which industrial relations is focused on the management of industrial conflict.

That the discipline places a normative emphasis on accommodation and stability has been noted and criticized by many scholars.[2] What has gone unnoticed, however, is that the construction of industrial relations as the study of job regulation through collective bargaining defines the discipline as male territory. As conventionally written, the history of the labour movement is the history of working-class men. Jamieson, Lipton, Logan, and Robin[3] tell us clearly that trade unions were a men's affair. Even those accounts influenced by the 'new' labour history of the 1970s – Heron, Kealey, Morton, and Palmer[4] – are stubbornly silent about the lives and experiences of women as workers and trade unionists.

A historical record that is principally concerned with documenting the growth and development of collective bargaining will necessarily ignore the many, many organizing drives and strikes that failed to build lasting unions. As a result, much of women's activism has slipped through the fissures in industrial-relations thinking. The history of women and unions has been 'invisible except in scraps.'[5] The sources are fragmentary and scattered: until recently, there were no published secondary- source materials on the union activity of women in Canada.[6]

When cobbled together the story of women's activism is impressive. Canadian women have been organizing unions for as long as unions have been organized. Among the earliest were unions of laundry workers, waitresses, candy makers, teachers, telephone operators, garment and textile workers, domestic workers, even unemployed women. There were, as well, some women members of 'men's' unions: tailors, retail clerks, bookbinders, boot and shoe makers, cannery workers, farm labourers, packing-plant and sugar-refinery workers. And there were strikes – many strikes – on occasion organized and led by women. There were strikes of waitresses (ten in Vancouver alone during the 1930s), laundry and sugar-refinery workers, garment and textile workers; and major strikes of telephone operators in Vancouver in 1902 and 1906 and Toronto in 1907.[7]

Women *were* there: they organized unions, they went on strike, they walked the picket line, and they fought with strikebreakers. But for women, stable, functioning unions were the exception rather than the rule. For a variety of reasons – not the least of which was the hostility of male trade unionists – women were less able than men to institutionalize their anger and resistance into permanent structures. And so, much of women's trade-union activity remains invisible; indeed, from an institutional point of view the history of women and unions is a legacy of failure.

Women have been invisible, as well, because much of their organizing activity has been directed towards the support of their men's (husbands', brothers', fathers') struggles and consequently has been of incidental interest to scholars. As is common in the social sciences, the study of industrial relations is premised upon a clear divide between work and home. Work that is done in the public sphere is part of the industrial-relations 'system,' while unpaid, domestic labour is not. The organizing of unions, consequently, is of disciplinary interest, while the organizing of women's auxiliaries, union-label campaigns, and picket-line vigils is not. Thus, although women's efforts on behalf of men have been vital to the success of many strikes that helped establish the union movement in Canada – think of Ford and Stelco in 1945–6 – the organizing of soup kitchens, clothing exchanges, and the like warrant nothing more than a footnote in conventional labour history.[8]

A history preoccupied with the growth and development of unions and collective bargaining, of necessity, values what men have done but marginalizes and trivializes what women have done. Such a *hist*ory leads readily to the conclusion that women and unions do not mix. The irrelevance of women's struggles to the study of industrial relations has generally been taken to imply that there were none. 'Myth had it that women were difficult to organize':[9] they were too timid or just not interested. And this remains the discipline's explanation for women's lower levels of unionization.

What is known about the relationship between women and unions in industrial relations is not from the study of women themselves but is largely a by-product of the many studies of union growth which have become the stock-in-trade of a number of scholars. This body of literature, which utilizes sophisticated statistical techniques to analyse patterns of union growth and decline, is at the leading edge of industrial relations. By regressing some measure of union attachment (union membership, having voted in favour of unionization in a representation election, or expressing a willingness to do so – note that most of these studies were done in the United States where representation elections are obligatory) against any number of independent variables, one of which is sex, researchers have confirmed, again and again, what the discipline believes it 'knows': women are less inclined to join unions than men.

Examined more carefully, however, the results of this research do not support conventional wisdom unequivocally. Much hinges on the nature of the data employed and, in particular, on the choice of the dependent variable. As Voos[10] has noted, those studies which analyse union-membership data do say that women are less likely to be union members than men and so tend to affirm the presumption that women, for whatever reasons, are less likely to join unions. However, when data from surveys of workers' attitudes towards unions are analysed they reveal a strikingly different relationship: on the basis of these studies one would have to conclude that American women today are *more* inclined to join unions than are men[11] – a conclusion consonant with recent experience. In all of the OECD countries union membership among women has grown remarkably over the last twenty years.[12]

Industrial-relations thinking has yet to catch up with the evidence, however. The rapid growth of union membership among women notwithstanding, the discipline's blinkered conceptualization of the relationship between women and unions remains undisturbed. When the literature is blunt and at its most sexist, the argument is simple: whether by nature or by socialization women are not willing to join unions. 'As many observers know, women are (generally) not union-oriented. They dislike the thought of strikes, pickets, violence.'[13] For many scholars it is self-evidently true that the future growth of the union movement is severely limited by the large number of women now working for wages. And the presumption is so widely accepted that many studies of union growth have employed gender as an explanatory variable without any discussion.[14] Others have justified the use of gender as an independent variable reciting the usual 'saturation school' arguments: principally that unionization is less cost-effective for women because they are only temporarily attached to the labour force and consider their wages as a supplement to the family income. Bye the bye, many of these studies assume that women are *less* likely to have a positive image of organized labour than men.[15]

In the less obviously gendered form of this literature, lower levels of union membership among women are said to result not simply from the fact that women are women but because women are commonly employed in certain kinds of 'hard to organize' jobs. So, for example, Antos et al.[16] concluded that almost 60 per cent of the sizeable difference in the levels of union membership between the women and men in their sample was largely accounted for by the different occupational and industrial location of the women. A similar finding was reported by Fiorito and Greer,[17] who argued that the lower rate of unionization among the women in their study was explained in large part by factors other than gender per se, that is to say, differences in union membership were related to differences in labour-force attachment, industrial and occupational distribution, and other factors that vary with gender. And from her review of the data, Voos[18] concluded that 'lower rates of organization among women do not reflect less demand for unionism because of lack of attachment to the labor force ... but rather that the process of filling union jobs (occupational selection by women and hiring decisions by employers) creates the overall negative association.'

But this is nothing more than a variation on a theme. The explanation that women do 'women's' work and so are hard to organize relies on the same tired set of gendered assumptions, albeit in a somewhat more sophisticated form: the 'polite version,' Smith calls it, of the 'older and deeper view that women are naturally timid and unwilling to fight and have no place in the rough arena of union struggle.'[19] Such an explanation tells us yet again that women workers are essentially women, not workers, and so are best understood by examining their personal characteristics and family situations. This mode of reasoning is evident even in those studies which employ job segregation as an explanatory variable. Why 'women's' work should be so hard to organize, particularly when wages and working conditions are abysmally poor – the very conditions that industrial-relations scholars would regard as caustive factors in the organizing drives of men – is never analysed or explained. And in the absence of any consideration of job segregation by sex as an institutionalized form of discrimination against women, the implication is that women choose 'women's' work, for example, part-time or temporary jobs, because it allows them to accommodate their family responsibilities, or that women are content with the low pay attached to 'women's' work because theirs is a 'second' income, or that women don't mind doing unskilled, monotonous 'women's' work because they are not permanently attached to the labour force, and so on and on. What could be plainer: women are women.

Industrial relations employs what Feldberg and Glenn[20] have labelled the 'gender model' to explain why women workers are less likely to be union members than men. In fact, the 'gender model' is standard treatment for women in the discipline. A similar set of arguments is offered to explain why women, once organized, are less likely to be actively involved in union affairs. In this case, the fact that women are women and consequently live 'women's' lives is advanced to 'explain' why they are less active in their unions and, in particular, why they are so under-represented among the leadership of unions, locally and nationally.

The (small) number of studies of women as leaders and union activists relies heavily on received wisdom of this sort. The commonly discussed obstacles to the participation and advancement of women in unions focus on their perceived 'difference': the double workday and family commitments, lack of self-confidence and self-assertiveness, and insufficient training and experience.[21] Considerably less attention has been paid to the difficulties placed in the path of women seeking positions of power in male-dominated organizations. Although discrimination is almost always listed as one of the obstacles that women must overcome, the systemic nature of that discrimination is rarely studied. Few researchers have bothered to examine how union policies and practices systematically discourage women's participation and exclude them from the leadership.[22] The literature is equally silent about women's struggles to change this reality. The comparatively few studies of women's efforts to organize women's committees and put issues like sexual harassment and pay equity on their unions' bargaining agendas have been conducted by academics 'outside' of industrial relations.

As a discipline, industrial relations is deeply committed to a gendered construction of women and 'women's' work. The basic assumption that underlies much of the analysis is that, whatever women are doing, they are women first and foremost and are driven by motivations uniquely female. At work or at the union hall, women are not really workers or trade unionists but women and so are defined by the roles of wife, mother, and daughter. That women do 'women's' work seems entirely natural to scholars of labour-management relations. Rather than being an industrial- relations phenomenon that needs to be understood from within, job segregation is taken as a given and so offered as a partial explanation for women's lower rates of unionization.

What we have here is 'bad' industrial relations, even when judged on its own terms. The argument that women are women, even when presented in its more sympathetic form drawing attention to job segregation and the double workday, is not a sound industrial-relations approach. Scholars of labour-management relations would never explain men's union activity by reference to 'male' characteristics; for example, researchers would never argue that men organize trade unions because they are the principal wage-earners or because men, by nature, are more aggressive and asssertive than women. What is important, men are never compared with women: men are assumed to be workers while women are not. Indeed, industrial relations constructs men *only* as workers and never as men. Gender is never a consideration: it is the work experience – how well the workers are paid, how hard they are pushed, the size of the work group, and so on (what Feldberg and Glenn have labelled the 'job model') – that informs an industrial-relations analysis of why certain groups of workers/men do or do not choose to unionize.

Men acting as men are unknown in industrial relations and yet it is their point of view that suffuses the discipline's approach to labour-management relations. Emerging as it did in the 1930s and 1940s, the academic study of industrial relations has long evidenced a great sympathy for the plight of working men humiliated and emasculated by the abuse of managerial power on the job. Stories of the indignities suffered by men in desperate need of employment to support their families – plying the foreman with liquor or painting his porch to secure a job – abound. Indeed, it is impossible to read labour history without imbibing the subtext which celebrates the organizing of trade unions as the means by which working-class men have achieved their due. And it is this perspective which underpins the discipline's understanding of the role and function of trade unions.

What has emerged is a profound identity between the interests of (white) working-class men and the meaning of trade unionism, so that, now, it is seemingly impossible to disentangle the ways in which trade unions act to protect the narrow economic interests of a particular group of men and industrial relations' conceptualization of trade unionism as a social force. Union men and scholars together agree that what unions have achieved – seniority rights, the 'family wage,' and 'fair' treatment for the select few – is precisely what unions are for. That these gains have been won by denying an equivalent measure of economic security to women and others who have

been systematically excluded is barely acknowledged, let alone analysed, in the literature.

Exclusion and segregation have long been the nub of male power
at work. Many are the examples of craft unions that denied women
access to training and jobs by refusing to accept them as members. In
this way cigar makers, bookbinders, moulders, and barbers tried to
prevent women from entering their trades;[23] when women were hired
anyway strikes were called to force employers to dismiss them.[24]
Commonly, skilled workers interfered with the organizing efforts of
women and other groups of less skilled workers by refusing to respect
their picket lines[25] – a practice that remains in place today. Nor were
the experiences of women in industrial unions remarkably different.
Again, women were organized only reluctantly, and often without
full membership rights or benefits.[26] Job segregation was the norm:
with the unions' agreement 'men's' and 'women's' jobs were clearly
demarcated and lower rates of pay negotiated for the latter. Even the
demand of equal pay for equal work – that is, the demand that men
and women be paid the same rate for the same job – proved to be
discriminatory. Though progressive on its face, 'equal pay for equal
work' was initially adopted by unions chiefly as a way of discouraging the employment of women.[27]

The multiple ways in which collective bargaining has been used to
ignore or marginalize the needs of women are part of the legacy of
trade unions that is 'missing' from the textbooks. Not one of
Anderson, Gunderson and Ponak, Craig and Solomon, Phillips, or
Sethi[28] conceptualizes trade unions as part of the male power structure. Accordingly, issues of craft autonomy and 'dual' unionism, the
designation of 'men's' and 'women's' jobs, discriminatory pay
schemes, truncated seniority structures, and the like – mechanisms
devised by unions to protect male privilege – form no part of the
story of unionism that is passed on from one generation of industrial-
relations scholars to the next.

Better-paying, 'men's' jobs have been effectively reserved for men
by seniority schemes which systematically hive women off into mini-
ghettos of lower-paid tasks. The discriminatory first assignment of
women to low-paying and unskilled entry-level positions has commonly been frozen into worklife-long disadvantage by seniority rights
that are less than establishment-wide. Fragmented, truncated, and
sex-segregated job ladders effectively restrict the range of jobs to
which women can aspire without suffering the penalties (loss of

seniority and loss of pay) which collective agreements routinely impose on workers who seek to jump from one seniority district to the next.[29] In heavy industry especially the application of seniority rules has proved to be highly prejudicial to women. Experience has shown that the toe-hold that women won in the steel industry during the 1970s was quickly lost in the economic downturn of the early 1980s. The contractual obligation to lay off first those hired last has all but eliminated women. More than ever, the industry is an enclave for older, white men.[30]

Because men and women rarely do the same work, aphorisms like 'pay the job and not the worker' and 'fair comparisons' have also had a discriminatory effect on women's wages. In the process of comparing like with like, 'women's' work is systematically undervalued by both employers and trade unions. Once again, it is what men do that constitutes the benchmark of value. And there are a myriad of ways by which the value of what women do is systematically downgraded. Skill is a notoriously gendered construct,[31] but so are effort, responsibility, and working conditions. Always, the effort entailed in manual work is measured by the physical demands of 'men's' jobs, while 'women's' work, no matter how exhausting, is defined as 'light'; nor is there any appreciation for the mental effort entailed in much of 'women's' work in service occupations. Responsibility, likewise, is a gendered concept which on the job is measured by the potential damage to capital equipment. Potential harm to children or sick people, by contrast, is not factored into pay schemes. And the sine qua non of poor working conditions, the grease and noise so characteristic of heavy industrial work, have an economic value that the dirt and noise of 'women's' work – sweat, urine, and tears – does not.

Exclusion and segregation continue to be the norm in unions and unionized workplaces and women who attempt to break through into men's privileged space are frequently punished. Derided, insulted, occasionally assaulted, women in a 'man's' workplace are immediately sexualized and treated as 'fair game.' For women, sexual harassment is not an aberration but a constant, a means by which men – managers and workers alike – police the dividing line between men's and women's worlds.[32] The experiences of women employed on 'men's' jobs in the steel, mining, and forestry industries are testament to the multiple, varied, and persistent resistance that is evoked by women challenging men's privileged position in the labour force.[33] Nor has the male preserve of the union hall been any friendlier. The business of unions is 'men's' work and women are not especially wanted. The widespread practices of belittling women, shouting them down at meetings, dismissing their concerns as trivial, and responding to their presence with sexual harassment are so common that they are rarely examined in detail and never from an industrial-relations perspective.[34]

That women are not, arguably cannot be, studied through the lens of industrial relations as currently constructed is patent. It is not simply that the discussion of the relationship between women and unions in the literature is 'bad' industrial relations ('bad,' that is, because it treats women as stereotypically defined by their gender while ignoring all the job-related factors that make up an industrial relations analysis of workers and unions); it is critically important to understand that the acceptability of such approaches is rooted in the discipline's refusal to conceptualize gender as a power hierarchy. What is missing from industrial relations as currently defined is an analysis of gender relations as power relations. This is to underline the fact that simply to treat women like men, that is, to construct them only as workers and trade unionists, would be a mistake. It is not the discipline's construction of women as gendered that is problematic (although the analysis has been far too simplistic and stereotypic); what is wrong with industrial relations is that, so far, scholars have not engendered men. To overcome its analytical shortcomings, the discipline must begin to address the reality that men at work, at home, and at the union hall are privileged by virtue of their gender.

Critical to an expanded understanding of the relationship between women and unions is an analysis of job segregation by sex. Institutionalized job segregation is fundamental to patriarchy because it ensures that women's place in the labour market is subordinate to men's and so reinforces the unequal division of labour within the household. Job segregation by sex 'constructs women's "primary" commitment as devotion to home and family whether or not they also work for pay.'[35] Defined as wives and mothers first, women are expected to take family life as their central responsibility around which all other commitments must be organized. There is no escape: women's subordinate position in the labour market reinforces their subordination within the family which, in turn, reinforces their subordination in the labour market[36] – which explain why, rather than disappearing as more and more women enter the labour force, job segregation remains stubbornly entrenched.

From an industrial-relations perspective job segregation can and must be theorized as a mechanism of job regulation, a creation of employers that has been further institutionalized by trade-union practices. There is nothing natural or inevitable about the sexual division of labour. In the past and in the present, 'women's' work has been characterized by low pay and rapid labour turnover, not because women refuse to invest in training or because women are not committed to their jobs, but because this form of work organization is profitable for employers and advantageous to male workers. It is not women's natural affinity for cleaning and caring or their determination to put their families first that lands them in dead-end jobs in the service sector, but employers' need for a low-cost, flexible workforce, that has created a 'secondary' labour market to which women have been systematically allocated.[37]

Placing job segregation squarely within the industrial-relations 'system' adds powerfully to an industrial-relations understanding of the relationship between women and unions. Without denying that much of what women do is influenced by the reality of their 'women's' lives, an analysis which takes into account the everyday of job segregation draws attention to job-related factors such as the low pay, close supervision, and job insecurity endured by many working women and so underscores why so many are favourably disposed towards trade unions. An analysis of job segregation also illuminates why so few of these women have been able to act on their desire for union representation. Employers that rely on women's labour fight unionization as hard as they fight to preserve their access to a cheap and flexible workforce. Eaton's and the chartered banks are cases in point. Without doubt their determination to undercut the momentum of organizing drives was motivated by the fear that collective bargaining would raise substandard 'women's' wages and constrain management's right to organize and schedule work as it sees fit. Without doubt, as well, Eaton's and the banks were greatly aided in their resistance to unionization by labour laws that institutionalize the bargaining advantage of employers in the service sector.

An analysis of job segregation by sex within industrial relations would likewise sharpen the discipline's understanding of how trade unions function. A history of deliberately excluding and segregating women on the job and at the union hall identifies unions as bastions of male power. And yet none of the commonplace practices adopted by unions which entrench male privilege has attracted critical interest: the point of view adopted by industrial-relations scholars has been thoroughly male.

Until job segregation by sex is made visible as an underlying mechanism of job regulation, women's needs and concerns will be defined as outside the boundaries of industrial relations. For the moment, issues like pay equity and sexual harassment fall within the parameters of the discipline, but only insofar as women are able to keep these matters on the bargaining agenda. In other, more fundamental respects, pay equity and sexual harassment are not theorized as industrial-relations phenomena. Neither the systematic undervaluing of 'women's' work nor the widespread practice of sexual harassment is conceptualized as an 'output' of the industrial-relations system. Only when the discipline removes its gender blinkers and accepts that job segregation by sex is a mechanism of job regulation that reveals a great deal about how the industrial-relations system works will scholars be able to see unequal pay and sexual harassment for what they are: integral parts of an industrial- relations system that is designed to keep women 'in their place.'

From the standpoint of women, trade unions are just one more tool of patriarchy. But women's voices are never heard in industrial relations; their point of view is never considered.

Self-consciously adding gender to the industrial-relations mix will overturn many of the discipline's most closely held assumptions. Simply acknowledging that men exercise power over women because they are men will compel scholars to think more carefully about the nature of conflict at work. Conventionally theorized as a result of the imbalance of power inherent in the employer-employee relationship, an analysis that puts women at the centre – the subject, not object, of the inquiry as Smith[38] would say – would force researchers to acknowledge that there is a gender, as well as an employment/class, dimension to conflict. To accommodate the standpoint of women, industrial-relations scholars will have to jettison, as well, its too-simple model of trade unions as acting to meet workers' needs. Unions, too, are part of the male power structure and active defenders of male privilege. As upholders of the concept of the 'family wage' (paid to men), male trade unionists have sought to maintain a division of labour at home and at work that perpetuates the gender hierarchy by assigning to women full responsibility for unpaid labour while claiming for men an unfettered right to the most secure and highest-paid form of wage labour.

Such a project will press against the boundaries of the discipline as currently defined, forcing scholars to reconceptualize the meaning of industrial relations so that women, as well as men, will be the focus of attention.

NOTES

1 John T. Dunlop, *Industrial Relations Systems* (Carbondale and Edwardsville: Southern Illinois University Press 1958)
2 Stuart J. Dimmock and Amarjit R. Sethi, 'The Role of Ideology and Power in Systems Theory: Some Fundamental Shortcomings,' *Relations industrielles* 41 (1986): 738; Anthony Giles and Gregor Murray, 'Towards an Historical Understanding of Industrial Relations Theory in Canada,' *Relations industrielles* 43, no. 4 (1988): 780; Richard Hyman, *The Political Economy of Industrial Relations* (London: Macmillan Press 1989) and *Industrial Relations: A Marxist Introduction* (London: Macmillan Press 1975)
3 Stuart Jamieson, *Times of Trouble: Labour Unrest and Industrial Conflict in Canada, 1900–1966*, Study no. 22, Task Force on Labour Relations (Ottawa 1966); Charles Lipton, *Trade Union Movement of Canada, 1827–1959*, 4th ed. (Toronto: NC Press 1978); Harold A. Logan, *Trade Unions In Canada* (Toronto: Macmillan Company of Canada 1948); Martin Robin, *Radical Politics and Canadian Labour* (Kingston: 1968)
4 Craig Heron, *Canadian Labour Movement* (Toronto: J. Lorimer 1989); Gregory S. Kealey, *Toronto Workers Respond to Industrial Capitalism, 1867–1892* (Toronto: University of Toronto Press 1980); Desmond Morton, *Working People*, rev. ed. (Ottawa: Deneau 1984); Bryan D. Palmer, *Working-Class Experience: Rethinking the History of Canadian Labour, 1800–1991*, 2nd ed. (Toronto: McClelland & Stewart 1992)
5 Dorothy Smith, 'Women and Trade Unions: The US and British Experience,' *Resources for Feminist Research* 10, no. 2 (1981): 53
6 Star Rosenthal, 'Union Maids: Organized Women Workers in Vancouver 1900–1915,' *BC Studies* 41 (1979): 36
7 Marie Campbell, 'Sexism in British Columbia Trade Unions, 1900–1920,' in Barbara Latham and Cathy Kess, eds, *In Her Own Right* (Victoria: Camosun College 1980), 167–86; Gillian Creese, 'The Politics of Dependence: Women, Work and Unemployment in the Vancouver Labour Movement before World War II,' in

Gregory S. Kealey, ed., *Class, Gender, and Region: Essays in Canadian Historical Sociology* (St John's: Committee on Canadian Labour History 1988), 121–42; Ruth Frager, 'No Proper Deal: Women Workers and the Canadian Labour Movement, 1870–1940,' in Linda Briskin and Lynda Yantz, eds, *Union Sisters* (Toronto: Women's Press 1983), 44–64; Elizabeth Graham, 'Schoolmarms and Early Teaching in Ontario,' in Janice Acton et al., eds, *Women at Work: Ontario, 1850–1930* (Toronto: Canadian Women's Educational Press 1974), 165–209; Marie Lavigne and Jennifer Stoddart, 'Women's Work in Montreal at the Beginning of the Century,' in Marylee Stephenson, *Women in Canada*, rev. ed. (Don Mills: General Publishing 1977), 129; Madelaine Parent, 'Women in Unions: Past, Present and Future,' in Participatory Research Group, eds, *Strong Women, Strong Unions* (Ottawa: Group and Canada Employment and Immigration Union 1985), 16–30; Joan Sangster, 'Women and Unions in Canada: A Review of Historical Research,' *Resources for Feminist Research* 10 no. 2 (1981): 2, and 'The 1907 Bell Telephone Strike,' *Labour/Le Travailleur* 3 (1978): 109; Mercedes Steedman, 'Skill and Gender in the Canadian Clothing Industry, 1890–1940,' in Craig Heron and Robert Storey, eds, *On the Job* (Kingston and Montreal: McGill-Queen's University Press 1986), 152–76; Rosenthal; Susan Wade, 'Helena Gutteridge: Votes for Women and Trade Unions,' in Barbara Latham and Cathy Kess, eds, *In Her Own Right* (Victoria: Camosun College 1980), 187–203

8 Creese; Frager; Rosenthal

9 Smith, 'Women and Trade Unions,' 53

10 Paula B. Voos, 'Criticism and Comment: Determinants of US Unionism,' *Industrial Relations* 22, no. 3 (1983): 445

11 Henry S. Farber and Daniel H. Saks, 'Why Workers Want Unions: The Role of Relative Wages and Job Characteristics,' *Journal of Political Economy* 88 (1980): 349; Jack Fiorito and Charles R. Greer, 'Gender Differences in Union Membership, Preferences, and Beliefs,' *Journal of Labor Research* 7, no. 2 (1986): 145; Thomas A. Kochan, 'How American Workers View Labor Unions,' *Monthly Labor Review*, April 1979, 23; Duane Leigh and Stephen M. Hills, 'Male-Female Differences in the Potential for Union Growth Outside Traditionally Unionized Industries,' *Journal of Labor Research* 8, no. 2 (1987): 131; Thomas S. Moore, 'Are Women Workers "Hard to Organize"?' *Work and Occupations* 13, no. 1 (1986): 97; Paul Rodan, 'Women and Unionism: The Case of the

Victorian Colleges Staff Association,' *Journal of Industrial Relations* 32 (1990) 386; Voos

12 Organization for Economic Co-operation and Development, *Supplementary Outlook, 1991* (OECD 1991)

13 Woodruff Imberman, 'The Hocus Pocus in Union Avoidance,' *Journal of Labor Research* 1, no. 2 (1980): 275

14 Joseph R. Antos et al., 'Sex Differences in Union Membership,' *Industrial and Labor Relations Review* 33, no. 2 (1980): 162; Farouk Elsheikh and George S. Bain, 'Unionisation in Britain: An Inter-Establishment Analysis Based on Survey Data,' *British Journal of Industrial Relations* 18 (1980): 169; Farber and Saks; Kochan; James G. Scoville, 'Influences on Unionization in the US in 1966,' *Industrial Relations* 10 (1971): 354

15 Jack Fiorito and Charles R. Greer, 'Determinants of US Unionism: Past Research and Future Needs,' *Industrial Relations* 21, no. 1 (1982): 1; Barry T. Hirsch, 'The Determinants of Unionization: An Analysis of Interarea Differences,' *Industrial and Labor Relations Review* 33, no. 2 (1980): 147; Leigh and Hills; Moore; William J. Moore and Robert J. Newman, 'On the Prospects for American Trade Union Growth: A Cross-Section Analysis,' *Review of Economics and Statistics* 57 (1975): 435

16 Antos et al. 164

17 Fiorito and Greer, 'Gender Differences in Union Membership, Preferences and Beliefs,' 161–2

18 Voos 450

19 Smith, 'Women and Trade Unions,' 53

20 Roslyn L. Feldberg and Evelyn Nakano Glenn, 'Male and Female: Job versus Gender Models in the Sociology of Work,' *Social Problems* 26, no. 5 (1979): 524

21 Gary N. Chaison and P. Andiappan, 'An Analysis of the Barriers to Women Becoming Local Union Officers,' *Journal of Labor Research* 10, no. 2 (1989): 149; Chaison and Andiappan, 'Profiles of Local Union Officers: Females v. Males,' *Industrial Relations* 26, no. 3 (1987): 281; Chaison and Andiappan, 'Characteristics of Female Union Officers in Canada,' *Relations Industrielles* 37, no. 4 (1982): 765; Alice Cook, 'Women and American Trade Unions,' *Annals of the American Academy of Political and Social Sciences* 375 (1968): 124; Dafna N. Izraeli, 'Avenues into Leadership for Women: The Case of Union Officers in Israel,' *Economic and Industrial Democracy* 3 (1982): 515; Karen S. Kozaria and David A. Pierson,

'Barriers to Women Becoming Union Leaders,' in *IRRA 33rd Proceedings* (Madison: Industrial Relations Research Association 1980), 49–54; Alison M. Turtle et al., 'Women's Participation in the New South Wales Teachers Federation,' *Journal of Industrial Relations* 26, no. 4 (1984): 451; Barbara M. Wertheimer and Anne H. Nelson, *Trade Union Women* (New York: Praeger Publishers 1975)

22 But see Edmund Heery and John Kelly, ' "A Cracking Job for a Woman" – A Profile of Women Trade Union Officers,' *Industrial Relations Journal* 20, no. 3 (1989): 192; Sue Ledwith et al., 'The Making of Women Trade Union Leaders,' *Industrial Relations Journal* 21, no. 2 (1990): 112

23 Creese

24 Frager 51

25 Robert H. Babcock, *Gompers in Canada* (Toronto: University of Toronto Press 1974)

26 Ruth Milkman, 'Organizing the Sexual Division of Labor: Historical Perspectives on "Women's Work" and the American Labor Movement,' *Socialist Review* 10 (1980): 95

27 Creese

28 John C. Anderson et al., eds, *Union-Management Relations in Canada*, 2nd ed. (Don Mills: Addison-Wesley 1989); Alton W.J. Craig and Norman A. Solomon, *The System of Industrial Relations in Canada*, 4th ed. (Scarborough: Prentice Hall Canada 1993); Gerald E. Phillips, *Labour Relations and the Collective Bargaining Cycle*, 2nd ed. (Toronto: Butterworth 1981); Amarjit S. Sethi, ed., *Collective Bargaining in Canada* (Scarborough: Nelson Canada 1989)

29 Maryellen R. Kelley, 'Discrimination in Seniority Systems: A Case Study,' *Industrial and Labor Relations Review* 36, no. 1 (1982): 40

30 Meg Luxton and June Corman, 'Getting to Work: The Challenge of the Women Back Into Stelco Campaign,' *Labour/Le Travail* 28 (1991): 149

31 Jane Gaskell, 'What Counts as Skill? Reflections on Pay Equity,' in Judy Fudge and Patricia McDermott, eds, *Just Wages: A Feminist Assessment of Pay Equity* (Toronto: University of Toronto Press 1991): 141–59

32 Lin Farley, *Sexual Shakedown* (New York: Warner Books 1980)

33 Debbie Field, 'Coercion or Male Culture: A New Look at Co-worker Harassment,' in Briskin and Yantz 144–60; Jennifer Penney, *Hard Earned Wages* (Toronto: Women's Press 1983)

34 But see Ledwith et al.; Heery and Kelly.
35 Ruth Milkman, 'Redefining "Women's Work": The Sexual Division of Labor in the Auto Industry during World War II,' *Feminist Studies* 8, no. 2 (1982): 337, 340
36 Heidi Hartmann, 'Capitalism, Patriarchy, and Job Segregation by Sex,' *Signs* 1, no. 3, pt 2 (1976): 137, 153
37 Joan Smith, 'The Paradox of Women's Poverty: Wage-earning Women and Economic Transformation,' *Signs* 10, no. 2 (1984): 291
38 Dorothy E. Smith, *The Everyday World as Problematic: A Feminist Sociology* (Toronto: University of Toronto Press 1987) 105

Authors

Pat Armstrong has been an activist in the student, women's and union movements since the 1960s. She is the co-author, with Hugh Armstrong, of *The Double Ghetto, A Working Majority,* and *Theorizing Women's Work,* and author of *Labour Pains: Women's Work in Crisis,* as well as various articles on families, pay equity, and health care. She teaches sociology at York University.

Patricia Baker is an anthropologist and assistant professor in the Departments of Sociology/Anthropology and Women's Studies at Mount Saint Vincent University. Her main research interest is in the experience of women in unions, particularly in Canada's financial industry, and she has recently published 'Some Unions Are More Equal than Others' in *Studies in Political Economy.*

Linda Briskin is an associate professor in the Division of Social Science, York University. She has written *Feminist Pedagogy: Teaching and Learning Liberation*; co-authored *Feminist Organizing for Change: The Contemporary Women's Movement in Canada*; co-edited *Union Sisters: Women in the Labour Movement*; and co-authored *The Day the Fairies Went on Strike* (for children). She has both an activist and scholarly interest in the documentation and development of new feminist strategies for making change.

Rebecca Priegert Coulter is an associate professor in the Division of Educational Policy Studies, Faculty of Education, University of Western Ontario. She has published articles on the history of juvenile delinquency and on the history of youth and work in Canada as well as on gender and education.

Carl Cuneo has taught in the Department of Sociology at McMaster University since 1973. He has published articles on the state, unemployment insurance, class, and gender, as well as the book *Pay Equity: The Labour-Feminist Challenge*. He is currently conducting research on work, gender, and trade unionism in the demise of Dominion Stores Limited.

Anne Forrest is an associate professor in the Faculty of Business Administration at the University of Windsor, where she teaches industrial relations and is involved with the Women's Studies Programme.

Judy Fudge teaches at Osgoode Hall Law School and researches and writes on the gender implications of labour law. She recently published *Labour Law's Little Sister: The Feminization of Labour and the Employment Equity Act*, and co-edited *Just Wages: A Feminist Assessment of Pay Equity*.

Pradeep Kumar is Professor in Industrial Relations and associate director of the School of Industrial Relations and the Industrial Relations Centre, Queen's University. His papers on various aspects of unionism and collective bargaining in Canada have appeared in the *Canadian Journal of Economics, Relations industrielles, Labour / Le Travail*, and the *Industrial and Labor Relations Review*. He is also the author of many books and chapters of books, and has served as consultant to numerous government agencies.

Ronnie Leah is an assistant professor, Department of Sociology, University of Lethbridge. She has edited *Coalition Building: Organizing the Popular Sector*; co-authored 'Saskatchewan Women Respond to Cutbacks: The Founding of a Provincial Women's Coalition'; and written 'Daycare, Trade Unions and the Women's Movement: Trade Union Women Organizing for Change,' and 'Linking the Struggles: Racism, Feminism and the Union Movement.'

Patricia McDermott is an associate professor in the Division of Social Science, York University. She has written extensively on pay equity and has co-edited *Just Wages: A Feminist Assessment of Pay Equity*. She is currently completing a book on gender and the law in Canada.

Donna Mergler is a professor of physiology at the Université du Québec à Montréal and a researcher at CINBIOSE (see Karen Messing). Her research centres on neurotoxicology, mental health in the workplace, and women's occupational health. She originated the research-action program in occupational health at the Université du Québec. The research team directed by Donna Mergler and Karen Messing won the 1990 Muriel Duckworth Prize for action-oriented research awarded by the Canadian Institute for Research for the Advancement of Women.

Karen Messing is professor of biology and director of CINBIOSE, the centre for the study of biological interactions between the environment and health at the Université du Québec à Montréal. Her research centres on women's occupational health and she is currently studying the health of cleaners. She is the author of *Occupational Health and Safety Concerns of Canadian Women*. The research team directed by Karen Messing and Donna Mergler won the 1990 Muriel Duckworth Prize for action-oriented research awarded by the Canadian Institute for Research and Study of Women.

Penni Richmond has coordinated the Women's Bureau of the Canadian Labour Congress (CLC) since 1989. Working through the CLC Women's Committee and women's groups around the country, she is focusing on anti-harassment training and action around employment equity and violence against women. She is a long-time activist in the Public Service Alliance of Canada and in community-based organizations such as Oxfam and the Development Education Centre (DEC).

Jane Stinson is a senior research officer with the Canadian Union of Public Employees (CUPE). She is currently on leave of absence from this position pursuing a master's degree in political economy at Carleton University. She is involved in a research project on computer-based homework in the federal government and is writing a thesis evaluating the effects of pay-equity legislation in Ontario.

Pamela Sugiman is an assistant professor of sociology at McMaster University. She is currently researching the relationship between gender and racial divisions of labour in the southern Ontario automobile industry and the UAW Canadian region from the 1920s to the 1960s.

Rosemary Warskett is completing her doctorate in sociology at Carleton University in Ottawa. Her thesis deals with pay equity and she has recently published 'Wage Solidarity or Equal Value' in *Studies in Political Economy*.

Julie White is an independent researcher working in Ottawa. She has written *Women and Unions, Women and Part-Time Work,* and *Mail and Female: Women and the Canadian Union of Postal Workers*. She is currently working on a new book that examines the status of women generally in the labour movement in Canada.

Armine Yalnizyan is Program Director at the Social Planning Council of Metropolitan Toronto, where she conducts research and policy analysis on labour-market issues. She has been chair of the Economy and Employment Committee of the National Action Committee on the Status of Women.